An Introduction to Foreign Language Learning and Teaching

LEARNING ABOUT LANGUAGE

General Editors:
Geoffrey Leech & Mick Short, Lancaster University

Already published:

An Introduction to Foreign Language Learning and Teaching

Keith Johnson

An imprint of **Pearson Education**

Harlow, England · London · New York · Reading, Massachusetts · San Francisco · Toronto · Don Mills, Ontario · Sydney
Tokyo · Singapore · Hong Kong · Seoul · Taipei · Cape Town · Madrid · Mexico City · Amsterdam · Munich · Paris · Milan

Pearson Education Limited

Edinburgh Gate
Harlow
Essex CM20 2JE
England

and Associated Companies throughout the world

Visit us on the World Wide Web at:
www.pearsoned.co.uk

First published 2001

ISBN 978-0-582-29086-0

British Library Cataloguing-in-Publication Data
A catalogue record for this book is available from the British Library

Library of Congress Cataloging-in-Publication Data
A catalog record for this book is available from the Library of Congress

10 9 8 7
09 08 07

Set in 10/12.5pt Palatino by 35
Produced by
Printed in Malaysia ,LSP

For Helen and Hugh

Contents

Author's acknowledgements

Large parts of this book began life as talks delivered to groups of students over a period of time. These student audiences found various ways of providing me with feedback, and I have found various ways of incorporating that feedback into this text. I am grateful for their help.

I have many individuals to thank. Nicki McLeod has been very facilitative in making resources available. Geoff Leech and Mary Ellen Ryder provided valuable comments on part of a draft version. Elizabeth Mann and Verina Pettigrew displayed a number of virtues, among which patience was to the fore.

Apart from myself, two people have read this book in draft form from beginning to end. One is Mick Short. The feedback he provided went way beyond anything one has a right to expect from a series editor. His comments have been plentiful, perceptive and constructive. Thank you, Mick. Thank you also Helen. As ever, you have managed to combine being a kind but firm critic with your role as spouse, remaining cheerful despite having had your life disrupted by book writing – surely one of the most disruptive of human activities.

Publisher's acknowledgements

We are grateful to the following for permission to reproduce copyright material:

Bangalore Regional Institute of English for an extract from their 'Newsletter' 1/2 1979; Ontario Institute for Studies in Education for extracts from *The Good Language Learner* by Naiman, Frohlich, Stern and Todesco; Pearson Education Ltd for an extract from 'Communicative writing practice and Aristolian rhetoric' by K. Johnson in *Learning to Write: First Language/second Language* edited by Freeman/Pringle/Yalden, 1983; Cambridge University Press for an extract from *The Cambridge English Course, Students Book 2* (Swan, M. and Walter, C. 1985); Center for Applied Linguistics for a Figure from *The Social Stratification of English in New York City* (Labov, W. 1966); Graphic News Ltd for graphic GN1704 NYK/copier graphic; Thomas Nelson and Sons Ltd for an extract from *Tandem Plus* (Read, C. and Matthews, A. 1991) and an extract from *Now for English* (Johnson, K. 1983); Oxford University Press for a Table from *Understanding Second Language Acquisition* (Ellis, R. 1985), © Rod Ellis 1985, reproduced by permission; Pearson Education Ltd for extracts from *Reading Tasks* (Benitez, L., Castrillo, J. M., Cerezal, N. and Suarez, C. 1988), an extract from *Teaching Oral English, Second Edition* (Byrne, D. 1986) and an extract from *Process Writing* (Arndt, V. and White, R. V. 1991); Penguin UK for extracts from *Success with English Coursebook* (Broughton, G. 1968).

While every effort has been made to trace the owners of copyright material, in a few cases this has proved impossible and we take this opportunity to offer our apologies to any copyright holders whose rights we have unwittingly infringed.

PART 1

BACKGROUND

Chapter 1

Five learners and five methods

Introduction

According to one estimate,[1] there are about a billion people in the world today learning English as a foreign language. A billion is a thousand million – a phenomenally large number of people! If you add to this the number of individuals who are learning foreign languages other than English – French, German, Italian, Spanish, Japanese, Chinese and many others – then you realize just how many people on the planet are engaged in the process of foreign-language learning.

Why the quite phenomenal expenditure of human energy in this direction? Why on earth do people bother to learn foreign languages on such a grand scale? In this chapter we shall consider some of the reasons why they do it, how successful they are at it, and some of the ways in which they may be taught. A major theme of the chapter will be *variety*. There are, we shall find, many different reasons for learning, many different degrees of success and many different ways of teaching.

Why do people learn foreign languages?

1.1 Reasons for learning

Before we look at other people, try to answer the 'Why Question' for yourself and for friends. First consider your own language-learning experiences, and ask yourself what your motives for learning were. Make a list of these. If you were obliged to learn, think what the motives of those who obliged you were. When you have thought about yourself, consider other people you know.

Think finally about the world beyond your immediate environment. Write a list of what you imagine to be the main motives for people world wide learning foreign languages. As you read on, note how many of the reasons on your list are discussed below.

In order to answer the Why Question, and to appreciate the variety of answers it may receive, we shall consider five individuals involved in foreign-language learning. They have been chosen to reveal some of the common motivations learners have.

Learner number one is Zhang. He lives in the Sichuan province of mainland China. He has a bachelor's degree from his local university in business studies, and he wants to do a master's degree overseas. He has applied to universities in Britain, the United States and Australia, and there is the chance that he may receive some scholarship money. But all the universities require him to take an internationally recognized English test before he is offered a place, and his score on the test must be very high. It is now January, and Zhang's test is in June. He does not enjoy language learning at all, but his situation explains very well why so very many of his daily waking hours are spent in the (for him) tedious business of improving his English.

Mike is an Australian, and his reason for learning Spanish could not be more different from Zhang's reason for learning English. Mike has just got married to Carmen, a Spanish girl he met in Sydney where she was among other things following an English-language course – yet more language learning! Mike has never been to Spain, and does not speak Spanish at the moment. But both these things must change. In the summer the two of them plan to visit Carmen's parents in Valencia and neither of her parents speaks English. Hence Mike is at present as intensely engaged in foreign-language learning as Zhang is.

Learner number three is an Indian girl whose name is Jasmine. She lives in Chennai (formerly Madras), the capital city of the Indian state of Tamil Nadu. Her native language is Tamil. The foreign language she is learning is another Indian language, though a very different one from Tamil. It is Hindi, considered a national language of India. In India many diverse, mutually unintelligible languages are spoken, and there is the need for one tongue to be spoken by all; the phrase <u>lingua franca</u> describes such a language, used as means of communication between speakers of other languages. Jasmine wants to continue living and working in Madras, but the job she has in mind will involve communication with Indians throughout the subcontinent. This is why she is learning Hindi.

Bryn is a Welshman. He lives in Wales, and is learning Welsh as a foreign language. You may find it odd for someone to be learning the language of their home country as a foreign language. But Bryn's situation and aspirations are not that uncommon. His parents have always spoken English at home, and his education has been entirely in English. Now, as a man in his early twenties, he feels the need to speak the language of his roots, to understand his own culture, to help strengthen the distinctiveness of Welsh society which he feels has long been under threat from England and the English. Bryn does not find learning Welsh particularly easy, but this does not bother him; he is very well motivated, and can indeed get quite lyrical on the topic – he really does regard Welsh as opening a window onto a new and meaningful culture for him.

Anna Vecsey is a scientist who works for a research institute attached to a university in Budapest, Hungary. She studied English at school, but her English is poor, and she is made constantly aware of her need to improve it. This awareness is particularly strong at the moment because her institute is about to host an international conference. The delegates will come from all over the world, and the language of communication will be English. Papers at the conference will be delivered in English, chat over coffee will be in English, and there is unlikely to be any respite even over dinner, where English will be spoken. English, English, English! As a consequence, Anna Vecsey has signed up for a language-improvement course at a local private language school.

These five characters illustrate some of the many reasons why people take time to learn a foreign language in today's world. The reasons are indeed various. Zhang is learning English in China for study purposes. Mike is busy with Spanish in Australia to integrate himself within his wife's culture, while Bryn in Wales is learning Welsh to strengthen his own cultural identity. Jasmine learns Hindi in India for purposes of *intranational* communication (that is, with people from within her country), and Anna in Hungary learns English to facilitate *international* communication (with people from other countries).

The multilingual world

It is not in fact difficult to understand the importance of foreign-language learning in today's world. As the planet becomes smaller, and the means for moving round it easier, so it has become more multicultural and multi-lingual. Not so long ago we used to be able to talk of nation states which could be associated with single languages – in France they spoke French, in Germany German, and so on. But it is no longer like that. Take a country like Australia. Clyne (1991) plots the immigration patterns into Australia since the Second World War. In the 1950s came the Latvians, Lithuanians, Estonians, Czechs, Poles, Hungarians, Croats, Slovenians and Ukrainians. Then there were Germans from Eastern Europe, refugees from Greece in 1967, from Hungary following the Soviet intervention of Hungary in 1956 and Czechoslovakia in 1968. The list really could be expanded very considerably, still talking about the same period – British, Maltese, Cypriots, Dutch, Germans, Italians, Yugoslavs, Lebanese, Turks, Chinese, Vietnamese, Cambodians. Clyne (1991) gives some revealing details of various censuses on language use in Australia. The 1986 Census for example looks at languages used in the home, state by state. No fewer than 63 languages are listed, and in fact some of these are language families ('Aboriginal languages' are for example grouped together). All this means that a stroll down a main street in any major Australian city is likely to be an informal introduction to the languages of the world! You are certainly not going to hear just English, the one language traditionally associated with Australia. The same is true in the United States, another country where a common perception is that just English is spoken. But the United States, like Australia and much of the rest of the world, is not monolingual. Today's world is truly multilingual.

In a multilingual world, it is natural to find large numbers of people who speak (and have therefore learned) more than one language. In many countries there are many more than two languages in operation, and it is not difficult to find examples where large numbers of languages are spoken on a daily basis. According to Crystal (1987) in many African countries, as many as 90 per cent of the population regularly use more than one language. The oft-cited champions in the language-learning stakes are the Vaupes River Indians, a tribe of around ten thousand Indians living in what is today Colombia. They have some dozen mutually unintelligible languages. Indeed, it seems to be the custom to find a marriage partner who speaks another language. This means that children have to start off by learning mum's language, dad's language, and a language common to the tribe. Many more languages may be added through an individual's life (especially if one were to become engaged to marry several times!).

The Vaupes Indians may be an extreme case, but multilingualism in the world is a hard fact, and with it comes the need to develop common languages for communication. It is indeed becoming the model for people to have one language to speak at home and another to communicate with some group of people outside. It is important for those of us who live with one language only to understand that we are the exception rather than the rule. Learning a foreign language may nowadays be regarded as a normal, almost everyday activity.

Individual learning differences

We have seen that people learn foreign languages for a great variety of reasons. Another dimension on which we find great variety is in the degree of success foreign-language learners enjoy. This is one way in which *first* language (L1) learning (learning your mother tongue as a child) and foreign language learning differ. Though there are many ways in which the following statements need to be qualified, it is broadly true that all children, whatever their 'talent' for language learning, whatever their social background, their level of educational achievement, all learn to speak their native or first language by a very early age. Some will take slightly longer that others, but they all get there.

A similar statement could not be made about foreign-language learning. It is unfortunately very far from the case that everyone who attempts to learn a foreign language 'succeeds'; indeed, the figures for successful school learning of a foreign language are in some countries (like England) depressingly, even shamefully low. With foreign-language learning, individual differences seem to make themselves felt. Some people do it very well. Sir Richard Burton (the nineteenth-century explorer who translated the Kama Sutra) appears to have spoken more than forty languages, and you may well be able to think of individuals in your own experience who seem to have a special talent for language learning. Others are hopeless; they may be well-intentioned, but they are simply dreadful, quite unable to put a sentence together in a foreign tongue, and incapable of modifying their native language accent in any way. You may be able to find examples of public figures in your own country who come into this category.

1.2 Differences in people you know

Consider some examples of successful and unsuccessful learners among those you know – people perhaps who at school have come top and bottom of the language-learning class. Why were they successful or unsuccessful? Can you account for their performance in any way?

Your answers will contribute towards a solution to the puzzle of what makes people good or bad at language learning.

Most of us fall somewhere between Richard Burton and the public figure with the appalling foreign accent. We manage to get by in a foreign language, though we mostly nowhere approach the level of the native speaker. At some point along the way we <u>fossilize</u> – that is, our foreign language stops moving forwards, and 'sticks'. First language learners do not fossilize in this way.

How can we account for these individual differences? We shall consider this question in some detail in Chapters 8 and 9. Meanwhile, box 1.3 offers a 'taster' of some of the fascinating findings that research in the 'individual differences' area suggests.

1.3 Individual learning differences. A 'taster' of some issues discussed at length in Chapters 8 and 9

- You do not have to be intelligent to learn a foreign language; but you do have to be intelligent to follow some methods.
- There are some people with a talent for foreign-language learning, but apparently not much else. Smith and Tsimpli (1995) devote a 240-page book to discussion of a boy called Christopher who suffers from brain damage, and who has to live in an institution because of his inability to handle life outside. Yet in one area, Christopher excels – he can speak sixteen foreign languages!

7

- Attitude towards the native speakers of the foreign language you wish to learn may sometimes be very important. Some people would argue that, if for some reason you intensely dislike the native speakers of a particular language, you are wasting your time trying to learn that language.
- Parental support is very important for children. If mother and father want a child to do well at learning a foreign language, this will help the process a good deal. As we shall see later, some parents regard language learning as a 'girlish' activity, supporting girls' learning but encouraging boys in other directions.
- Factors like those just considered can 'trade each other off'. Naiman *et al.* (1978) make mention of one girl in Canada who had many qualities that suggested she should be a good foreign-language learner. Her teachers described her as 'attentive, very jovial and relaxed, obviously enjoying some of the activities'; French was, she said, her favourite subject, and outside the classroom she would listen to French radio and would talk to her friends in French, just for fun. She was not afraid of making mistakes, was very motivated, and a hard worker. Everything is there to make her a good learner, except that she lacked something – talent (aptitude) perhaps. As a result she was second lowest in her class.

Language teaching: a variety of methods

We have noted great variety both in the reasons why individuals learn foreign languages, and in their success at doing so. We also find variety when we turn to the other subject of this book: language teaching. It would be an understatement to say that there is no consensus of opinion as to what is the best way to teach a foreign language. To illustrate the point, consider the following five language-teaching classrooms. They are very different from each other.

1.4   Methods you have experienced

Before looking at the five methods, reflect on the language-learning methods you yourself have experienced. Describe them in as much detail as possible. What were their main characteristics? Did you have to know a lot of grammatical terms to be able to use them? Was there a lot of parrot-like repetition involved? Did they concentrate on reading and writing more than listening and speaking? What did you find to be their strengths and weaknesses?

Classroom 1 is in Canada, and the pupils are nine-year-old children. Their native language is English, but this is hard to believe as you listen to what goes on during the school day. From the time they arrive till the time they leave, the pupils are spoken to almost entirely in French. They are greeted by their teacher in French, their lessons are conducted in French, teachers speak to them in the playground and the dinner hall in French, and say goodbye to them at the end of the day in French. When the pupils started at this school, they themselves replied to the teachers in English (that is, the teachers spoke French and the pupils responded naturally in English), but over time this has changed, and now the pupils themselves are increasingly using French. This mode of teaching is commonly referred to as *immersion*. It is based on the idea that learners can 'pick up' a foreign language in much the same way as children 'pick up' their native language.

In **Classroom 2**, the teenage English pupils are learning Italian. The book they are using is full of extremely complicated grammar rules, explained in English. The teacher spends some twenty minutes of the lesson explaining the grammar point of the day, in English, using diagrams on the blackboard, and plenty of grammatical terms (talking of 'tenses', 'nouns', 'adverbs' and the like). The learners are then given a series of translation exercises to do, both from English into Italian and vice versa. One glaring characteristic of the sentences the learners are given to translate is that one can never imagine anyone ever saying them. They are sentences clearly concocted to practise grammar points – Dobson *et al.*'s (1981) example of a typical sentence from this method is *The flowers of my grandmother are in the garden of the Dutchman.* When did you, or anyone else, last say that? This method is called *grammar-translation* and, although its heyday is now really past, it is still used in many parts of the world today, to teach many languages.

Classroom 3 is using a method called *total physical response* (TPR) for the teaching of beginner German. Even though the learners are truly beginners – in their first month of learning – German is the only language used throughout the lesson (though, unlike in the Canadian immersion example, the learners' L1 is used outside the classroom). At this stage it is only really the teacher who talks, and what she says in German is easy for the learners to understand, because all sentences are instructions for action – *Stand up, Walk over there, Stop, Turn round, Sit down.* The teacher first demonstrates these actions herself; then she chooses members of the class to do them. It will be a while before the learners themselves are asked to speak, but when they do, it will be in the foreign language, and to ask other members of the class to follow similar action sequences. As with the immersion approach, part of the rationale for-TPR lies in a parallel with first language learning, in which a close relationship between words and actions is developed.

Classroom 4 uses a version of a method which will be familiar to many of you. It is known as *audiolingualism*. The lesson (teaching Spanish in France) focuses on a grammar point, but unlike in Classroom 2 there is no explanation whatsoever, and the learners' native language is hardly used at all. The grammar point is made clear in the textbook by the use of example sentences, accompanied by pictures which help make meanings obvious. The time spent on exemplifying the grammatical point is quite short, and it is not very far into the lesson that the learners are given a series of rapid-fire exercises (or <u>drills</u>) to practise the grammar point. One of audiolingualism's central tenets is that learning a language is largely a question of habit formation, and for this reason a good part of the lesson is spent on drills, in an attempt to make using the grammar point an automatic habit.

Classroom 5 does not look like a classroom at all. The learners (in fact they are called *clients*), are sitting in a circle with the teacher (called the *counsellor*) walking round the outside. The clients (who happen to be Americans learning Russian) are attempting to hold a conversation with each other, in Russian, on a topic chosen by them. As they are intermediate clients, they are able to muddle through quite well, but every so often they need to ask the counsellor for help with words or phrases. This the counsellor gives in a whisper, and the clients' conversation continues. At the end of the session the procedure becomes more recognizable as conventional language teaching. The counsellor writes some grammar, vocabulary and pronunciation points on the blackboard, and talks the clients through them. This method is called *community language learning* and, as the use of words like 'counsellor' suggests, is modelled on counselling procedures associated with psychotherapy.

We have in this chapter considered five different learners and five different teaching methods. It would of course be an exaggeration to say that there are as many methods of teaching a foreign language as there are learners. But there are, clearly, very many ways of skinning the language-learning cat. Chapter 10 provides a detailed survey of recent language-teaching methods.

Plan of the book

Part 1 of this book deals with background issues. In Chapter 2 we ask: What does learning a language involve? What exactly needs to be learned, and what can be taught? We seek answers to these questions by analysing language into its component parts, and considering which of those component parts need attention from the learner, and which from the teacher. In Chapter 3 we deal with some key ideas about language and language learning that have had particular influence in the field.

Then, in Part 2, we focus on language learning. In Chapters 4 to 7 we survey some of the theories that have been prominent in recent times. Chapters 8 and 9 look at some of the factors that have been associated with success in language learning. Several of these have already been mentioned in box 1.2.

In Part 3 our attention turns to language teaching. Chapter 10 gives a brief recent history of teaching approaches, talking in more detail about the methods seen in the five classrooms above, and others besides. In Chapter 11 we look at issues related to the planning of language teaching within a social and even political context (teaching a foreign language can be a very political act indeed). Chapter 12 also deals with planning, but of specific programmes. It is about syllabus design. Chapters 13 and 14 look at what actually happens in classrooms – the nuts and bolts of how to teach a language. Chapter 15, the final chapter, is about testing.

Some terminology and some conventions

Terminology plagues the language learning and teaching worlds. For many people ESP stands for 'extra sensory perception', but to language teachers it means 'English for Specific Purposes' (teaching English, for example, for business studies, or to airline pilots). Associated with ESP are EST (English for Science and Technology) and EAP (English for Academic Purposes). Then there is TESOL (teaching English to speakers of other languages), TEFL (teaching English as a foreign language) and even TENOR (teaching English for no obvious reason – the opposite perhaps of ESP).

Some pieces of terminology need attention at the very beginning. TEFL has already been mentioned, but there is also TESL – teaching English as a second language. What is the difference between a foreign and a second language? For some a second language is one that is used (probably as a *lingua franca*) in the learner's home country – French for people in ex-French colonies, for example – while a foreign language is one without that special status. But nowadays many do not make this distinction, and it has become the case that 'second language learning' often refers to the learning of any language other than the mother tongue. It is perhaps lamentable that the word 'second' as opposed to 'foreign' has taken on this general meaning, because 'foreign' is the more general word. We shall accordingly use the word 'foreign' throughout this book.

Another way of saying 'foreign language' is 'FL', and we shall often use phrases like 'FL acquisition', and speak of a learner's 'FL'. We shall also refer to a learner's mother tongue as his or her 'L1'; so the phrase 'an L1 German speaker' would mean a person whose native language is German.

A further term that needs explanation is 'applied linguist'. Anyone who applies the findings of linguistics to some area is an applied linguist. So for example a speech therapist who uses linguistics to help in the understanding and treatment of speech defects is an applied linguist. One major application of linguistics is in the areas of foreign-language learning and teaching. In this book we shall often speak of applied linguists, referring to those interested specifically in the FL learning and teaching fields.

Three conventions: the book makes liberal use of boxes. Sometimes these contain examples or reference materials not perhaps important enough to be an integral part of the text. Sometimes they contain points to think about, which might form the basis for workshop activities if you are working with others in a group. These boxes are tinted.

The second convention is that important new pieces of terminology are underlined. When they are first introduced, they are often first expressed in everyday terms, with the 'technical' term italicized and put in brackets afterwards. An example is the way the word <u>drill</u> is introduced in discussion of Classroom 4 above.

Finally: this book is being written in the midst of the Great English Gender Crisis. It is now no longer acceptable to use *he, his* and *him* in a generic way, while alternatives like *(s)he, his or her* are clumsy and long-winded. Our solution is to have an entirely female world in one chapter and an entirely male world in the next. So in Chapter 2 all teachers, learners and others are 'she', while in Chapter 3 they are all males. An odd solution perhaps, but one which nicely reflects the lack of resolution to this crisis in the English-speaking world in general.

Note

1. The source is the 1997 British Council/British Tourist Authority advice pack entitled *Marketing English Language Courses*. I am indebted to David Crystal for making this information available. His own estimate is for a lower number.

Chapter 2

What is there to learn?

What exactly is involved in learning a foreign language? What kinds of 'knowledge' and 'skill' need to be mastered? If you are asked questions like this, your initial (and natural) responses will probably involve words like 'pronunciation', 'vocabulary' and 'grammar'. These are the questions we shall ask in this chapter. One intended outcome is to make you realize how complex an operation learning a foreign language is. There is indeed an immense amount to be mastered.

Questions like the ones above need to be approached in two stages. Firstly, we will identify what different types of knowledge and skill are involved in *using* a language: the skills and knowledge that the competent language user possesses. This will involve the areas already mentioned – like pronunciation, vocabulary and grammar – as well as some less obvious ones. The result of this stage of enquiry will be a list of all the levels on which a language can be analysed: the levels which the discipline of linguistics is concerned with.

But describing these different levels of knowledge and skill will only half-answer our questions. This is because not everything involved in using a language needs to be learned afresh by the learner. A rather extreme example will clarify this. One of the things that the speakers of nearly all languages do is to produce sounds by pushing air from the lungs, through the vocal cords and up into the mouth. We may legitimately say that this skill is part of what is involved in speaking a foreign language. But the learner has already mastered this skill in relation to L1 learning. It does not have to be either learned or taught. So the second stage of enquiry asks the extent to which mastery of these levels involves new learning.

To develop some feel for the complexities of the 'what is involved in learning a foreign language' question, we may add to the extreme example of breathing a more modest and more revealing one. Part of the English grammatical system involves use of 'articles': the words *the*, *a* and *an*. We may legitimately say that in order to use English properly, this article system has to be mastered. But this will entail very different amounts of learning for speakers of different languages. For some learners, there will be rather a small amount of learning involved, because their own L1 has a comparable system. So L1 speakers of German, for example, will have relatively few problems with the English articles (which are in many respects very much simpler than the German ones). But the situation will be dramatically different for the speakers of L1s which do not have a comparable article system, or indeed any article system at all. So for Japanese or Russian speakers the operation involves very much more than learning the words *the*, *a* and *an*. With these learners, the whole issue of what an article is, and what it 'means' has to be tackled, and a pause for thought will make you realize what a phenomenally difficult issue this is likely to be.

We shall see in Chapter 4 that one way of finding out what a particular learner will find easy or difficult in the FL is to undertake a comparison of FL and L1, in order to identify similarities and differences. This correctly suggests that the answer to our questions 'what exactly is involved in learning a foreign language?' and 'what kinds of "knowledge" and "skill" need to be mastered?' are not just complex, but will also differ from learner to learner.

Categorizing the levels of knowledge and skill involved in language use

How does one begin to categorize the levels of knowledge and skill involved in language use? One possible 'way in' is to look at, and categorize, the mistakes that a learner makes. Box 2.1 gives you an example of learner language to think about in this way:

2.1 'Cats' – useless domestic animals

Below is an essay produced by a foreign-language learner on the topic of 'Cats'. The essay is full of mistakes and inadequacies of various kinds. Identify as many different *categories* of error as you can. For example, the essay contains a number of spelling mistakes, so one category for your list would be 'spelling'.

By identifying categories of error you are in fact identifying categories of knowledge and skill involved in FL use.

> The cats are useless
>
> The cats ~~are~~ *is* useless as domesic animal.
> Specially in cities there is no problem of
> ~~Cates~~ and mices. In my life, ~~we~~ *I haven't* kept a cat
> in the house. I think, the decision come from that
> my life is full of hard work. Perhaps, you might
> say: It is a nice thing to find a game *(cat)* for
> your childern, as demostic animal. I reply; OK.
> ~~for~~ I ~~life~~ like *this* thing <u>one time</u> a week while
> I don't leave my children to play with useless
> game. My brother has a son, and this ~~son like~~ *he had*
> ~~his~~ *a* cat. Later on, the cat was died. However
> the boy was in deep sorrow and still of this
> feeling for a long time.

We shall now consider how others have attempted to categorize linguistic levels. The framework we shall focus on is one developed by Canale and Swain (1980) to describe what they (and many others) call 'communicative competence'. This term is worth a moment's thought. 'Competence' is the term linguists use to describe roughly what we have so far rather ponderously been calling knowledge and skill, and this section's heading might therefore have read 'categorizing the levels of competence involved in language use'. The use of the word 'communicative' allows us to avoid a more restricted term like 'grammatical' – worth avoiding because, as we shall see, there is much more to using a language than grammar.

Canale and Swain's (1980) model of communicative competence identifies three levels of analysis: what they call grammatical, sociolinguistic
and strategic. We shall introduce one change in terminology: because the
word 'grammatical' has various meanings, we replace it with the word
'systemic', which we define below; otherwise our framework is identical to
Canale and Swain's. We shall deal with each of the levels of analysis in
turn. For each, we have two aims: firstly to clarify just what is associated
with the category, then to develop, in relation to each, some feel for what
needs to be learned by (and taught to) the FL learner. The final result will
be to give us some sense of what, in general terms, is involved in learning
a foreign language.

Systemic competence

The word 'systemic' means 'as a system', and the term **systemic competence**
therefore covers knowledge and skill related to the way the language works
as a system. This involves many different levels, including pronunciation
(phonetics and phonology) as well as grammar (morphology and syntax).
We may also take it to include word meanings (semantics). Also under this
category come other skills which will have made an appearance in your
response to box 2.1, like handwriting, spelling and punctuation. We may
be tempted to call these 'mechanical' skills, though a moment's thought
will indicate that often they are very far from being purely mechanical –
try for example to explain the difference in use between a comma and a
semi-colon. Not so easy!

The following sections give examples of these areas of competence, but
do not provide anything like full coverage of them. The examples nearly
all relate to the English language. Readers who already have a good understanding of how English works as a system may wish to pass over some
of the boxed examples and exercises.

We start with an area which will not have occurred in your consideration
of box 2.1, because that is an example of written, not spoken, English.

Pronunciation

It comes as a surprise to many that there are definite 'rules' which govern
how we pronounce our native language. Box 2.2 illustrates a pronunciation
rule of English associated with a very simple grammatical area indeed –
how we form the plurals of regular nouns in English. We do this, of course,
by adding an *s*. But think now about pronunciation, about how the plural is
said, not *written*. There are in fact three different ways in which the final *s*
may be pronounced. Before reading what these are, look at box 2.2 and
attempt to identify them for yourself:

2.2 The plural *s*. It couldn't be simpler – or could it?

Below are three English nouns with their plural forms. Say the words, both singular and plural, to yourself and try to isolate how the *s* is pronounced or said. It is different in each of the three cases. Then think about what is controlling how the *s* is pronounced. Unless you know it already it is unlikely that you will be able to work out exactly how the rule works, but you may be able to guess what kind of factor is controlling it.

(1) *book*   *books*
(2) *rug*   *rugs*
(3) *horse*   *horses*

In the explanation that follows, note the use of slanted brackets //. These conventionally denote a sound. So /s/ is not the letter *s*, but the sound /s/. Often, of course, the sound /s/ is represented in writing with the letter *s*, but this is not always the case – the word *bounce* for example contains the /s/ sound, but it is written as *ce*. If you have not done it before, it is quite difficult to think in terms of sounds, not spellings. As you read the following lines, you will perhaps need to remind yourselves constantly to 'think sound'. Here is the explanation: in box 2.2, plural (1) is pronounced as /s/). (2) is pronounced more like the first sound of the word *zoo*, and we represent this as /z/. (3) is pronounced /Iz/. What controls the way the noun plural *s* is pronounced is what sound comes immediately before it. In (1), a /k/ comes just before the 's', and we pronounce the final letter as /s/. Because /g/ comes before the 's' in (2) we pronounce it /z/. Because the sound /s/ comes before 's' in (3) we pronounce it /Iz/. With this final example it is particularly important to 'think sound' not spelling: the spelled word *horse* ends with a *e*, but this *e* is not pronounced at all.

All native speakers of English 'know' the rules that are exemplified here, from an early age. They may not be able to express them in the way that linguists would (linguists would speak about whether the preceding sound were <u>voiced</u> or <u>unvoiced</u>). But if you gave a young child a test on this rule, you would find that she would pass with flying colours even at the tender age of six. Berko (1958) in fact does just this. She was interested in (among other things) how well young children know these 'plural pronunciation rules'. Her test uses invented nouns, because in that way you can be sure the child has not heard the word before, and is just repeating it from memory. One of the items on her test is the invented noun *wug*, the name she gives to a small bird-like animal. She shows the children a picture of one wug, then two, and asks the children to finish the sentence: *there are two* _____. Because the final sound of *wug* is a /g/ (as in *rug*), the plural *s* will be pronounced /z/ (and not /s/ or /Iz/). Of the sixty native-English-speaking children she tested in the five and a half to seven age group, an astonishing 97 per cent produced the correct pronunciation – of a word they had never heard before!

The 'plural pronunciation rules' are just one of a vast number that native speakers follow on the pronunciation level. Box 2.3 contains further examples of two major related areas, stress and intonation.

2.3   Blackbirds and swimmers

1. Consider the word *blackbird* and the phrase *black bird*. The first refers to a specific type of bird (whose Latin name is *Turdus merula*); the second refers to any bird that is coloured black. How would you use stress to make it clear which you were referring to? For example, if you said *I saw a blackbird in my garden yesterday* how would it differ from *I saw a black bird in my garden yesterday*. Be as explicit as you can about the difference.

2. The sentence *John can't swim, can he?* can mean at least two things. John is a small baby. In (a) below you are seeking confirmation of the fact that John can't swim, and the sentence might be paraphrased *it's true that John can't swim, isn't it.*

   (a)   *Let's not go swimming tomorrow. John can't swim, can he?*

   But in (b) the sentence might be paraphrased *it's not true that John can swim, is it?*:

   (b)   *You want to go swimming tomorrow? Good heavens! John can't swim, can he?*

   Say the sentences (a) and (b) over to yourself several times. You probably use different intonation for *John can't swim, can he?* in (a) and (b). Attempt to describe what this difference is.

It is important to realize that the rules exemplified in box 2.3 are (just like those in box 2.2) ones which native speakers know instinctively, and use as part of their repertoire of rules of the language. But are such rules instinctive to all humans, or do they need to be learned by learners of English as a foreign language?

You can probably readily imagine that some FL speakers of English will have problems with the particular rules that we have looked at here. Spanish speakers, for example, are likely to have problems with the /z/ and /Iz/ pronunciations of the plural form, because in Spanish they are all of the /s/ type. The intonation example (*can he?*) may remind you of foreign films that have been dubbed into English, where the dubbing voice never seems able to get the intonation of this question type right. Indeed, intonation is notoriously likely to cause problems, because so often it is associated with strong feelings. I remember an occasion when a courteous and friendly Italian student was asked to leave her British host family, apparently largely because of her intonation patterns. When she asked for help, for example, her intonation (going downwards, or <u>falling</u> at the end) would make it sound as if she were giving an order – *Please would you help me carry this bag!* The family thought she was rude and brusque. Further, you will probably have no trouble in accepting the general notion that pronunciation causes FL speakers all kinds of difficulties. You will probably have noticed that immigrants may spend very many years indeed in the target language country and still fail even to approximate native language pronunciation; such individuals will, probably for all their lives, maintain their foreign pronunciation. Sound habits die very hard indeed.

A further example of deep-seated pronunciation problems: it is well recognized that speakers of some oriental languages have problems with the English /1/ and /r/ sounds, so that sometimes a word like *rice* comes to be pronounced like *lice*, and *like* may be *rike*. The reason is that in these languages /1/ and /r/ are simply not distinctive sounds – there are no word pairs, like English *rice* and *lice* where the /1/, /r/ difference is crucial to distinguish words (they are not, in linguistic parlance, <u>phonemes</u>). The speakers of these languages simply do not 'hear' the difference between these two sounds; and since they cannot hear it, they cannot produce it.

Readers who are native speakers of English may appreciate these sorts of difficulties more strongly with the realization (of the obvious fact) that native speakers of English will experience similar types of difficulty learning an FL. An oft-cited and clear example relates to the learning of Russian. In both English and Russian there are two rather different ways of pronouncing the sound /1/. In the English word *like*, for example, the tongue touches the gums behind the top teeth, and the front part of the tongue is raised upwards. The resulting sound is what is called the 'clear /1/'. The so-called 'dark /1/' is found in a word like *real*. Here the tongue again touches the gums behind the top teeth, but the part of the tongue that is raised is much further back.

The above paragraph illustrates that English uses both the clear and dark /1/ sounds. But you might find it difficult without any phonetic training actually to hear the difference between the two sounds, and to identify one from the other. This is because in English the difference is not crucially important, in the sense that there are no words which differ only because a clear or dark /1/ is used (a linguist might say that the clear/dark /1/ distinction is not <u>phonemic</u> in English). But this is not true in Russian, where the distinction does actually differentiate words. So, for example, there are two different Russian words roughly written in Latin script as *lyk* which means 'the hatch (of a ship)' when the /1/ is clear, and 'onion' when the /1/ is dark; an important distinction, especially if you are a sailor about to dine. Note that the clear–dark /l/ distinction is an exact parallel for English learners of Russian with the /l/–/r/ difficulty experienced by some oriental learners of English.

One further area to which your consideration of the Cats Essay in box 2.1 will have drawn attention is spelling, and its relationship to pronunciation. English (along with some other languages) seems to employ eccentric and bewildering ways of connecting sounds with spellings, and this understandably always causes great problems for the learner. Box 2.4 is a humorous poetic reflection on this ubiquitously fascinating topic. To appreciate the poem fully, pause over words that are spelt similarly (like those in line 2) and relish the differences in their pronunciation.

2.4 Hints on pronunciation for foreigners

I take it you already know
Of tough and bough and cough and dough?
Others may stumble but not you,
On hiccough, thorough, laugh and through,
Well done! And now you wish, perhaps,
To learn of less familiar traps?

Beware of heard, a dreadful word
That looks like beard and sounds like bird,
And dead: it's said like bed, not bead –
For goodness' sake don't call it 'deed'!
Watch out for meat and great and threat
(They rhyme with suite and straight and debt).

A moth is not the moth in mother
Nor both in bother, broth in brother,
And here is not a match for there
Nor dear and fear for bear and pear,
And then there's dose and rose and lose –
Just look them up – and goose and choose,
And cork and work and card and ward,
And font and front and word and sword,
And do and go and thwart and cart –
Come, come, I've hardly made a start!
A dreadful language? Man alive
I'd mastered it when I was five.

T. S. W. (only initials of writer known)

(From a letter published in the London *Sunday Times*, 3 January 1965)

The moral of all this is that the general area of 'sounds' is one in which learners have a good deal to learn. Exactly how much, and exactly what, will of course depend on the learners' L1. But we have said enough here to establish the importance of the area. There is perhaps also a moral for language teaching; as Abercrombie (1949: 11) is moved to claim: 'the language teacher . . . will inevitably be a phonetician'.

Morphemes

A second level on which a native speaker displays knowledge is that of the morpheme. A morpheme is often defined (in Richards *et al.* 1985 for example) as 'the smallest meaningful unit in a language'. Morphemes are the building blocks of words. Box 2.5 illustrates:

2.5 Identifying and analysing morphemes

Consider the word *unbelievable*. This is made up of three morphemes. Identify what they are. Try to paraphrase what each 'means'.

The 'core' of box 2.5's word is the unit *believ(e)*. To this has been added the morpheme *able* which attaches to verbs and changes them into adjectives, and means something like 'capable of'. *un* is another morpheme which is often put on the front of an adjective to mean 'not'. That all native speakers know this is evidenced by the fact that they will often coin new words using the *able* morpheme. In my notes on a draft of this chapter I used the word *relatable* (in the context of saying that two points I was making were 'relatable' to each other). My word processor's spelling check denied the existence of this word *relatable*. But neither you nor I have problems working out what it means; we know what the constituent parts signify, so can easily work out what the whole means.

We all have minor problems with the morphemes of our own language on occasions. Native speakers of English may pause, embarrassed, when they want to express the notion of 'not authentic', being uncertain as to whether the correct word is *inauthentic* or *unauthentic*. But someone learning a foreign language has to master all kinds of morphemic rules which are right there in the centre of how the language works. A learner of English, for example, has to know that -ed is the morpheme used to express (simple) past time (as in *I walked*), and that certain sorts of present time are expressed through use of the verb ending *-ing* (as in *He is walking*). She has to know that the *s* morpheme we considered in box 2.2 marks plurality in nouns, as well as possessiveness (in this latter sense it is accompanied by an apostrophe when written – *the doctor's* and *the doctors'*). Even to express the simplest of propositions involves a 'mass of morphology'.

As with pronunciation, you will probably have no trouble with the notion that morphological difficulties can be huge for the foreign learner. Where the language being learned is one in which there is a complex and rich morphology these difficulties will be particularly daunting. Consider the 'endings' to nouns and adjectives, for example. In English the rules are very simple. We have already seen that there is a morpheme which indicates plurality, a final *s* in the case of regular nouns . We have also seen that a final *s* marks possessiveness (the possessive <u>case</u> as it is called by some linguists). These are the main grammatical morphemes that can be added to the end of nouns. Adjectives in English are even simpler: their form does not change at all according to what noun follows them. Those of you who have learned French will know that the rules are more complex in this respect. French nouns have different genders, masculine and feminine, and the form of the adjective will depend on the noun's gender (*le petit homme* – 'the small man' versus *la petite femme* – 'the small woman'). But Russian is in quite a different league of complexity! For starters, there are *three* genders (masculine, feminine and neuter), not two. Within these genders there are different noun types which take slightly different endings. Next, there are *six* cases which are marked with different endings. The possessive which we have discussed in relation to English would be one of them, but there would be others to mark whether a noun was the subject of a sentence, its object, its indirect object and so on. Singular and plural are also marked. Then there is the fact that adjectives as well as nouns have endings, and that the noun/adjective endings are often different from each other. Box 2.6 illustrates just one small part of the entire picture. The first table shows the forms of just masculine nouns. There are three main types, shown in the three columns. Each row shows a different case (Nom. for Nominative, Acc. for accusative; see Note 1 for details of the others). The second table shows the forms of one main adjective type (called 'hard' – in fact there are two categories of 'hard adjective'; just one is given here in order not to make the picture too hopelessly complex!). You do not need to be able to read the script to understand the point being made. Just look at the endings of the words and note how they differ. This should give you an idea of the nightmare that some learners of Russian as a foreign language face in the morphology department (as well, one might add, as native-speaker Russian children learning their L1).

Another characteristic of morphology is that even if it is 'simple' (as English morphology tends to be) this does not appear to mean that it will be easily learned. An oft-cited example of this is the final *s* morpheme in English marking the third person singular of a verb in the simple present tense (*He likes* in contrast to *I like*). On many levels this *s* morpheme really is rather easy – after all, there are not many morpheme endings to remember in English, and the form of this one could not be simpler. Yet various studies (including Dulay and Burt (1973) and others we shall mention in Chapter 4) show that learners acquire this form rather late. Indeed, if you live in an English-speaking country which has an immigrant population, you may be able to think of immigrants who have lived there for years and yet still forget this final *s*. Part of the problem is doubtless the comparative communicative redundancy of the form; if a learner says *He like* instead

2.6 A mass of Russian morphology

The two tables below give just a few details of the morphology of Russian nouns and adjectives. The information is taken from Fennell (1961):

I. Masculine Nouns

Singular

Nom.	стол	герóй	автомобúль
Acc.	стол	герóя	автомобúль
Gen.	столá	герóя	автомобúля
Dat.	столý	герóю	автомобúлю
Instr.	столóм	герóем	автомобúлем
Prep.	столé	героé	автомобúле

I. Hard Adjectives

(a)

	Singular			Plural
	Masculine	Feminine	Neuter	All Genders
Nom.	нóвый	нóвая	нóвое	нóвые
Acc.	⌠нóвый	нóвую	нóвое	⌠нóвые
	⌡нóвого			⌡нóвых
Gen.	нóвого	нóвой	нóвого	нóвых
Dat.	нóвому	нóвой	нóвому	нóвым
Instr.	нóвым	нóвой(ою)	нóвым	нóвыми
Prep.	нóвом	нóвой	нóвом	нóвых

of *He likes*, the chances are that she will be understood; the message will be conveyed. As another example of the actual difficulty of apparently 'easy' morphemes, research done by Lightbown (1987) on French-speaking learners of English found that accuracy for the basic -*ing* morpheme went from 69 per cent in Year 1, to only 39 per cent in Year 2, though it went back up to above 60 per cent in Year 3.

Syntax

Monsieur Jourdain, a character in Molière's play *Le Bourgeois Gentilhomme*, does not know what the word *prose* means, and is filled with astonishment when he is told that he has been speaking it all his life (*Good Heavens! For more than forty years I have been speaking prose without knowing it*). A similar astonishment is sometimes expressed when native speakers (of English, or any other language) find out that their own language has a syntax. They know that foreign languages have grammar rules that can be learned. But, because they have acquired their native language in a seemingly unconscious way as a child, they are unaware that their own language has rules, and are unable to articulate what those rules are. They have been speaking with syntax all their lives without knowing it!

Box 2.7 invites you to explore part of the syntax of a reasonably simple area of grammar, related to how we form <u>interrogative</u> sentences in English. A major use of interrogatives is to ask questions.

2.7 Forming English interrogatives

(a) below illustrates a sentence together with its interrogative form. State as precisely as possible what 'operations' are performed on the statement to change it into an interrogative.

(a) *John is playing tennis* ⇒ *Is John playing tennis?*

Now form the interrogative equivalents of (b) and (c) and again explain how you do it. Try to explain it in such a way as to clarify the similarities of interrogative formation in (a), (b) and (c).

(b) *John can play tennis*   ⇒
(c) *John should play tennis* ⇒

Now look at (d). What happens to the statement here to form an interrogative? How is it different from the other examples?

(d) *John plays tennis* ⇒ *Does John play tennis?*

Form interrogatives out of (e) and (f):

(e) *John and Mary play tennis*
(f) *John played tennis*

Is it possible to devise a general rule that will explain how all the interrogatives you have seen – (a) to (f) – are formed? This is discussed in Note 2.

If your L1 is not English, or you have studied or speak any language other than English, you might like to think how the English way of forming interrogatives differs from how it is done in the other language. English in fact has a rather unusual way of interrogative formation, particularly where some form of the verb *do* is used. This is the reason why for many learners of EFL these forms cause problems. A common mistake is for learners to produce *plays John tennis?* or *played John tennis?* You might wish to speculate why they should do this.

As with the other linguistic areas we are dealing with in this chapter, we have here done no more than touch upon the huge problems which syntax may give the EFL learner (remembering always that degree of difficulty will depend on similarities and differences between English and the learner's L1). Box 2.8 below provides a few further examples.

2.8 More areas of syntactic difficulty

Swan (1995) is a reference book on English usage. It contains examples of typical mistakes that EFL learners use. Six of these characteristic errors are given below, with the 'correct' version provided in brackets.

For each error attempt to articulate the rule that has been broken, and how it has been broken. Where possible speculate why the error occurred. In some cases it may be that you can find the possible cause in the structure of another language that you know. For example, you may find yourself thinking 'that's how you say it in French'.

(a) *They know each other since 1980 (They have known each other since 1980)*
(b) *I've known her since three days (I've known her for three days)*
(c) *Always check the oil before to start the car (Always check the oil before starting the car)*
(d) *I'm going to the mountains about twice a year (I go to the mountains about twice a year)*
(e) *Tell me when are you going on holiday? (Tell me when you are going on holiday)*
(f) *Do you can tell me the time? (Can you tell me the time?)*

These errors are discussed in Note 3.

Vocabulary

We have already seen, in the section on morphology, that 'word building' is a skill that L1 speakers possess. There are other skills to do with words (or lexis as linguists calls it) that the native speaker has. One of these relates to the area of collocation, the way that words are conventionally used together. To illustrate this, consider the following example taken from McCarthy (1990: 12). He looks at the four adjectives: *large, great, big* and *major*. These are very close, though not identical, in meaning. So it is very often a question of convention, rather than precise meaning, that decides when one rather than another can be used. Box 2.9 below shows whether these adjectives co-occur with the four nouns that appear across the top of the table. A tick means that collocation occurs, a cross that it does not, and a question mark that there is a degree of uncertainty. These collocations, by the way, hold for British English, and there are doubtless differences for English as spoken in other parts of the world.

2.9 Some English collocations (from McCarthy (1990))

	problem	amount	shame	man
large	?	✔	✘	✔
great	✔	✔	✔	✔
big	✔	✔	✘	✔
major	✔	?	✘	✘

Box 2.9 shows among other things that in British English we say something is *a great shame*, but not *a big shame* or *a large shame*. You can well imagine that FL learners will find these conventions very difficult to master. Because they are often simply convention, it is often just exposure to the language that is needed, rather than any significant degree of understanding or intellectual effort.

Mackey (1965, cited in Wilkins 1972a: 120) exemplifies some of the difficulties that occur if the learner expects the <u>lexical field</u> of words to be the same from one language to the next. Box 2.10 illustrates some English uses of the word *head*, and shows the French equivalents. The learner who thinks she can use the French word *tête* wherever the English *head* is used is in for a shock.

2.10 Some French ways of saying what in English is called 'head'

	of a person	*tête*
	of a bed	*chevet*
	of a coin	*face*
	of a cane	*pomme*
head	of a match	*bout*
	of a table	*haut bout*
	of an organization	*directeur*
	on beer	*mousse*
	title	*rubrique*

It is easy to find amusing examples of unusual collocations made by learners. The student who came up to me at the end of a lesson and complimented me on my *delicious lesson* was making a mistake of collocation. *Delicious* does carry the general meaning of 'very good' that (I assume) he intended, but it is used for food, not lessons. Remaining with the topic of food, consider the following list of menu mistakes from around the world:[4]

2.11 Would *you* eat these dishes?

Stuffed nun	(Indian restaurant)
Smoked Solomon	(Jakarta)
Turdy delight	(Israel)
Pig in the family way	(West Germany)
Terminal soup	(Istanbul airport)
Steamed dick with vegetables	(Chinese restaurant)
Quick Lorraine	(London)
Roast Headlamp	(Greece)
Squits with source	(Alpes-Maritimes)
Boiled god in parsley	(London)
Calve's dong	(Athens)
Fish Rotty and spaghetti Bolograse	(North Yemen)
Battered soul	(Switzerland)
Hard-boiled eggs, filled with a delicate curried mouse	(Manchester)

One lexical area which learners of English as a foreign language find particularly difficult are the so-called 'phrasal' verbs. These are verbs which are composed of a verb plus a <u>particle</u> – a word like *up*, *in* or *over* (some of which are prepositions). Examples of phrasal verbs are *look up*, *put off*. Sometimes these verbs have a literal meaning, which learners can easily work out. Hence in (a), the meaning of *look up* is quite clear – it is the meaning of *look* plus the meaning of *up*:

(a) *Mary looked up the chimney and saw a bird's nest there*

But these verbs often have a meaning that cannot be worked out by combining together the meanings of the constituent parts. Hence the meaning in (b) is not so easy to guess:

(b) *Mary looked up the word*   (i.e. in her dictionary)

These verbs have rules about word order which are also difficult. Hence you can put *up* after the noun in (c), but not in (d). A star * beside a sentence means it is not acceptable in English:

(c) *Mary looked the word up*
(d) **Mary looked the chimney up*

As for *look up*, so for *put off*. If you take the meaning of *put* and add it to the meaning of *off*, you do not arrive at the sense of 'postpone' which is one of the verb's meanings. All very bewildering. You may like to think of some other verbs like this, where there is a literal meaning that is the 'sum of the parts', as well as one that cannot be so easily guessed.

In this treatment of systemic competence we have left many stones unturned. Some of these you will have come across in box 2.1 where you considered the Cats Essay, and it may now be of interest to you to revisit your categorization of errors in that essay, to see how may of your categories you feel fit under the title of systemic competence.

The picture which should be emerging as this chapter progresses is of the complexity of learning a foreign language. It is indeed a complex and multifaceted process. This will become increasingly apparent as we turn to Canale and Swain's second area.

Sociolinguistic competence

Rules of use

Though most of you will have some idea of what Canale and Swain's first category entails, it may well be that the other two will be less familiar. Canale and Swain divide their **sociolinguistic competence** into two categories. The first they call (sociocultural) rules of use.[5] An example of theirs: imagine a man and a woman go into a restaurant and are approached by the waiter, whom they have never seen before. If the waiter were to address them by saying *OK chump, what are you and this broad gonna eat?*, then they would doubtless be shocked and bewildered, perhaps even enough to beat a hasty retreat. Notice that the rude waiter is not breaking any rule of grammar (as he would have done if he had said *What are you and this broad gonna eating?* for example). He is instead offending against a 'rule of use' – one which deals with how it is appropriate to address customers in a restaurant. The example illustrates that it is possible to break rules of use in a perfectly grammatical way.

Rules of use are often less easy to state than rules of grammar, and sometimes need careful thought before they can be articulated clearly. Box 2.12 invites you to think about rules of use:

2.12 Thinking about rules of use

Here are some questions to stimulate you into thinking about rules of use in your L1:
1. In many languages there is a conventional greeting question that people ask when they meet a friend or acquaintance. In some languages, like English, the question is something like *How are you?* What is the conventional greeting question in your language? What is the expected reply?

   Think of two ways of greeting, one extremely informal and one very formal. Give examples of concrete situations in which you would

---

use one, then the other. Imagine what would happen if the informal greeting were used in a very formal situation, and vice versa.

What do you say when you are introduced to someone for the very first time? Is it different from a normal greeting?

2. Imagine that you are in a railway carriage. It is very hot, and you'd like the window opened. Before opening it, you want to check that everyone else in the compartment is happy for you to do this. How would you ask? Then think of two other ways – one that you feel would be excessively polite, another that would be too direct.

Language groups often differ in terms of how polite you are expected to be, when asking someone a favour, for example. In some language groups you are expected to be very polite and indirect. In others is it considered normal to be forthright, making your meaning straight-forward and clear. You might be able to think of a language group which in your mind is associated with being very polite. And one associated with directness?

3. Imagine you are walking along the street and you want to know the time. You stop someone and say *Excuse me, do you have a watch?* They reply *Yes I do, thanks*, and walk off. What would your reaction be? Try and say in what way the person has violated a rule of use.

Does sociolinguistic competence need learning? Surely, you might think, the same rules apply universally! The following two anecdotes illustrate that this is not at all the case. One of them is associated with the area of greeting questions. My first teaching job abroad was in the country now called Croatia, where I was fortunate to spend time in a small, almost deserted village on one of the beautiful Adriatic islands. Each day as I left the house, I was approached by the very elderly lady who lived next door. She always said the same thing: *Where are you going?*, to which I would reply *To the shop* or *Down to the sea*, or whatever. I must confess to becoming a little irritated over time with the lady's question. 'Why doesn't she mind her own business?' I would silently complain; 'you can't even leave the house without her wanting to know where you're going!' It was only some years later, when I had travelled a little more widely, that I realized what had been happening here. Her question was exactly equivalent to the British English *How are you?* said as a conventional greeting. The question *Where are you going?* is just a way of saying *hello,* and the expected response might be *Out.* This response performs the same function as the English *Fine* in response to the question *How are you?* What would be completely incorrect would be for either of these questions to be taken at face value as serious requests for information. If you were to reply to *How are you?* with a list of ailments, your interlocutor would be justifiably bewildered. A 'rule of use' about the way we greet would have been broken. Box 2.13, taken from Garfinkel (1967), illustrates just this situation.

2.13   Mistaking a greeting for a request for information

Garfinkel (1967: 44) reports on a sociological experiment where student experimenters are asked to engage an acquaintance in ordinary conversation, then to insist that the acquaintance clarify the sense of some ordinary remarks. One of the conversations went like this (S = subject, E = experimenter):

> S: *How are you?*
> E: *How am I in regard to what? My health, my finances, my school work, my peace of mind, my . . .*
> S: (Red in the face and suddenly out of control) *Look! I was just trying to be polite. Frankly, I don't give a damn how you are.*

Can you think of any other situations where to ask for clarification of some ordinary remark would seem strange?

The point is that in some countries of the world the conventional question asked on meeting is not *How are you?* but *Where are you going?* and the expected response in such situations is not a true statement of one's movements, but a simple formulaic phrase. In other parts of the world the greeting question is *Have you eaten?* My response to the Croatian lady's question was as mistaken as E's response in box 2.13. The moral is simple: since greeting questions differ from culture to culture, a language learner from a different culture needs to learn them. Many rules of use need to be learned.

Keenan and Ochs (1979) provide the second anecdote:

2.14   How to obtain sweet potatoes

Keenan and Ochs (1979) describe aspects of the Malagasy language, spoken in the African Republic of Madagascar. 'Regarding request behaviour', they say, 'the European may often find himself as having been understood to have made a request where in fact none was intended. For example, on one occasion, Edward [an American] in making idle conversation with a neighbour, happened to remark on the large pile of sweet potatoes in front of the man's house. About twenty minutes later, having returned to our own house, we were surprised to see the man's son appear with a plate of two cooked sweet potatoes! On reflection, it was clear that our casual remark was interpreted as a request by our neighbour' (p. 156).

Malagasy is, incidentally, one of those languages where the conventional greeting question is *Where are you going*? (Keenan and Ochs (1979: 149).)

Thomas (1983) deals in detail with what she calls 'pragmatic failure', the sorts of things that go wrong when people try to communicate messages. She begins her paper with the following quotation from Miller (1974) which seems to imply that rules of use should occupy a central position in foreign-language learning: 'most of our misunderstandings of other people are not due to any ability to hear them or to parse their sentences or to understand their words . . . a far more important source of difficulty in communication is that we so often fail to understand a speaker's intention'. There are different sorts of pragmatic failure; one common one occurs when the rules of use differ in native and target language.[6] One of Thomas's examples deals with the phrase *would you like to*. This is very often used in English as a polite command, as for example when a teacher says to a pupil in class *Would you like to read?*. The teacher saying this is not really giving the pupil any option – it is truly intended as a command. Thomas, working as a teacher of English in Russia, would sometimes say this to her pupils. On a number of occasions the reply came back: *No, I wouldn't*. The pupils replying in this way were not being cheeky or rude – they genuinely thought their preferences were being consulted. Box 2.15 contains various other illustrations of pragmatic failure from Thomas (1983), again related to her Russian experiences.

2.15 Some differences in English and Russian rules of use

1. In Russian *konesno* means 'of course' and it is often used to convey an enthusiastic 'yes' (something like *yes indeed* in English). But often Russian speakers will use *of course* in a wrong sense in English, as in the following:

   A: *Is this a good restaurant?*
   B: *Of course.*

   What Speaker B (a Russian) here means is 'Yes it really is;' but the actual effect of this answer to an English speaker would be something like 'What a stupid question!'

2. *Po moemu* ('in my opinion') and *kazetsja* ('it seems to me') are often used in Russian much as we use *I think* in English. Often this causes no problems at all (Thomas's example is *St Sophia's is, in my opinion, the finest example of Byzantine architecture in the Soviet Union*). Problems come when Russians use the expressions for less weighty opinions, where their use sounds pompous to say the least – *It seems to me there's someone at the door*, or *In my opinion the film begins at eight*.

3. The usual way to ask directions in Russian is by use of the simple imperative, as in *Tell me (please) how to get to . . . .* In English we prefer something a little more indirect (like *Excuse me, please, could you tell me . . .*) Russians who transfer use of the Russian way into English risk sounding brusque and discourteous.

Rules of discourse

Canale and Swain's second category of sociolinguistic competence concerns what they call 'rules of discourse'. The word discourse is used to refer to the way that pieces of speech or writing are joined together to form stretches (involving one or more participants – a conversation is a piece of discourse involving two or more participants). 'Rules of discourse' are essentially 'joining together rules'. Box 2.16 invites you to consider two different types of discourse rules:

2.16 Two ways of breaking discourse rules

Here are two short 'texts'. Both are a little odd as regards 'rules of discourse'. Articulate as precisely as you can exactly what makes each text odd:

(a) *John saw a man in the park. The man's name was Jack. The man was wearing a coat. The man had a hat on. The man was carrying a stick.*
(b) (spoken in a street, between two strangers):

   X: *Excuse me, can you tell me the time?*
   Y: *The clouds in the East are gathering, and war may ensue.*

Try to express the way in which the rules being broken in (a) and (b) are different.

Notice first that as with the rude waiter's 'rules of use' example, these sentences do not contain grammatical mistakes. What is odd is how they are joined together. In Text (a) it is a little strange how the words *the man* are repeated. It is clearly the same man who is being referred to in each sentence, and we are even told his name (Jack). So why, in sentence 3 do we not read *Jack* or *He*, instead of *The man*? Probably you would also expect sentences 3 and 4, and maybe 5 to be joined together to form a longer sentence – *He was wearing a coat and hat, and was carrying a stick.* As well as being grammatical, the sentences in Text (a) make perfect sense. But the grammatical means of joining sentences together are a little strange, though not actually wrong. The sentences are cohesive; they do show cohesion of sorts. But the cohesion is rather unusual.

Text (b) is concerned with coherence, not cohesion. The sentences are well-joined together grammatically speaking. The problem lies on the level of 'making sense unity'. Indeed, in the circumstances Speaker X could be forgiven for beating a hasty retreat. Y's response clearly breaks the rules of discourse which require a response to have some relevance to the question asked. The result is that X probably wonders whether Y is mentally unhinged, or drunk, or otherwise incapacitated (though, again we note, in a perfectly grammatical way). Disobeying rules of discourse can lead to the strait-jacket!

Notice in this context that sentences may seem on the surface to be entirely unconnected, yet may in fact be perfectly coherent. A much-quoted instance (cited in Brown and Yule 1983: 196) is:

A: *There's the doorbell*
B: *I'm in the bath.*

Though the sentences in this example may seem as unconnected as those in Text (b), you will find it easy to imagine the context in which they hang well together.

Do rules of discourse need learning? As with rules of use, one's first reaction might be that the same rules apply universally. But, again, this is not the case. Look back to the Cats Essay, in box 2.1, and try to find one example of a cohesion error and one of coherence. Their presence shows that FL speakers do indeed make such errors. But, you may wonder, are these errors language/culture-based or just to do with the fact that the learner is writing in a slapdash fashion?

Though slapdash writing will of course result in poor cohesion and coherence, these can also be caused by language-related differences. Particularly vivid examples of this are found in the work of Kaplan and in the area of study called 'contrastive rhetoric', where the writing styles of different language groups are observed. Kaplan (1966) reports on the analysis of some seven hundred compositions written by students from different language groups. He plots differences in writing styles associated with the different language groups. Box 2.17 illustrates one paragraph from a composition written by an Arabic-speaking student. Does anything strike you about the way sentences are joined together?

2.17 Part of a student composition (from Kaplan 1966)

At that time of the year I was not studying enough to pass my courses in school. And all the time I was asking my cousin to let me ride the bicycle, but he wouldn't let me. But after two weeks, noticing that I was so much interested in the bicycle, he promised me that if I pass my courses in school for that year he would give it to me as a present. So I began to study hard. And I studying eight hours a day instead of two.

Kaplan notes that 80 per cent of these sentences begin with a co-ordinating element (a word like *and* or *but*), and that there is also an absence of subordination – both trends which continue throughout the whole essay. He associates these characteristics with Arabic, and perhaps all Semitic languages.

The fact that errors with rules of discourse can be blamed on slapdashness makes them particularly serious in some contexts. In Johnson (1977) I report on the reactions of university tutors to errors occurring in overseas students' writing. Grammatical mistakes are often simply ignored, but discourse errors – particularly of coherence – are often treated very severely. This is because such errors are often automatically associated with slovenly, slapdash writing. Rules of discourse, like rules of use, often need to be learned.

Strategic competence

Canale and Swain (1980: 30) describe their third area – 'strategic competence' – as 'verbal and non-verbal communication strategies that may be called into action to compensate for breakdowns in communication . . .'. This is a very important type of competence for the learner to develop, because she will inevitably face many breakdowns in communication when struggling to use the foreign language with her restricted linguistic resources.

Communication strategies have been much studied, and different ways of classifying them have been developed. Box 2.18 gives some examples of the way learners cope with communication breakdowns.

2.18 Some communication strategies

Bialystok (1990) gives some examples of the communication strategies used by nine-year-old English-speaking children learning French. One major strategy-type is described as *paraphrase*. For example, the learner who wishes to express the notion of 'playpen', but who does not have the French word, says *On peut mettre un bébé dedans. Il y a comme un trou* (*You put a baby in it. It's like a hole*).

Tarone (1977), whose classification Bialystok uses for her data, gives an example of paraphrase which involves 'word coinage'. The learner wants to describe an animated caterpillar. She calls it a *person worm*.

On other occasions, the learner will simply use the native language for an unknown item. One learner trying to define what a 'swing' is, said *C'est une sorte de, tu peux dire, chaise que quand tu 'move'* (*It's a kind of, you could say, chair for when you move*).

Some of the strategies learners use involve non-linguistic means such as mime. Tarone's example of mime is the learner who claps hands to indicate the word *applause*.

Think of your own language-learning experiences. Can you identify any other communication strategies that you yourself have used?

Does strategic competence need to be learned? Several things need to be said about this issue. Firstly, it is certainly true that many traditional teaching methods not only ignore strategic competence, but may actually hinder its development. These are methods which never involve the learners in taking any risks. The only speaking or writing they are asked to do involves reproducing material that has recently been practised, while their listening and reading practice entails going through texts word by word so that 'total comprehension' is achieved. But the communicative situations the learner will experience when using a foreign language will commonly involve risk-taking. The learner will regularly want to say and write things which have *not* been recently practised, and they will need to understand messages when they do not understand nearly every word contained in that message. The result is learners who become silent, tongue-tied, when they are asked to say something they cannot say, or understand something containing words they have not met before.

But the question of *how* best to facilitate the development of strategic competence is a difficult one. Some believe that there is benefit to drawing learners' attention to the different types of strategy, like the ones in box 2.18. Others believe that we should put learners into simulated communicative situations where they have to take risks so as to facilitate the development of communication strategies. There is some evidence that strategic competence will develop by itself, as long as the learner is exposed to communicative situations. Schmidt (1983) discusses the fascinating case of a learner called Wes. He was a thirty-two-year-old Japanese artist spending time in Honolulu. His language development was followed over a three-year period. By the end of this time, Schmidt says, 'Wes's grammatical control of English had hardly improved at all' (p. 144). But his strategic competence had improved a lot. Schmidt again: 'Since Wes clearly has a very limited command of the grammatical aspects of English, communication breakdowns do occur when he is talking to native speakers. Yet Wes is almost always able to repair these breakdowns, and it seems that his confidence, his willingness to communicate, and especially his *persistence* in communicating what he has in his mind and understanding what his interlocutors have in their minds go a long way towards compensating for his grammatical inaccuracies' (p. 161). One might almost say that Wes's English improved little over the period, but what he could do with it improved greatly.

The tale of Wes points up a dilemma associated with the development of strategic competence. It is natural that we should want our learners to develop the means of 'getting by' with imperfect language resources. But we do not want to develop this so effectively that the language resources themselves never become developed. Learning how to paraphrase is indeed a useful skill, but better still is knowing the correct words themselves, making paraphrase unnecessary.

Conclusion

In this chapter we have looked at some of the skills involved in using a foreign language, and have considered whether these skills need to be learned. Perhaps you have been shocked by the sheer amount that there is to master, and are left wondering how on earth anyone ever manages the task!

'How people learn foreign languages' will be the subject of Part 2 of this book. Underlying the various theories of FL learning we shall consider there, as well as the views of FL teaching we shall meet in Part 3, are a small group of key ideas which it will be useful to discuss at the outset. This we shall do in Chapter 3.

Notes

1. The other cases mentioned in box 2.6 are genitive (Gen.), dative (Dat.), instrumental (Instr.) and prepositional (Prep.). For details of the uses of these cases, you are invited to consult any one of a number of books offering a background to language studies and linguistics – Crystal (1987) for example.

2. In (a) the <u>auxiliary</u> part of the verb (*is*) is put before the subject noun (*John*). Sentences (b) and (c) contain modals (*can* and *should*). In some ways these act like auxiliaries – as here where they are put before the subject noun to form interrogatives. Sentences (a), (b) and (c) all have two verb forms – an auxiliary or modal and the main verb (*play*). But in (d) to (f) there is just a main verb. In English you need an auxiliary or modal to form the interrogative, and where there is not one present, the verb *do* is brought in to fulfil this purpose. So in (d) to (f) the interrogatives begin with a part of *do*. All the interrogatives in the box have the same order of elements: auxiliary (or modal) + subject noun + main verb. The interrogative of (f) highlights another aspect of the system, that it is the auxiliary or modal which shows the tense. (d) is in the simple present tense, and (f) in the simple past. This is indicated by *do* in (d) and *did* in (f). Notice that in the non-interrogative sentences (d) and (f), tense is indicated by the form of the main verb (*plays* is simple present, *played* simple past).

3. Here are short answers to the questions. Yours might well be longer and more detailed:
   (a) In English, the present perfect tense (*have known*) is used for an action that began in the past but is continuing until the present. In many other languages the simple present tense (*know*) would be used.
   (b) *since* is used in association with a moment of time – as in sentence (a): *since 1980* – while *for* is used in association with a period of time (*for three days*). Many languages do not make this distinction.
   (c) In many languages a word like *before* can be followed by an infinitive (*to start*). In English the *-ing* form is used, and this causes problems for many learners.
   (d) One use of the English present continuous tense (*I'm going*) is to express an action taking place as you speak. A common way of expressing habitual action (e.g. one that takes place twice a year) is by using the simple present

(*I go*). As with all rules, though, there are exceptions – *He's always talking* is an example of the present continuous being used to express an (annoyingly) frequent action. Many languages do not have both these tenses, or do not use them in the same ways.

(e) Many learners find indirect questions difficult in English. The actual question asked here might be *When are you going on holiday?* Here the word order is *are you* to indicate the direct question. With the words *Tell me* in front, the question becomes an indirect one – a type of statement in fact – and in that case the word order is *you are* (as in most statements).

(f) Box 2.7 contains the answer to this. There we saw that *do* is often used to form questions in English. But where there is a modal like *can* you simply put this before the subject – *You can* becomes *Can you?* A learner struggling with this complicated way of asking questions is likely to over-generalize, and use *do* in all her questions.

4. I am indebted to Maria Sifianou for providing the list of menu mistakes

5. The word <u>pragmatics</u> has come to be used in relation to Canale and Swain's sociocultural rules of use. Cook (1998a: 249) defines pragmatics as 'the study of how language is interpreted by its users in its linguistic and non-linguistic context'.

6. Thomas (1983) identifies two sorts of pragmatic failure. The examples in box 2.15 are of what she calls <u>pragmalinguistic failure</u>. This can occur when a language user assumes that a rule of use in her L1 is the same in the FL. <u>Sociopragmatic failure</u> is primarily to do with cultural rather than linguistic differences. An area where this type of failure occurs relates to taboo subjects. A subject that is talked about normally in one culture may be almost taboo in another.

Chapter 3

Some views of language and language learning

Introduction

As perhaps in all areas of human knowledge, in the field of applied linguistics nothing ever happens in a vacuum. New ideas do not just spring out of thin air: they often come out of old ideas, and from ideas in other areas of knowledge. In this chapter we shall look into the background to two sets of ideas which have had a great deal of influence on the direction of foreign language learning and teaching studies. These ideas are not easy ones to grasp, and for this reason you may find this chapter the most challenging of the book. But understanding the ideas and where they come from really will enrich your insight into the field.

A central conflict: empiricism and mentalism

There is a conflict that continually rears its head throughout this book. This is what Diller (1971) says about it: 'the great theoretical division between linguists – the empiricists versus the rationalists – also divides the language teaching methodologies'. Not just teaching methodologies, we might add, but also theories about how foreign languages are learned.

We shall spend a large part of this chapter clarifying what empiricism and rationalism (or 'mentalism' as we shall call it) are, and exploring how these opposing philosophies have exerted their influence in two particular areas – linguistics and learning theory (including the study of L1 acquisition). But first, box 3.1 invites you to reflect on some issues relevant to what we shall be discussing.

Structural linguistics

At the end of the nineteenth and beginning of the twentieth century, a stimulus for the development of contemporary linguistics came from what at first sight might appear as an unlikely source. This was the rapid

3.1 Contrary opinions

For every point of view that exists, there is always an opposite one. Below are some opposite points of view about foreign-language learning and teaching. Match the opposites together (the suggested pairings are given in Note 1. Then ponder the opinions, particularly in the light of your own foreign-language learning experience. Which opinions do you have most/least sympathy with?

All the issues raised here will make an appearance later in the book, particularly in Chapter 10, which deals with the recent history of language teaching.

(a) Learning a language is like learning any other habit. You don't have to think about it; it just develops automatically.

(b) Of course, to learn a language you have to hear others speaking it. But learners develop the language 'inside themselves', forming their own views about how it works, and following their own sweet way.

(c) Amount of practice is not important. Sometimes you can learn a word after just hearing it once – particularly if you hear it in a context where its use is particularly vivid.

(d) Practice makes perfect, so the more you practice, the more thoroughly you learn. The teacher should make you repeat sentences lots of times.

(e) We don't need to worry when a learner makes an error. After all, children make lots of errors when learning their L1, and these nearly always disappear over time. Indeed, errors can be a good thing. As the saying goes: 'we learn through our mistakes'.

(f) Thinking about how the language works is a very important part of learning. Understanding can be a very useful tool.

(g) We learn languages by copying what others say. That's why exercises which ask you to 'listen and repeat' are so useful.

(h) When you are learning a language the teacher must ensure you make as few mistakes as possible. This is because practice makes not just perfect, but permanent as well. A mistake repeated will often become ingrained.

disappearance of scores of American Indian languages. Box 3.2 overleaf records the pessimistic thoughts of one linguist and anthropologist, J. W. Powell, on this matter.

Realization of the near extinction of so many languages led some linguists – particularly Franz Boas, whose huge *Handbook of American Indian Languages* (1911) is a monument to the movement – to develop what is sometimes called 'field linguistics'. As this name suggests, this sort of linguistics involved going 'out into the field' to collect data, very often from a language that

3.2 Languages dying out

In his paper 'Indian Linguistic Families of America North of Mexico', J. W. Powell says:

> The field [studying American Indian languages] is a vast one . . . and the workers are comparatively few. Moreover, opportunities for collecting linguistic material are growing fewer day by day, as tribes are consolidated upon reservations, as they become civilised, and as the older Indians, who alone are skilled in their language, die, leaving, it may be, only a few imperfect vocabularies as a basis for future study. History has bequeathed to us the names of many tribes, which became extinct in early colonial times, of whose language not a hint is left and whose linguistic relations must ever remain unknown. (Holder 1966: 102)

was in the process of dying out. These data would then be used as the basis for the linguist to work out the language's structure. This idea, of working from data to an understanding of underlying structure is an important one. Two terms coined by another early twentieth-century linguist of the period, the Swiss linguist Ferdinand de Saussure, are useful to clarify the idea. He uses the French word *parole* (literally 'word') to describe actual concrete instances of language use – the utterances recorded by the field linguist, for example. To describe the more theoretical, underlying structure of the language Saussure uses another French word *langue* ('tongue', 'language'). We can use these terms to express our important idea: it was believed that you could collect specimens of *parole*, and then use this recorded information to work out *langue*.

Linguists (with Saussure at the forefront) developed a set of analytic techniques which they believed would enable them to achieve this aim of working from instances of a language's use to an understanding of how that language was structured. These procedures for analysing languages are still used by some linguists today, and involve techniques for breaking speech up into segments (words, phonemes, morphemes, etc.), and for classifying items into categories (like nouns, adjectives and adverbs). A central technique associated with these procedures involved looking at the 'distribution' of items – exactly where they could and could not occur in relation to other items: box 3.3 gives you an example of a distributional point.

It was the American linguist Leonard Bloomfield who put together and systematized these analytic procedures in a highly influential book called *Language*, which appeared in 1933. The linguistics of Bloomfield and his colleagues has come to be called structuralism, and one of its central aims was to be *scientific* in its approach to linguistic analysis. As to what 'being scientific' entailed, in this Bloomfield is part of the philosophical tradition known as empiricism. This tradition goes back to the seventeenth-century English philosopher John Locke (and beyond), and is associated in

3.3 Looking at distribution

There are various positions in a sentence that a word like *sometimes* can occupy. Here are two examples of the <u>distribution</u> of *sometimes*:

(a) *He sometimes played the bagpipes*
(b) *He played the bagpipes sometimes*

Try substituting *sometimes*, in both these sentences, with each of the following words in turn: *often; frequently; well; rarely; regularly; terribly*.

Some, but not all, of these words have the same distribution. Which? Try to find something in common about the ideas expressed by those with the same distribution as *sometimes*. (It would, incidentally, be easy to find exceptions to what it is that you discover.)[2]

Bloomfield's own time with the logical positivist philosophers like Rudolph Carnap, working in Vienna. This tradition placed central importance on 'sense data' – concrete, material things that can be seen, touched, heard, recorded, measured – as the starting point and basis for scientific enquiry. In the study of language, this leads precisely to the procedure of using actual instances of speech (*parole*) as the starting point for analysis. Here are two quotations (cited in Stern 1983: 137) which illustrate Bloomfield's desire to be scientific, and show what that entails:

- 'science shall deal with only such events that are accessible in their time and place to any and all observers'
- 'science shall deal with only such terms as are derivable by rigid definition from a set of . . . terms concerning physical happenings'

For Bloomfield, then, science (and linguistics as science), was concerned with the observable and the physical.

In its concern with these attributes, structural linguistics became linked with a school of psychology also aggressively interested in the observable and the physical. This school was known as behaviourism.

Behaviourism

Four of the principal protagonists in behaviourism were: a nineteenth-century Russian, Ivan Pavlov; an early twentieth-century American, John Watson (sometimes called the father of behaviourism); another early twentieth-century American, Edward Thorndike; and a mid-twentieth-century American, Burrhus Skinner.

Behaviourism was concerned with how learning took place. The three basic behaviourist ideas about learning are:

Background

(a) *Conditioning* (Pavlov and the dribbling dogs)

Learning is seen as a question of developing connections (known as stimulus-response bonds) between events. The process of developing connections is called conditioning. Pavlov's dogs are the best known example of the conditioning process. In one famous experiment (described in box 3.4), Pavlov taught dogs to salivate when they heard a bell ringing. Salivation is of course an entirely natural thing for a dog to do in the presence of food – no learning at all is required – and for this reason the response is known as an unconditioned reflex. But it is not normal for a dog to salivate when a bell rings, so we are here indeed talking about learning. The dogs were conditioned to respond in the way they did; their response is a conditioned reflex.

3.4 How to teach dogs to salivate when a bell rings, in two easy lessons

1. Ring a bell, and soon after give the dog food.
2. Repeat many times. Soon the dog will associate the bell with food, and will salivate when the bell rings.

(b) *Habit formation* (Skinner and the sporty pigeons)

The behaviourists shared with the structural linguists a view of science which was grounded on the importance of physical events (what we earlier called 'sense data'). Hence they did not take easily to the idea of some unobservable, abstract entity called the 'mind' being involved in learning. For them, learning was a question of habit formation. When the behaviour to be learned was complex, it was developed by a process called shaping. To shape a behaviour, you break it down into small parts, and teach each one at a time, until eventually the whole complex behaviour is built up. By shaping, Skinner was able to teach pigeons unlikely behaviours, like playing table tennis (see box 3.5), and in this way Skinner had remarkable success in teaching animals behaviours which are both complex and unnatural for them. As we shall see in Chapter 10, the concept of shaping plays a role in some language-teaching methods.

(c) *The importance of the 'environment'* (writing on a 'clean slate')

We can draw a distinction, useful in many discussions about learning, between the *organism* and the *environment*. The organism is the person or animal that does the learning. The word 'environment' is here being used in a very wide sense to refer to anything external to the organism – an event or a situation, or even another person (a teacher or parent for example) – may be seen as part of the environment in this sense. Different learning theories give different degrees of importance to the organism and the environment. In behaviourism, the environment is

3.5 How to teach a pigeon to play table tennis, in five easy lessons

1. First stand your pigeon behind a ping pong ball. Whenever it approaches the ball (by chance at first), give it some food. Soon your pigeon will have been conditioned to approach the ball.
2. Now only give the pigeon food when it actually touches the ball.
3. When the pigeon has learned to touch the ball, start to reward it only when it pushes the ball forward.
4. Continue training in the same way until the pigeon can knock the ball over a net.
5. Your pigeon is now ready to confront an opponent (another pigeon). You now only reward them when they push the ball past their opponent. The championship can commence.

all, and the role of the organism is considered insignificant. Two vivid metaphors are often used to describe this view of the organism. The child is said to be born as a 'clean slate' (the Latin phrase is *tabula rasa*) onto which experience 'writes' or 'draws' its 'messages'. A second, similar, metaphor is of the child as a piece of unused photographic paper, which, when 'exposed' to the world and to experiences, begins to reflect images of these. The simple diagram below shows a way of representing the roles of organism and environment in behaviourism; the size of the boxes indicates relative importance to the learning process.

Environment   Organism

Anyone interested in applied linguistics will need and want to know more about behaviourism than is given here. Many introductory texts dealing with learning theory will give the appropriate background. See for example Borger and Seabourne (1966), or Robinson (1995).

Mentalism (rationalism)

Skinner applied his behaviourist views to language in a book, published in 1957, called *Verbal Behaviour*. Chomsky's 1959 review of this is a major and devastating attack on behaviourism in linguistics. Chomsky writes from within a philosophical and linguistic tradition known as 'mentalism' or 'rationalism', which stands in opposition to behaviourism in nearly all respects. Mentalism is the belief that the mind (and all things associated with it, like consciousness, thoughts, etc.) are important for determining not just human behaviour, but also the way we 'do' science. Chomsky revolutionized linguistics and introduced a theory known as transformational generative grammar (TG for short). His book *Syntactic Structures* (1957) introduced the theory, and his 1965 *Aspects of the Theory of Syntax* modified the model. Chomsky's views of both language and language learning have been highly influential in the study of foreign-language learning (and language teaching as well). Lyons (1970) provides a brief and accessible account of Chomsky's early beliefs (his thinking has developed considerably since the TG days which we shall concentrate on here). A more recent (and more technical, hence rather less easy-to-follow) account of Chomsky's views is found in Cook and Newson (1995). We shall here look firstly at his views on language and linguistics, then on first language acquisition.

Transformational linguistics

As we have seen, a main idea of the structuralists was the belief that the starting point for language analysis should be 'the observable'. A central plank of Chomsky's argument is that if we insist on restricting ourselves to the study of the observable, we shall fail to understand the most important aspects of language. We can illustrate this by looking at two of Chomsky's most famous sentences:

(1) *John is easy to please*
(2) *John is eager to please*

Structural linguistic techniques would recognize the clear structural similarity between these sentences. They both start with the noun, followed by part of the verb *be*, followed by an adjective (*easy/eager*), finishing with *to* and a verb (*please*). But, despite these similarities, there are fundamental differences between the sentences. These are brought out by the fact that we can say (3), but not (4):

(3) *It is easy to please John*
(4) **It is eager to please John*

Without entering into the technicalities of Chomsky's analysis, we can understand the gist of his argument by thinking about the relationships between the verb *please*, and the adjectives *easy* and *eager*. In sentence (2), the person wanting to do the pleasing is John. But sentence (1) means something like 'it is easy for someone (else) to please John'; the sentence has a 'passive sense': 'John is easy to be pleased'. The relationship of the elements in the sentences are, then, quite different, and this accounts for the fact that we can say (3) but not (4). The important point is that these different relationships do not manifest themselves in the 'observable' sentences (1) and (2) themselves, which are superficially similar. It is only at a deeper level of analysis – when you start to think about the impossibility of saying (4) – that the true relationships become apparent. It is this, more revealing, but also more abstract (and unobservable!), level of analysis that Chomsky introduced into his linguistics. He called it <u>deep structure</u>. In terms of his analysis, he would say that sentences (1) and (3) are similar at deep structure level, while sentences (1) and (2), though superficially highly similar, are dissimilar at the deep level.

It is important to understand how Chomsky's willingness to talk in terms of a deep structure which goes beyond the observable, leads him to abandon the structuralist belief that considering *parole* leads to an understanding of *langue*. In our example, the instances of *parole* (that a field linguist recording English might testify) are sentences (1), (2) and (3). Sentence (4) would never be heard, because it cannot exist – further evidence of the main point – that unobserved truths are important in understanding how *langue* works.

We may call this type of analysis 'mentalist' because it believes that in order to say important things about language it is necessary to go beyond the observable. This is where the essential methodological differences between Bloomfield and Chomsky become evident. Chomsky is always asking whether one can say certain sentences (like (4) for example). The person he asks is often himself, as a native speaker of the language in question. He is prepared to 'create his own data'; to rely on native speaker intuition; and, above all, to ask about what you *cannot* say as much as what you *can* say. It is considerations like this that lead Chomsky (1966) to say, referring to the structuralists' techniques mentioned earlier: 'I think there are by now very few linguists who believe that it is possible to arrive at the phonological or syntactic structure of a language by systematic application of "analytic procedures" of segmentation and classification.' Pause to reflect on this sentence for a moment. It will play an important part in the argument below.

Mentalist learning theory

The 'analytic procedures' just mentioned were developed for the linguist, particularly the field linguist anxious to describe a language before it disappears. As we have seen, Chomsky's views amount to a claim that, however much the linguist uses these techniques, he will never arrive at a proper understanding of how a language system works.

Let us now turn our attention to another individual, in another situation. This is the young child born into a language community and attempting to learn his first language (e.g. English). This child has something in common with the field linguist. Both are faced with a new language which at first they know nothing of. Both have to use whatever resources are at their disposal to come to grips with the language. The young child is indeed a type of field linguist. How does the child manage to crack the secrets of his first language? Ask a behaviourist this question, and the answer would speak in terms of applying (in an unconscious way of course) the same kinds of analytic procedures that the field linguist uses, one of which you explored in box 3.3.

But for Chomsky this way of 'working out' a language's structure is as unlikely for the child as it is for the field linguist. However long the child listened to *parole* and unconsciously applied the linguist's 'analytic procedures' he would never reach *langue*. Chomsky's statement given at the end of the last section, then, embodies a belief in how languages are *not* learned. The child does not listen, apply some rather general techniques, and eventually end up speaking the language. Environmental help plus the use of some general procedures are just not enough.

How then does the child manage to learn his first language? Chomsky sees this problem as part of a more general one that he calls 'Plato's problem'. This problem is: how is it that human beings, whose contacts with the world are so brief and limited, know as much as they do? The association with Plato comes about because in *The Meno* Plato describes the philosopher Socrates demonstrating that an ignorant slave boy knows the principles of geometry. Socrates leads the boy through a series of questions to discover geometric theorems. Plato's answer to the problem was reincarnation – we know so much because we bring knowledge with us from previous existences. Chomsky's formulation of Plato's problem in relation to language is this: how does a child learn such a complicated system as language in such a relatively short time? The acquisition is quick, what is acquired is complicated; therefore the achievement needs explanation. As we have seen, one sort of explanation is that the child receives excellent teaching, from the 'environment' in general and the mother in particular. Chomsky has always denied the feasibility of this explanation. He points out that the data the child gets from the environment (parents and other adults) are 'degenerate' in the sense that they are full of false starts, poor examples, and do not contain anything like the full information the child would need to be able to work out how the language operates. Certainly they are not at all the kind of carefully planned and well articulated language data that most trained FL teachers strive to give their learners. This argument against the 'child receives excellent teaching' explanation is sometimes called the poverty of stimulus argument.

How on earth then *does* the child learn? Chomsky's answer is that the child is born with a powerful piece of machinery – what he calls the language acquisition device (LAD) – which enables him to do the complex task. This piece of machinery contains a kind of blueprint of how language works. It is the existence of this blueprint that makes it unnecessary for the child to undertake the kind of analytic procedures the field linguists developed. These procedures are not necessary because the child already knows a lot about language when he is born. Though at first sight it may seem surprising, Chomsky (1987) notes that his answer to the problem is not so dissimilar to Plato's. Today (in the tradition of Western thought at least) we no longer believe in reincarnation. But the effect of a 'piece of machinery' like the LAD, developed by evolution and genetically passed on from age to age, is not really so different!

Chomsky's views about the LAD amount to a claim about 'what does the work' in L1 acquisition. The child's environment does of course have some role to play – after all, if the child hears no language then he will certainly not learn an L1. But this role is minimal, and the real work is done by the child himself. The diagram below shows this view of the relative roles of environment and organism in L1 acquisition. It stands in dramatic contrast to the diagram on page 43:

Environment   Organism

Chomsky's views on language acquisition stimulated a huge number of studies on the subject, and most reach conclusions that negate behaviourist views. Box 3.6 illustrates the kind of data the transformational grammarians were fond of. You are invited to look at this box before reading the next paragraph.

If 'practice makes permanent' and learning proceeds through habit formation (as behaviourists claim), then we might expect the badly formed sentence *Nobody don't like me* to become well and truly permanent, since it is repeated eight times. But doubtless it does not become permanent. What is likely to happen is that when the child is good and ready to produce the right form, he will do so irrespective of how many hundreds of times he may, up until that point, have produced the wrong form. One might take the exchange as an example of how little the child is affected by

---

3.6 A child that nobody don't like

In the following exchange, reported in McNeill (1970: 106), the linguist parent is attempting to correct the child (learning English as an L1):

> Child: *Nobody don't like me.*
> Parent: *No, say nobody likes me.*
> Child: *Nobody don't like me.*

The child and parent repeat this exchange *eight* times. Then, exasperated at the parent who seems more interested in grammar than in what is being expressed, the child says, with some passion:

> Child: *Oh, nobody don't likes me.*

Two questions:

(a) what does this example suggest to you about the role of *habit formation* in learning the L1?
(b) where does the child's incorrect sentence *Nobody don't like me* 'come from'? Where does the child get it from?

---

his 'environment' – the child carries on in his own sweet way despite all parental attempts to change linguistic behaviour. And where does the child's utterance 'come from'? It has almost certainly never been *heard* by the child in his 'environment'. The child himself has invented it. It comes – like all L1 acquisition for Chomsky – from somewhere inside the organism itself.

Before leaving Chomsky, it is worth noting where his view of an innate LAD takes him. It must of course be the case that all children possess the same piece of machinery. The notion that there is one LAD for those born in Japan, another for Italian children, another for the Dutch, is absurd. The idea only makes sense if we say that all children, wherever and whenever they are born, possess the same blueprint for language. If this is the case, then it follows that all the world's languages must share important characteristics – those aspects of all human languages that our innate blueprint maps out. During recent decades, Chomsky and like-minded linguists have taken up a quest which has in fact fascinated linguists for centuries – to explore the possible nature of what is called Universal Grammar (UG). Finding deep underlying similarities between the world's languages, which are superficially so diverse, has become a major preoccupation of Chomskyan linguistics.

The behaviourist/mentalist conflict

We have here been developing two opposing views of language and language learning; views which can be linked up to more general philosophical positions about the world and knowledge of it. As we look at the development of thought in both the language-learning and language-teaching spheres, we shall see the conflict between these two views enacted time and time again.

A familiar pattern in much language literature from 1940 to 1970 is for fairly drastic empiricist views to be replaced by fairly radical mentalist ones. Time and time again the movement is from Bloomfield/Skinner inspired to Chomsky-inspired. But there is often a further movement since 1970 – towards less radical positions, towards middle ground. An example is found in an area we have just been discussing: the question of the role of the environment in first language acquisition. As we have seen, for the behaviourist it was all important, while for Chomsky it could not be less important. But (as we shall see in Chapter 5), studies since 1970 have shown that Chomsky's view that the language the child receives is 'degenerate' is not really true. That language may be less important than the behaviourists would have it, but it has more effect than Chomsky would accept. We will find this sequence:

empiricist view ⟶ mentalist view ⟶ more sensible middle view

occurring time and time again in the following chapters. Perhaps indeed the use of the word 'sensible' here reflects the human tendency to believe that the present time is always the most sensible in history. We often view the past as moving from extreme to extreme, believing it is only today that we are enlightened enough to adopt some sensible middle position!

At the beginning of the 1970s another change occurred in linguistics which was highly influential in language learning and teaching studies. It was a movement away from the kind of linguistics Chomsky was associated with towards one where the use of language in society became a predominant interest. Some people refer to this movement as the 'sociolinguistic revolution',[3] and to this we now turn. But first:

3.7 An earlier exercise revisited

In box 3.1 you considered some contrary views about language learning and teaching. Look again at these views. For each pair of contrary views, decide which is associated with an empiricist position, and which with a mentalist one.

Do these views (plus what you have just been reading about) enable you to make any general statements about the implications of empiricism and mentalism for both language learning and teaching? What does each approach say about how we learn? And about how we should teach? Your thoughts at this stage may be vague; but they should become clearer as the book proceeds.

The 'sociolinguistic revolution'

If you have ever seen a transcript of your voice recorded onto tape as you were taking part in some form of 'natural' conversation or discussion, you will probably have been shocked at the number of 'ums' and 'ahs' you make, the number of times you start a sentence one way and finish it in another, the number of times you make grammatical and lexical slips. This is a common experience. Many of us think of ourselves as incisive, fluent, coherent speakers, and our self-esteem takes a cruel blow when we see what we have said written down. The speaker in box 3.8 was not drunk, tired, drugged or mentally deranged. The slips and hesitations made are normal to nearly all speakers in informal situations.

3.8   Up the Amazon

Below is a part of a passage of normal speech, transcribed. It is taken from Hughes and Trudgill (1996: 52):

Um . . . in the days before husbands and children, um I did quite a lot of travelling and um . . . one of the th . . . places I went to was to the Amazon and um I hadn't really as why I . . . I knew my husband and um . . . then but . . . just as a friend really and so we um decided that we, or he decided that we would go to Brazil and er I'd been travelling anyway . . . came back for Christmas, two days to wash my rucksack and off we went to Rio . . . and um I hadn't given it any thought at all and the next thing I knew we went up to Manaus . . .

If you were given a copy of a similar transcription of your own speech, you would probably have little difficulty in editing out all the slips and hesitations, to convert it into a far more elegant piece of discourse. It may be said that the slips you made were 'performance related', and that your actual 'competence' in the language is more truly reflected in the corrected version. This latter version, one might say, more truly represents your true ability at English.

Chomsky draws this distinction between competence and perform-ance, and it is one that is similar to Saussure's between *langue* and *parole*. Saussure's *langue*, the underlying language system, is akin to Chomsky's 'competence', and Saussure's *parole* is related to Chomsky's 'performance'.[4] Chomsky states quite clearly that his concern as a linguist is not with performance but competence, and a highly abstract version of competence at that. In his influential 1965 book, which set out one version of trans-formational grammar, he speaks in terms of the competence of the 'ideal speaker–listener, in a completely homogeneous speech-community'. He is not interested in the way that John or Mary actually speak. One of them might have a speech defect, the other a particular way of pronouncing their 'r' sounds; one may have a London accent, the other a Liverpool one. But these are performance features, and Chomsky is interested in the abstraction, the underlying.

At the beginning of the 1970s the views of linguists coming from different traditions and countries, but sharing a more social approach to language study, came to have their voices heard. Sociolinguists (those interested in how language is used within society) began to show discontent with the Chomskyan way of doing things. One of the notions that came under attack was this idea of the 'ideal speaker–listener'. The American sociolinguist Dell Hymes, for example, was interested in the language of disadvantaged children, people who could hardly be described as ideal speaker–listeners. He wanted to be able (directly or indirectly) to help such children, and he found little in the rather rarefied atmosphere of Chomskyan linguistics of relevance for him.

We have already seen in Chapter 1 that Chomsky's other notion – of the 'homogeneous speech-community' – is not one that has much currency in today's world. Stern's (1983: 231) quotation summarizes arguments that we have already seen: 'since World War Two the profound social and political changes in the world have left a recognition that the reality of the language situation can no longer be forced into the simple mould of the single-language nation state with its single-medium school'. Little surprise that with perceptions like these in the air, Hymes should describe Chomskyan linguistics as a 'Garden of Eden' view.

In an important article entitled 'On communicative competence', Hymes (1970) argues that linguists, particularly of the transformational school, have been concerned exclusively with what he calls 'the possible'. They have focused their attention on what the rules of the language system permit as possible structures, what we called 'systemic competence' in Chapter 2. If, Hymes argues, we restrict linguistics in this way, we shall learn nothing about how language is used as a means of communication among humans. Hymes suggests various other factors, apart from 'the possible' that we need to study. One of these Hymes calls 'the feasible'. There are sentences which, though perfectly grammatical, would never be said by anyone because they are so difficult to process. Box 3.9 overleaf exemplifies one of these.

A further factor might be called 'the performed'. There are many phrases and sentences which, though they might well express what a speaker wants to say, do not happen to be used. We saw examples in Chapter 2, where we suggested that there is no real reason why a sentence like *It's a big shame* (as opposed to *It's a great shame*) should not be used. But it never is (in standard British English at least). Note that *It's a big shame* is perfectly grammatical – it just does not happen to be the way we express the idea.

3.9 The woman who married a mouse!?

An example of a sentence that is perfectly grammatical yet too difficult to process is: *the mouse the cat the dog the man the woman married beat chased ate had a white tail.*

Split this up into smaller sentences to reveal what this sentence means. Start at the front of the sentence with the mouse. Your first sentence might be *The mouse had a white tail.* Then move on to the cat: *The cat . . . .* And so on.

Invent another similarly complex sentence, also containing five verbs, but having nothing to do with mice.

The final factor is the one that has had the greatest effect on the study of language learning and teaching. It is what Hymes calls 'the appropriate', and it deals with the 'rules of use' discussed in Chapter 2 under the heading of 'sociolinguistic competence'. Many examples were given in Chapter 2, one being Canale and Swain's inappropriate way the waiter spoke to the restaurant guests: *OK chump, what are you and this broad gonna eat?*

Hymes's (1970) complete list of factors is given in box 3.10 (with some added comments provided on the right):

3.10 Hymes's communicative competence

1. Whether (and to what degree) something is formally possible — Roughly (but not exactly) equivalent to 'systemic competence', and what Chomskyan linguistics is concerned with

2. Whether (and to what degree) something is feasible in virtue of the means of implementation available — *the mouse the cat the dog the man the woman married beat chased ate had a white tail*

3. Whether (and to what degree) something is appropriate (adequate, happy, successful) in relation to a context in which it is used and evaluated — related to the 'rules of use' discussed in Chapter 2 under the heading of 'Sociolinguistic competence'

4. Whether (and to what degree) something is in fact done, actually performed, and what its doing entails — *It's a great shame* versus *It's a big shame*

An example of the 'sociolinguistic' approach

The work of Hymes and other sociolinguists on rules of use is a central part of what we have been calling the 'sociolinguistic revolution'. Here is an example of the kind of study that the approach led to. Sinclair and Coulthard (1975) set themselves the task of analysing interactions between teachers and pupils in the school classroom. Not surprisingly, at various points in their investigation they come across situations in which teacher and pupils misunderstand each other. In one lesson, for example, the teacher plays a recording of a television programme 'in which there is a psychologist talking with a "posh" accent. The teacher wants to explore the children's attitude to accent and the value judgements based on it' (p. 29). When the recording is finished the teacher questions the students about the psychologist:

> Teacher: *What kind of person do you think he is? Do you* – (pupil bursts out laughing) – *what are you laughing at?*
> Pupil: *Nothing.*

The pupil says *Nothing* because he thinks the teacher is angry with him for laughing. He interprets the teacher's *What are you laughing at?* as an implied command to stop laughing. In fact the teacher does not mean it in this way. He intends it as a serious question; if he can make the pupil explain his mirth, this will provide him with an excellent opening for the topic he wishes to discuss. As the conversation proceeds, the pupil realizes what the teacher really meant and the misunderstanding is cleared up.

It is easy to see why this misunderstanding should have taken place. Some question forms in English – such as *What are you laughing at? Why are you shouting? What are you standing up for?* – may be interpreted either as straight requests for information or as commands to do something (expressed in a rather indirect way). A parent may, for example, ask a child *Why are you shouting?* out of genuine curiosity at what the child is doing. But it might also be a veiled way of saying *For goodness' sake talk softer.* Because sentences like these have two possible interpretations, the question arises how a pupil (or indeed any native speaker) knows in any given situation which interpretation is the correct one. In the case we have considered there was misunderstanding; but more often than not the listener will know immediately and unequivocally whether the speaker was asking for information or giving a command. Sometimes the speaker will give a 'linguistic signal' to make the meaning clear; for example, intonation or tone may indicate that a command is being given. But often there will be no overt signal, and only the context will help the listener towards the correct interpretation.

3.11 Help or information?

In one of the boxes in Chapter 2 an example was given of a misunderstanding where a request for help was wrongly interpreted as a request for information. Try to find this example.

Also in Chapter 2 there is an example of an utterance intended as an order being wrongly interpreted. The utterance involves the structure *Would you like . . . ?* Find this example also. The answers are in Note 5.

Sinclair and Coulthard try to draw up rules which specify what situational factors have to be present for a sentence to be interpretable as a command. One rule says that 'any declarative or interrogative [uttered by a teacher in a classroom] is to be interpreted as a command to stop if it refers to an action or activity which is proscribed at the time of the utterance' (p. 32). According to this rule, utterances like *I can hear someone laughing, Is someone laughing?*, and *What are you laughing at?* are to be taken as commands to stop laughing in situations where laughing is felt to be a 'forbidden activity'. Where laughing is *not* a forbidden activity these three utterances would receive quite different interpretations. The first might simply be an observation, the second and third requests for information. The pupil's misunderstanding in the episode outlined earlier happens because (contrary to the teacher's intentions) he perceives of laughing as forbidden activity at that particular moment.

In fact Sinclair and Coulthard give three rules for the interpretation of sentences as commands. But the details of the analysis are not relevant here. What is important is the nature of the questions the linguists are asking. They are not questions about the structure of the sentences, but about their use.

The work of Sinclair and Coulthard has been introduced to illustrate the shift in emphasis that occurred in the early 1970s in linguistics. As if further exemplification were necessary, the titles of two books influential at that time may be cited. The first is a book by the linguist Michael Halliday concerned with the way children acquire their L1. Books in the transformational school about this (of which there were very many), are predominantly concerned with the stages children go through when they acquire structures – how children 'learn to form', one might say. Halliday's 1975 book is entitled *Learning How to Mean*, and this clearly shows that the interest is not in syntax for its own sake, but in how language is acquired to perform actions.

The title of another book influential in the field is even more revealing. It was published in 1962, two years after the author's death. He was John Austin, a British philosopher with a particular interest in matters linguistic. The book is called *How to Do Things with Words*. The title says it all, and this idea of 'doing things with words' well captures a notion which played an important role in the 'movement' we have been describing. It is the notion of the <u>speech act</u>. We might say that Sinclair and Coulthard are looking at the teacher's utterance *What are you laughing at?* in speech act terms. The study of speech acts forms an important branch of linguistics central to the movement we have been discussing. This is <u>pragmatics</u>, defined by Widdowson (1996: 130) as 'the study of what people mean by language when they use it in the normal context of social life'.

Conclusion

In this chapter we have considered ideas that were developed some decades ago. We have spent time on them because of the influence they have had, and continue to have, on theories of language learning and teaching. The next chapter begins our consideration of language learning. In it, we shall immediately see evidence of how the empiricism/mentalism conflict has made itself felt – in this instance in the analysis and interpretation of learner errors.

Notes

1. The pairs are: (a) and (f); (b) and (g); (c) and (d); (e) and (h).
2. The words *often*, *frequently*, *rarely* and *regularly* can all be put either before the verb or at the end of the sentence. The other two words, *well* and *terribly* cannot normally go before the verb. The words with the same distribution as *sometimes* all express the notion of frequency – *how often* an action takes place. Based on these words, you can say that adverbs of frequency can be placed before the main verb or at the end of the sentence. But it is easy to find exceptions. *On Tuesdays* for example expresses frequency, but you would not normally put this phrase before the main verb.
3. This term is a useful label, but we are here using it to refer to developments that go beyond what are usually considered as sociolinguistics. As is mentioned on page 55, the concept of the speech act, and the study of pragmatics in particular play an important part in the 'movement'.
4. Though similar, Saussure's and Chomsky's terms are not equivalent. Chomsky's 'competence' is a psychological concept, while Saussure's *langue* has a social dimension – it is the language of the entire speech community.
5. In Example 3 of box 2.12, the question *Excuse me, do you have a watch?* is wrongly interpreted as a request for information. On page 31, the teacher's utterance *Would you like to read?* is not recognized as a command.

PART 2

LEARNING

Chapter 4

Learners and their errors

An FL learner's language is perhaps never more interesting than when she gets things wrong. When she produces correct, error-free utterances, they may tell us little about what is going on in her mind. But as soon as an error is made, we can look at its nature and try to work out why it was made. Errors can hold vital clues about the processes of FL learning. It is rather like the pain that may tell the doctor more than all the parts that do not hurt. Box 4.1 gives a simple illustration.

4.1 Being hungry or having hunger?

If you are hungry in German, you say *Ich habe Hunger*, literally **I have hunger*. You would not say **Ich bin hungrig*, literally *I am hungry*, which is of course the normal English way of expressing the idea.

If a German learner of English says **I have hunger*, you can be almost certain that she is translating literally from German; she is 'working through' German. But there is a second type of mistake which many learners make, irrespective of their native language. It is to say **I hungry*. If our German learner says this, we cannot say that she is 'working through' German, because this is not the German way of expressing the idea. She is in fact doing something which young children learning English as an L1 do, leaving out the verb *be*.

In this chapter we shall discuss these two different sorts of error.

The incorrect sentence **I have hunger* illustrates a type of error that formed the basis of a theory about foreign language learning which was developed by applied linguists in the 1950s and 60s. We shall begin by discussing this theory.

Contrastive analysis (CA): a theory about FL learning

The rationale for this language-learning theory lies within behaviourism, and the belief that learning is a question of habit formation. The behaviourists believed that when a new habit was learned, old (already learned) habits would have some effect on the learning process. Looking at the effects of one habit on learning another is known in psychology as the study of transfer. Two sorts of transfer are important to us. *Positive transfer* is where the two habits share common aspects, such that knowing one will help with learning the other. So if you are learning to ride a motor bike, it may be that being able to ride a normal bicycle will help the process. In this case we would say that there is positive transfer from bicycle to motor-bike riding. *Negative transfer* is also called interference. When I bought my new car, the direction indicator (to signal a left or right turn) was on the side of the steering wheel where my old car had its windscreen wiper. The result was that for my first few weeks in the new car, every time I wanted to turn left, the windscreen would get cleaned.

4.2 Further examples of transfer

Think of some more examples of learning to do (non-linguistic) activities. They might be learning a particular sport or a particular musical instrument. Think of some behaviours which might help or hinder your learning of these activities. Think of at least one example of *positive*, and one of *negative* transfer.

It is easy to think of language-learning parallels to these examples. Chapter 2 contains many. We noted, for example, that a German learner of English will not have great difficulty with the concept of the article system, because both languages have systems that are conceptually similar. We can therefore say that learners are likely to experience some positive transfer from native to target language. We also saw there that Japanese does not have a comparable article system, so Japanese learners will experience negative transfer from the L1 when learning German or English. Our German learner who said *I have hunger* for *I am hungry* would also be displaying negative transfer or interference.

One of the major figures interested in such matters was Robert Lado, whose influential book *Linguistics across Cultures: Applied linguistics for language teachers* appeared in 1957, the same year that a book mentioned in Chapter 3 appeared – Skinner's account of language in behaviourist terms, called *Verbal Behaviour*. Lado was interested in what made some things easy for learners and other things difficult. He believed that by comparing the native language (its structure, its sounds, its lexis) and the target language, we would be able to find out about ease and difficulty of learning, and this belief was a kind of manifesto for what came to be called the 'contrastive analysis (CA) hypothesis'. Here is a clear statement of it, from Lado (1957: 2): 'those elements that are similar to the [learner's] native language will be simple for him, and those areas that are different will be difficult'. This hypothesis led to a very large number of research projects throughout the world, which aimed to compare various languages in order to identify potential learning difficulties. The Center for Applied Linguistics, founded in Washington in 1959, was particularly active in this area, with large-scale projects comparing aspects of English with German, Spanish, Italian, Russian and French. Box 4.3 gives you a taste of what CA involves.

4.3 CA in action: personal pronouns in English and Polish

Here is an example of part of an English–Polish contrastive analysis, abridged from Krzeszowski (1990: 41–3).

Krzeszowski notes first that the English system of personal pronouns includes the following items:

	Singular	Plural
1st person	*I*	*we*
2nd person	*you*	*you*
3rd person	*he/she/it*	*they*

The equivalent Polish system is:

	Singular	Plural
1st person	*ja*	*my*
2nd person	*ty*	*wy*
3rd person	*on/ona/ono*	*oni/one*

In some ways these two systems are identical. For example, both distinguish singular from plural, and both differentiate 1st, 2nd and 3rd person pronouns. Notice also that for the 3rd person singular both English and Polish distinguish masculine, feminine and neuter pronouns. We might expect a Polish learner of English to receive positive transfer as regards these aspects, experiencing no problems with them when learning English.

But, Krzeszowski notes, there are also important differences. One of these relates to the 2nd person singular and plural forms. Many languages, like French with its *tu* and *vous*, and German with its *Du* and *Sie*, have a 2nd singular pronoun which is used between friends, and a more formal plural form for use with colleagues or strangers. Polish *ty* and *wy* are used in this way. But English pronouns do not mark this distinction. Once upon a time they did: in Shakespeare's age, for example, the pronoun *thou* was the singular, familiar form. But this form has now dropped out of common usage.

Another difference may surprise you. It is to do with the 3rd person plural forms in Polish, *oni* and *one*. The distinction here is between what is called *virile* and *non-virile*. The virile form *oni* refers to groups of people in which there is at least one male person, while non-virile *one* is used for all other plural nouns.

This is only part of the picture. An added complication is that, although both languages have masculine, feminine and neuter 3rd person singular forms, these work in quite different ways. In English, the gender of whatever is referred to is important: *he* is usually used for nouns that refer to male people or creatures; *she* is used for females, and *it* for other nouns. In Polish the gender of nouns is grammatical. This means that (again as in French and German) nouns are masculine, feminine or neuter, without regard to whether they refer to males, females or other. So very many inanimate objects will be masculine or feminine – in French a station is, for example, feminine: *la gare*. Krzeszowski illustrates this difference between Polish and English by means of the following sentences:

(1)   *Zgubilem swój stary portfel. On byl juz dosc zniszczony.*
(2)   *I lost my old wallet. It was already rather worn out.*

In Polish, the noun for wallet (*portfel*) is masculine, hence the pronoun is on (meaning, literally, 'he'). In English, we use the pronoun 'it' because a wallet is an inanimate object.

This last difference well illustrates how contrastive analysis can be used to predict learner errors. Krzeszowski (1990: 43) notes that Polish learners of English do in fact experience negative transfer here, often using *he* instead of *it* in sentences like (2) above.

Because it makes sense to suppose that as a general rule learners will learn simple things before more difficult ones, it was imagined that CA projects like those undertaken by the Center for Applied Linguistics would tell us something about the *order* in which learners would acquire items in the target language. We might expect that a learner will acquire parts of the target language which are similar to her native language before those that are different. It follows from this that learners with different native languages will acquire items of a target language in different orders. So, to take up an earlier example: we might expect Germans learning English to master the article system before Japanese students learning English.

4.4   Transfer in language learning

Consider your own FL language-learning experience. Make a list of three examples where you are aware of making mistakes in an FL which are due to negative transfer from your L1. If you have any FL *teaching* experience, you may also think of L1 transfer mistakes that your learners make in the FL.

Positive transfer is sometimes more difficult to detect than negative. Try to think of three examples where your L1 and an FL you have learned are similar, and where positive transfer might occur.

The early days of CA were heady ones, and it was believed that comparing native and target languages would tell you almost everything you needed to know to devise a language-teaching programme. This extreme view came to be known as the strong CA hypothesis. Here is an expression of it, from Lee (1968: 180): 'the prime cause, or even the sole cause, of difficulty and error in foreign language learning is interference . . . '

The problem with the strong CA hypothesis is that it is clearly not true. We have touched on one example already, in box 4.1, where we noted that some learners, even of languages like German, do produce sentences like *I hungry, even though contrastive analysis would predict *I have hunger. Where does the error *I hungry come from? If it is not caused by negative transfer, then this would be a case where the strong CA hypothesis breaks down.

Problems like these led to the development of what Wardhaugh (1970) calls the weak CA hypothesis. This is more reasonable in its claims. It says that CA may help us identify and explain some learner errors once they have occurred. But the hypothesis is 'weak' because it does not claim any predictive power for CA, to foresee errors with any certainty in advance. So, if the German learner does say *I have hunger then the contrastive analyst can draw on her knowledge of German to provide an explanation for the mistake. But the weak theory allows that the learner may also produce errors like *I hungry, which cannot be explained in terms of interference. The problem with the weak hypothesis is that it does not seem worth the immense effort of large-scale comparison of languages (such as those the Washington Center for Applied Linguistics undertook), just to be able to explain a proportion of error occurrences.[1]

It was behaviourist learning theory that gave birth to CA, and the Chomskyan attacks on behaviourism which we considered in the last chapter contributed significantly to its temporary demise. But notice the word 'temporary'. CA became unfashionable for a time; but it was never truly killed off and still attracts interest today, though not within the original behaviourist framework. This continued interest is not really surprising. All language teachers know that L1 to FL interference not only happens, but is an important aspect of language learning. The behaviourist framework may be discredited, but it would be a grave mistake to lose the idea of transfer with it.

Although it will take us outside the historical perspective we have been following, we will briefly look at issues related to transfer that have continued to interest applied linguists beyond the behaviourist era. One such issue is: when does transfer occur? Does it happen in some situations more than others? A number of studies have looked at various factors which might influence its occurrence. One factor is learner level. It has been suggested that lower level learners are particularly prone to negative transfer. Having fewer resources at their disposal in the target language, perhaps they rely heavily on their native language to help them in times of trouble.

When they do not know a word or a structure, for example, they may simply fall back on their L1 equivalents and use these. Box 4.5 shows one study where this was found to be the case.

4.5 Transfer in Spanish beginners and intermediates

(a) Taylor (1975) reports on a study involving 20 native Spanish-speaking students learning English as a foreign language. Ten were elementary students and ten intermediate. The learners heard 80 sentences in Spanish and had to write translations in English. The errors they made were then analysed, to see (among other things) which errors could be attributed to transfer. It was found that the elementary students made many more transfer errors than the intermediate group.

(b) Here are three examples of the transfer errors Taylor's subjects made. Use these sentences to work out ways in which Spanish and English are different. Express these differences as precisely as you can.

What understand the children?
Can the director to speak with me now?
Will not to watch TV the boys tonight?

But the question is more complex than Taylor's findings suggest. Firstly, there is plenty of evidence of non-transfer errors occurring in the language of beginners; indeed, you may well imagine a beginner producing utterances like the *I hungry* we saw earlier. Also, there are some areas of transfer – related to the more complicated grammatical structures, for example – which only come to light when the learner has reached a certain level.

Another factor which many think has an effect on amount of transfer is *language area*. It is generally recognized that pronunciation is an area where much transfer occurs. You can probably think of examples in your own experience where it is possible to identify the native tongue of a speaker of your language because of her accent. There is also a lot of transfer at the lexical level, as box 4.6 suggests:

4.6 Words, and how they are pronounced

(a) Think of an example of someone you know who uses your native language as an FL. Focus on their pronunciation. What makes their accent sound 'foreign'? Identify as many foreign characteristics as you can, including intonation and stress perhaps.

(b) Ringbom (1978) reports on a major study of lexical transfer. He looks at how a large number of Swedish and Finnish students translate words (contextualized in sentences) into English. The transfer he finds often manifests itself in quite strange, even bizarre, ways. Two examples: the Finnish word for 'jam' is *hillo*; at least one learner mixes

---

the Finnish and English word together to produce a non-existent word *jillo. The Finnish word for 'blush' is *punastua*. This reminds one learner of the English word 'punish', so this is used to translate *punastua*.

Swedish and English share many similarities, but Finnish is very different. Ringbom notices that learners seem to be aware of this fact. The Swedes in his study seem to expect English words to be similar to Swedish ones, and are 'much more confident in making guesses' (p. 86). An example is the word *dozen*, which is fairly similar in form to both Swedish (*dussin*) and Finnish (*tusina*) Despite this similarity, many more Swedes than Finns try to guess at the English word. Many Finns just leave it out.

We are now about to leave CA and consider another approach to learner errors. Before we do, it is worth pondering exactly how much value CA will be to language teachers. Box 4.7 invites you to do this.

4.7 The learners' L1: to speak or not to speak?

It is a common situation in the world today that FL teachers are native speakers of their learners' target language, and are teaching students who share a common L1. This would be the case, for example, where an English-speaking American goes to teach English in Japan, to learners who all have Japanese as their L1.

An issue: how important is it that such teachers should speak the L1 of their learners? Some would say it is essential, and that our American should only be allowed to teach English in Japan if she speaks Japanese. Others say it is less crucial.

Ponder both sides of this issue. Think (particularly in the light of what we have been discussing in this chapter) of how knowing Japanese will help the American. But think also of ways in which it will be of restricted value, and of how many factors other than knowing the learners' L1 will be important to her.

Your conclusions?

Non-contrastive errors

4.8 A strange way to ask a question

Imagine that a learner produces the utterance *Did she wanted*? Specify first how this sentence deviates from the correct form. Then try to imagine how this error came about. A linguist assures you that the sentence is not based on the learner's L1. Where, then, does it come from? How might you account for it?

In English questions, we often place the tense marker (the element which indicates the time of the 'action') on the auxiliary verb. In box 4.8's question, the auxiliary is *do*, and the form *did* is what indicates that the action took place in the past. The learner gets this part right. But she in fact marks tense twice – as well as having *did* she also puts an *-ed* on the end of the verb *want*. The morpheme *-ed* is indeed the way that tense is marked in non-question forms – so *she wanted* is right, for example. But the tense marker goes from main verb to auxiliary verb in questions.

Where does the error 'come from'? Although it is not impossible that for some learners of some L1 there may be elements of transfer at work here, it is unlikely to be the main cause, since languages do not usually mark tense like this, on both an auxiliary and on the main verb. The fact that the learner remembers to put *do* in the past tense, but forgets that she should not put the main verb *want* in the past tense strongly suggests that her error comes about because she is a little mixed up about how questions are formed in English. Maybe she has developed a mistaken view of how English works. Or perhaps in the heat of a conversational moment she forgets what she has learned and puts every verb in sight into its past form!

By the end of the 1960s interested in CA had waned, and the field was ready for a less restricted view of learner errors – one which would deal not just with interference, but also with errors of the **Did she wanted?* sort. One paper which clearly shows this shift towards a more wide-ranging consideration of error types is Richards (1971). The paper's title – 'A non-contrastive approach to error analysis' – reveals this new perspective.

Richards is interested in errors whose 'origins are found within the structure of English itself', or the way it is taught; that is, in non-contrastive causes. He calls non-contrastive errors of this sort <u>intralingual</u>, meaning 'coming from within the language itself', as opposed to <u>interlingual</u> meaning 'coming from differences between L1 and FL'. Another term which Richards uses to describe some non-interlingual errors is <u>developmental</u>. This term is revealing, and points up an important characteristic of these errors – that they are often similar to the errors made by children learning their L1. This similarity is mentioned in box 4.1, in relation to the German learner's use of the **I hungry* form which, we noted, cannot be explained in contrastive terms.

Richards identifies four general types of intralingual errors, and these are illustrated in box 4.9. Although his categories seem to overlap a little, they constitute an important early attempt at classification. Box 4.10, on page 68, invites you to explore the idea of intralingual errors.

Richards's paper was one of a number with similar perspectives written around the beginning of the 1970s. Other important ones are Selinker (1972), Corder (1967) and Nemser (1971). The term <u>Error Analysis</u> is often used to describe this perspective, which provides a wider coverage of errors than the more restricted Contrastive Analysis.

4.9   Richards's (1971) error types

1. Over-generalization	includes 'where the learner creates a deviant structure on the basis of his experience of other structures in the target language' (p. 174)	*He can sings* The learner knows *He sings, He wants*, etc. Putting the -s on the end of *sing* after the verb *can* is a false over-generalization.
2. Ignorance of rule restrictions	'failure to observe the restrictions of existing structures' (p. 175) (closely related to over-generalization)	*I made him to do it.* Here the learner ignores the restriction on *make,* that it is not followed by *to* and a verb (unlike, for example, *want* in *I wanted him to do it.*
3. Incomplete application of rules	'the occurrence of structures whose deviancy represents the degree of development of the rules required to produce acceptable utterances' (p. 177)	*You read much?* Here the learner may clearly be asking a question (intonation and/or the context may make this clear), but the correct question form is not used.
4. False concepts hypothesized	'faulty comprehension of distinctions in the target language' (p. 178)	A learner may come to believe that *was* is how past time is marked in English, and produce sentences like *One day it was happened . . .*

The creative construction hypothesis: a second theory about FL learning

Things are taken a step further by two American applied linguists, Heidi Dulay and Marina Burt. In the first of two exciting and important papers, Dulay and Burt (1973), they begin to develop an alternative to CA which they call creative construction theory. They are particularly interested in errors the learner brings upon herself – like Richards they use the word 'developmental' to describe these. To understand why the word 'creative'

> ### 4.10 No mices? Then the cats are useless
>
> Here are two sentences from the 'The cats essay' you saw in Chapter 2 (box 2.1). Concentrate on the italicized words:
>
> (1) Specially in cities, there is no problem of rates and *mices*.
> (2) *The cats* are useless (The essay's title).
>
> It is almost certain that *mices* in (1) is an intralingual error. What exactly is happening here? Describe as precisely as you can how this error comes about. Can you relate it to any of Richards's category types described in box 4.9?
>
> Without knowing something about the writer's L1 we cannot say whether *the cats* in (2) is an interlingual or intralingual error. For the sake of argument, imagine that it is intralingual, and that the writer intended to say *Cats are useless*. What does the sentence as it stands mean, and when might it be used? Specify how this meaning is different from what the writer intends it to say? Now imagine that you have to explain to the writer what he has done wrong and what he should have written. What would you say?
>
> Gluttons for punishment might also consider the essay's first phrase, which is correct:
>
> (3) The cat is useless . . .
>
> Explain why *the cats* in (2) is wrong, but *the cat* in (3) is right.
> The 'answers' are given in Note 2.

appears in the theory's name, ask yourself again where a sentence like *did she wanted*? 'comes from'. We have noted that it is unlikely to be modelled on the learner's L1. It is even more unlikely that the learner has ever heard it uttered by a native speaker – or even another learner (though the latter cannot be entirely discounted, of course). The place it is most likely to 'come from' is the learner's own head; it represents her own attempt to put into practice rules about question formation that she has learned. There is, in other words, a sense in which she has 'created' the form.

Dulay and Burt's 1973 paper reports two studies. In the first, they are interested in what proportion of errors is caused by interference, and what proportion may be said to be developmental. As we have seen, CA – which at that time was still the predominant view of many applied linguists – had made extravagant claims about interference. Indeed, you will recall that in the strong version of CA, transfer was considered almost the only reason for learner error. Dulay and Burt hoped that by experimentation they would be able to come up with an actual percentage of interference errors.

Dulay and Burt took 145 Spanish-speaking children living in the United States, and analysed 388 of their errors, attempting to classify these as contrastive or developmental. If, to pursue our earlier example, a child produced *I have hunger then this was taken to be an error of transfer (this is the Spanish as well as the German way of expressing the idea). But if the learner produced *I hungry (not the direct equivalent of a Spanish expression) then this was taken to be a developmental error. Dulay and Burt make the important point (which we noted earlier) that this error, of omitting a part of the verb be, is one that L1 children also commonly make. It seems to represent a 'developmental' stage learners go through when acquiring a language naturally. Although it is not always easy (as Dulay and Burt concede) to put an error into the contrastive or developmental categories with complete certainty, they do manage to come up with figures that cover most of the errors made.

It is easy to imagine how these figures rocked the hitherto CA-dominated world. They are:

Interference	3% of the errors considered
Developmental	85% of the errors considered
Others	
(i.e. where no decision could be made)	12% of the errors considered

In the second part of their study they were interested to find out whether there was any evidence for learners acquiring some important morphemes of English in a specific order. The quest to discover a morpheme acquisition order is firmly based on work that was being done in the study of L1 acquisition, particularly by the linguist Roger Brown. Box 4.11 shows how Brown (1973) finds that four children he studied learned 14 basic morphemes of English in the same order.

4.11   An L1 morpheme acquisition study, and an FL order

R. Brown (1973) studied three children – Adam, Eve and Sarah – over the period they were acquiring some basic English morphemes. English was their emerging L1. He plotted their progress monthly until they had acquired the morphemes he was interested in. Then he compared the order in which they learned these morphemes, and he found a remarkable degree of consistency from one child to the next. This led him and others to the idea that maybe L1 learners have a kind of 'internal syllabus' (a 'programme inside their heads'), that leads them to acquire their native language in the same way.

His study led to a number of others, looking both at the L1 and (like Dulay and Burt) at foreign-language learning. Below is the order of some of the morphemes in a paper of Dulay and Burt's (1974) described below:

---

the, a (articles, as in *I saw the boy*)

↓

-ing (as in *He is walking*)

↓

-s (plural nouns, as in *The cars went past*)

↓

-'s (possessive, as in *The boy's hat*)

↓

-s (3rd person of simple present tense, as in *She wants*)

Dulay and Burt's study looked at eight morphemes. They did indeed find an acquisition order common to their learners (though it was a different one from the order Brown and others found for L1 children).

What would happen if children with different L1s were considered? Would the same morpheme acquisition order be found? As we noted earlier, CA would predict otherwise, since the belief was that a learner's acquisition order would be based on the differences and similarities between target language and L1. Imagine, for example, two learners – Learner A and Learner B. Learner A's native language has a form similar to the English possessive *-s*, while Learner B's does not. CA would expect Learner A to acquire this morpheme in English before Learner B. If this does not happen, and both learners acquire this and other morphemes in the same order, this would indeed be a final nail in the coffin of the strong CA hypothesis.

In a second paper (1974), Dulay and Burt looked at two groups of children, Spanish and Chinese speakers, and tackled the question: do learners with different L1s acquire morphemes of a foreign language in the same order? The answer, according to their study, was yes. The acquisition order of the two groups was virtually the same. This led them to an exciting and rather far-reaching speculation – that there is perhaps a universal morpheme acquisition order which all learners follow, irrespective of their mother tongue.

Some details of their findings: the English auxiliary verb *be* was acquired at about the same time by both groups, even though there is no comparable verb in Chinese but there is in Spanish (suggesting to adherents of CA that the Spanish speakers would acquire it before the Chinese). Similarly the plural morpheme *-s* was acquired by both groups at roughly the same point in the sequence, even though there is one in Spanish but not Chinese. If this study and ones like it are taken at face value, then the lid of CA's coffin is firmly in place.

Both the Dulay and Burt studies were with children, and the question arises whether the same results would be found for adults. This was studied by Bailey, Madden and Krashen (1974), who found roughly the same acquisition order with adult FL learners.

Let us pause and take stock. We seem here to have findings which suggest:

- most errors are developmental, not the result of interference
- both children and adults follow a sequence in the acquisition of grammar items in the FL. There is what might be called an 'internal syllabus'
- this sequence is 'universal', occurring whatever the learner's L1

This research has been much criticized for its methodology, and in a moment we shall consider some of these criticisms. But before this, two observations:

Firstly, you need to be clear on the intellectual roots of these ideas, which should be related to what was discussed in Chapter 3. The shift from Contrastive Analysis to Error Analysis is a clear instance of the movement from behaviourism to mentalism that we plotted in that chapter. CA has its basis in behaviourist learning theory, while the work of Dulay and Burt is pervaded by Chomskyan ideas. Take the very notion of 'creative construction'. We have seen that Chomsky's view of L1 acquisition places a great deal of importance on the role of the acquiring organism – language comes from inside the individual, it 'grows' rather like a plant grows. The sentence we discussed earlier – *Did she wanted*? is similarly one that comes from within. The very word 'creative' carries echoes of Chomsky and his language-acquisition views. The phrase 'internal syllabus' which we used earlier similarly suggests the notion of 'everything being within the organism'. Indeed, it would not be far-fetched to suggest that Chomsky's LAD contains or implies some kind of 'internal syllabus' for FL acquisition.

The second observation also relates to this notion of an 'internal syllabus', which we earlier glossed – in box 4.11 – as a 'programme in the learner's head'. Consider for a moment the possible implications for *language teaching* of this notion. Most learners in most classrooms have a syllabus imposed on them from outside. The textbook or the teacher (and often, ultimately, the Ministry of Education) tells them what morphemes and grammatical structures they will learn, in what order. There is, in other words, an 'external syllabus' imposed on the learners. But if learners really do have their own learning order, is there any point in imposing another order on them? What point in having an *external* syllabus if learners have their own *internal* one? This exciting idea has hovered round the edges of much discussion about language teaching over recent years, and tends to evoke strong passions. Some rightly point out that Dulay and Burt's subjects were living in the target-language environment, potentially hearing English all the time in their surroundings. This is crucially different, it may be argued, from people learning the target language in their own native country, perhaps in classes which meet for just a few hours each week, with no word of English ever heard between classes. So findings true in one situation may not hold in the other. But there are counter-arguments: perhaps the differences between the situations are not that significant; perhaps a good teacher should make the FL classroom as much like the L1 environment as possible. These are important ideas and arguments which we will return to more than once in later chapters.

4.12   Yes, but what does it mean in practice?

The previous paragraph contains some ideas that are potentially challenging to conventional ideas about language teaching. Two of them are:

(a) The question is asked: 'is there any point in having an *external* syllabus if learners have their own *internal* one?' Imagine that you answer this question by saying 'No there isn't. Let's get rid of external syllabuses.' Yes, but what does this mean in practice? What might language teaching not based on any external syllabus 'look like'? Note that there may be more than one possible answer to this last question.

(b) The suggestion is made: 'perhaps a good teacher should make the FL classroom as much like the L1 environment as possible'. Yes, but what does *this* mean in practice? A teacher will never be able to make her language classroom resemble the L1 environment in all respects. But is there anything she can do to move in this direction? What?

Both these issues will be raised in later chapters, the first in Chapter 12 (p. 222), the second at various points, particularly in Chapter 10.

Since the heady days of Dulay and Burt's work, many criticisms have arisen which cast doubt on their findings.[3] An obvious restriction of this work is its small scope. First of all, it deals with a very small number of language items – a handful of morphemes only – and ignores nearly all the various language levels we looked at in Chapter 2. Secondly, the number of learners covered in the studies is very small. Thirdly, only two language groups – Spanish and Chinese – are involved. Yet, on the basis of such small samples, the authors seem to make sweeping claims, cavalierly using words like 'universal'.

There are also problems with the research methodology used, and even Dulay and Burt's percentages for interference and developmental errors have been bitterly disputed. Box 4.13 is taken from Ellis (1994) and shows that it would be unwise to base your views about the importance (or otherwise) of transfer errors on Dulay and Burt's figures. Certainly many experienced teachers would strongly contest the idea that interference plays the small part that the figure of 3 per cent suggests.

4.13 Percentages of interference errors found in various studies.
From Ellis (1994: 302)

Study	% of interference errors	Type of learner
Grauberg (1971)	36	L1 = German adult, advanced
George (1972)	33 (approx.)	Mixed L1s adult, graduate
Dulay and Burt (1973)	3	L1 = Spanish children, mixed levels
Tran-Chi-Chau (1975)	51	L1 = Chinese adult, mixed level
Mukkatesh (1977)	23	L1 = Arabic adult
Flick (1980)	31	L1 = Spanish adult, mixed level
Lott (1983)	50 (approx.)	L1 = Italian adult, university

Conclusion

This chapter has been about learner errors. We have seen how important a part they may play in understanding the processes of foreign-language learning. Indeed, we have considered two theories that are centrally based on two differing views of learner errors.

Both these theories have had their moment at the centre of the applied linguistic stage and, although neither continues to hold that position, neither has yet made its final exit. We have seen that the 'CA hypothesis' received major setbacks as Chomskyan mentalism (here in the form of Dulay and Burt's work) replaced behaviourism. But we have also seen that CA today still remains a subject of interest to applied linguists.

The second of these theories, 'creative construction' has also been attacked, and the various problems and doubts we have just discussed certainly led to a diminution of interest in morpheme acquisition studies in the 1980s. But even more than with CA, 'creative construction' is still very much alive and kicking. Its underlying ideas continue to excite, and persist in finding a place in discussion about language learning and teaching even today. The idea of the internal acquisition order is an attractive one which for many has a ring of truth to it. As we shall see in the next chapter, it is certainly another idea that refuses to go away.

We shall also see in the next chapter, and indeed in later ones, that errors continue to play an important part in the study of foreign-language acquisition. We have begun to look at errors, but we are by no means finished with them.

Notes

1. If you want to know more about this period in the history of CA, see James (1980); and Ellis (1994: Chapter 8).
2. *Mice* is an irregular plural form of *mouse*. The learner knows that the morpheme [s] is associated with noun plurality, and adds it to the word *mice*. So *mices* is 'doubly plural'. Over-generalization (or possibly 'ignorance of rule restrictions' – the two are difficult to distinguish) is at work here – the learner over-generalizes the use of the normal plural marker [s].

    One use of the definite article *the* is to refer back to something already mentioned. So *The cats are useless* may be used to refer to specific cats, that have probably already been mentioned by the speaker. For example: *Mary's got three dogs and two cats. The dogs are very helpful to her. But the cats are useless.* One use of the plural form, without any article, is to express a generalization. *Cats are useless*, without the definite article would refer to cats in general. Another way of expressing the same idea is by use of the definite article and a singular noun. So the learner's *The cat is useless* is correct. Another example of these two ways of expressing a generalization might be *Horses are beautiful animals*, and *The horse is a beautiful animal*.
3. McLaughlin's 1987 book has a succinct discussion of some of these criticisms (pp. 33–4).

Chapter 5

Acquisition: some characteristics

Language acquisition: a powerful and exciting concept

If ideas can symbolize the spirit of an age, then the symbol of the recent applied linguistic age is undoubtedly 'language acquisition'. But what does this term mean? What exactly is 'language acquisition? In the next section we shall try to answer these questions; for the moment we may characterize it as the process by which individuals 'pick up' a language through exposure to it. There are two immediately obvious sorts of language acquisition. The first is L1 acquisition, which every normal child manages at an early age. The second is FL acquisition where someone, child or adult, picks up a language, for example while they are living in the target-language country.

Chomsky's ideas are responsible for the interest in L1 (and, indirectly, FL) acquisition that there has been over the past few decades. For him, L1 acquisition is a conundrum, even a miracle. The big question (which, as we saw in Chapter 3, he refers to as 'Plato's problem') is: how is it that the very young child, so poorly developed in many areas, is able to learn the rudiments of his native language so quickly and so successfully? Chomsky's answer was, as we have seen, that the individual has a machine in the head, an LAD, that does the job for him.

The words 'quickly and successfully' hold the key to the applied linguists' interest in the acquisition idea. In an important article that appeared in 1968, Newmark and Reibel make the point that L1 acquisition is the quickest and most successful instance of language mastery that we know of. Since this is so, they argue, we might do well to study in some detail what is known about the L1 acquisition situation. What does the child do that makes acquisition so quick and successful? How do the adults who talk to the child behave? What assistance do they give to the acquisition process? What are the important aspects of the acquisition environment?

If we have answers to these questions, perhaps they will be of inspiration to applied linguists interested in foreign-language teaching. Of course, you will immediately say, there are huge differences between L1 acquisition and what goes on in foreign-language classrooms around the world. There are also big differences between FL acquisition in the *target-language country,* and language teaching for a few hours a week in the *learner's native country*, and we made mention of these differences towards the end of Chapter 4 (p. 71 above). But even bearing these considerable differences in mind, perhaps we really should ask the questions above and, for both L1 and FL, find out what we can about the mysterious phenomenon of language acquisition. It is certainly the case that applied linguists from the end of the 1960s have been inspired by such questions. The notion of language acquisition really is a powerful and exciting one.

In this chapter we shall look at some of the ideas associated with both L1 and FL acquisition. In the next, we consider some theories that have developed from these ideas.

5.1 Thinking about L1 acquisition

Paragraph 3 of the section above poses the following questions:

1. What does the child do that makes L1 acquisition so quick and successful?
2. How do the adults who talk to the child behave? What assistance do they give to the acquisition process?
3. What are the important aspects of the acquisition environment?

In the course of this chapter we shall provide some answers to these questions. Now would be a good time for you to ponder how *you* would answer them.

The learning/acquisition distinction

One of a number of applied linguists associated with the ideas outlined above is the American Stephen Krashen. In various of his publications (e.g. Krashen 1982) he argues that there are two distinct ways of mastering an FL, and he calls these <u>acquisition</u> and <u>learning</u>. Acquisition first: he describes this process as a 'natural' one, where there is no 'conscious focusing on linguistic forms' (of the sort that you find in most classrooms). It is what we have already informally called the process of 'picking up' a language, just as you do if you go and live in the target-language environment. Indeed Krashen says that the minimal condition for acquisition to occur is 'participation in natural communication situations'. As we saw earlier, FL acquirers sometimes make the same kinds of mistakes as L1 acquirers (our earlier example – Chapter 4, p. 59 above – was omitting the verb *be*, as in **I hungry*), and indeed Krashen claims that what is known about L1 acquisition is in general applicable to FL acquisition. He also uses the term 'creative construction' to describe the process, clearly indicating that he comes from the same stable as Dulay and Burt.

Learning, on the other hand, is a conscious process, and it usually takes place in the language classroom. For Krashen it is particularly marked by two characteristics. First, there is *error correction*. When learners make mistakes, it is normal for the classroom teacher to draw explicit attention to them, and to correct the errors. As we shall see later, with some exceptions parents do not usually do this. The second characteristic is what Krashen calls *rule isolation*. In the language-teaching classroom it is normal for a lesson to focus on one language point. It may be a grammatical item like a particular tense, or a pronunciation point, or some 'rule of use'. The word 'isolation' indicates that in this procedure language points are dealt with one by one, in isolation. Again, as we shall see, L1 parents do not usually focus on individual items in this way.

The acquisition/learning distinction is not without its critics, and several writers have pointed out that it is not a very clear-cut one. Little or nothing is said by Krashen about the different processes involved in each, and (it might be argued) the only real difference is in terms of the environments in which these two processes occur. So, to put it in crude terms, acquisition is what happens when you go and live in the target-language country, while learning is what happens in classrooms. But even this apparent difference can be questioned, because there is almost certainly overlap between what happens in these two environments. Certainly I can think of examples in my own experience where I have been living in an FL environment and generally acquiring the language, but at the same time augmenting that acquisition by using grammar books to help me 'learn'. Equally (though less easy to demonstrate) I feel that sometimes as a learner in an FL classroom there have been points that I have 'picked up' (perhaps just by listening to and 'soaking up' the language the teacher produced) rather than 'learned'. These experiences suggest that when we attempt to master a language (in whatever environment) we are doing a bit of learning *and* a bit of acquisition.

Despite these difficulties, many find the acquisition/learning distinction a useful one, and we shall use it here as the framework for our discussion. In this chapter and the next we shall concentrate on acquisition, and in Chapter 7 we shall look mainly at learning. In order to identify important aspects of acquisition, we shall consider two sorts of people and their behaviour. We look first at the people who give acquirers their language, and we shall call these people 'language providers'. In the case of L1 children, they are those (often the parents) looking after the children, sometimes referred to as caretakers. In the case of FL learners they will be people who communicate with the acquirer, including in the classroom. Then we shall look at acquirers themselves, and the language they produce. Some of what we say in the following discussion will apply more clearly to L1 than FL acquisition. At other times it may be the other way round. We can justify moving freely from one to the other on the assumption that, in some respects at least, the two are indeed comparable.

Once we have looked at both 'language providers' and 'acquirers' we shall, in Chapter 6, consider some of the ways in which applied linguists have brought the ideas we have been discussing together to form theories of foreign-language acquisition.

As the chapter unfolds, it will become clear that three concepts are central to it. The first is the concept of <u>input</u>. This is the language that the learner receives from those who communicate with him. Secondly there is the language that he himself produces, which we call <u>output</u>. The third concept is <u>affect</u>. Psychologists and applied linguists use this noun and the associated adjective 'affective' to refer to 'feelings' and 'to do with the feelings' respectively. The word root is the same as in the more everyday English words 'affection' and 'affectionate'. Affect, as we shall see, is important for language acquisition.

5.2 Acquiring and learning: a consumer's comparison

Acquiring a foreign language can be very successful, but it can have its drawbacks. The same is true of learning.

Reflect a little on the pros and cons of each process. If you have experience in your own life of acquiring and learning different FLs, be sure to base your reflections on this.

Language providers and their language (input)

There is one point of view that says that the best language teachers in the world are those parents or caretakers who provide children with the input that leads them to acquire their L1. After all *all* children, bar those with some severe impairment, successfully acquire their L1 to an astonishing degree. From this point of view, therefore, it makes sense to look closely at what those language providers both *do* and *do not* do when they give children language input. Perhaps these 'L1 language teachers' have some secrets to convey to FL language teachers . . . about what to do, and also what not to do . . .

Some things that caretakers do *not* do

Whether or not caretakers can justifiably be called 'L1 language teachers', one thing that they do not do is give 'language teaching lessons' – or at least not of the sort that FL teachers traditionally provide. To appreciate this, consider one FL teacher in action. The evening before his English class, he consults the syllabus provided by his country's Ministry of Education, to decide what language items to teach the next day. The syllabus tells him that the students are ready for the simple past tense (*Yesterday I* <u>worked</u> . . . ,

Last year I visited . . .). So he prepares his lesson round this. When he enters the class, he begins by talking in the L1. *Good morning,* he says in the L1, *today we're going to look at the simple present tense in English – how it is formed and how it is used.* He then explains how the tense is formed for regular verbs, by adding -*ed* to the verb stem. He also describes how questions and negative forms are made, and gives some examples of the tense's use. He has prepared some simple drill-like exercises to follow. In one, he says sentences in the simple present (like *He works*), and expects the learners to change the sentences into the simple past (*He worked*). Learner errors are immediately corrected. In his next lesson he will elaborate on this basic introduction to the tense.

There are at least four things here that L1 caretakers **do not** do:

1. They do not follow a syllabus. Our FL teacher might say *My learners are now half way through their intermediate course, and the syllabus says that the time has come to introduce the simple past tense.* As we shall see later, caretakers have a very good sense of the rough linguistic level of their children. But no caretaker would say *Sarah is now three and a half, so next week I'm going to introduce the simple past tense to her.* There is no syllabus document lurking in the nursery cupboard.
2. Caretakers do not normally provide explanations for their offspring. They may find themselves *using* the simple past tense, but there would be no talk about -*ed* or verb stems.
3. Caretakers do not drill. They might, very indirectly, encourage the child to produce some piece of language, but the 'change the simple present into the simple past' formula would not normally be used. Nor anything like it.
4. As an introduction to the fourth point, look at box 5.3 on page 80 below. Point 4 is that caretakers do not often correct errors of grammar. What they *do* frequently correct is the 'truth value' of what a child says; whether, that is, a statement is true or false. But grammatical errors are often not consciously drawn attention to. The examples in box 5.3 show this. So even though child utterance (a) is poorly formed, he receives parental approval because it is true. Child utterance (b) on the other hand is 'corrected' because it is false, even though its grammar is perfect.

   Although adults may be tolerant of poor grammar, there are some linguistic areas they do care about. Two of these are rude words, and forms that they consider socially unacceptable (so a dialect form like *I ain't* might well get remarked upon).

One way of expressing these four ideas is to say that caretaker communication is largely message-focused, and not normally form-focused. In other words, much of the caretaker's effort is put into getting the message

---

5.3 What parents *do* and *do not* correct

Brown and Hanlon (1970: 47–9) study the L1 development of three pre-school children (Adam, Eve and Sarah). As part of that study, they look at adult responses to child utterances. Here are four of their examples:

Child	**Adult**
(a) *Draw a boot paper*	*That's right. Draw a boot on paper*
(b) *There's the animal farmhouse*	*No, that's a lighthouse*
(c) *Mama isn't boy, he a girl*	*That's right*
(d) *And Walt Disney comes on Tuesday*	*No, he does not*

Look first at the child utterances. Some of them contain mistakes (which might be called 'grammatical'), some not. Identify each. Then look at the adult responses. Some signal approval, some disapproval; again identify each.

Based on these four sentences, what can you say about what adults *do* and *do not* correct?

---

across, into being understood, and not in dwelling on the nuts and bolts of the language. The concentration tends to be on content and not means, the 'what' and not the 'how'.

Any reader who is a parent will understand why words like 'normally' have frequently been used in the above discussion. We are here discussing what generally, but not always, happens. So, many caretakers will *occasionally* focus on form, correct, and give explanations, particularly if the child asks a language-related question. Caretakers who are professionally engaged in language studies or language teaching are probably particularly abnormal in this respect. I personally find myself even *drilling* our young child on occasions! For the antics of another language-studies related person, turn back to box 3.6 in Chapter 3, where the linguist caretaker tries very hard to correct the child's error.

A final point on the *do nots*. We have here been discussing L1 acquisition specifically. But some (if not all) of the points made apply equally to FL acquisition, where a learner acquires the language in the FL environment. Towards the end of Chapter 2 (p. 35 above), we met a Japanese adult called Wes, studied by Schmidt (1983). Wes was living in Hawaii and picking up English from the environment. Schmidt has the following comment to make about Wes's language providers: 'I have observed Wes', he says, 'in interaction with many native speakers, including at least a dozen language-teaching professionals, and have not noted a single instance of feedback explicitly focused on grammatical form . . .' (p. 166).

Some things that caretakers *do* do

5.4 Thinking about caretaker talk

You will probably readily agree that parents 'modify' their language when talking to a young child. But how exactly? How is their language different from when they are talking to another adult? Make a list of as many characteristics of caretaker talk as you can think of.

Clark and Clark (1977 – Chapter 8), and Snow and Ferguson (1977 – an entire book devoted to the matter) provide excellent accounts of the important characteristics of caretaker talk. Here is a rough guide to what caretakers do, taken from the above-mentioned sources and elsewhere:

- Caretaker talk is intelligible, and grammatically well formed (indeed, it is perhaps not quite as 'degenerate' as Chomsky claimed – see p. 46 above). Newport, Gleitman and Gleitman (1977) transcribed passages of caretaker talk and compared them with passages of adult/adult speech.[1] They found only 4% of the caretaker talk sample impossible to transcribe, in comparison with 9% of the adult/adult speech.

- Caretakers talk lots about the here-and-now (a term in common use in the field). This means that they talk to children about objects that can be seen, and events that are happening in front of their eyes. As Cross (1977: 169) notes: 'the vast majority of expressions the child hears encode events that are perceptually, cognitively and semantically available and salient to the child'. This emphasis on the here and now enables caretakers to use gestures to point at things being discussed, and in general to

make full use of the situation to help clarify what is being said.

- Caretakers simplify. Some points:
  (a) Snow (1972) found that adults use fewer grammatical morphemes in speech with two-year-olds than with ten-year-olds, and fewer with ten-year-olds than with adults.
  (b) Caretaker sentences tend to be shorter. Phillips (1973) found that utterances to two-year-olds averaged less than four words each. Adult/adult speech averages over double this figure.
  (c) Caretakers avoid pronouns. You have doubtless noticed the way that adults prefer to repeat nouns rather than use pronouns. So you find *Mummy will lift Tommy up* rather than *I'll lift you up*, and *The boy was running. The boy climbed the tree* instead of *The boy was running. He climbed the tree.*

- Caretakers 'model' interactions for children. Even before the child can speak, caretakers sometimes hold 'monologue conversations' with him, demonstrating to the child what a conversation is 'like'. Here is an example from Snow and Ferguson (1977):

Mother: *Hello. Give me a smile then*
Child: [Yawns]
Mother: *Sleepy, are you? You woke up too early today*
Child: [Opens fist]
Mother: *What are you looking at?*

- Caretakers repeat a lot. It is not thought that this occurs simply to provide more input (in the behaviourist belief that repetition is important). Rather it is to make sure that the child understands. Newport *et al.* (1977) give the following example: *Go get the duck – the duck – yes, get it – that's right – get the duck.* You can easily imagine the movements, particularly pointing, that accompany this utterance.
- Caretakers <u>rough tune</u>. By 'tuning' we mean adjusting input to the

child's language level. What caretakers do *not* do is 'fine tune' in the way that many foreign-language teachers do. Fine tuning means keeping careful tabs on what language is known to the audience, and using just that language. There is, as we have seen, no syllabus lurking in the nursery cupboard. But this does not mean that caretakers are oblivious of child language level. They rough tune their language. This means that they have a very good general sense of what the child will understand, and they apply that general sense as they talk – avoiding ways of expression that are clearly over-complex. For example, no one would dream of using, with a three-year-old, a sentence like *I can scarcely believe my eyes. You certainly have increased in size since the time that I last saw you, some weeks ago now.* Common sense tells the speaker that, in all sorts of ways, this sentence would be inappropriate.

Language acquirers and their output: five interesting characteristics

What is it that acquirers do, and what characteristics does their output have? In this section we shall identify perhaps the five most interesting characteristics of acquirers and their output. Two have in fact already been identified, in the work of Dulay and Burt discussed in Chapter 4. Their subjects were living in the target-language environment, and they were acquiring rather than learning English. *Interesting Characteristic 1*, according to Dulay and Burt, is that their subjects engaged in a 'creative construction' process. *Interesting Characteristic 2* is that acquirers' language appears in a fixed, natural order. Krashen (1982) among others calls this the 'natural order hypothesis'.

Here now are the other three.

Interesting Characteristic 3: acquirers go through a 'silent period'

5.5 The beginnings of FL acquisition: two examples

Here are two examples of the beginnings of FL learning:

(a) Krashen (1983) tells the story of a four-year-old Japanese girl called Hitomi, who lived with her parents for a while in an apartment neighbouring on Krashen's . Hitomi spoke no English on arrival in the US, and Krashen tells of his attempts to get Hitomi to speak in the early months of her stay. He would say things like *Hitomi, say 'hi'*, but here would be no reaction. He tried *Hitomi, say 'ball'*, and even *I won't give you the ball till you say ball*. All these attempts met with silence.

Hitomi was more or less silent for five months ('more or less' because children in these circumstances do produce set phrases, like *Leave me alone*. They have picked such phrases up as entire units, without really understanding how they are made up).

Krashen notes two interesting characteristics about Hitomi's speech, when it eventually came. Firstly, it resembled the speech of his own children, particularly in the way it developed from shorter to longer utterances. By the time Hitomi returned to Japan, Krashen notes that her English was approaching that of his own children. There are indeed similarities between L1 and FL acquisition.

Secondly, Krashen asks the question: 'What was going on during the first five months?' His answer: 'She was listening. . . . When she started to talk, it was not the beginning of her language acquisition. It was testimony to the language acquisition she had already done.'

(b) Ervin-Tripp (1974) describes a group of 31 English-speaking children attending school in Geneva, where French was the language of instruction. Ervin-Tripp's observations go back to the time the children arrived and first began being exposed to French. 'Some of the children', she notes (p. 115), 'said nothing for many months . . . My own children began speaking six and eight weeks after immersion in the school setting.'

These two examples reveal a truth about learners in many acquisitional situations – that they go through a 'silent period'. This means that quite a considerable period of time may pass between the acquirer first being exposed to a new language and his beginning to produce it. We might also suppose that this process applies with individual language items (like Hitomi's *ball*), as well as for general production. In other words there is likely to be an interval between the acquirer first hearing a particular structure or word, and his use of it.

Interesting Characteristic 4: affect is important

A small anecdote will illustrate how important affect can be in foreign-language acquisition. Some years ago I worked in Italy, in an institution which taught English as a foreign language. Most of the teachers were native speakers of English, brought out from Britain in the first instance on one-year contracts. I remember one year that two women in their early twenties – let us call them Teacher A and Teacher B – came at the same time to the institution as teachers. They were similar in some ways: neither had been to Italy before, except on short holidays, and neither spoke any Italian. They were both good teachers. Teacher A immediately fell in love with Italy. She looked around her and saw energy, colour, a sense of style, great architecture and art, blue sea, warm sun, delicious food. Teacher B looked on the same world, but saw something completely different. Instead of energy she saw disorganization, instead of seeing colour she heard noise, and for her the 'sense of style' counted as 'obsession with super-ficiality'. Even the warm sun was viewed as an attractor of mosquitoes, and the delicious food was just precursor of an upset stomach. Teacher A extended her contract for a further year. Teacher B could not wait to return home.

The effect of these developing attitudes on the teachers' learning of Italian was dramatic. Within a few months Teacher A was able to communicate very adequately, and as well as beginning to take lessons, she also started reading widely. It is perhaps not necessary to comment on the 'progress' of Teacher B's Italian. Attitudes towards the speakers and culture of the target language can indeed influence the path of acquisition.

Some characteristics of affect are associated with age, which is why some age groups seem more likely to be successful in foreign-language learning than others. Box 5.6 contains an illustration:

5.6 Children, cultural differences, and learning a foreign language

Two researchers, Lambert and Klineberg (1967) looked at children of different nationalities, and studied their views of foreign peoples. Their conclusion is that at the age of about ten children are at their most recept-ive for the acceptance of cultural differences. Because attitudes towards cultural differences may be important for FL learning, Gardner and Lambert (1972: 145) are led to wonder whether this is not an argument for introducing language learning at this age.

Think about what makes ten such a good age for attitudes towards cultural differences. Write down some reasons. Think also about the periods *before* and *after* ten. What affective characteristics might you expect to find at those ages which will not work against the acceptance of cultural differences?

Gardner and Lambert's answer to the question in box 5.6 is that children before and after the age of ten (or thereabouts – we can of course only speak of approximate ages here) have a tendency to link 'different' with 'bad'. You may also have noted when pondering this issue, that not long after the age of ten comes adolescence. In many respects, adolescence is a time for reflection on one's individuality, where one is notoriously 'closed' to anything different outside the self. It is also, of course, a period of great self-consciousness, and this can be very detrimental to FL learning. Speaking a foreign language, perhaps with a poor accent and lots of mistakes, risks ridicule. The last thing many sensitive adolescents want is ridicule.

Affect is, of course, relevant to language learning as well as acquisition, but it is the acquisition–affect relationship that is particularly sensitive. Krashen (1981) captures this relationship in a vivid way when he notes that, if you want to predict how well someone will *acquire* a language, find out about their attitudes. If you want to find out about *learning*, then there may be other characteristics worth exploring (for example, how talented they are at languages).

We shall consider the issue of affect in much more detail in Chapter 8.

Interesting Characteristic 5: learner language is 'simplified' language

In all speech communities in the world, special ways of communicating have developed for use with groups of people who, for one reason or another, are likely to have problems with the 'normal' language. These groups include children, foreigners, the mentally handicapped and the deaf. These modes of communication are called <u>simplified codes</u>, capturing the fact that all have elements within them that are simplifications or 'reductions' of the language on which they are based. In this section we shall concentrate on one type of simplified code, of interest precisely because it has been compared with FL learner talk. This simplified code is pidgin.

A pidgin language is one which has been developed to meet the communication needs of two groups speaking different L1s. Pidgins often arise in colonial situations. For example, when Britain colonized parts of West Africa (Nigeria for example), a means of communication between colonizers and colonized was required, and the result was English-based pidgin languages. Though these areas are no longer colonies, it is common for these pidgin languages to be used today. Associated with the term pidgin is <u>creole</u>, strictly speaking a pidgin used as an L1. A creole would come about if two pidgin speakers married and had a child who spoke the pidgin as his first language. Though the pidgin/creole distinction may be clear-cut in theory, in practice linguists talk of the <u>creole continuum</u> to capture the idea that languages may lie somewhere between a pidgin and a creole.

Looking at pidgin languages is both interesting and fun. As something of a diversion, you may wish to spend a moment mulling over an example of one. Box 5.7 contains the transcript of an advertisement broadcast on the Solomon Islands Broadcasting Service in 1971. The Solomon Islands are in the SW Pacific Ocean. They were placed under British protection at the end of the nineteenth century, and gained independence in 1978. The Capital city is Honiara Town. The major language of communication is called Solomon Island Pidgin, and it is based on English.

5.7   The 'number wan blade' in Honiara Town[2]

Read through the transcript below several times. The first time, just identify what is being advertised. Then try to work out as many of the words as possible (this will largely be a question of guesswork). A loose 'translation' into standard English is given in Note 2 at the end of the chapter. Only refer to this when you need to.

Paul: *Hei, Peter! Baibai yu leit long parti blong Mary, ye.*
Peter: *Orait, orait. Mi kam nau.*
Paul: *Yu sheiv tudei, or no mor?*
Peter: *Mi sheiv tudei, bat-e wichwei, yu tink mi luk-e no gud yet?*
Paul: *Yes. Yu luk-e not veri klin this morning, and this taim mi teikim kam wan-fela 'Gillette Thin Blade' – nju kain bleid, ye. Himi savi meikim yu klin an smuth, gud tu. Yu trai im!*
Peter: *Thank yu, Paul. Mi savi this-fela 'Gillette Thin Blade' – himi namber wan, an mi tink mi savi sheiv long him plenni taim. Bat, samting no mor, hau mach nau him kostim ye man?*
Paul: *Himi kost ten sens long wan paket, Peter, and-e tu sens for wan-fela bleid. Eniwai, las taim taim yu go long party blong Mary, yu enjoi-im?*
Peter: *Oh, mi laikim tu mach, man.*
Female: *Mai keranki, yu luk smart tu mach tudei, Peter!*
Peter: *Yes. Yu savi lilim difrens abaut the 'Gillette Thin Blade' – bikors this ai fil fresh, klin an gadim smuth feis tu.*

The applied linguist who is associated with the study of pidgin languages in relation to FL learner talk is John Schumann, whose 1978 book contains a quite detailed comparison between these two types of simplified code. A number of his examples of learner talk are taken from a learner named Alberto. He was a thirty-three-year-old Costa Rican who had studied English for a time at home and who had been living in the United States for four months at the time that he was studied. Box 5.8 overleaf contains some examples of his language, showing how it shares characteristics with pidgins.

5.8 The pidgin in Alberto

Here are four characteristics of pidgins, taken from Schumann (1978). Below them are four examples of Alberto's language (also take from Schumann 1978). You should find it quite easy to match the characteristics with the examples. The 'answers' are given in Note 3 at the end of the chapter.

1. Pidgins often simplify word order. In a pidgin spoken in the Melanesian Islands, for example, questions and statements have the same word order. So *You are building a house* and *Are you building a house?* are both *Yu wokim haus* in this pidgin. Statements and questions would be distinguished by intonation.
2. Pidgins often do without 'function' words – words expressing grammatical relations. The pidgin used by immigrant workers in Australia, for example, dispenses with all the complicated ways of expressing negation we use in standard English (*do not, did not, will not* and so on). You simply put the word *no* in front of the verb – *I no come*, for example.
3. The vocabulary of a pidgin is often rather restricted (<u>underlexicalization</u>), and speakers have to be quite inventive to find ways of expressing ideas using available words. Two West African pidgin examples: the word for *calf* is *kaw pikin* (baby cow), and *puppy* is *dok pikin* (baby dog).
4. Getting rid of complicated 'endings' (<u>inflectional morphemes</u>). One West African pidgin, for example, has one word *cop* for all the English forms associated with the verb *eat*. So *cop* can mean: *eat, ate, eaten* and *eating*.

Now here is Alberto:

A *One boy is . . . playing two plate* [= cymbals]
B *This is a chicken* [statement] *and This is apple?* [question]
C *I talk to you Spanish and Yesterday I talk with one friend*
D *I no drink, smoke*

In the next chapter we shall see that Schumann uses the similarities between pidgins and learner language to develop an entire theory of FL acquisition. It is a theory that is based on the *role* that pidgin languages play in the lives of those who speak them. It tries to get to the very heart of why pidgin languages have the form that they do.

In this chapter we have gathered together some of the observations that applied linguists have made about acquisition, in relation to both L1 and FL. But are these points just a collection of 'interesting characteristics', or can they be linked together to form a coherent theory of language acquisition (particularly for FLs)? The answer is that they can, and that the characteristics we have been considering have led not to one, but to a number of theories. We shall now look at some of these.

Notes

1. In their research, Newport, Gleitman and Gleitman collected data from fifteen children and their mothers, in two two-hour sessions held six months apart.

2. Here is a loose translation of the advertisement:

   Hey, Peter! You'll be late for Mary's party soon. Okay, okay, I'm coming. Haven't you shaved today? Yes, I have, but what's wrong, do you think I don't look right? Yes, you don't look very clean-shaven this morning, but I just so happen to have brought a Gillette Thin Blade with me. It's a new kind of blade which will give you a really close shave. Here, try it! Thanks, Paul. I know these Gillette Thin Blades. They're really good. And I expect you can use them lots of times. But, just one thing; how much do they cost? They cost 10 cents a packet, and 2 cents a blade. Anyway, did you enjoy Mary's party last time? Oh yes, it was really good. Goodness gracious, you look really smart today, Peter! Yes, you can feel the difference with the Gillette Thin Blade, because I feel fresh and clean-shaven, and I've got a smooth face.

3. The intended matches are: 1–B; 2–D; 3–A; 4–C.

Chapter 6

Acquisition: some theories

Though we shall make mention of other theories of language acquisition, this chapter will focus on two: Krashen's Input Theory and Schumann's Acculturation Theory.[1] As its name suggests, the first places great emphasis on the input language providers offer. The second is particularly concerned with the importance of affect.

Krashen's Input Theory

Krashen's theory is in fact an amalgam of five hypotheses:

6.1 Krashen's Input Theory: the key points

1. **The acquisition–learning distinction.** Learning and acquisition are separate processes.
2. **The natural order hypothesis.** There is a natural order of morpheme acquisition that applies to FL acquisition.
3. **The monitor hypothesis.** Acquisition is more 'important' that learning. The main role of learning is a secondary one: to monitor what we say and write in the FL.
4. **The input hypothesis.** The most important thing to provide acquirers with is 'comprehensible input'.
5. **The affective filter hypothesis.** Learners need the right 'affect' for acquisition to take place.

Numbers 1 and 2 have already been discussed and, although points relevant to the other three have also been raised, they need more detailed attention.

The monitor hypothesis

Box 6.2 overleaf is about pronunciation of the sound [r] in New York. What has this to do with FL acquisition? The answer will slowly reveal itself:

6.2 Pronouncing [r] in New York

One way in which varieties of English differ is in whether the [r] is pronounced after a vowel, in words like *far*, and *hard*. This is what linguists call the <u>post-vocalic [r]</u>. Some varieties, like standard British English for example, do not pronounce this [r], while other varieties (like Scottish) do. In some places, pronouncing the [r] is considered prestigious, and leaving it out may be thought to be 'slovenly'. One such place is the New York area in the United States.

In a famous sociolinguistic study which took place in New York, the linguist William Labov (1966) studied the use of post-vocalic [r] by different social groups in five different situations. These situations ranged from very informal (in 'Casual speech') to reading out pairs of words – like *beer* and *bear* – in a careful way to make their pronunciation clear. These pairs are called 'Minimal pairs'. The diagram below shows two things about pronunciation of the post-vocalic [r]. One of them is to do with differences from situation to situation. The various situations are listed along the bottom of the diagram. What can you say about the use of this [r] in relation to situation? The second point is to do with differences in use between social classes (indicated by the different lines on the diagram). What can be said about this?[2]

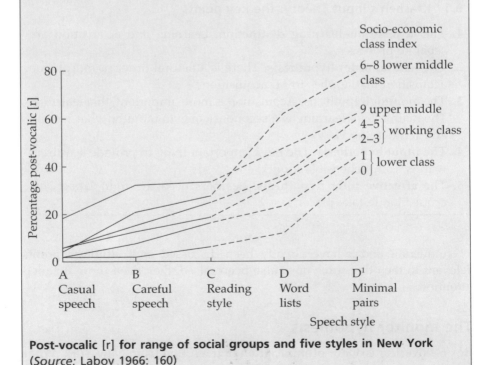

Post-vocalic [r] for range of social groups and five styles in New York (*Source:* Labov 1966: 160)

We can all, whatever our L1 is, think of occasions where we speak differently from the way we normally do. We may 'put on an accent', or be particularly careful about our grammar and choice of words when speaking to an important person, being interviewed for a job, or in any other situation where we feel 'on show'. There are many people who will have a local dialect that they used as a child, and will still use as adults in informal situations. But for special occasions (or even just slightly formal occasions like when at work in the office) they may modify that dialect towards a more standard form. In some situations, caused by drunkenness, stress or tiredness for example, the more standard way of speaking may involuntarily disappear. I once had a friend who spoke with a perfectly standard British English accent until he had had a few glasses of beer. He then broke into the most incomprehensible regional dialect, quite impossible to understand unless you came from within fifty miles of his birthplace (a distance which decreased as the amount of beer consumed increased). The information in box 6.2 about New York pronunciation of the post-vocalic [r] provides a good example of how intricate and sensitive the phenomenon of modifying language according to situation can be.

The modification of speech patterns, particularly in situations where there is form-focus, is known as <u>monitoring</u>. Box 6.2 shows how this has been studied in relation to L1 use. Krashen applies the concept to FL learning. He (along with others) notices that there is much <u>variability</u> in FL learners' language production. Sometimes for example they will get a structure right while on another occasion they will get it wrong. He conjectures that on some occasions learners will be making a particular effort with their language (for example when they are writing something formal, talking to someone important, doing a language test). On other occasions – as when chatting informally to friends, they will be more interested in *what* they are saying than in *how* they are saying it. In these former situations, we may say that the learners are monitoring their own speech – checking it carefully before they produce it. In the latter situations there is no monitoring.

Krashen links FL monitoring to the learning/acquisition distinction. He says that in informal speech the language the FL learner produces is the result of an acquisition process – the learner uses the language she has 'picked up'. It is only in more formal situations that what has been learned comes into play and, even then, it is in a rather restricted role. That role is to monitor production, to inspect and sometimes to alter output generated by the acquired system. As we have just seen, there will be more monitoring on some occasions than others.

An example of FL monitoring: there is a notoriously unfriendly rule of English grammar which says that most verbs take an -*s* in the third person singular of the simple present tense – so we say *She likes*, in contrast to *I like*, *They like*. The rule is simplicity itself, and is usually taught early on in language-teaching courses. But, although the rule is simple, we describe it as 'unfriendly', because learners are highly liable to forget it when com-municating naturally. So they will practise sentences like *She likes* ad infinitum (and indeed *ad nauseam*) in the language classroom, but then – to the teacher's fury – stroll out of the class and slip *She like* into their conversation. Why? Because in class the learner is alert to things linguistic, and is attending to her own language as she produces it. Her internal monitoring device is at its highest setting. It is then that what she has learned in class comes into play. Outside class she uses the form often acquired by those living in the target-language environment: *She like*.

Box 6.3 is Krashen's own illustration of his monitor hypothesis (from Krashen 1977: 154):

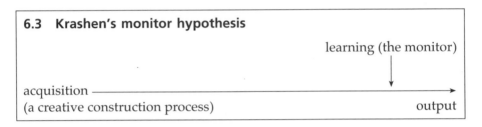

6.3 Krashen's monitor hypothesis

learning (the monitor)

acquisition ⎯⎯⎯⎯⎯⎯⎯⎯⎯⎯⎯⎯⎯⎯⎯⎯⎯⎯⎯→
(a creative construction process)   output

Output is the language the learner produces. The arrow between acquisi-tion and output shows the central importance of acquisition. When giving an informal lecture, Krashen (1983) uses a vivid colloquial phrase which exactly captures this idea: 'acquisition', he says, 'is where the action is'. The position of the learning arrow close to output indicates that it is often a 'last-minute process'. Indeed, monitoring may also occur *after* performance, resulting in the learner correcting herself after she has spoken or written. Notice also the use of Dulay and Burt's creative construction term to describe acquisition.

The input hypothesis

'The hypothesis states simply', say Krashen and Terrell (1983: 32), 'that we acquire (not learn) language by understanding input that is a little beyond our current level of (acquired) competence.' To make this idea concrete, consider the imaginary situation given in box 6.4:

6.4 Can you speak Flipspraek?

Imagine that three friends of yours, native speakers of English, are learning an (imaginary) language called Flipspraek. They are at different levels: Friend 1 is almost a beginner, Friend 2 is more advanced and Friend 3 is the best of all. The three friends go to stay with a family in Flipspraekland. Early on in their stay someone in their host family says to all three of them:

(a) *Glop ti indo ap tugen, molim maegt ti blippo un grinop int mag?*

Since Friend 1 does not understand a single word of this utterance, she can only smile sweetly and nod her head energetically.

Friend 2 understands some words. These are written in English in (b):

(b) *If you're indo ap tugen, molim could you blippo a grinop for me?*

Do you think that Friend 2 knows enough to understand the meaning of the whole utterance? Or to decipher any of the individual unknown words? Consider what she is likely to *understand* and *not understand* of the utterance.

Friend 3 understands a little more, and this is what she 'hears':

(c) *If you're indo into town, please could you post a grinop for me*

Is Friend 3 able to work out roughly what *indo* and *grinop* mean? What are you able to say about their meanings?

Friend 3 is likely to surmise that *indo* is some verb of movement, even though she cannot be sure whether it signifies 'going', 'driving', 'walking', or something else similar. In the same way, she cannot know whether a *grinop* is a 'parcel' or a 'letter' or a 'postcard'; but she is probably fairly certain that it is some item that can be posted.

This example shows how language 'a little beyond our current level of (acquired) competence' can often be worked out by a learner. Friends 1 and 2 have little hope of understanding *indo* and *grinop*, because they understand so little of the context in which the words occur. For Friend 3 on the other hand, the Flipspraek sentence is likely to lead to a degree of learning. She may not be able to work out the exact meaning of the two unknown words, though with time and a few more examples of their use, this will doubtless come. But the general meanings will be clear.

Krashen's claim is that learning will occur when unknown items are *only just* beyond the learner's present level. As with Friend 3, context will help this to happen, but so will other devices found in simplified codes and employed by caretakers – such as using gestures (e.g. pointing at things), focusing on the here and now, repeating items. Above all the learner needs the help of a friendly language provider, who will rough tune, and modify her language so that it does not wander too far away from the learner's level of competence.

Krashen has a formula that neatly expresses his idea of <u>comprehensible input</u>. He describes the acquirer's present level of competence as i, and the level immediately following i as $i+1$. The input hypothesis claims that learners progress by understanding language containing $i+1$; language just above present competence. In this formulation, we may say that rough tuning consists of knowing, roughly, what a learner's i is, and hence being able to gauge $i+1$.

How convincing is this idea? As box 6.4 above illustrates, it has a ring of truth to it. But there are problems. An anecdote will illustrate one. Years ago I knew a six-year-old English child named Suzi. One of her favourite television programmes was a very adult one. It dealt with the lives and loves of a group of rich Americans. The plot was extremely complex, as was the language. Why, I used to ask myself, does Suzi like this programme so much? It cannot, I thought, contain much input that is comprehensible to her, either in terms of content or language. But there must have been a level on which understanding took place, otherwise there would not have been such interest. But $i + 1$? It seemed to be, if anything, more like $i + 110$! Does that mean she learned nothing from it, linguistically? I have no way of knowing. But the degree of attention she gave to it suggests that she was at least receptive to learning taking place. Another problem is that it is almost impossible to measure a notion like i, and this makes it very difficult to assess the hypothesis properly. Part of this particular issue is taken up in Chapter 14 (p. 274 below), where an implication is that people rarely know or do not know something in black-and-white terms. People usually 'half-know' things, or know 'little bits of things'. This makes it difficult to judge what i is, and also what $+ 1$ might mean.

The affective filter hypothesis

We have already seen (and will see further in Chapter 8) that affective factors can have a strong influence on FL learning. A helpful way of conceptualizing that influence is to regard affect as a 'filter' through which FL input has to pass before it is acquired. Where the feelings of the learner are 'positive', we might say that she is more 'open' to input. Her filter is clean, and language passes easily through it. A learner with 'negative' feelings will, on the other hand, be 'closed' to input. The filter will be clogged, and little gets through.[3] Recall Teachers A and B in Chapter 5. Teacher A fell in love with Italy, and her attitude left the filter clean for Italian to come in. Teacher B's negative feelings well and truly clogged the filter.

This notion of the affective filter is used by Dulay and Burt (for example in Dulay *et al.* 1982), and finds its place in Krashen's Input Theory. Box 6.5 is taken from Krashen and Terrell (1983: 39):

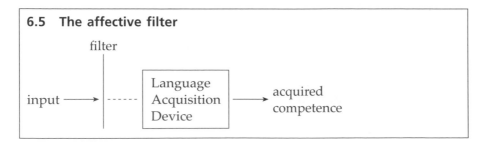

6.5   The affective filter

Krashen's model joins together the five hypotheses described in box 6.1 above to produce a theory of foreign-language acquisition in which central importance is given to the nature of the input given to learners. Krashen and Terrell (1983) attempt to relate the hypothesis to a language-teaching method, which they call the Natural Approach. The approach involves simulating aspects of acquisition in the classroom. A silent period, for example, is allowed, and great emphasis is placed on providing learners with roughly tuned $i + 1$. The approach is briefly discussed again in Chapter 10.

Output and interaction

Krashen's Input Theory and its key notion of 'comprehensible input' have not been without their critics. One major objection relates to the fact that, though comprehensible input may play an important role, it is not in itself enough: understanding is not quite the same as acquiring. One argument along these lines is put forward by Swain (1985). Her Output Hypothesis is based on the idea that understanding language and producing language are different skills, and that the second can only be developed by pushing the learner to produce output – actually to say and write things.

A second hypothesis is based around a notion that involves both input and output. This is the notion of interaction. When a learner interacts with someone – it may be another learner or a teacher (native speaker or otherwise) – the learner receives input, and produces output. The Interaction Hypothesis is associated, for FL learning, with Allwright (1984) and Long (1983). The hypothesis claims that it is in the interaction process that acquisition occurs: learners acquire through talking with others.

Because learners do not know the language perfectly, it is natural that their attempts to interact should sometimes go wrong. Misunderstandings may occur. When these happen, those involved in the interaction have to try and 'repair' it by a process known as negotiation of meaning (defined by Ellis 1997: 141 as 'the interactive work that takes place between speakers when some misunderstanding occurs'). This will involve saying things again, perhaps using other words and simpler structures, using lots of gestures, and in general employing the strategies we associated in the last chapter with simplified codes. A number of applied linguists have suggested that the process of negotiating meaning may be particularly useful to language acquisition, and various experimental studies have tried to show this. Box 6.6 overleaf describes one paper on this subject.

6.6 Negotiating comprehensible input

An important paper in the discussion of negotiation of meaning is Long (1983). Long begins his paper by arguing that *modifications to input* made by native speakers (NSs) in conversation with non-natives (NNSs) play an important role in making input comprehensible to learners. But *modifications to interactional structure* are, he argues, probably more important. Long uses the following examples to illustrate the difference between these two sorts of modification:

(1) NS : *What time you finish?*
    NNS : *Ten o'clock*

(2) NS : *When did you finish?*
    NNS : *Um?*
    NS : *When did you finish?*
    NNS : *Ten clock*
    NS : *Ten o'clock?*
    NNS : *Yeah*

The point to notice is that in (1) the NS modifies her utterance, leaving out the auxiliary (a characteristic, as we have seen, of pidgins). This is a 'modification to input'. In (2) the NS makes no such modification – the verb *did* is included. But (2) does contain two NS strategies for negotiating understanding. Firstly the NS repeats the initial sentence (*When did you finish?*) when at first the NNS fails to understand it. Secondly, she checks the NNS's utterance *Ten clock* by repeating it in its correct form. These strategies are called 'self-repetition' and 'confirmation check' respectively.

The kinds of interactional modification found in (2) are what Long regards as particularly important to ensure that the learner receives comprehensible input. In his paper he puts forward a classification of interactional modifications, developed either to avoid communication misunderstandings occurring, or to resolve them once they occur. The two examples given above are from his classification.

Schumann's Acculturation Theory

We have already seen more than once that attitudes towards society are important in FL learning. The American applied linguist John Schumann's Acculturation Theory places social considerations at its centre. His focus is almost exclusively on those who are acquiring a foreign language in the target-language environment, like Spanish L1 speakers living in the United States, or English L1 speakers exposed to Arabic in Saudi Arabia. The theory claims that the important factor in FL learning success is the learner's view of the L1 speakers and their society, and her aspirations regarding becoming a member of that group – how much she wants to 'be like' the FL speakers, to 'be a part of' the FL society.

We have already seen that Schumann (1978) establishes similarities between pidgin languages and FL learner talk. The next issue he considers there also concerns these two simplified codes. It is the issue of <u>fossilization</u>, the word used to describe what happens when a learner's FL development grinds to a halt. Schumann was part of a team involved in a study described in Cancino *et al.* (1978). The study looked at six Spanish-speaking subjects, aged between five and thirty-three, living in a target-language country and acquiring English. One of the six was the Costa Rican Alberto who has already been mentioned. The researchers plotted the progress of these learners over a period of ten months, particularly focusing on the acquisition of one structure – making sentences negative in English (<u>sentence negation</u>). At the beginning of the study all six of the learners made sentences negative by the highly effective but inaccurate means of putting the word *no* in an utterance. Examples are *I no can see, They no have water*, and if you look back to box 5.8 above you will find another. Two things are noteworthy about the learners' progress over time. The first is that by the end of the ten months, all except Alberto had gone well beyond the 'putting-*no*-in-the-sentence' solution, and had acquired the rudiments of the English negation system. This fact is noteworthy because it suggests that, if left to their own resources (that is, acquiring the language in the natural environment without tuition), some learners will indeed progress. Just like L1 acquirers, they are able to 'grow out of' their mistakes and move towards mastery of the language. It is a fact that has highly thought-provoking implications for the attitude of language teachers towards learner errors. One legacy of behaviourist thinking is the still widespread view that errors should be avoided at all costs, because 'practice makes permanent', suggesting that if errors are left uncorrected they will never be grown out of. But it is clear that in the case of L1 learning, and for nearly all of Cancino *et al.*'s subjects, practice certainly does *not* make permanent.

The second noteworthy point relates to Alberto. He was the exception to the rule. Over the ten-month period, he made no progress at all, and finished as he started, with the 'putting-*no*-in-the-sentence' solution. Box 6.7 overleaf chronicles a similar sorry tale.

Any of you who have had contact with immigrants coming to live in your own country, and trying to pick up your own L1 will know that cases like Alberto's and Zoila's are unfortunately not that rare. Some learners seem to reach a stage beyond which they fail to progress. Stabilization of erroneous forms occurs, and fossilization sets in. Notice that the word 'fossilization' might also be used to describe what occurs with pidgin languages; they reach a certain point in their development where they no longer continue to 'move towards' the standard base language.

6.7 A sorry tale

Shapira (1978) provides another example of fossilization, to equal Alberto's. She studied Zoila, a twenty-five-year-old Guatemalan woman. Zoila was a native speaker of Spanish who had lived in the United States for three years at the time of the study, working as a housekeeper in English-speaking families. Shapira plotted Zoila's progress with ten selected morphemes. The sad conclusion: 'during the 18 month observation period, there appears to have been little, or quite insignificant, development in the acquisition of any of the 10 grammatical categories studied'. The title of Shapira's paper is 'The non-learning of English: a case study of an adult'.

Fossilization is a phenomenon of great interest both to FL acquisition researchers and to language teachers. The reasons are rather obvious: if we can find out why fossilization occurs not only will we understand the processes of foreign-language acquisition better, but we may even be able to do something (in the classroom perhaps) to prevent its occurrence. Schumann (1978) therefore now turns to these fascinating and vital questions: why does FL fossilization occur, and what stops it from occurring? Again note that a related question might be asked about pidgin languages: why do pidgins stop moving towards the standard base language; what makes a pidgin stop?

6.8 Thinking about fossilization

In the paragraphs you are about to read, suggestions are given as to what might cause fossilization. Before you read these paragraphs, consider how you would answer this question. What are your thoughts on the causes of fossilization?

If possible base your considerations on some 'fossilized individuals' that you have yourself come across.

A common view of fossilization, and possibly one that occurred to you when looking at box 6.8, is that it happens when the language a learner has acquired is sufficient to meet her needs. In these circumstances there is, quite simply, no reason for the learner's language to continue progress towards the 'norm'. Imagine for example a learner visiting an English-speaking country as a tourist. One of her needs is quite likely to involve ordering meals in a restaurant. Perhaps she will use a structure like *Give to me* for this (e.g. *Give to me fish and chips*). This structure is 'unacceptable' in various ways, and certainly no English-language teacher would condone its use. But it is also likely to succeed! That is, its use is likely to result in the appearance of a plate of fish and chips, or whatever. And, if it works, the argument goes, what incentive is there for the learner to abandon it, and develop some more acceptable phrase such as *I'd like . . . please*?

This view of fossilization is described in more detail in box 6.9, where objections to it (particularly in relation to L1 acquisition) are also put forward.

6.9 Some views on fossilization

Vigil and Oller (1976) develop what they call the feedback model of fossilization. This argues that whether or not a form fossilizes will depend on the reaction the speaker receives when using it. '. . . any forms', they say, 'that elicit favourable feedback will tend to fossilize.' The listener reaction of *I understand* will, in other words, lead to fossilization, while the reaction *I don't understand* will lead to change/improvement. The principle is clear: a learner who is managing to have her needs met by an imperfect 'pidgin-like' form has no motive to improve.

Selinker and Lamendella (1978) bitterly attack this position. The main objection relates to L1 acquisition and the fact that L1 children do not fossilize the pidgin-like forms they develop in the process of acquisition, even though caretakers in general both understand what their children are saying, and indicate that understanding to the child.

The feedback model is related to the one that Schumann follows. He bases his argument on the position expressed in Smith (1972), who argues that language serves three general functions. Two of these are particularly relevant to us.[4] The first is what Smith calls the *communicative*, and it relates to the simple transmission of information. So when someone asks what the time is, or indeed requests a plate of fish and chips, it is this function that is being fulfilled. Smith's second function is the *integrative*. Here the user wants her language to mark her as a member of some social group. Some aspects of L1 use are easy to associate with this function. For example, people may deliberately either maintain or avoid a local dialect to make a statement about the social group to which they belong. Using or not using a particular dialect is sending signals to the world about how you see yourself in relation to some group.

The Fish-and-Chips Syndrome (mentioned earlier) well illustrates the communicative/integrative distinction. Providing the utterance results in fish and chips, then it succeeds on a communicative level. But, for a learner who has some integrative ambitions, who wants perhaps to be seen as urbane, a well-travelled person-of-the-world who is as at home ordering food in English as in her native language, the utterance would send all the wrong signals. It might succeed communicatively (and digestively) but fail integratively.

Schumann uses the communicative/integrative distinction to explain why both pidgins and FL learners fossilize. It is commonly the case, he notes, that pidgins are used mainly for the communicative function, while the L1 is generally reserved for the integrative. Because they are designed to fulfil such a restricted function, Schumann argues, pidgins are as developed as they need to be; further 'sophistication' is unnecessary. Similarly with FL learners; where they are using the FL for simple communicative purposes, early fossilization is likely to occur. Where, on the other hand, the learner wishes in some way to integrate with the speakers of the FL, to be considered as one of them (the integrative function), then there is a motivation for fossilized forms to be replaced by the standard ones. Schumann uses the term <u>acculturate</u> (meaning to 'become a part of a culture') to express his central idea: it is that the occurrence or otherwise of fossilization will depend on the degree to which the learner wishes to acculturate to the FL language and society.

Schumann's theory attempts to identify the factors which will enable us to predict whether fossilization will occur in the language of a particular learner or group of learners. His factors are divided into two broad categories: *social* and *psychological* distance. Examples of each are given in box 6.10. In order to clarify how these factors are relevant, consider the first: 'social and economic dominance'. Remember that we are dealing with learners staying in a target-language country. A question to ask, Schumann is saying, relates to the relationships between the learner's L1 culture and the culture of the target-language speakers. If one or other culture regards itself as socially or economically dominant, then this may prevent the learner from making the effort to progress with the language. For example, if the learner comes from an economically rich country and is staying in a poor country, then the motive for integrating within that (poorer) culture may not be present; the learner may be content to 'get by' with pidgin-like forms which fossilize early.

How useful is Schumann's list? One possible criticism is that it is not always straightforward what each factor will predict regarding FL acquisition. To return to the 'social and economic dominance' example: it may be that a member of a socially dominant society will not readily learn the language of a less dominant one. But the converse may not be true – it is easy to imagine that a member of a less dominant society will make efforts to learn the language of a more dominant one. You may also feel that, though some factors may in some circumstances be important, they need not necessarily be so. Consider 'degree of enclosure' for example. Though it might deter some individuals, it is unlikely to stand in the way of a determined learner. Finally, you need to ask whether a list like Schumann's can ever be anything like complete. Spend a moment thinking whether there are any factors you might add to those in box 6.10. You can probably find quite a few.[5]

6.10   Some factors in Schumann's Acculturation Theory

SOCIAL DISTANCE

These are factors dealing with the learner's relationship to the culture of the target FL speakers. Here are some examples:

- **Social and economic dominance** Is either the L1 or the FL culture regarded as socially or economically dominant over the other?
- **Degree of enclosure** Where the learner is living. In some countries, guest workers (for example) are put together in special compounds with their own living quarters. In other situations, the learner may be living among the 'local inhabitants'.
- **Cultural congruence** How close the FL and L1 societies are. Do they share a religion? A history?
- **Length of residence** How long is the learner staying in the FL country?

PSYCHOLOGICAL DISTANCE

- **Language shock, culture shock, culture stress** Shock = initial reaction; stress = longer-term reaction. Language shock is suddenly finding you don't have the right word, that you can't express yourself, that you may appear comic. Culture shock involves the realization that you are not in control of your environment, and have to expend much energy on the mere process of living.

Schumann uses his factors to give examples of good and bad profiles. A *bad* profile is Americans living in Riyadh, the capital of Saudi Arabia, during the 1970s. There were roughly 20,000 in the city which then had a population of only 300,000. Perhaps some Americans will view themselves as culturally dominant, and certainly the cultures are incongruent. The Americans all lived together (high enclosure), and were staying in the country for a short while. The prediction is that they would not learn much Arabic. As an example of a *good* profile, Schumann cites American Jewish immigrants settling in Israel. Being Jews in a Jewish society, there is high cultural congruence. Enclosure is likely to be low, with them living not necessarily together with other American immigrants, but in districts suited to their social status; and, of course, they are going for life-long length of residence! They are likely to succeed in learning Hebrew.

The theory also works reasonably well for the six learners whose development of the negative Schumann and his colleagues were studying. Of the six, only Alberto fossilizes. The five others are upper middle class professional immigrants. They are not enclosed, but live, mix and socialize with similar professionals regardless of racial origin. Alberto is a lower class worker immigrant; he lives (and socializes) with other Spanish-speaking factory workers; and he only has a sixteen-month visa.

And learning?

In the first sentence of Chapter 5, we said that the recent past in applied linguistics was the 'age of language acquisition'. In the course of this chapter and the last we have seen how much creative energy has been put into exploring the acquisition idea. We have also seen (perhaps as a consequence) how little importance, in a model like Krashen's, is given to learning. Acquisition really is where the action has been.

But what about learning? Krashen associates learning with classrooms, picking out error correction and rule isolation as its essential characteristics. But learning, with these characteristics, is surely what is going on throughout the world. A good proportion of those billion people learning English as a Foreign Language, for example, are probably learning in classrooms, and paying very little attention at all to the ideas about acquisition we have been considering. After all, these ideas have been developed largely by looking at learners living in the target-language country, exposed to the language all the time – a far cry from the learner in her native country, attending class for just a few hours a week. As a consequence, if you ask most teachers about the role learning plays, they are likely be uncomfortable with the view that it just gives students knowledge which comes into play only in formal, monitored situations. Surely, many teachers would protest, it is more central than that. Acquisition may be the exciting, colourful cutting edge of current thinking. But (many would argue) learning is what teachers believe in, and learning is what students do.

So learning is what we shall now look at . . .

Notes

1. In fact both theories are referred to as 'hypotheses' – the Input Hypothesis and the Acculturation Hypothesis. But this usage can be confusing, particularly since Krashen's theory has a 'sub-hypothesis' also called the 'input hypothesis'. To avoid this confusion, we shall talk of Krashen's Input Theory and Schumann's Acculturation Theory, reserving the word 'hypothesis' for some of the ideas that go to make up the theories.
2. The situations differ in the degree of attention the speaker is likely to give to what she says, with 'casual speech' at one end, and 'minimal pairs' at the other. The diagram shows that all speakers, whatever their social group, use the post-vocalic [r] more in situations where there is more *form-focus* (this phrase was introduced on p. 79). The diagram also shows differences in social class. In general, the pattern is for 'higher' classes to pronounce the post-vocalic [r] more than 'lower' ones. The one interesting exception is the lower middle class, who appear to pronounce the [r] more that the upper middle class. Perhaps this is a case of social pretension; the lower middle class sense that pronunciation of the post-vocalic [r] is the socially superior thing to do, and hence rather overdo it.
   This discussion of the post-vocalic [r] owes much to Holmes (1992).

3. We have here changed the image of the filter a little. For Krashen it is 'up' or 'down', while for us it is 'clean' or 'dirty'.
4. Smith's third function, not discussed, is called the 'expressive'. This goes beyond the integrative, and through it the user seeks respect in the particular realm of language use, perhaps as a story-teller or a poet.
5. The list in box 6.10 does not contain all Schumann's factors. But, even if it did, you would easily be able to find more that he does not list.

Chapter 7

Learning . . . and acquisition again

Are there any recent theories of learning? Is there just behaviourism (the learning theory of earlier decades), or does some more up-to-date theory exist, that does perhaps for learning what Krashen and Schumann do for acquisition? The answer is yes, there are indeed recent theories of learning which spring from current approaches to psychology and which offer real alternatives to the acquisition view. McLaughlin (1987) calls them 'cognitive theories'. McLaughlin *et al.* (1983) outline one such theory, while Johnson (1996) and Skehan (1998) develop others. Theories like these attempt to explain how learners sitting in classrooms, receiving tuition from a teacher, can come to master a language as proficiently as by the acquisition route. We begin this chapter by looking at some of the concepts underlying these cognitive theories. These concepts are the <u>declarative/procedural knowledge distinction</u>, together with the notions of <u>automization</u> and <u>restructuring</u>. We shall then think about how these concepts might relate to the acquisition view we have just finished describing. The result of our deliberations will be an attempt to outline one framework which can account for both FL learning *and* acquisition.

Declarative and procedural knowledge

This is an old distinction made in philosophy, between 'knowledge about' and 'knowledge how to'. It is a distinction that makes perfect sense to those involved in skill training of any kind. Driving instructors, for example, understand that 'knowing about' driving (what a steering wheel is and what function it performs, etc.) is quite different from 'knowing how to' drive. Indeed a driving test which concentrated on declarative and not procedural knowledge would be a recipe for disaster. Language teachers also understand the distinction well. They realize that having declarative knowledge of a language is quite different from being able to speak it. The world is full of people who know a great deal *about* English, but who find it difficult to create a sentence in the language. Box 7.1 describes one.

7.1 Putting dad to shame

(a) I once had a neighbour who was an eminent professor from overseas. He was an expert on the English language, and had written many a learned paper describing aspects of English grammar. But his use of English was almost non-existent. He could not understand what was said to him, and his attempts to speak were filled with errors and such poor pronunciation that it was almost impossible to understand what he was saying. He had high declarative knowledge, but poor procedural knowledge. This situation did not change over the year that he was in England.

The professor was accompanied by his family. This included his eight-year-old daughter, who was attending the local school. Though her English was almost non-existent when the family arrived, within a year it was of a very high standard indeed. It was certainly very much better than her professorial father's. Her procedural knowledge was very good, but her declarative knowledge was probably very small.

(b) Think of some individuals you have come across who 'know about' a foreign language, but cannot speak it well.

(c) Now a burning issue to ponder. You probably agree that 'knowing about' a language is very different from 'knowing how to' speak it. But can 'knowing about' help you in the process of learning 'how to'? If your aim is to speak a language fluently, is there any value to understanding how it works?

Why is this a burning issue? What would be the implication for language teaching if we decided that declarative knowledge did not help in the development of procedural knowledge?

Automization

Automization means 'making automatic', and box 7.2 (overleaf) gives a clear example of the process at work. It is a very important process, and indeed two cognitive psychologists, Shiffrin and Dumais (1981), describe it as 'a fundamental component of skill development', playing a vital role in the development of any skill (including, presumably, the skill of using a foreign language).

Exactly why is automization important? Precisely what role does it fulfil? When a skill is newly learned, its performance takes up a great deal of conscious attention – what is sometimes called <u>channel capacity</u> ('room in the mind'). Take an aspect of learning to drive a car as an example. Learners who have just been taught how to change gear will at first only be able to do it if they concentrate on the gear change and nothing else. They need to take their eyes off the road, to look down at the gear-stick, to think about which

7.2 A seven-year course in cigar rolling

Crossman (1959) studied several girls whose job was to roll cigars in a factory, using a purpose-built machine. These girls were studied over a period of about seven years, during which time they each made over ten million cigars. They continued to improve over this time, getting faster and faster at the job. Indeed, by the time the study finished it was only the slowness of the machinery that was preventing the girls from getting faster. When it comes to rolling cigars, practice does indeed make for speedy performance!

direction to move it in, to remember which pedal is the clutch and which foot should be put on it. Then they have to co-ordinate all these actions together; there is a lot to do at once. Until the learner has progressed from this stage, he is a danger to himself and anyone near him. Taking eyes off the road is clearly dangerous, and a driver simply cannot stop doing everything else whenever a gear change is called for. One might say that there are 'higher level skills' which require available channel capacity. In driving, these skills include paying attention to what is happening around you, anticipating the movement of other traffic and of pedestrians. Will that lorry pull out? Is that man about to cross the street in front of you? Are the traffic lights about to change? Channel capacity can only be made available to consider such matters if 'lower level' skills like changing gear have been made automatic so that they occupy no 'room in the mind'. When novice drivers have automated gear changing, they will be able to perform the action without even being aware that they are doing it. The role of automization in skill learning is therefore to free valuable channel capacity for those more important tasks which require it.

7.3 'Higher' and 'lower' level skills

(a) The paragraph above talks about 'higher' and 'lower' level skills in relation to car driving. Can you identify similar levels for another non-linguistic skill? Choose a skill you are familiar with (it might be a sport, for example) and list some 'lower' and 'higher' level skills. If you cannot think of a skill yourself, take playing a musical instrument (in an orchestra) as your example.

(b) In the following paragraph, the concept of automization is applied to language learning. Before you read it, consider what 'lower' and 'higher' level skills are involved in language use.

Begin by thinking of the following 'skills' related to English. Which of them might be considered 'lower' level and which 'higher' level?

- differentiating the two *th* sounds in the words *this* and *thing*
- understanding the main message a speaker is conveying
- understanding the difference between *I have seen* and *I saw*
- describing what you want sufficiently accurately to ensure that you get it
- forming correct past tenses

Try to add to these examples some more of your own.

It is easy to apply the automization concept to language learning. When the learner first comes across a new tense, for example, he may need all his available effort to produce it. What auxiliary is used? What ending goes on the auxiliary? What part of the main verb is needed? As with changing gear in a car, there is at first precious little time for anything else. The higher level skills in language use relate generally to understanding messages being conveyed to us, and ensuring that our own messages are properly conveyed. You may yourself be able to think of language learners who are struggling so hard with the mechanics of the language that holding a conversation with them is very hard work indeed. You are in the conversation to find out something from them, and tell them something in turn. But all their attention seems to be on trying to produce the correct tense. Indeed, you have probably passed through this learning stage yourself. It is the pre-automization stage. Over time the learner will come to use that tense so automatically that it occupies no thought space for him to do so, at which point he is free to think about *what* he is saying, not *how* he is saying it.

Therein lies the importance of automization. But how does it come about? How does the learner move from the first stage of full conscious attention to the stage of effortless production? One theory, associated with the American cognitive psychologist John Anderson and his colleagues, was developed in relation to the learning of skills in general, not specifically language learning. In fact in the first instance it was applied to the learning of geometry.[1] The following paragraph describe the model briefly.

In much traditional teaching, the teacher starts by giving the learner declarative knowledge on the chosen topic, telling him *about* what he has to do. The driving instructor, for example, may well begin to teach gear changing by describing the required movements and how they are done. Similarly the language teacher may begin his treatment of a particular tense by giving an explanation of how it is formed. Anderson's model conceptualizes automization as the process of converting that declarative knowledge into procedural knowledge. The model has two main stages.[2] Stage 1 is called the *declarative stage*. Here, the learner is given knowledge which is memorized. When he wants to perform an action, the stored knowledge has to be dredged from memory. Whether the action is gear changing or using a new tense, the learner more or less suspends performance of other actions, and consciously brings back to mind what to do next. We shall call Stage 2 the *proceduralization* stage.[3] At this stage, the learner converts 'knowledge about' into 'knowledge how to'. The knowledge, in other words, becomes *proceduralized* or *automized*.

7.4 Required attention minus one

(a) Anderson's model deals with the process of proceduralization. But how, in actual practice, is proceduralization achieved? The cigar maker in box 7.2 illustrated the process at work. What causes the skill to become automated in that case? Is there anything further a learner might do to help the process on its way? What about the teacher – how can he help?

(b) In Johnson (1996) I argue that one way of helping to develop proceduralization can be expressed by means of a formula: $ra - 1$. This stands for 'required attention minus one'. It works like this. Imagine that a learner has ten units of conscious attention; he has a channel capacity of ten. (It is important to realize that this figure is plucked out of the air just to help explain the idea – the conscious mind cannot of course really be divided into units.) When the learner first learns some new piece of grammar (let us say the simple present tense), he needs all ten units to get it right, and has no channel capacity left over for anything else. This is like the car driver who has to stop doing everything else when changing gear. At this stage, the teacher gives exercises that use just the simple present tense, and nothing else. But quite soon the teacher introduces exercises which involve the learner in doing just a little bit more – just enough more, let us say, to take up one 'unit of attention'. The 'little bit more' might involve using more language, or having to think more about what to say in the exercise. The learner now has only nine units of attention available for the simple present tense, which really needs ten. He is put under a small amount of pressure. Over time he will learn to give only nine units of attention to the tense. When the teacher sees this, some further complication is introduced into the exercise, requiring two 'units of attention', leaving only eight for the simple present. The strategy works, then, by giving the learner increasingly demanding activities, pushing him towards producing the tense with less and less channel capacity available. The formula $ra - 1$ captures this idea of constantly giving the learner just one unit less that he requires to do the task comfortably. In the end, if the strategy is successful the learner reaches the state where he can use the tense using zero units of attention. The tense will, in other words, be fully automated. In terms of our formula, we can say that automization has happened when the ra needed to undertake a given skill equals zero.

Restructuring

Although automization is very important in skill development there is, in fact, McLaughlin (1987: 138) says, 'more to learning a complex cognitive skill than developing automaticity through practice'. The additional element is to do with the concept of <u>restructuring</u>. As people learn, the way they 'view' what they are learning changes. McLaughlin uses an example from Cheng (1985) to illustrate restructuring at work. The example involves the simple mathematical problem of adding up ten twos. The first way is to view the problem as one of addition. This way entails nine operations, each adding two to the running total $(2 + 2 = 4 + 2 = 6$ and so on). The second way is to see the problem as a multiplication one. This involves just one operation $(2 \times 10 = 20)$. A young child will use the first solution until he has been taught his multiplication tables. When this has happened, he will be able to 'restructure' the problem, seeing it as multiplication rather than addition.

McLaughlin gives another example from Cheng to show how automization alone, without restructuring, cannot account for skill learning. The example is to do with piano playing. At a certain level, a player will be able to play in a rhythm involving four beats. He will also be able to play in a rhythm involving three beats, and both these skills may become highly automated. But sometimes the pianist will be asked to combine these skills together – for example to play in a four-beat rhythm with the left hand and a three-beat rhythm with the right hand. This will be difficult for the pianist, however well automated each of the individual skills is. In order to master the combination of four and three, the pianist has to 'view' what he is doing differently – to 'restructure' it.

One important characteristic of restructuring, McLaughlin (1987 and 1990) points out, is that it often occurs suddenly; the 'new way of seeing things' happens in a flash. In this respect restructuring is quite different from automization, which usually occurs over time as more and more practice is given. A learning theory needs to have some way of accounting for 'sudden flash' learning, because it does happen. Perhaps you can think of an example in your own experience of where you have had a 'sudden flash' of understanding, or where you have suddenly been able to do something which a few moments before you were unable to do.

Learning and acquisition: two pathways

In this chapter and the last, we have discussed two 'pathways' to mastery of a foreign language, which have been called 'acquisition' and 'learning'. Is it possible to develop one framework which will account for both learning and acquisition? In Johnson (1996), I argue that the concepts of declarative and procedural knowledge can be used to talk about both learning and acquisition. The 'Learning Pathway' is, I suggest, as described in Anderson's model. It starts with declarative knowledge and moves to procedural knowledge, and I call it DECPRO – from DEClarative to PROcedural. A main process in this sequence is *proceduralization* or *automization*. The process is important because, as we have seen, declarative knowledge without procedural knowledge is insufficient.

But procedural knowledge without declarative is also insufficient. An example will illustrate. In Chapter 2 I mentioned that my first teaching job abroad was in the country now called Croatia. I can still remember the first sentences that I picked up in Croatian. They included *I'd like a steak with an egg, How much does that cost?*, and (for reasons too complex to go into) *Can you tell me where the gas cylinder depot is?* I learned these sentences as 'single entities', or <u>chunks</u> as they are sometimes called, having no understanding whatsoever how they were constructed, and indeed only the vaguest idea of what the individual words meant. I would not have been able to use these chunks as models for producing other similar sentences. I could not, for example, have used the model of *How much does that cost?* to say *How much does that weigh?* or even *How much is it?* But the chunks were very useful to me, not least because I could produce them very quickly, without the kind of effort which (we saw earlier) a learner has to make at the first stages, dredging up rules from memory, and holding up conversations while he does so. This strategy of picking up chunks is typical of the 'Acquisition Pathway'. It is what many do when they acquire an FL in the country where it is spoken. We might say that acquisition involves the 'direct proceduralization of knowledge'. The *starting point* is procedural knowledge.

Procedural knowledge alone is inadequate. It is a common fate for immigrants to develop the ability to say a few sentences with apparent fluency, but without real understanding of the rules behind what they are saying. But these rules are necessary for progress in the language to continue, and without them fossilization sets in. This is precisely what would have happened to my Croatian had I been content with the chunks. The acquirer, in other words, has to move on from chunks to a more general understanding of how the language works. The progression here is from procedural to declarative. It is a process of *declarativization,* and in Johnson (1996) I describe this 'Acquisition Pathway' as PRODEC – moving from PROcedural to DEClarative knowledge.

Box 7.5 shows the two pathways that we have been discussing:

7.5 Two pathways

DECPRO: the Learning Pathway
declarative knowledge → procedural knowledge
(a proceduralization process)

PRODEC: the Acquisition Pathway
procedural knowledge → declarative knowledge
(a declarativization process)

We have argued that both procedural and declarative knowledge are important to the learner. Not only must both be developed, but also maintained. Sometimes maintenance is quite a problem, and it often happens that declarative knowledge is lost once it has been proceduralized. An example often given is that you can only remember phone numbers you use a lot by actually dialling them; they are proceduralized 'actions' for you, and you have lost declarative knowledge of them. Box 7.6 gives another illustration.

7.6 Losing your 'internal map'

For many years I lived in the town of Reading in Berkshire, England. I left there some years ago, but recently had to return. Before this return journey, I tried to remember in my head how to get from the motorway to the place I was visiting, a journey I had done hundreds of times in the distant past. But I had lost my 'internal map' (declarative knowledge) of the town and, however much I tried, I simply could not recall the way. But as soon as I actually arrived at the end of the motorway on the journey itself, I had no trouble at all in finding the way – I just 'followed my nose'. The earlier declarative knowledge was gone, but the procedural knowledge remained.

Can you think of an example in your own experience where you lost declarative knowledge of an action, but where procedural knowledge remained?

So there are two pathways – learning and acquisition – and two processes associated with them, proceduralization and declarativization. Is one pathway better than the other, more likely to lead to success? In Johnson (1996) I claim not, and argue that both pathways lead to the same place, but following different routes.[4] You can begin your journey with either declarative or procedural knowledge. Your starting point will determine which route you follow to your desired destination of mastering the FL. The argument goes like this: 'if your starting point is declarative knowledge, your task is to maintain this, and to proceduralize it. But, if your starting point is procedural knowledge, then your task is to maintain this, and to declarativize it.' Box 7.7 overleaf puts flesh onto these bones. It looks at the issues related to each pathway, stating them this time from the point of view of a teacher not a learner.

Combining formal and informal instruction

As you might expect, a number of the issues in box 7.7 to do with declarativization and proceduralization, will reappear in Part 3 of this book, which focuses on teaching. Chapter 10 for example looks over the recent history of language teaching, and we shall see there that it is possible to identify approaches which place emphasis on the development of either declarative

---

7.7 Declarativization and proceduralization: the jobs to be done

for the Learning Pathway (DECPRO):

(a) How to develop initial declarative knowledge in the learner. What *is* the best way to give learners an understanding of how the language works?

(b) How to proceduralize that knowledge, once imparted. Changing 'knowledge about' into 'knowledge how to' is (we realize today) an immense problem.

(c) How to *maintain* declarative knowledge (because, as we have argued: (i) it is important to keep it, and (ii) there is a tendency for it to disappear.

for the Acquisition Pathway (PRODEC):

(a) How to give initial procedural knowledge. What sorts of activities will help learners to acquire? How can we create, in the classroom, the conditions for acquisition to occur?

(b) How to declarativize that knowledge, once developed. Turning procedural knowledge into declarative knowledge.

(c) How to *maintain* procedural knowledge.

---

or procedural knowledge. At the declarative end of the spectrum we find 'formal' approaches where lots of attention is given to grammar explanation, accompanied by a severely restricted amount of very controlled practice. Other, more informal methods, place the emphasis on 'learning how to' rather than 'learning about'. Little attention is given to learning rules, and students are encouraged to undertake communication activities where actual use of the language is required.

7.8 Declarative and procedural classrooms

In Chapter 1 (p. 9) we looked into five very different language classrooms. Go back to these descriptions. Identify one classroom where the focus of attention is most obviously on declarative knowledge. Then find one where the main focus is on procedural knowledge.[5]

If both declarative and procedural knowledge really are important for students, then this suggests that successful approaches will give due attention to both. There is in fact some indirect evidence which may be considered relevant to this suggestion. It takes two forms. Some research suggests that there is benefit to adding some procedurally oriented practice to teaching which is basically focused on the declarative. This is supported by work by Savignon (1972), Spada (1986, 1987), and Montgomery and Eisenstein (1985).

Box 7.9 gives details of the last of these, where the conclusion is that 'a combination of form-orientated and meaning-orientated language teaching was more beneficial than form-orientated teaching alone'.

7.9 Adding some acquisition to learning

Montgomery and Eisenstein (1985) report on an experiment with a group of students following an ESL (EFL) language course at a Community College in New Jersey. The course lasted 9 hours a week and was grammar based. A group of 14 students were given an extra programme, described as an oral communication course (OCC). This course revolved around a number of trips made to places of interest in the community. The students would prepare for the visit, and there were also follow-up activities after it. The course was very message-focused, with the emphasis being on finding information out during the visit. As an example visit, Montgomery and Eisenstein cite an excursion to a bank. As preparation the students work out questions they wanted to ask at the bank. Once there, they were looked after by a hostess, were shown round, and had a chance to ask their questions ('interestingly', Montgomery and Eisenstein note, 'while the students came with 15 prepared questions, a total of 55 questions were asked' – p. 324). Follow-up work included writing a letter to the bank thanking them for the visit.

At the end of the programme the students who had followed the ESL plus the OCC programme were assessed. Their performance was compared with that of 14 otherwise similar students who had followed only the ESL programme. The students in both groups showed improvement, but the 'OCC + ESL' students did better. Montgomery and Eisenstein note that 'in terms of statistical significance, the area of strongest improvement for the OCC students, as compared with ESL-only students, was in grammatical accuracy. This is surprising, since there was no formal teaching of grammar in the OCC course and minimal error correction' (p. 329). Another factor that makes this finding surprising is that, as noted above, the ESL course was specifically grammar based.

A further benefit to the OCC training was motivational. Montgomery and Eisenstein again: 'at least equally important [to the language improvement] is that the OCC students reported extremely positive attitudes towards the OCC programme' (p. 331).

The authors are careful about their conclusions. After all, the students following the OCC course were receiving *additional* language work – so we would expect superior test results! Nevertheless, the authors feel able to conclude that (p. 329): 'a combination of form-orientated and meaning-orientated language teaching was more beneficial than form-orientated teaching alone'.

The second type of research evidence suggests that language-teaching programmes that concentrate on the development of procedural knowledge can benefit if a declarative element is added. Ellis (1994, whose Chapter 14 contains a useful summary of research in these areas), mentions Harley (1989) and White (1991) in this respect. Both report experiments involving the introduction of formal instruction into an informal approach to language teaching. In both cases the effect was beneficial, though (as box 7.10 shows) this is only part of the picture:

7.10   Adding some learning to acquisition

Harley (1989) describes an experiment which introduces an element of 'formal' language teaching into an immersion programme (Classroom 1 in Chapter 1 was using this sort of programme, in Canada, where Harley's experiment also took place). These programmes may be said to provide an environment in which acquisition can occur, and indeed applied linguists like Krashen have given enthusiastic support to them.

Harley was looking at an immersion programme for the teaching of French to children around the age of 11, in the Canadian province of Ontario. She began by noting that, however impressive the overall results of immersion might be, the learners continued to make mistakes. She decided to focus on one area of error, the use of two tenses in French, called the *imparfait* and *passé composé*. The pupils knew how to form these tenses, but had problems differentiating their meaning. Usually immersion programmes do not involve any form-focused language teaching, but Harley decided to introduce some into this programme, to see whether it would help the pupils over their problems with these tenses. So, for eight weeks an 'experimental group' was given tuition in the use of these tenses, alongside the normal immersion programme.

After the eight weeks, the pupils were given tests to see if any improvement had occurred. Their performance was compared with that of pupils who had not received the form-focused tuition. The results of the tests show that improvement in the area had indeed been made by the experimental group. But this is only part of the story, because after some months further tests were given, and these show that the benefit to the experimental group had disappeared. In Harley's own words: 'the findings of the study indicate that there were some immediate benefits to the students who were exposed to . . . experimental treatment . . . However, in the long run, the experimental students did not do significantly better than comparison students on the set of tests designed to measure their competence in a specific area of French grammar' (p. 354).

What would be your own guess as to why the effects of the formal tuition seemed to be short-lived? Harley's own speculation is that perhaps a longer period of tuition might have had a more lasting effect.

Both these sorts of evidence are far from conclusive. But, taken together, they may suggest that, where there is DEC, PRO needs to be added and, where there is PRO, DEC can be useful.

Conclusion

Now for a dramatic change of focus. So far in Part 2 we have been looking at theories of FL learning. In Chapters 8 and 9 we turn our attention to the characteristics that make learners different from each other. You might say that we are about to move from a consideration of 'learning' to a focus on 'learners'.

Notes

1. This description of Anderson's learning model is based on two sources, Anderson (1982) and Neves and Anderson (1981).
2. There is a third, less important stage, which is not discussed here. Anderson (1982) calls it the 'Procedural Stage'.
3. The use of the term *proceduralization* in this sense departs somewhat from the terminology of Anderson and his colleagues.
4. Though I argue that one pathway is not inherently superior to the other, there may be many reasons why, in a particular situation, one is to be preferred to the other (or is, quite simply, more likely to happen). For example, if a student is living in a country where the target language is spoken, in a situation where there is some pressure to communicate in that language, then it may be that PRODEC becomes the predominant pathway.

   In this and the preceding chapter, we have (for the purposes of discussion) treated our two pathways as totally distinct. This has perhaps left the impression that someone wishing to master a foreign language follows either one or the other of these two routes (possibly making a conscious choice between the two at the beginning of the process deciding whether to be a 'learner' or an 'acquirer'). But this is not of course what happens, and you may well find yourself protesting thus: individuals, surely, both acquire and learn, sometimes one or the other, or even a mixture of the two all the time. Your protest would be right.
5. In Classroom 2 (the grammar-translation class) the emphasis is almost entirely on declarative knowledge. The students are learning *about* Italian. Classroom 1 (immersion) is perhaps the one where there is most focus on procedural knowledge.

Chapter 8

Individual language learners: some differences

8.1 A good language learner: the ingredients?

A major theme of this chapter and the next is what makes people good or bad language learners.

What do *you* think makes a good language learner? Make a list of the qualities you think a good language learner possesses. Think about bad language learners also. What makes them bad?

Try to think of specific individuals you know. You might start by thinking about yourself. Are *you* a good or a bad language learner? What makes you so?

A few years ago I joined a class to learn Russian. There were about twelve people in the class. Our learning experience had much in common. We all had the same teacher, of course, and followed the same textbook. It is true that some worked outside the class more than others . . . and yes, remembering back, there was one student who had a friend of a friend who was Russian, and she managed a bit of conversational practice outside class. But even in this respect the differences were small – we all had full-time jobs and were usually unable even to finish the modest pieces of homework that we were given. Yet, despite these similarities of learning experience, what was really dramatic was the very different levels of success reached by individuals in the class. At one extreme was the poor fellow who by the end could barely manage a heavily accented *Good morning*, and whose progress with the alphabet never really got beyond a heartfelt expression of sheer amazement at how clever Russian children must be to master it. At the other was the lady with a clear 'flair' for languages who seemed to pick up words and structures on hearing them once only, and who seemed to be moving rapidly towards being able to read *War and Peace* in the original. Between those two fell the rest of us, displaying a truly diverse spread of achievement.

Why these differences? Apart from the odd 'environmental' advantage (like the student who had the chance to converse with a Russian) most of the differences must have lain within ourselves – with what we ourselves brought to the learning task. But what exactly are the factors (or <u>variables</u> as they are called) that make the difference? In past decades applied linguists have given a great deal of attention to trying to identify them and to developing some kind of a profile of what the 'good language learner' is like.

The variables that contribute to individual differences are usually divided into three broad categories. Some are called *cognitive*, meaning that they relate to the mental makeup of the person. Intelligence is one such factor; another is language aptitude, the phrase used to refer to an ability specific to language learning and different from general intelligence. Other variables are called *affective*, a word that we have already come across (in Chapter 5), meaning 'related to the feelings'. The most commonly studied affective variables are motivation and attitudes. The third set of factors we shall look at are the *personality* variables. The one that springs most readily to mind is 'extroversion/introversion', but there are other less obvious (and possibly more important) ones.

In this chapter we shall look at variables related to two of these three categories – cognitive and affective. Personality variables will be saved for Chapter 9, where we also look more closely at the concept of the 'good language learner'. We will explore not just what good language learners are like, but also at what they 'do' – the strategies and processes they follow to help them learn a language successfully.

The cognitive variables: intelligence

8.2 Intelligence and FL learning

Do *you* think there is any relationship between intelligence and language learning? Do more intelligent people learn languages better, or faster?

As always, if you can, make your starting point specific individuals that you know personally.

Earlier in this century, intelligence was considered an important factor for FL learning. It was believed that a certain degree of intelligence was useful, if not essential, for success. This was a reason why learning foreign languages was often left until university level, so that only the most intelligent would take it on. It was also a common belief that FL learning actually helped to developed the intelligence, and even today one occasionally hears (in Britain at least) the learning of Latin supported in this way. It may not be a useful language to know, some people argue, but learning Latin helps build intellectual powers. Occasionally this argument is expressed in its 'pain is good for you' form – Latin is so hard, and hurts so much, that it must be doing you good!

8.3   Learning to say *a cup of tea* by the Pain Is Good For You Method

Howatt (1984) amusingly describes the German grammars of a certain Rev. Tiarks, a Minister of the German Protestant Reformed Church in London during the nineteenth century. His textbooks for learning German were extremely popular, and are definitely based on the Pain Is Good For You Method.

Here is Howatt's description of parts of Tiarks's *Introductory Grammar of the German Language* which first appeared in the 1830s:

> The book takes us through the parts of speech in German with their various declensions and conjugations. Then there is a set of short reading texts including some poems which will 'make a salutary impression, both moral and religious, on the mind of the young student' . . . The Rev. Tiarks' pomposity and humourlessness are rather exhausting. So, too, is his thoroughness . . . The Third Declension of German nouns, we are told, 'originally contained all substantives of the masculine gender ending in *e*: but those given in Note 1 have lost the final *e*, and now end in a consonant'. Note 1 dutifully lists forty-three *e*-less masculines, including useful words like those for *demagogue, ducat, herdsman, hussar, Jesuit, quadrant, theologian* and *fool*. The grey obscurity of Tiarks's prose continues relentlessly throughout the book. In describing how to translate a *cup of tea* into German, we are informed that 'those words, the measure, weight, or number of which is expressed by the above-mentioned substantives, are not put in the genitive, unless a part of a certain quantity or quality is meant; but in the same case with the preceding word'. At the end of the slog, the pupil is rewarded with the Reverend's selection of uplifting poems and a few edifying texts on cowherds and Frederick the Great. Howatt (1984: 137)

As we saw in Chapter 3, Chomsky's views about language stimulated a large number of studies of how children acquire their first language. In these it was a common belief that L1 learning, at least as far as speaking and listening were concerned, is relatively unrelated to cognitive development. One of the major figures in this field was Eric Lenneberg (1921–75). In his 1967 book he argues that, at the time language acquisition takes place, the child is at a rather low level of mental development. A rather sobering and dramatic 'fact' he cites is that in normal children L1 acquisition is related in terms of developmental stage to the ability to control bowels! So almost everyone learns to speak their L1 irrespective of intelligence.

Although the work of Lenneberg and others is concerned with L1 and not FL acquisition, it was very much in the spirit of Chomsky's views not to consider intelligence and FL language learning to be related. In the FL area, two Canadian researchers are particularly associated with looking at the relationship between intelligence and FL proficiency. Robert Gardner and Wallace Lambert's influential book (1972) is called *Attitudes and Motivation in Second-Language Learning*. It has an appendix which includes a paper entitled 'Language aptitude, intelligence and foreign language achievement'. In it, they report on a 1961 study done on 96 children learning French in Louisiana. The basic finding is that there is little relationship (correlation) between intelligence and achievement in FL learning.

Canadian scholars like Gardner and Lambert have for a long time been major contributors to the field of applied linguistics, one important reason being that Canada is a bilingual country, with French- and English-speaking provinces. Issues of foreign-language learning are hence of particular interest to Canadians. One of their major contributions was to pioneer immersion programmes. The first experiment with immersion took place in St Lambert, a suburb of Montreal in 1965, and is described in Lambert and Tucker (1972). Box 8.4 overleaf gives some details.

In the following years immersion programmes mushroomed in Canada. In the early days the children on these programmes were in selected schools; they had passed certain tests and hence were considered 'intelligent'. One Canadian researcher, Genesee (1976), was interested to know whether these programmes were worth running with less intelligent pupils. To find this out, he used a basic research method which you will find in different permutations (related to different variables, not just intelligence) throughout this chapter. He first tried to find out how good all the pupils in his study were at French, by giving them various tests. He then tried to measure their intelligence, by other tests. Finally he attempted to correlate French achievement with intelligence, using statistics to find out whether being 'good at French' was related to 'being intelligent' (and whether 'bad at French' correlates with 'not-so-intelligent'). Genesee was interested to look not just at overall ability in French, but at performance in different skill areas like listening, reading, speaking and writing. So in fact he gave his subjects five sub-tests in French, dealing with the different skills. In order to measure intelligence, he gave the subjects an IQ (for 'Intelligence Quotient') test. Doubtless many of you will have come across IQ tests in some context or other. You may have suffered them at school, since in some countries (including Britain) they have been used to measure intelligence as a means of helping to make decisions about a child's future. You can also find something that passes for them in books and magazines purchased at railway stations, where you are invited to 'measure your own intelligence', or 'find out how clever you are'. Genesee's attempts to correlate French achievement and intelligence find no relationship between intelligence and what he calls 'communication skills' (basically, speaking and listening). But he *does* find a correlation between intelligence and what he calls 'academic language skills' – that is, reading and writing. This suggests that being intelligent will help you to learn reading and writing,

8.4 Parent power at work in St Lambert, Montreal

The 'St Lambert experiment' is an example of parent power. It started when a group of twelve parents met, on 30 October 1963, 'to discuss what they considered a lamentable situation in the local school system' (Lambert and Tucker 1972: 220). Children from an English-speaking background were going through the system 'with little more knowledge of French than their parents had had'. In a country committed to bilingualism, this was considered unacceptable by the parents.

Their idea to begin an immersion programme was met with a good deal of scepticism. Here is what the Association of Catholic Principals of Montreal said: 'we are of the opinion that the average child cannot cope with two languages of instruction and to try to do so leads to insecurity, language interference, and academic retardation' (Lambert and Tucker, p. 5). Research available at that time tended to support that view. West (1926) for example reported 'a large academic handicap for children trained through a foreign language' (p. 6). But, thanks to the parents' persistence and the support of experts at McGill University in Montreal, the project got under way. The first class of English-speaking children to be taught in French was set up at kindergarten level in September 1965, with a second group starting in September 1966. McGill was asked to evaluate the experiment.

Lambert and Tucker's description of the experiment includes the comments of one Mme Benoîte Noble, an experienced teacher from France, who attended classes. Here is what she says about the kindergarten class: 'the teacher circulates all the time, keeping up a steady flow of conversation, commenting, approving, asking questions. The children speak English to her. She repeats their sentences in French, answers them, and tries to have the child repeat the answer in French after her. However, she never puts pressure on the child to do so' (p. 237).

This is what is happening by grade 5: 'the children read very well, with practically no accent. When they speak, an English accent is apparent and they make grammatical mistakes that a French-speaking child would not. They answer orally questions asked about the reading, and then answer other questions in writing.' (p. 241) Overall, 'the teachers speak French all the time; they like, are even enthusiastic about, their work; they are competent, experienced elementary school teachers, not second-language specialists' (p. 242).

The St Lambert experiment was counted a great success, and was the first of a large number of immersion programmes in Canada.

but not speaking and listening. So the answer to the question 'does intelligence relate to FL learning?' may be: 'it depends on which language skills you are talking about'.

The distinction between 'communication skills' and 'academic writing skills' reappears in the work of Cummins (1980). He distinguishes between 'basic interpersonal communicative skills' (BICS for short), and 'cognitive/academic language proficiency' (CALP). The latter, Cummins finds, is 'strongly related to general cognitive skills . . . and to academic achievement' (Cummins 1980: 176).

8.5 Intelligence and different language skills

As we have seen, more than one applied linguist has suggested: (i) a relationship between 'academic skills' and intelligence, but (ii) no relationship between 'communication skills' and intelligence.

Think about both (i) and (ii). Do these suggestions sound sensible to you? If so, can you explain these relationships? Why should 'academic' but not 'communication' skills involve intelligence?

Genesee's findings lead towards another interesting perspective. Perhaps IQ correlates not with FL learning ability, but with *ability to profit from certain types of instruction*. Perhaps, that is, you have to be intelligent to succeed in learning languages when using particular methods. This idea was investigated by Chastain (1969). He compared IQ scores with the achievement results of students learning a foreign language by two different methods. One of these was the popular method known as audiolingualism. We came across a version of audiolingualism in Chapter 1's Classroom 4, and you will read much more about it in Chapter 10, which deals with the recent history of language teaching. At its basis is the behaviourist view that language learning is a question of habit formation, in which the 'mind' has no role. The other method was called 'cognitive code' (also to be touched on in Chapter 10). In 'cognitive code' teaching learners are expected to understand grammatical explanations and to learn rules; so it might be said that the method involves exercise of the intelligence. Sure enough, Chastain found that the more intelligent learners did well in cognitive code classes, but that there was no such correlation for the audiolingual classes (where intelligence did not seem to relate to success). So a further answer to the question 'does intelligence relate to FL learning?' may be: 'you have to be intelligent to learn from those methods which utilize the intelligence'.

We shall leave intelligence for the moment. But this is not the end of the story. We shall find ourselves having cause to mention it again very soon.

The cognitive variables: aptitude

8.6 Christopher (from box 1.3, page 7 above) again

Savants are people who may be backward in most areas yet who have extraordinary skills in just one area. Christopher is a savant who is described by Smith and Tsimpli (1995). He was born in 1962, and was diagnosed as brain-damaged at the age of six weeks. Smith and Tsimpli (1995: 1) describe him like this:

> Christopher is unique. He is institutionalised because he is unable to look after himself; he has difficulty in finding his way around; he has poor hand–eye co-ordination, turning many everyday tasks such as shaving or doing up buttons into a burdensome chore; but he can read, write and communicate in any of fifteen to twenty languages.

Christopher's languages include (Smith and Tsimpli 1995: 12): Danish, Dutch, Finnish, French, German, Modern Greek, Hindi, Italian, Norwegian, Polish, Portuguese, Russian, Spanish, Swedish, Turkish and Welsh. Notice what a variety of language families are represented here.

Smith and Tsimpli note that one of the astonishing things about Christopher is the *speed* with which he learns. An example with yet another language, not listed above:

> when he began learning Berber . . . he took to the language enthusiastically, seeming 'thoroughly to enjoy teasing out the details of the subject agreement system; and after a few minutes he was able to suggest the correct verb form to accompany a masculine as opposed to a feminine subject . . . despite there having been only two relevant examples' (Smith *et al.* 1993: 286). Moreover, on the occasion of his second lesson (three weeks after the first) he was able to translate simple sentences on demand, despite having spent only an hour or so on revision in the intervening period. (Smith and Tsimpli 1995: 18)

How can this be? How can individuals like Christopher, with such gross cognitive deficits, be so good at just one thing – FL learning? His case seems to provide strong evidence for the idea that there is such a thing as an aptitude for FL learning that is separate from general cognitive ability. We have already noted that this idea was appealing to the Chomskyan way of thinking, because – at least as far as the L1 is concerned – acquisition is not seen as intimately connected with general cognitive growth. It may be that this idea, related though it is to the L1, stimulated interest in the FL aptitude area in the 1960s. Certainly we do find at that time an upsurge of interest in the subject.

A second reason for this upsurge in interest is the purely practical desire to predict – to be able to recognize who will succeed at language learning before they do any. To understand this idea, you need to distinguish

---

8.7 FL learning and other subjects

In the popular imagination, language-learning ability is associated with being good at certain other skill areas. People say 'if you're good at languages you're probably good at Subject X as well'. One 'Subject X' is music. People sometimes express the view that being good at foreign languages goes with being good at music.

Can you think of any other subjects? Do you have any ideas about what these subjects may have in common with language learning?[1]

---

aptitude from achievement and proficiency. Achievement and proficiency tests measure 'how well you have done'. An aptitude test looks at 'how well you would do'. It has a strong predictive element to it. The hope of the 1960s was that, rather than spending a great deal of money teaching individuals who might not have any natural talent, aptitude testing would be able to identify in advance those worth focusing the training effort on.

8.8 A Big Question

There is one question which will dominate this section: how on earth can aptitude be measured?

Give some initial thought to the question, and to what kinds of quick test might be given to individuals to predict their success in FL learning.

Do not expect at this stage to reach any firm conclusions. A few thoughts will do.

What *is* language aptitude? According to Carroll (1973: 5) it is the 'rate at which persons at the secondary school, university and adult level [will] successfully master a foreign language'. Notice that this definition accepts that everyone can acquire; it is just that some people do it *faster* than others. This definition takes us only so far, and box 8.8's Big Question can only really be answered usefully if we can somehow develop a more detailed notion of what language aptitude entails. One of the big aptitude tests, developed by Carroll and Sapon (1959) was called the Modern Language Aptitude Test (MLAT for short). It has five sub-tests. The way the authors developed their test was interesting. They drew up a long list of factors which they thought might be related to language aptitude. Then, over time, they undertook research to see which of these factors actually correlated with actual language-learning performance. As a result, their list was reduced to manageable size. Four major areas were in fact identified (in Carroll 1965). We shall look at the two most important of these – *phonetic coding ability* and *grammatical sensitivity* – in some detail, just making mention of the other two (*inductive learning ability* and *rote learning ability*).

Phonetic coding ability

8.9 Spelling clues

One of the sub-tests in MLAT is called 'Spelling Clues'. An approximate phonetic spelling of an English word is given. These are the italicized words on the left below; the first, *luv*, represents the word *love*. You have to find the word on the right which has approximately the same meaning. The answer to (1) is *affection*. Example (1) is taken from MLAT itself; the other examples are invented, following the MLAT principle.

In order to get an idea of what it feels like to do part of an aptitude test, work through the examples below. The test is written specifically for native speakers of English. If you are not one, do the examples anyway; you might also like to invent some examples of your own, for your own native language.[2]

(1)	*luv*	carry	exist	affection	wash	spy
(2)	*cawz*	men	jobs	cattle	helmets	ravens
(3)	*wor*	hat	battle	train	waterfall	window
(4)	*layk*	river	handbag	pond	similar to	dam
(5)	*hansum*	good looking	money	football	writer	journey
(6)	*cntri*	open	plant	habit	walk	nation

What on earth has this sub-test of MLAT got to do with ability to learn a foreign language? The answer is suggested by a phrase often used to describe someone with linguistic flair. We say they have 'a good ear' for languages, and this expression carries the idea that language aptitude has a component which deals with sound. Carroll, along with others in the field, accept that this is the case, and accordingly the first of his four areas is called *phonetic (or phonemic) coding ability*. He defines this (1965: 128) as 'the ability to code auditory phonetic material in such a way that this material can be recognised, identified, and remembered over something longer than a few seconds'. This ability is important because 'individuals lower in this ability will have trouble not only in remembering phonetic material, words, forms, etc., but also in mimicking speech sounds' (p. 129).

It is important to understand that this skill is something more than the simple ability to hear differences between sounds. There is more than the ear involved. One extra element is memory, and the quotation above talks about phonetic material *remembered*. There is also the element of being able to associate sounds with symbols, what might be called 'sound–symbol association ability'. This element is particularly strongly present in the MLAT sub-test you looked at in box 8.9, where you are asked to make associations in the L1 between sounds (the 'approximate phonetic spellings' on the left) and meanings (the appropriate words on the right). In addition, Carroll talks about 'coding' material, and this suggests how not just the ear but also the brain is involved. Carroll is speaking of the ability to see some kind of order in the stream of foreign sounds bombarding the FL learner. Gardner and Lambert (1972: 289) describe this same ability in similar terms, as 'a higher cognitive skill in which the individual actively seeks to impose a meaningful code on . . . material'. Their own research shows how important this ability is for FL learning. So does the work of Pimsleur *et al.* (1964), which is described in box 8.10.

8.10 How to do badly at French

Pimsleur *et al.* (1964) were interested in the problem of why so many people do badly at FL learning. Their estimate was that '10 to 20 per cent of all students now studying foreign languages are beset by a frustrating lack of ability in this area'. (p. 115)

Their large-scale study took place in a city in the American mid-West which they called by the pseudonym of 'King City'. They looked at 12 schools in King City – 7 junior high and 5 high, attended by about 11,500 students. Information was collected in a variety of ways, including by classroom observation, discussions with teachers, interviews with students, and through a number of tests looking at various variables of possible relevance. Motivation was one such variable, and this was measured by two tests which they called Interest I and Interest II.

There were also two tests which looked at 'ability with sounds'. Here are their descriptions of these tests (p. 121):

- Chinese Pitch Test. 'A 30-item test of auditory discrimination in which the student must distinguish Chinese tones.'
- Sound–Symbol Test. 'A 44-item rapid-fire test in which the student hears a nonsense syllable and must match it with the correct spelling in his booklet; this test measures sound–symbol association.'

The results? Those identified as under-achievers did particularly badly in three tests: Interest I, the Chinese Pitch Test and the Sound–Symbol Test. 'Such a finding appears to indicate', Pimsleur *et al.* concluded (p. 123), 'that the so-called "talent for languages" [language aptitude, that is] resides principally in the domain of auditory ability, which may be described as the ability to receive and process information through the ear.'

Grammatical sensitivity

Box 8.11 overleaf may perplex you. How can it be, you may wonder, that asking questions about the function of words in a person's L1 will help to know how good they will be at FL learning? Carroll's claim is that there is

8.11 Words in sentences

Another of MLAT's sub-tests is called 'Words in sentences'. In this, you are given a 'key sentence' which has one item italicized and in capital letters. In (1) below this is the word *LONDON*. After the key sentence come one or more other sentences with five items italicized and given a letter: A, B, C, D or E. You have to decide which item 'does the same thing' in its sentence as the word in capitals in the key sentence. In (1) below the answer is A, because (to use MLAT's own words): 'the key sentence is about "London" and the second sentence is about "he"'. Examples (1)–(4) are the practice items in MLAT itself; the other examples are invented, following the MLAT principle.

   Work through the examples below. The test is written specifically for native speakers of English. If you are not one, do the examples anyway; as with box 8.9, you might also like to invent some examples of your own, for your own native language.[3]

(1) *LONDON* is the capital of England.
     He liked to *go fishing* in *Maine*
     A B   C D   E

(2) Mary is cutting the *APPLE*
     My brother John is beating *his dog with a big stick.*
       A   B   C D   E

(3) *MONEY* is his only object.
     Not so many *years ago, most farming* was done by *hand.*
                  A   B   C   D   E

(4) There was much *TALK* about a rebellion.
     Where is *John*?   There is no *doubt* about *it.*
              A   B   C
     There lay the dead *horse.*   There I found my *answer.*
                         D   E

(5) I gave *HIM* the book.
     When *Peter's mother* died, *Mary* wrote *a letter to him.*
            A   B   C   D   E

(6) Peter likes swimming *AND* Mary likes dancing.
     Yesterday *we all* went *to* the theatre, *but* Mike stayed *at* home.
                A B   C   D   E

a connection. *Grammatical sensitivity* is to do with how aware you are of the workings of your first language. In Carroll's words (1973: 7), it is 'the individual's ability to demonstrate his awareness of the syntactical patterning of sentences in a language'. There is a longer quotation below from Carroll

(1973). In it, he suggests that individuals possess this grammatical sensitivity to varying degrees, and claims that it is related to success in a foreign language:

> although it is often said that linguistic 'competence' in the sense defined by Chomsky (1965) involves some kind of 'knowledge' of the grammatical rules of the language, this 'knowledge' is ordinarily out of conscious awareness . . . nevertheless, some adolescents and adults (and even some children) can be made to demonstrate an awareness of the syntactical structure of the sentences they speak . . . Even among adults there are large individual differences in this ability, and these individual differences are related to success in learning foreign languages, apparently because this ability is called upon when the student tries to learn grammatical rules and apply them in constructing and comprehending new sentences in that language. (p. 7)

It is important to understand that this awareness is not the same thing as knowing grammatical *terminology*. So, for example, someone may never have heard the word 'adjective' or have the remotest idea what it means, but may at the same time have some kind of subconscious awareness of what an adjective is. It is rather like Socrates's slave boy whom we met in Chapter 3 (p. 46 above). The philosopher was able to show that the boy had an understanding of the principles of geometry without being able to articulate a single mathematical rule.

Research in the area suggests that grammatical sensitivity is indeed an important skill for the FL learner to possess. According to Skehan (1989: 27) the sub-test of MLAT that measures it (described in box 8.11) 'has proved to be the most robust of all the sub-tests used in the language aptitude field, and withstands study-to-study variation'. Gardner and Lambert (1972) record a particularly interesting finding. They observe that grammatical sensitivity correlates with grades in *all* areas of academic achievement, not just FL learning. This brings us back to the notion of 'general' intelligence; for, although grammatical sensitivity is clearly a language-related concept, Gardner and Lambert are suggesting that it has relevance to non-language areas. The implication is that FL learning and other sorts of learning are somehow linked together.

Inductive learning ability and rote learning ability

We shall pass briefly over Carroll's other two areas. One is *inductive learning ability*. This is the ability to 'examine language material . . . and from this to notice and identify patterns of correspondences and relationships involving either meaning or grammatical form' (Carroll 1973: 8). Though Carroll is just talking about language learning here, you might think that the ability to identify 'patterns of correspondences' and 'relationships' will be useful in learning almost any subject. So perhaps once again we are dealing with an ability related to general intelligence. Finally there is *rote learning ability*.

This is to do with the ability to learn things by heart. In the language field, it relates particularly to the area of vocabulary learning.

Boxes 8.9 and 8.11 illustrate how two of Carroll's areas can be tested. Box 8.12 describes MLAT as a whole. Think about which of the four areas we have described are being tested in each sub-test:[4]

8.12   The sub-tests of MLAT

(a) Number learning. Subjects (Ss) are given numbers in an artificial (made-up) language. They are asked to reproduce these numbers in combined sequences: e.g. they might be taught 1 and 5, and be asked to produce 15.
(b) Phonetic script. Ss are given a rudimentary phonetic 'alphabet', and are then asked to underline words they hear on tape.
(c) Spelling clues. This is the sub-test illustrated in box 8.9.
(d) Words in sentences. This is the sub-test illustrated in box 8.11.
(e) Paired associates. Ss learn some Kurdish vocabulary items for 2 minutes, and are then tested on it.

Another important test, developed at around the same time as MLAT, is Pimsleur's (1968) Language Aptitude Battery (LAB for short). Although LAB differs from MLAT, there are striking similarities. For example, two of LAB's underlying components deal with 'verbal intelligence' and 'auditory ability'. Both have clear counterparts in MLAT.

Aptitude tests like MLAT and LAB were reasonably successful as predictive tools, able to identify those who would and those who would not succeed at FL learning. But these tests were born out of the 1960s and 1970s, and interest in them has waned since then. There has been some further research, but not much. Skehan (1989) discusses the idea that tests like MLAT are entirely concerned with what in Chapter 2 we called systemic competence. But, as we saw in that chapter, there are other areas of competence relevant to communicative ability. It is possible that there are different 'aptitudes' related to these different areas. Recall Wes, the Japanese artist we also met in Chapter 2 (p. 35 above). His strategic competence was particularly far advanced. Perhaps we can say that he has good 'strategic aptitude', but not-such-good 'grammatical aptitude'. Skehan identifies the search for possible different sorts of aptitude as a worthwhile research agenda. The views of Krashen (1981) on aptitude are also worth recalling. In Chapter 5 we noted his view that if you want to predict how well someone will *acquire,* you should find out about her attitudes. But it is when you want to find out about *learning* that the aptitude test comes into its own. So, the suggestion is, MLAT may give you valid information about possible classroom learning success, but it will not tell you how well a person will pick up an FL living in a country where it is spoken.

The affective variables

Motivation

> **8.13 Why, why . . . oh why?**
>
> In Chapter 1 we considered the motives for language learning of five individuals. Look back to that chapter (p. 4 above) and remind yourself of those five types of motivation. Also in that chapter (box 1.1, p. 3 above) you were asked to think of other reasons for language learning. Remind yourself of your thoughts there also. Have any further motives occurred to you since then?
>
> Can you identify, from among all these motives that you have been thinking about, some that you predict will be the most likely to lead to language-learning success? Do these particularly strong motives have anything in common? In other words, is it possible to make any kind of general statement about what particularly motivates language learning?
>
> These issues will be considered in the present section.

In all areas of human activity, there are many reasons why people do things, and learning foreign languages is no exception. Among the wealth of motives for FL learning, one of the more grotesque is what is known as 'machiavellianism' – where one learns the foreign language not for love of the target country and its culture, but to contribute to its destruction. Spies sometimes have to be word-perfect in the target language in order to carry on their sinister trade. In this context the notion of 'target' has rather unpleasant military overtones!

Consider particularly two of the individuals mentioned in Chapter 1. Bryn the Welshman is learning Welsh because 'he feels the need to speak the language of his roots, to understand his own culture, to help strengthen the distinctiveness of Welsh society . . .' (p. 4). People with Bryn's kind of motivation often do well in FL learning. The other learner is Zhang from China. He is learning English so that he can study abroad. The key to his ambition is a good score on an English test.

These two learners exemplify a distinction that is commonly made in motivational studies, between <u>integrative</u> and <u>instrumental</u> motivation. We say that someone is 'integratively motivated' if they are learning the foreign language through a desire to learn more about a culture, its language and people – to 'integrate' more within the target-language society. Bryn is integratively motivated. Instrumental motivation involves learning in order to achieve some other goal. So, if you learn French because you will get a better job if you speak that language, then your motivation is, like Zhang's, instrumental.

If asked, you would probably predict that Bryn will do well at Welsh, and indeed integratively motivated people often do succeed at language learning. Here is another example, from a 'Good Language Learner' study that we shall look at in detail in Chapter 9. One of the best pupils described in this study is known as Student B. Here is his own statement (Naiman *et al.* 1978: 86) about why he is learning French: 'I'd like to know how to speak French – fluently; I'd like to be bilingual, as this is a bilingual country.' He wishes, that is, to play his part as a member of a bilingual society. There is plenty of other evidence to show the positive effects of integrative motivation. Indeed, one way of viewing Schumann's Acculturation Theory (which we looked at in Chapter 6) is to say that it is based on the notion of integrative motivation and its importance. Gardner and Lambert (1972) is another major study of this area. They looked at learner groups in Montreal, Louisiana, Maine, Connecticut and the Philippines. They find a high correlation between integrative motivation and proficiency. The correlation is particularly striking in Montreal.

8.14 Striking in Montreal

Why 'particularly striking in Montreal'? Can you think of any reason why integrative motivation should relate to FL proficiency particularly in that context? To ponder this question you need to bring to mind anything you know about the language situation in Canada in general and Montreal in particular. In Gardner and Lambert's study, by the way, the foreign language in question was French.

We will be considering this issue of motivation and context later in this section.

Though some studies find that integrative motivation is more effective than instrumental, there is also no shortage of research showing the importance of instrumental motivation as well. An oft-cited study is Lukmani (1972) who found that instrumental motivation correlated with success at English. Box 8.15 gives the details. Gardner and Lambert (1972: 130) find the same in the Philippines: 'we found that students who approach the study of English with an instrumental outlook and who receive parental support in their views are clearly more successful in developing proficiency in the language than are those who fail to adopt this orientation'.

Earlier we spoke of a 'wealth of motives' for foreign-language learning. Precisely because of that wealth, many have found the integrative/instrumental distinction a little simplistic, unable to capture all that needs to be said about motivation. One major study which reaches this conclusion is Burstall *et al.* (1974). She and her colleagues undertook a large-scale research project concerned with the teaching of French at primary schools in Britain. The resulting 'Burstall Report' was extremely influential. Its main

8.15 Sixty girls from a Mumbai high school

(a) Lukmani (1972) is a good example of a study showing the importance of instrumental motivation. Her experiment dealt with speakers of the Marathi language, used in the Bombay (now Mumbai) area of India. She noted that there are many studies showing the importance of integrative motivation to language learning. She was interested to find out whether instrumental motivation can also have a strong effect.

Her subjects were sixty girls from a high school in Mumbai (Bombay). They all came from lower middle class families in a comparatively non-westernized section of society, and had been learning English for seven years. Various means were used to find out about the girls' motivations, as well as their English proficiency. One of the questionnaires dealing with motivation gave a variety of possible reasons for learning English, and asked the subjects to say how important each was to them.

The girls' motivation proved to be predominantly instrumental. The three most common motives mentioned were (in this order): (1) getting a good job; (2) coping with university classes; (3) travelling abroad. What is more, the subjects' instrumental motivation scores correlated significantly with their English proficiency. 'In other words', Lukmani says, 'the higher their motivation to use English as a means of career advancement, etc., the better their English language scores.' (1972: 272)

(b) Look back to box 8.13 and the list of motives for language learning you drew up there. Try to identify which of these motives might be called integrative, and which instrumental. How well does the distinction work when applied to all these motives?

finding cast doubt on whether there was any real advantage to an early start in FL learning, and this finding influenced policy (in England and outside) for a long time. Part of the study looked at how a number of psychological variables relate to the learning of French in English schools. Regarding motivation, the report finds that the motivational characteristics of individual pupils appeared to be neither exclusively integrative nor wholly instrumental. The motives of the pupils were often complex, and difficult to categorize completely in terms of the integrative/instrumental distinction.

8.16 Gender differences

Another finding of the Burstall report relates to gender differences in motivation. Before reading the next paragraph, think whether you would predict any differences between boys and girls as regards motivation for learning a foreign language at school.

Two other findings in the Burstall Report are relevant to us. The first relates to gender differences. Burstall found consistently more integrative motivation in girls. One reason perhaps is that girls appear more confident of parental support for language learning. Whatever the rights and wrongs of the matter, some parents seem to regard learning languages as suitable for girls, while the boys are encouraged in the direction of subjects (like electronics and mechanics perhaps) which some might regard as more 'macho'. Secondly, she found a difference between 'word' and 'deed' in integrative motivation studies. When asked, nearly all the pupils talked about their strong desires for intercultural contacts. But did they really mean it? This points to a very common problem in the study of many affective areas, and in fact one which Schumann and his colleagues encountered when studying Alberto. The fact is that, if you ask someone about their feelings for a foreign culture, for example, many are unlikely to admit negative feelings to a stranger (the researcher). But their true feelings might be quite different.

In general, writers have tended to find the integrative/instrumental distinction unsatisfactory. Gardner (1985), for example, accepts that the picture is complicated by such factors as the 'machiavellianism' we mentioned earlier. Spies may be rare individuals but, even when dealing with 'normal' people, attitudes towards languages and cultures are often far from straightforward.

The study of motivation also raises the interesting 'chicken-and-egg' issue of cause and effect. Motivation may lead to success; but success can also lead to motivation – and it may be very difficult to work out which of these two is in fact happening. Burstall *et al.* (1974) came to the conclusion that high motivation in the pupils she was studying was the *result* of success, not vice versa. There are some other studies that suggest the same. The idea that success leads to motivation is referred to as the 'Resultative Hypothesis'.

Attitude

8.17   Poor attitudes – what effect?

How important do *you* think attitude towards the speakers and culture of the target language is? Can a learner with poor attitudes in these areas succeed? If possible, think of someone you know who has poor attitudes in these areas. How successful have they been as FL learners?

Think about how such attitudes might affect learning. Are there any specific aspects of the language that are particularly likely to suffer though poor attitudes?

There are various sorts of attitude which may be relevant to language learning. By far the most studied is attitude towards the target-language speakers, sometimes called the *reference* or *aspirational* group. If you are learning French, how important is it that you should like French speakers?

Some of the Canadian work looking at the learning of French in Montreal came to the conclusion that attitude towards reference group is extremely important, such that students with prejudiced attitudes are likely to do poorly in school French, whatever their aptitudes or motivation. Jakobovits (1970) is particularly firm. His view is that if you dislike French speakers you are wasting your time even attempting to learn French.

But is attitude towards reference group *always* so important? Surely there are many situations where learners know very little indeed about the reference group. Indeed I fear that it is not unknown to meet learners who are not terribly sure where the countries speaking the target language are located in the world.

Learner level is likely to be one factor governing how important this type of attitude might be. It is possible that at the advanced level attitude towards reference group will be more important than lower down. At the advanced stage 'getting inside the culture' is important. It is then that you study the literature and culture of the target language, and for these activities a degree of sympathy towards that language and culture will be necessary. One might also say that having a good accent becomes more important at the higher level. Developing a good foreign accent may certainly be said to depend on a sympathy for the culture and people.

8.18 Accent and attitude

Do *you* think a good target-language accent depends on attitudes towards reference group? Did you identify it as an important language area in box 8.17?

Why should accent depend on such attitudes?[5]

But what about at the elementary level? At that stage learners do not have to put much of themselves into the lessons. Indeed, learning may be seen as just an 'academic exercise'. Green (1975) studied the learning of German in British schools. One finding was that liking German seemed to have no relationship to favourable views towards German people. This is a conclusion that can perhaps be explained in terms of learner level.

Geographical setting is almost certainly another important factor. You will by now have realized that many studies of individual differences emanate from bilingual Canada. In bilingual countries, cultural stereotyping is often very strong. Hence in a city like Montreal, English speakers will often have strong views about French speakers, and vice versa. These views are likely to be highly influential in language learning. French speakers who strongly dislike English speakers are likely actively to resist learning English (and may often refuse to speak it even if they are able to). But in other parts of the world, and in relation to certain languages, serious cultural stereotypes may not even exist. To pluck an example at random: it may well be that most Romanian children have no discernible attitudes towards Spain and the Spanish language. There will doubtless be a degree of non-serious stereotyping (with the Spanish it may be to do with bullfighting and flamenco), but nothing more than this. In that type of situation, one would not expect attitude towards reference group to be important. Perhaps this accounts for Gardner and Lambert's findings, mentioned earlier, that integrative motivation was most important in Montreal but less so in places like the Philippines.

8.19 Other types of attitude

At the beginning of this section we noted that there are various sorts of attitude which may be relevant to language learning. But so far in this chapter the only attitude type we have really considered is 'attitude towards reference group and culture'. Think of some other attitude types which you feel may also be important. One way of doing this would be to write a list, with each item beginning 'Attitude towards . . .'

Here are some other attitude types that have been discussed in relation to language learning:

Attitude towards success (sometimes called <u>need achievement</u>) This is 'the degree to which a student strives for accomplishing goals in life'. It may be that people tend to divide themselves into 'high achievers' and 'low achievers' in general. The 'high achievers' will strive to do well at everything, including learning languages. It is interesting to note that Pimsleur's aptitude test, the LAB, looks at the overall grades of learners in all subjects, in order to help predict success in language learning. The testers are trying to identify 'individuals that do well overall'.

Attitudes towards teacher It is a common belief that you will not learn French if you dislike the French teacher. This is doubtless sometimes true. In the Good Language Learner study we shall look at in the next chapter (Naiman *et al.* 1978), one of the weakest students on which a special study was done is one of the few (of those studied in depth) to report not getting on very well with the teacher. But it is often *not* true, and indeed the same Good Language Learner study reports that bad learners as well as good learners liked their teacher (a finding reported in box 9.8 of Chapter 9). It seems that in many cases, learners are quite capable of 'distinguishing the messenger from the message'.

8.20 Messengers and messages

Can you think of examples in your own experience where attitude towards the teacher seems to have had an effect on learning? A case perhaps where someone you know disliked learning a language (and did badly at it) because he or she disliked the teacher? Or where liking for a teacher seems to have affected language learning positively?

Attitude towards your own country Perhaps what you think of your own country, and not just of the country of the target-language speakers, will influence how well you succeed in the FL. One relevant type of attitude is associated with a feeling of 'ethnocentrism', a belief in the superiority of your own country (your <u>membership group</u> as it is sometimes called). You can imagine that this belief will hinder the learning of a foreign language – after all, if you believe your own country to be *that* important, then it is up to the rest of the world to learn *your* language, not you theirs. This unhelpful attitude is often said to be held by some countries where English is the main L1. A further fascinating factor is called 'anomie'. This is a feeling of a lack of attachment to your own culture. In some parts of the world, some individuals may yearn to be of a different culture, having a strong desire to be living somewhere else. The effects of anomie on language learning may not be simple. Where the 'somewhere else' is a country speaking the target language, anomie might be a powerful stimulus to learning. For example, someone who dreams all the time of living in America is likely to find the dreams helpful for learning English. But, if the reference group is felt in some way to be responsible for the negative feelings of anomie, this may prevent learning. So people living in border areas may develop a dislike for a neighbouring country and its language, perhaps because they perceive of it as a threat to their own country in some way. Bryn, the Welshman from Chapter 1, harboured such feelings towards England (though in his case the threat did not of course prevent him from learning English).

Spolsky (1969) researched these two factors, ethnocentrism and anomie, in the United States, but did not in the event find much correlation between them and language-learning success. He concludes that attitude towards reference group (the factor we began our discussion with) is more important that of membership group.

Earlier in this chapter, in relation to both Schumann's Alberto and the Burstall Report, we mentioned the difficulties in finding out what people really think, particularly where attitudes are concerned. How can you find out? The obvious method is to ask them, and indeed attitude questionnaires (or <u>scales</u>) have been commonly used for this purpose. Jakobovits (1970) contains examples of various such scales. Usually these are made up of statements which have to be agreed or disagreed with (to different degrees – a scale of 1–6 is common). Below are two statements from an 'Anomie Scale' and two from an 'Ethnocentrism Scale' (in that order). The scales are written for Canadians, and are taken from Jakobovits (1970: 266–7).

1. Having lived this long in this culture, I'd be happier living in some other country now.
2. The big trouble with our country is that it relies, for the most part, on the law of the jungle: 'get him before he gets you'.

3. The worst danger to real Canadians during the last 50 years has come from foreign ideas and agitators.
4. Certain people who refuse to salute the flag should be forced to conform to such a patriotic action, or else be imprisoned.

Box 8.21 illustrates another common technique for finding out about attitudes.

8.21 Finding out what they *really* think?

One way of finding out people's true feelings is to use a technique known as the 'semantic differential'. In this, subjects are asked to indicate feelings towards a group of people (for example) by indicating their impressions on a scale. For example, in one study by Gardner (reported in Stern 1983: 276, after Gardner and Lambert 1972: 157), subjects were asked about 'French people from France', and about 'my French teacher'. Subjects had to put a cross on each line to indicate their impressions. For example, if they felt French people from France to be very interesting, they would put a cross as indicated in line 1 below. Here are some of the items that the scale included:

1. Interesting   -x- : — : — : — : — : — : —   Boring
2. Prejudiced   — : — : — : — : — : — : —   Unprejudiced
3. Brave   — : — : — : — : — : — : —   Cowardly
4. Handsome   — : — : — : — : — : — : —   Ugly
5. Colourful   — : — : — : — : — : — : —   Colourless
6. Friendly   — : — : — : — : — : — : —   Unfriendly
7. Honest   — : — : — : — : — : — : —   Dishonest
8. Smart   — : — : — : — : — : — : —   Stupid
9. Kind   — : — : — : — : — : — : —   Cruel
10. Pleasant   — : — : — : — : — : — : —   Unpleasant

In another study (Lambert *et al.* 1960), subjects had to listen to a passage read in two languages, French and English. Subjects were then asked to mark their impressions about the speaker (whom they could not see). The scale used was like the one above, but included the following fourteen items:

height	good looks	leadership	sense of humour
intelligence	religiousness	self-confidence	dependability
entertainingness	kindness	ambition	sociability
character	likability		

This study was done in Canada, and revealed some interesting attitudes of French-speaking and English-speaking Canadians about themselves and each other.

To what extent can (and should) teachers attempt to control attitudes? As we noted in our discussion of learner level, in many situations learners do not arrive in class with fixed attitudes, and the teacher's role then is more like 'attitude former' that 'attitude changer'. But where negative attitudes do exist, it needs to be realized that, though they can be changed, attitudes tend to be somewhat deep-seated and enduring. Psychologists have done fascinating work in attitude changing, in non-linguistic areas. A problem of attitude change was, for example, posed in the Second World War when the war with Germany, but not with Japan, was finished. The natural reaction of allied troops was to want to go home, and they had to be persuaded to continue fighting. But it would be unrealistic to expect teachers to engage in elaborate attitude changing programmes. A little gentle persuasion perhaps, but not much more. Dörnyei and Csizér (1998) suggest 'ten commandments for motivating language learners' that the teacher can follow. Their commandments include exhortations like: 'familiarise learners with the target language culture', 'personalise the learning process', and 'create a pleasant, relaxed atmosphere in the classroom'.

But how important really are attitude and motivation? Though there can be no doubt that highly motivated learners with the right attitudes will have a head start, these are not necessarily enough. We conclude this chapter with part of a sad story. It shows that attitudes and motivation will not take you all the way. A second instalment of the story comes in Chapter 9.

8.22   The Sad Story of Student A: Part 1

The sad story comes from Naiman *et al.* (1978), and is about one of the students they studied in depth. They call her Student A. She has much going for her. She is full of the right attitudes, and has plenty of integrative motivation. Here are some of the things said about her:

- 'she appeared to be attentive, very jovial and relaxed, obviously enjoying some of the activities'
- 'she indicated that French was her favourite subject and expressed a general love of languages'
- 'outside the classroom she occasionally listened to the French radio station and talked to her friends in French – "for fun"'
- 'according to her teacher, Student A was a "beautifully adapted person", not afraid of making mistakes, very motivated, and a hard worker'

But life can be very cruel. Despite these very positive traits Student A is, sadly, second lowest in class. Why do you think this happened?

A possible explanation will be given in Chapter 9.

Notes

1. A subject often mentioned in this respect is mathematics. Perhaps FL learning shares with mathematics, and music, the ability to see patterns, and relationships. This ability is discussed on page 143.
2. The intended answers are: (1) affection; (2) cattle; (3) battle; (4) pond; (5) good looking; (6) nation.
3. The intended answers are:

    (2)   D   Like *apple*, *dog* is the direct object of the sentence.
    (3)   D   Like *money*, *farming* is the subject of the sentence.
    (4)   B   In the third and fourth sentences, the word *there* has a different meaning from the one in the key sentence. In the second sentence the meaning is the same, and the words *talk* and *doubt* both come after the verb BE.
    (5)   E   *Him* in the key sentence means *to him*, and like *him* in the following sentence is the indirect object.
    (6)   D   The words *and* and *but* are used in the same way, to join what otherwise might be separate sentences together.

4. *Number learning* clearly involves inductive learning ability. The main component of *Phonetic script* is phonetic coding ability, as is the case with the *Spelling clues* test. As box 8.11 illustrates, *Words in sentences* is said to involve grammatical sensitivity. Ability at rote learning is a main part of the *Paired associates* sub-test.
5. Accents are a very strong marker of identity, and of association with a social group. Many people cherish local or class accents in their L1 for that reason. Some such attitudes make their way into FL learning, where a learner may only put effort into improving her accent if she wants to feel part of the target-language society. Sometimes you even hear of learners who have a very good 'ear', and who are capable of a near-native accent in the FL. But they may intentionally keep some foreign-ness in their accent, just to indicate to the world that, however well they speak the FL, their true identity is not as a member of the target-language group.

Chapter 9

Good language learners and what they do

The Sad Story of Student A suggests perhaps that there are factors other than those we have so far considered that can contribute to individual success or failure in language learning. Perhaps the key to her lack of success has something to do with the personality variables we shall now consider. When we have discussed these, we shall look in detail at the study Student A's story comes from, Naiman *et al.* (1978). This was the largest of a number of studies undertaken in the 1970s, looking at what makes a good language learner. As we shall see, these studies partly attempt to identify the characteristics that go to make up good language learners. But they also consider an issue we shall finish the chapter with. This is the question, not of what good language learners are *like*, but of what they *do*. What processes do they use in the course of learning that make them so good at it?

Personality variables

Extroversion and introversion

> **9.1 Extroverts and introverts**
>
> Before you read below about research that has been done in this area, here are three issues for you to consider:
>
> (a) You probably have a general idea of what makes an introvert and an extrovert. Try to make this general idea as specific as possible. What exactly is an introvert? And an extrovert?
> (b) A research issue: how can you find out whether a person is an extrovert or an introvert? Can you think what kind of research techniques might tell you?
> (c) Which do *you* think are likely to learn languages better – extroverts or introverts? What advantages and disadvantages are there to being an extroverted FL learner? What about an introverted one?

Skehan (1989), a book all about individual differences, begins his discussion of extroversion/introversion and foreign-language learning by giving Eysenck's (1965: 59–60) descriptions of extrovert and introvert personalities:

> The typical extrovert is sociable, likes parties, has many friends, needs to have people to talk to, and does not like studying by himself. He craves excitement, takes chances, often sticks his neck out, acts on the spur of the moment, and is generally an impulsive individual. He . . . always has a ready answer, and generally likes change . . .
>
> The typical introvert, on the other hand, is a quiet, retiring sort of person, introspective, fond of books rather than people; he is reserved and distant, except with intimate friends. He tends to plan ahead . . . and distrusts the impulse of the moment. He does not like excitement, takes matters of everyday life with proper seriousness, and likes a well ordered mode of life . . .

Skehan (p. 100) identifies two characteristics of the extrovert. One is sociability (the gregarious, people-oriented side of the extrovert), and the other impulsivity (the extrovert's preparedness to take risks). A test which aims to measure such characteristics is Eysenck's Introversion–Extroversion scale. It operates in much the same way as Jakobovits's scales described earlier, consisting of statements to which the subject agrees or disagrees to a greater or lesser degree. Two questions from Eysenck's scale will give you the flavour:

- Do you sometimes say the first thing that comes into your head?
- Can you usually solve a problem better by studying it alone than by discussing it with others?

Skehan points out that, given what has been said about introverts and extroverts, there is a conflict of expectations for learning in general, and for language learning in particular. Eysenck, for example, suggests that extroverts are easily distracted from study and find difficulty concentrating, suggesting that they do not make very good learners overall. But when it comes to language learning many feel that extroverts should have the advantage. After all, they engage in conversation a lot, exposing themselves to input and producing output – both characteristics which, as we saw in Chapter 6, are thought important for language learning. Among the attempts to relate these factors to language learning is Pritchard's (1952) paper which finds a correlation between the 'sociability' side of the extrovert's personality (measured by observing how much pupils talked in the school playground) and fluency in spoken French.

In Naiman et al.'s (1978) Good Language Learner study, Eysenck's scale is used with a large number of pupils. No correlation is found with language-learning success. The researchers express surprise at this result, because their informal observations of the pupils did suggest an advantage to the extroverts. They speculate whether the Eysenck scale was in fact doing its job.

Common sense might suggest that there could be a connection between extroversion and *oral performance*. But you may also feel that introverts are really just as competent in all areas, the only difference being that the introverts do not speak so much. You might then ask yourself whether you really have to speak a lot to learn a language. Can you not take everything in without opening the mouth much at all? It is a good question to ask.

9.2 Introverts, extroverts, input, output and interaction

In Chapter 6 we saw that different theories and hypotheses make claims about the important of input, output and interaction. The Input Theory was discussed at length but, if you need to refresh your memory about the Output Hypothesis and the Interaction Hypothesis, go back to page 95.

Think about what each of these three views implies about introverts and extroverts, and how successful each will be at FL learning. An example of the kind of thought you might have: the Output Hypothesis claims that it is important how much language the learner himself produces. Since extroverts are likely to produce more than introverts, we might imagine that this hypothesis would predict more success for extroverts.

Tolerance of ambiguity

Perhaps there are people you know who become very agitated if the future is unclear to them. People like this simply must know, in any given situation, what is going to happen to them next. Others, on the other hand, seem quite happy living in a state of uncertainty. The term tolerance/intolerance of ambiguity is used to describe these personality traits. Budner (1962) describes intolerance of ambiguity as 'the tendency to perceive . . . ambiguous situations as sources of threat'. As with several other variables we have been considering, this factor is measured by a scale. Budner's Intolerance of Ambiguity scale invites subjects to agree or disagree with statements such as 'what we are used to is always preferable to what is unfamiliar'.

9.3 Tolerant or intolerant?

Can you think of individuals you know whom you could call tolerant or intolerant of ambiguity, in the terms just discussed? How does this show itself?

Can you imagine any way in which this characteristic might relate to language-learning success? Would you expect learners tolerant or intolerant of ambiguity to be better language learners? Why?

Naiman *et al.* (1978) administer Budner's test and attempt to correlate results with French proficiency. Interestingly, this is one of the few personality traits where a correlation *is* found, particularly with results on a listening comprehension test. The suggestion is that those who are tolerant of ambiguity are better language learners than those who are not.

This piece of research finds another interesting, and related, connection. This is between intolerance of ambiguity and the degree to which learners want their L1 to be used in class. The researchers find differences between learners regarding attitude towards the teacher's use of the FL in class. Some learners are quite happy to be 'immersed' in the FL, even though they may not understand everything that is being said. But other learners are disoriented by not understanding, and are upset that the teacher does not use the L1 to help communication where necessary. *He keeps talking away in French*, they might say. *How am I supposed to know what he's saying? He ought to say it in English*. Naiman *et al.*'s study shows that the individuals who do not mind use of the FL in class are the ones shown by Budner's test to be tolerant of ambiguity. Those who object to overuse of the FL are intolerant of ambiguity. There is also a suggestion in the research that those tolerating more use of the FL fare better as learners. Putting all these connections together, we find that not minding extensive use of the FL is connected to being tolerant of ambiguity, and both these factors are related to success in FL learning.

This connection between proficiency and tolerance of ambiguity is particularly strong at the early learning stages, and this leads Naiman *et al.* to wonder whether individuals who are intolerant of ambiguity might decide to give up learning the language at an early stage.

Empathy/ego permeability and sensitivity to rejection

Another fascinating factor which has been studied in relation to FL learning is known as 'empathy' or 'ego permeability'. Ego permeability has been defined as the 'act of constructing for oneself another person's mental state' (Naiman *et al.* 1978: 32). To paraphrase this: some individuals may be said to be 'open' to the personalities of others; their 'egos' are 'permeable'. It is an attractive idea to imagine that empathetic individuals, with permeable egos, will be good language learners.

Guiora *et al.* (1972) carried out controversial work in this area. The problem is how you *measure* a notion like empathy, which is as vague as it is interesting. Guiora *et al.* thought that perhaps it could be measured in relation to alcohol intake. The idea is that the more alcohol one drinks, the more permeable one's ego becomes – one becomes more friendly, more garrulous, and (so the theory goes) more sympathetic to the concerns of others. The researchers plied subjects with controlled amounts of alcohol, and did indeed find an improvement, related to alcohol intake, in an individual's foreign-language pronunciation. The best accent was achieved after an ounce and a half of alcohol had been drunk; thereafter the obvious happens and pronunciation, like other aspects of behaviour, deteriorates. But H. D. Brown (1973) points out that alcohol also has the effect of relaxing the muscles, and this might account for any pronunciation improvement. Naiman *et al.* (1978) use an empathy scale developed in Hogan (1969), but they find no correlations with language-learning success.

It is easy to laugh at the 'alcohol research'. But it does highlight a problem that much research in this area shares. It is the dilemma that the things that we can measure easily are the obvious and uninteresting ones, while the interesting things are indeed difficult to measure in the rigorous way that a 'scientific' approach would need. You may feel that the ego permeability idea really is an interesting one. But how do you measure it?

A similar point might be made about another factor, known as 'sensitivity to rejection'. Individuals differ in their response to being 'rejected' by others. Some are very hurt by it, while others can laugh it off. It is an interesting idea to imagine that sensitivity to rejection relates to language learning. After all, when you communicate in a foreign language it is easy for you to make a fool of yourself. When you express yourself badly in the FL, you are truly opening yourself to the possibility of ridicule – and hence to a kind of rejection. Good learners must have shoulders broad enough to take this 'rejection'. Mehrabian (1970) developed a 'Sensitivity to Rejection' scale, and Naiman *et al.* (1978) gave this questionnaire to their learners. They found no correlation between sensitivity to rejection and language-learning performance. But perhaps once again this is because no really satisfactory way of measuring the variable was available.

Cognitive style and field dependence/independence

When we are given a problem to solve, we all have our own preferred ways of tackling it. These 'ways of thinking' are sometime referred to as 'cognitive styles'. Messick (1970) calls them 'habitual modes of information processing'. Interesting research has been done into different cognitive styles of individuals. In the language-learning field, some of the most interesting is related to what is called field independence. Witkin (cited in McDonough 1981: 131) describes this as 'an analytical, in contrast to a global, way of perceiving [which] entails a tendency to experience items as discrete from their backgrounds and reflects ability to overcome the influence of an embedding context'. In simpler words: some individuals seem more able than others to extract things from the context in which they are met, and to see them as separate entities. People who can do this easily are said to be 'field independent', while those who do not are 'field dependent'. One area in which this has been studied is visual perception, and there exists an 'Embedded Figures' test. This asks subjects to find a given shape and isolate it from a complex figure which contains it. Box 9.4 gives an example.

9.4 What Embedded Figures tests look like

Below is an example of an item from an Embedded Figures test. It is an invented example, but is based on what is found in actual tests, like Witkin *et al.* (1962). The task is to find the figure (a) 'embedded' in each of the figures (b), (c) and (d). Try it: this example is not difficult, though some of the items in Embedded Figure tests can be very hard.

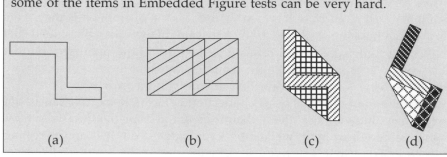

(a)　　　　　(b)　　　　　(c)　　　　　(d)

But there is more to field independence than visual memory. Indeed you may have come across an Embedded Figure test as part of those tests which (we mentioned in the last chapter) you can buy on railway stations to 'measure your own intelligence'. Their presence in IQ tests suggests that the ability to isolate shapes in this way has a cognitive side to it, and is felt to relate to general intelligence.

Naiman *et al.* (1978) gave their subjects a field independence test. The results were interesting. They found positive correlations between field independence and language-learning success, particularly at later learning stages. The field independent subjects seemed to be better learners. The researchers also make fascinating and explicit claims about the sorts of errors field dependent people make. For example, in one test the study used, subjects were given sentences in French which they were asked to repeat. This is sometimes used as a crude way of assessing proficiency – the better speakers make fewer mistakes and the worse make more. Below is one of the sentences from the test. English equivalents for each word are given underneath it, and a freer translation underneath that. To understand the example it helps a lot if you know French, though this is not absolutely necessary:

Hier　　quelqu'un nous a raconté une belle histoire
Yesterday someone to us has told　a nice story
Yesterday someone told us a nice story

You can see from this sentence that in French the word *nous* can mean *to us*, and it is put in front of the verb. But the word *nous* can also mean *we*, and in this meaning it would also come before the verb. In other words, *nous* before a verb can mean either *we* or *to us*.

When some field-dependent subjects repeated this sentence, they changed it to become:

*Hier   quelqu'un nous avons raconté une belle histoire.
*Yesterday someone we   have   told   a nice story

What is happening here? The learner heard the word *nous* and automatically thought of it as meaning *we*. So he wrongly replaced *nous a raconté* (*to us has told*) with *nous avons raconté* (*we have told*). It is as if they were 'seduced' by seeing the word *nous* in front of the verb, and assumed that it must be the subject of the sentence (*we*). They failed to perceive the underlying structure of the sentence.

Naiman *et al.* (1978) gave a number of personality and cognitive style tests to their subjects, only some of which have been described here. Of these, only two gave positive correlations with language-learning success – tolerance of ambiguity and field independence. The researchers themselves were disappointed not to have more results in this area. As we have mentioned on more than one occasion, they speculated that perhaps it is the difficulty in measuring some variables that made for such disappointing findings.

In this section we have considered some of the personality variables studied in relation to language learning. But there are others we have not covered. Principal among these are anxiety and one of a rather different sort to those we have looked at: age. Box 9.5 invites you to think about these two variables.

9.5 Thinking about anxiety and age

(a) Being an anxious person is likely to affect many aspects of an individual's life. What about using a foreign language? What effects would you expect anxiety to have on that? Would all the effects be bad? Is there anything good about being anxious?

(b) In Chapter 5 we saw that age affects an individual's attitude towards cultural differences. Box 5.6 on page 84 will remind you of what was said. Think now about age in more general terms. Think particularly about starting a language early in life (at the age of eight, for example). What advantages and disadvantages do you see to that? What about making a late start (say over the age of 45). Is the picture gloomier the older you get, or does the older person have any advantages?[1]

In this chapter and the last we have treated variables in isolation. But remember that within any real live learner many more than one variable is present. These variables exist in different strengths; sometimes one will be so strong as to dominate all the others; sometimes they will be of equal strength and will 'cancel each other out'. Certainly it is possible for a learner to compensate for some important characteristic that is missing, and it is equally possible for some strongly present negative element to destroy what might otherwise be a promising learner profile. 'Profile' is the important word in this context. If we want to make predictions about performance, we need to bear in mind *all* the characteristics a learner possesses, taken together. This issue of variables needing to be weighted when considering a learner profile is central to a model of FL acquisition developed by Spolsky (1989). He lists a full 74 factors (or 'conditions' as he calls them) that contribute to language-learning success. He notes that 'the effect of any one condition can be masked by the strong influence of other conditions; thus aptitude might be masked by attitude . . .' (p. 204). He uses the term 'preference model' to describe a framework which, like his, takes different variable weightings into consideration.

This is the point for us to revisit the Sad Story of Student A. As you will recall from box 8.22 above, she had very good attitudes and strong motivation. It was a mystery why she did so badly at learning French. Perhaps the answer lies in the Embedded Figures test she was given by Naiman *et al.* (1978). This revealed that she was highly field dependent, apparently not a good characteristic for language learners. For her this might be what Shakespeare's Hamlet calls the 'vicious mole of nature' – the one small feature that grows until it destroys all the good that surrounds it.

Good language learner studies

9.6 Doing the right things

At the beginning of the last chapter (box 8.1 on page 116) you were asked to consider what characteristics a good learner might possess. You were asked to think about bad learners as well. Here are some related questions:

What do you think good language learners *do* as they learn? What kinds of strategies do they use? Try to be as specific as possible. Do they, for example, learn lists of vocabulary items by heart? Do they pay a lot of attention to grammar? What else? And what about bad learners?

As always, try to think of specific individuals you know – including yourself perhaps.

You will by now have gathered that at this point in the book our main interest is in an abstract, fictitious, and perhaps even mythological character – the Good Language Learner. How can we find out what good language learners are like? Carroll's (1967) suggested way of doing this was inspirational. Why not, he suggested, gather together a group of people who were self-evidently good language learners, and try to find out what they have in common? Like most brilliant ideas, it seems entirely obvious once someone has thought of it.

Around the mid-1970s, a number of studies did just this. The largest so-called 'good language learner' study is one that we have mentioned many times already – Naiman *et al.* (1978) – and in this section we shall spend time describing what was done and found in some detail. Another study, Pickett (1978), has much in common with parts of Naiman *et al.*, but is much more modest in scope. A further two studies, by Stern (1975) and Rubin (1975), are well known. They are theoretical, and do not involve any direct research. You might regard them as statements of belief as to what good learners will (or should) be like, and part of their interest is that they give a clear idea of the view of language learning predominant at that time. Rubin's study is particularly interesting for its speculations regarding what strategies good learners use, and Naiman *et al.* use these speculations as the basis for part of their study. Box 9.7 lists Rubin's good learning strategies, as adapted by Naiman *et al.* Compare the list with the one you developed in box 9.6 above. Take time, also, to reflect on Rubin's list itself. Which strategies on the list do *you* feel are particularly important?

9.7 Seven hypotheses about good language learners
(from Rubin 1975, adapted by Naiman *et al.* 1978)

1. The good language learner is a willing and accurate guesser.
2. The good language learner has a strong drive to communicate, or to learn from communication. He is willing to do many things to get his message across.
3. The good language learner is often not inhibited. He is willing to appear foolish if reasonable communication results. He is willing to make mistakes in order to learn and to communicate. He is willing to live with a certain amount of vagueness.
4. In addition to focusing on communication the good language learner is prepared to attend to form. The good language learner is constantly looking for patterns in the language.
5. The good language learner practises.
6. The good language learner monitors his own and the speech of others. That is, he is constantly attending to how well his speech is being received and whether his performance meets the standards he has learned.
7. The good language learner attends to meaning. He knows that in order to understand the message it is not sufficient to pay attention to the language or to the surface form of speech.

Naiman *et al.* (1978)

Naiman *et al.*'s study really was large-scale. It had three main aims. One was to identify the strategies that good learners used. In particular: were Rubin's strategies (in box 9.7) used by good learners? Secondly, were there any correlations between successful learning and the variables we have been looking at, particularly the personality and cognitive style ones? A third and less central aim was to learn something about what teachers do in classrooms.

The study was done in Canada using subjects whose L1 was English. It had two main parts. For the *adult interview study* they identified 34 individuals who were self-evidently good language learners. They also chose, for comparison, two people who were bad at languages. All the chosen subjects were given a questionnaire in two parts. Part 1 asked about their experiences and background; Part 2 tried to find out about their learning strategies. Three of the good learner subjects were then chosen for special in-depth case studies.

The *main classroom study* dealt with pupils learning French at school. Two French proficiency tests were given to twelve classes of learners taken from different schools chosen to represent the variety of schools in the area. 72 pupils were selected from those who took the tests. These were given a series of personality and cognitive style scales, including some which we have seen already: the Embedded Figures test (for field independence); the Intolerance of Ambiguity scale; the Sensitivity to Rejection scale; the Empathy scale (for empathy/ego permeability); the Introversion–Extroversion scale; an attitude test. Each pupil was also observed in class for a total of 250 minutes, with many aspects of their behaviour noted down. Both students and teachers were interviewed. Six pupils were selected for in-depth case studies, one of these being the Student A we have already met.

The Naiman *et al.* study provides a veritable treasure trove of interesting pieces of information. Some of the small, but nevertheless fascinating findings are given in box 9.8:

9.8   Some small-but-fascinating findings from Naiman *et al.* (1978)

None of the findings below is particularly central to Naiman *et al.*'s good language learner study. But they are interesting pieces of information to have. Are you surprised by any of them? Do any of them need an explanation? What might it be?

- 'poor students tended to prefer written work, such as grammar exercises' (p. 81)
- in the classes observed during the study, there was more oral than written work. 'However, there was still very little emphasis given to

free discussion as opposed to the more structured activities like class exercises, tests, reading etc.' (p. 92)

- the researchers were surprised that good learners *did not* do any of the following very much: correct themselves, repeat things without being asked to, ask the teacher questions. But the good learners *did* put up their hands a lot (p. 53)

- 'it is interesting to note that more bottom than top students wanted to be asked [questions by the teacher] more frequently. This may indicate that they feel neglected or that they recognize the need for greater participation' (p. 79)

- teachers most often corrected student mistakes in an explicit way, saying exactly what was wrong rather than giving hints. Very few explanations of why something was wrong were given. When a learner got something right, the correct response was often repeated by the teacher, as a reinforcement (p. 94)

- 'it is interesting to see that not only top students had a favourable attitude towards their teacher . . . but also bottom students' (p. 78)

- how to find out about attitudes: 'a brief, but carefully designed, interview with a student may indicate a great deal more about his overall attitude towards language learning, and therefore the probability of his success, than the results of an involved attitude battery' (p. 67)

Treasure troves apart, what about more major findings, related to the study's three main aims? As regards *learning strategies*, five of Rubin's strategies found some support, particularly in the adult interview study. These were:

1. Active learner participation. The better learners did appear to be making positive efforts to create opportunities to use the language. As one of the good adult learners put it: 'I would try to get involved as much as possible . . . Language is a skill you've got to use all the time . . . Participation seems really essential' (p. 10).

2. The better learners realized that they did have to come to grips with language as a system. They showed willingness to learn grammar. In the questionnaire, learners were asked whether they learned systematically or unconsciously. 94 per cent of the good learners answered that their approach was highly conscious and systematic. They wrote statements like 'just absorbing the language doesn't get you very far'. Naiman *et al.* add an interesting comment. 'It may be significant', they say, 'that the two subjects [in the adult interview study] who regarded language learning as a totally unconscious process were the unsuccessful learners' (p. 11). It would be difficult, perhaps, to square this finding with Krashen's views (as described on p. 76 above, for example).

3. But at the same time the good learners saw it necessary to view language as communication, realizing the need to go and seek opportunities to talk to real people. The learner who was about the best of the adults studied claimed to have a girl friend in every language. He says the language comes alive when you get to know individuals who speak it!

4. Good learners do appear to monitor their own interlanguage, constantly correcting themselves. In one class, the best pupil answered (silently, to himself) all the teacher's questions, whoever the teacher had addressed them to. He compared his own answers with those given by others in class.

5. Good learners realize that learning a language involves affective problems, which they have to come to terms with. They know that you have to be prepared to appear foolish while you are learning. One learner picked up Icelandic from a five-year old, and only realized later that some of the expressions he was learning were childish (*Mr Copper-wopper* for policeman, for example). Another learner notes that 'one good character- istic is to be outgoing, to be willing to take risks'. For her this involved being prepared to go up to native speakers and practise on them, even though it was sometimes obvious that the native speakers would rather be speaking amongst themselves, without the presence of a non-native who would need 'special attention'.

Another major finding regarding learning strategies was to do with how you find out about them. The researchers found that information on strategies is more usefully collected through interviews, not observation. They had hoped that watching pupils in class would give them plenty of information on strategies. But this did not happen. This is not so surprising when you think how much of language behaviour in general is covert. There is not much to see or hear – most of what happens goes on in the head. Reading and listening are the obvious examples of covert language behaviour.

9.9 Seeing into the unseen

How can you find out what is going on when a learner reads or listens? Just watching the learner will not tell you much. What other research techniques are available for seeing into the unseen?

What about when a learner writes? The *results* of writing are visible but, as with reading and listening, a lot is unseen and goes on in the head.

These issues will be looked at later in this chapter (on p. 155 below).

We have already come across two of Naiman *et al.*'s three main findings to do with *cognitive styles and personality traits*. Here are the three:

- Tolerance of ambiguity correlated at lower levels, and may perhaps be important in decisions concerning whether or not to continue with the language.
- Field independence correlated at higher levels.
- A general measure of attitude (not just one of integrative or instrumental motivation) does correlate with success, particularly at early stages. It is perhaps *necessary*, but it is not *sufficient*.

The Sad Tale of Student A illustrates this last point. As we saw, she is full of the right attitudes, and has plenty of integrative motivation. But this is not sufficient to guarantee her success.

Naiman *et al.* also report three main findings regarding *what teachers do*:

1. As was suggested in box 9.8 above, the study revealed a predominance of question/answer techniques in class, with little free discussion or cultural background work.
2. Because of the size of classes, it sometimes happened that large numbers of pupils would be 'ignored' for some periods of time. But teachers did not concentrate more on better pupils, and less on those who were doing badly. The teachers' treatment overall was even handed.
3. Teachers are in general rather good at identifying good and bad learners. Tests of various sorts provide objective information on pupils and their progress. But a teacher's subjective judgement can also be trusted.

Since Naiman *et al.* there have been a number of other good language learner studies, including ones by Gillette (1987) on the learning of Spanish and French, and Lennon (1989) on Germans learning English. These studies, like the others we have mentioned, raise an issue which has perhaps been in your own mind as you read: to what extent can we really expect all good learners to be similar, and to follow the same strategies? After all, as we noted in Chapter 1 (p. 10 above), there are 'very many ways of skinning the language-learning cat'. It is true that we have to expect differences as well as commonalities, and Naiman *et al.* find just this. For example, they note that there is a lot of variation among the good learners over such matters as preference for formal versus informal learning conditions, and in their preferred way of being taught. There were also substantial differences in learning styles. Some learners would learn vocabulary by memorizing lists of words, for example, while others found different ways of doing this. In another more recent good language learner study, Stevick (1989: 128) witnesses the same thing. His seven successful learners 'differ markedly with regard to what . . . they prefer to do and not to do'. Observations like this lead Ellis (1994: 546) to the conclusion that 'it is easy to overstate the commonalities in strategy use among good language learners'.

But some commonalities there undoubtedly are, and the good language learner studies have contributed immensely in our efforts to identify them.

Learning strategies

As we have seen, learning strategies were a topic of major interest to the good language learner studies. In fact research like Naiman *et al.*'s led to a spate of enquiries into learning strategies during the 1980s and 1990s.

But what exactly is a learning strategy? Box 9.10 contains some examples:

9.10 Six learning strategies

Here are six examples of learning strategies, taken from a category system developed by Oxford (1990). Use these examples to try and develop your own definition of what a learning strategy is. In a moment you will be able to compare your definition with Oxford's.

A *Taking risks wisely* 'Pushing oneself to take risks in a language-learning situation, even though there is a chance of making a mistake or looking foolish. Risks must be tempered with good judgement' (Oxford 1990: 144).

B *Remembering new language information according to its sound* One of Oxford's examples is a way of learning FL vocabulary. You think of a word in your L1 (or any other language) which sounds like the word you are trying to learn. You try to associate the two words. For example, if you are trying to learn the Russian word *brat* (meaning 'brother'), you could associate it with the English word *brat* (an 'annoying person'). Bringing to mind this association may help you remember the Russian word. Under this heading, Oxford (p. 42) also mentions the use of rhymes to remember a word .

C *Finding out about language learning* 'Making efforts to find out how language learning works by reading books and talking with other people, and then using this information to help improve one's own language learning' (p. 139).

D *Cooperating with peers* 'Working with other language learners to improve language skills. This strategy can involve a regular learning partner or a temporary pair or small group. This strategy frequently involves controlling impulses toward competitiveness and rivalry' (p. 147).

E *Switching to the mother tongue* 'Using the mother tongue for an expression without translating it, as in *Ich bin eine girl* [used when a native speaker of English learning German cannot remember the German word for 'girl']. This strategy may also include adding word endings from the new language onto words from the mother tongue' (p. 50).

F *Repeating* 'Saying or doing something over and over: listening to something several times; rehearsing; imitating a native speaker' (p. 45).

Here is Oxford's own definition (1990: 8) of learning strategies: they are 'specific actions taken by the learner to make learning easier, faster, more enjoyable, more self-directed, more effective, and more transferable to new situations'. Actually, if you were to attempt a more elaborate characterization, you would face problems. One would be to distinguish learning strategies from another sort of strategy discussed by applied linguists – communication strategies. These are the 'techniques for coping' that learners develop in relation to strategic competence. Recall the Japanese artist Wes from Chapter 2 (p. 35 above), and the sorts of ruses he developed for getting his message across using his rather restricted knowledge of English. These 'ruses' are communication strategies. The problem of definition comes about because communication strategies can also be learning strategies. Here is an example from Hawkins (1998). A learner may develop the habit of asking people he is talking with to explain the meaning of a word. This is a communication strategy because it helps the learner over a linguistic deficit. But it can also be a learning strategy – it may be a very good way of getting to learn the meanings of new words.

A second point relevant to the definition of learning strategies is whether or not the word strategy should be confined to conscious actions. Learners do lots of things in the process of learning that come naturally and are out of conscious control. Are these strategies, or should they be called by some other name, such as 'processes'? Although applied linguists disagree over this, most say that learning strategies involve some degree of 'consciousness'. Does it really matter, you may ask? From one point of view it matters very much. As we shall see in a minute, attempts have been made to 'teach' strategies. You might argue that it is only really possible to teach things that are at least potentially conscious.

Rubin developed her list of learning strategies in 1975. Since then much more elaborate classifications of learning strategies have been devised. One of the best known appears in Oxford's (1990) book *Language Learning Strategies*. Her classificatory system makes a distinction between what she calls 'direct' and 'indirect' strategies. She explains these (1990: 14–15) by an analogy from the theatre. When using direct strategies, the language learner is like the performer in a play. An actor's task is to come to grips with the play itself. Similarly the language learner's direct strategies help him to come to grips with the language. They deal with things like memorizing vocabulary, and for getting to understand new grammar rules. The language learner's indirect strategies are more akin to the role of the play's director. They deal with regulation and control. In the case of the language learner, this would include planning issues (like how many hours you spend on learning, and what you do in preparation for each lesson), as well as issues to do with affective demands – coping with the 'strain on the nerves' that speaking and learning a foreign language can involve.

Oxford's classification has six main categories of strategy, three under the heading of 'direct', and three under 'indirect'. These are shown in box 9.11:

9.11   Oxford's (1990) Strategy System described in her own words (1990: 14–16)

(a)   **Direct strategies 'working with the language itself'**
    1. **memory strategies** for remembering and retrieving new information
    2. **cognitive strategies** for understanding and producing the language
    3. **compensation strategies** for using the language despite knowledge gaps
    Indirect strategies 'for general management of learning'
    4. **metacognitive strategies** for co-ordinating the learning process
    5. **affective strategies** for regulating emotions
    6. **social strategies** for learning with others
(b)   In box 9.10 (page 152) you were given examples of six strategies, marked A to F. Each of these strategies is an example of one of the strategy types (1–6) above. Try to match the examples in box 9.10 with Oxford's strategy types, by associating the letters (A–F) with the numbers (1–6) above.[2]

Another book dedicated to the study of learning strategies is O'Malley and Chamot (1990). Their classificatory system is different from Oxford's, but one common element is the category of *metacognitive strategies*. These important strategies 'involve thinking about the learning process, planning for learning, monitoring the learning task, and evaluating how well one has learned' (O'Malley and Chamot 1990: 137). Here are three examples of metacognitive strategies (described using O'Malley and Chamot's own words; 1990: 137):

- *Directed attention*: deciding in advance to attend in general to a learning task and to ignore irrelevant distractors; maintaining attention during task execution.
- *Self-management*: understanding the conditions that help one successfully accomplish language tasks and arranging for the presence of those conditions; controlling one's language performance to maximize use of what is already known.
- *Problem identification*: explicitly identifying the central point needing resolution in a task or identifying an aspect of the task that hinders its successful completion.

How useful are metacognitive strategies to the learner? There is a lot of recent research to suggest that metacognition is very important for academic success in general, not just in language learning. Here is an example of their importance in an area not related to language use. Schoenfeld (1985) is interested in how people solve mathematical problems. Look at his observations on one expert problem-solver: 'the critical point to observe . . . is that a monitor-assessor-manager was always close at hand during the solution attempt. Rarely did more than a minute pass without there being some clear indication that the entire solution process was being watched and controlled . . . there was an extraordinary degree of executive control at all times . . . Plans and their implementations were continually assessed, and then acted upon in accordance with the assessments . . .' (pp. 310–13). Goh (1998) reaches similar conclusions in her study, which is directly concerned with language learning. She notes that learners who have a high degree of meta-cognitive awareness seem better able to control and manage their learning in terms of understanding and storing new information as well as finding the best ways to practise and reinforce what they have learned.

An even clearer conclusion about strategy use comes out of one of the studies reported in O'Malley and Chamot (1990). They give tasks to learners at different levels. These include filling in blanks with vocabulary items, writing about a picture, and listening to a dialogue. The researchers try to find out what strategies learners are using as they do the tasks. The conclusion: 'in general, more effective students used a greater variety of strategies and used them in ways that helped the students complete the language task successfully. Less effective students not only had fewer strategy types in their repertoires but also frequently used strategies that were inappropriate to the task . . .' (1990: 140). Others, like Goh (1998) reach similar conclusions. Good learners, it seems, have a rich repertoire of strategies from which they can draw.

This study by O'Malley and Chamot reintroduces an issue brought up earlier, in box 9.9 on page 150. This is the question of how we can hope to 'see into the unseen', to find out what is going on in a learner's head as he learns to use language. One technique, employed by Naiman et al. and many others, is simply to ask the learner. Interviews and questionnaires can be used to persuade learners to state what their learning strategies are.

But there is another set of techniques, also involving introspection, which has the potential to tell us a great deal about strategy use. They are called think-aloud techniques. In these, the learner is given language-learning tasks to do, and is asked to say aloud whatever thoughts go through his head as he does them. He may be asked to do this after the task has been done, but a common version of these techniques is known as concurrent verbalization. This involves the learner in actually talking as the task is being done. O'Malley and Chamot use this type of verbalization in the study we have just discussed. Think-aloud techniques give the researchers some 'way in' to the otherwise silent world of learning strategies. But they are not everyone's cup of tea. At the very least, learners will usually need some training to be able to verbalize as they work. Even then, by no means everyone is able to think aloud successfully. Some subjects protest strongly against the technique, saying that they can either do the task, or talk about how to do it . . . but not both at the same time! Box 9.12 vividly records the protest of one person who was subjected to concurrent verbalization.

9.12 Talking drivel

(a) This subject was asked to verbalize simultaneously as she did a task. The task was not directly to do with language learning, but what she says about think-aloud techniques is very relevant to learning-strategy research. After struggling to verbalize her thoughts for over an hour, she lost patience with the technique. An explosion occurred:

> . . . the main problem is that I am so aware of the need to keep talking that I don't get a chance to think anything through. I'm desperate to be able to switch off, sit back, think about the task in peace and quiet, think something through. I'm not going to be able to come up with anything satisfactory because of this necessity to keep talking. And I'm talking drivel. I found that if I mention an idea, if I didn't have to verbalize it, I'd be rejecting it in seconds, probably as rubbish. But because I've got to verbalize, I find myself following it through, talking about it, exploring it. It's drivel.

(b) If you want to know what concurrent verbalization feels like, try doing it while solving an anagram. Here is the name of a Shakespeare play, with the letters mixed up; the title has three words: AJIMRDOONUELTE. Speak aloud (in your L1) as you solve this anagram. Say everything that is going through your mind as you do the task. If you wish you can tape record what you say. Listening back to what you said will give you an idea of what concurrent verbalizations sound like, and what it can reveal about processes.[3]

If a good repertoire of learning strategies will benefit the learner, the next question we need to ask is: can strategies be taught? What do you think? You are invited to look back over some of the specific strategies that we have mentioned (for example in box 9.10 on page 152). How would you go about teaching these? What kinds of exercises or activities could be given to learners to help develop strategies like these? If you ask applied linguists such questions, at present you are likely to receive answers that are statements of faith rather than views based on hard evidence. But the interest in learning strategies has understandably led to attempts to try and teach them. A pioneering attempt is found in Ellis and Sinclair (1989). What they offer is in effect a self-training manual, divided into two stages. Stage 1 is called *Preparation for language learning*. It deals with a series of questions such as 'What sort of a language learner are you?', 'Why do you need or want to learn English?' and 'How do you organize your learning?' Stage 2 is entitled *Skills training*. The areas it looks at are: learning vocabulary, learning grammar, listening, speaking, reading and writing. In relation to each, there are exercises that help you to reflect on how you are going about your learning. As an example, for vocabulary learning you are asked which method of learning you prefer – learning words by topic, by translating them into your FL, by writing them down, and so on. Then there are associated activities. The idea of learning vocabulary by topic, for example, is explored by giving you a collection of words and asking you to sort them into 'topics'.

Oxford's (1990) book might also be described as a training manual, and includes many interesting exercises geared to develop learning strategies in students. Box 9.13 describes one which many others have thought to be useful – getting one's learners to keep diaries of what happens as they learn.

9.13   Dear Diary . . .

Below is part of Oxford's (1990: 190–1) description to teachers on how to get learners to keep diaries:

Instructions
Tell your students the following in your own words: Use a diary or journal to express your feelings about learning the new language. Feel free to write whatever you want, but write something every day. The diary describes *how you are learning the language and how you feel about it*. Diary entries do not have to be long and involved. In fact, a few lines or a few paragraphs a day might be enough. When you want to explore a particular problem or a happy event in more detail, you can write more than usual. The diary is for you, and you can use it any way you want: to describe emotions, desires, issues, difficulties, achievements, other people, learning strategies, conversations, how you spent your time. You will probably want to use the diary to evaluate the general progress (or lack of it) that you feel you are making . . .

As well as books like these which deal with learner training in depth, it is now quite common for teaching materials and coursebooks to incorporate exercises geared to develop learning strategies. J. McDonough (1998) gives the example of a coursebook called *Signature* (Phillips and Sheerin 1990). This is a standard three-level course for adults learning English as a foreign language. One element which dates it in the 1990s is that it includes exercises aimed at training the learner in efficient dictionary use, as well as sensitizing them to the need to develop good learning strategies.

But the jury is still out. As J. McDonough (1998: 195) puts it, there is not yet 'much hard evidence that strategy training leads to improvement in language-learning outcomes'. We do not yet know whether strategies can be taught.

This chapter concludes Part 2 of the book, and our look at language learning. In Part 3 the focus switches to language teaching. In a perfect and logical world, you would expect what we say about language teaching to be firmly based on what we know about language learning. Certainly in Part 3 we shall make efforts to refer back to Part 2 as often as possible, and we will indeed often find ourselves seeking justifications for teaching procedures in terms of what is known about learning. But alas, as many have lamented since time immemorial, the world is neither perfect nor logical. It is a sad .and shameful truth that in applied linguistics, as elsewhere, division and compartmentalization exist where there should be unity and oneness. There are, in fact, two worlds rather than one. The world of language teaching, which we are about to enter, exists alongside the world of learning. But they really *are* different places . . . in which, unfortunately, they often seem to be driving on different sides of the road!

Notes

1. You might expect anxiety to have some bad effects on language performance, particularly in speaking, when you are likely to feel particularly exposed. But, in all areas of learning, a degree of anxiety may be useful if it makes you more aware and alert.

   We have seen various examples in the book (in box 7.1 on page 105 for example) of how young children have the advantage of being able to pick up languages in a natural way. But they also tend to be poor at learning rules and generalizations. Elderly people are perhaps slower to learn, but can be more organized, and often have the very great advantage of being well-motivated.
2. The matchings are: 1B; 2F; 3E; 4C; 5A; 6D.
3. The comments of the subject verbalizing simultaneously have been modified slightly, and abridged. The Shakespeare play is *Romeo and Juliet*.

PART 3

TEACHING

Chapter 10

Language teaching: a brisk walk through recent times

Introduction

There are, as we saw in Chapter 1, many ways of skinning the language-learning cat. The history of language teaching does indeed display a bewildering variety of different methods and approaches, all jostling for our attention, often by means of extravagant claims of the 'learn a language in three months without any effort at all (even while you're asleep)' variety. This chapter's 'brisk walk' will take us along a path through the forest of methods, paying some attention to the background ideas and intellectual traditions which lie behind the actual classroom procedures. But reflect first on your own experience:

10.1   Methods: a consumer's view

Think about your own classroom language-learning experiences. Identify some of the main characteristics of each 'method' (or 'approach') that you have experienced. Has a specific name been used in relation to each method?

For each method, try to list some of the advantages and disadvantages you noticed, viewed from your position as a learner – the 'consumer'.

In the late sixties, Kelly (1969) produced an overview of language-teaching history which began in the period around 500 BC. His long historical perspective carries a message for anyone looking at the development of language teaching. It is that there is nothing new under the sun. As he himself puts it (1969: 394): 'ideas accessible to language teachers have not changed basically in 2000 years'. It is indeed a sobering thought to find that issues which we consider today to be at the cutting edge of debate, and methods we like to think of as 'state of the art' are likely to have been around in Aristotle's time. Each generation, in ignorance and through vainglory, pats itself on the back for re-inventing the wheel.

A second introductory point: in this chapter we describe methods as if they existed in some pure, uncontaminated form. But in fact you rarely come across pure, uncontaminated examples of any method. This is because methods are put into practice by human textbook writers and human teachers. These groups of people have the wisdom to inject their own beliefs, preferences and experience into what they produce. So you almost never find a pure example of audio-visualism (to select one of the methods we shall describe). What you find instead is 'Textbook writer A's version of audio-visualism', or 'audio-visualism as taught by Teacher B'. Richards (1985) has a delightful phrase to describe this phenomenon. He speaks about the 'secret life of methods', capturing the idea that, behind all the public statements about what a given method is like, there lurks a back-street existence – the secret life that the method really follows.

Seven questions to ask about a method

Before beginning our 'brisk walk', it will be useful to try and identify some ways in which methods are different from each other. Here are our 'seven questions to ask' about any method you come across. Answers to them will help you to view methods in relation to each other:

1. What are the method's 'Big Ideas'? Many are based on a small number of central insights, which act as guiding inspiration. If you can identify these Big Ideas, you are well on the way to 'understanding' the method.
2. What are the theoretical underpinnings behind the method? In an ideal world, it would be supported by a view both of *language* and of *language learning*. This rarely happens. Sometimes just one of these – a view *either* of language *or* of language learning will be behind the method. Sometimes, shamefully, neither is there. As you read about the various methods in this chapter, try to relate them to the theories of language and language learning discussed earlier in this book.
3. How much 'engagement of the mind' does the method expect? As you will have gathered from Chapter 3, different learning theories have very different views about the role of the mind in learning. At one extreme is behaviourism, where the mind plays no part at all, and learning is viewed as habit formation. In mentalist views this is not true at all. A useful way of characterizing language-teaching methods is to identify how they stand in relation to this factor.
4. Is the method *deductive* or *inductive* in approach? Deductive learning is where the learner is first given a rule. These rules are then demonstrated working in practice. The sequence is from 'rule' to 'example', and the term RULEG is a useful way of remembering it. In the contrasting sequence, EGRUL, examples are first given, and the learner works out the rules for

herself. Often the rules are given at a last stage, and indeed are sometimes never explicitly stated at all. EGRUL is inductive learning.

5. Does the method allow use of the L1 in the classroom? Some methods shun this at all costs; 'the L1 must never be used, however desperate the struggle to communicate becomes' is a common dogma. In some others, you may find a major part of each lesson is given in the learners' L1, with the target language only making an occasional guest appearance. Sometimes the 'deductive versus inductive' question may determine this issue. A deductive method involves giving rules, and in practice this will often have to be done in the learners' L1. It is often not practicable to explain grammatical rules to a learner (particularly at the early learning stages) in the target language.

6. Which of the four skills are given emphasis in the method? The four skills are listening and speaking (the 'spoken' skills), reading and writing (the 'written' skills). Methods can differ dramatically as to where they place the emphasis. In some, learners do nothing but read and write; in others they do little other than listen and speak.

7. How much importance does the method give to 'authenticity of language'? In our survey, we shall see that there are methods which take great pains to make the language the learner is exposed to as 'realistic' as possible. In other methods, no effort at all is made in this direction.

Some of these points have already been covered in earlier portions of this book, and by its end all seven will have been given an airing. At this stage we want them just to give us a starting point on that path through the forest. We shall pick up the path back in the nineteenth century . . .

The grammar–translation method (GT)

GT has been mentioned before in this book. The first time was in Chapter 1's Classroom 2 in which English pupils were learning Italian using this method. Box 10.2 contains an example of a GT textbook used to teach that same language:

10.2   Learning Italian – an 'easy' method?!

Here is an example of part of a lesson taken from a grammar–translation textbook, Genzardi's *The English Tourist in Italy: A practical and easy method of learning and speaking Italian* (1910). When you look at this example, do not worry if you do not understand all the linguistic terminology used.

The lesson is about *Reflective Verbs* (*Verbi Riflessi*). It begins with a list of the various forms of the verb *to flatter – lusingare*. Here is the first list (of the <u>Indicative mood</u>):

I flatter myself	*io mi lusingo* or *mi lusingo*
thou flatterest thyself	*tu ti lusinghi* or *ti lusinghi*
he flatters himself	*egli si lusinga*
she flatters herself	*essa si lusinga* or *si lusinga*
we flatter ourselves	*noi ci lusinghiamo* or *ci lusinghiamo*
you flatter yourself or yourselves	*voi vi lusingate*
they flatter themselves	*essi si lusingano* or *si lusingano*

Other, more complex, tenses and forms follow. One of them, for example, is: *that you may have flattered yourself: – che voi vi siate lusingato.* There are also complex footnotes. One reads: *Reflective verbs in Italian are conjugated with a pronoun in the accusative, which, as well as the nominative, precedes the verb. The personal pronoun nominative may be omitted in Italian.*

The presentation of the verb forms is followed by a vocabulary list of 26 items, all of them reflective verbs, presumably to be learned by heart. Here are the first four items:

to complain	*lamentarsi*
to withdraw	*ritirarsi*
to wash one's self	*lavarsi*
to get up, rise	*alzarsi*

Then there are two translation exercises: the first from English to Italian, the second the other way round. More is said about these exercises in a moment, and box 10.3 below gives a longer example. To give you a taster of what they are like, here are the first few lines from the *Reflective Verbs* lesson:

He parted from his wife last year, when they were in Paris. At what o'clock shall you get up tomorrow? I shall get up early, because I have many things to do. I rejoice with you at your happiness. Get up soon, it is late; why did you not rise at six, as you promised me last night, before going to bed?

The next lesson then begins. It covers a different grammatical area.

Think about this example in relation to the 'seven questions to ask' introduced earlier in this chapter. The example will answer some, but not all, of these questions.

GT grew up in the early to mid nineteenth century. One of its Big Ideas is a sequence of classroom activities. The sequence starts with the statement of rule, often followed by a lengthy vocabulary list, intended to be learned by heart. Then there are translation exercises into and out of the target language. Most of these exercises involve the translation of single, or pairs of, sentences, with whole passages for translation reserved for the end of a course. Because this sequence of classroom events was associated with what happened in Prussian schools, in the US it was sometimes called the 'Prussian Method'. Two of the best-known figures associated with GT are

Karl Plötz (1819–81, a German who wrote textbooks for the teaching of French) and Heinrich Ollendorff (1803–65), who initially wrote courses teaching German to French speakers.

GT teaching could be dreadful. Howatt (1984: 136) vividly describes GT at its worst as 'a jungle of obscure rules, endless lists of gender classes and gender-class exceptions, self-conscious "literary" archaisms, snippets of philology, and a total loss of genuine feeling for the language'. We saw an example of GT approaching its low point in Chapter 8, where box 8.3 on page 118 illustrated the complex tangle of the Rev. Tiarks's German textbook (following what we jokingly called the 'Pain Is Good For You Method'). But Howatt also points out that not all GT teaching was as bad as this.

Here are some more of GT's Big Ideas. Many may have occurred to you when you considered box 10.2 above:

1. Despite Genzardi's claim about an 'easy method', GT is *hard*, and involves very much *engagement of the mind*. One reason is that modern languages were fighting to become accepted as subjects suitable for study within universities, and did not want to be seen as 'soft options' in comparison with Latin and Greek. Here is a remark, from a British University Commission Report for the year 1888, which indicates the kind of objections academics could raise against modern-language teaching. You can almost hear the snobbish sneer in the voice: 'the intellectual energy expended by the classical student was at least three times as great as that expended by the student of modern languages who attained the corresponding result'. One way for modern languages to prove their intellectual value to the world was to make the explanations difficult!

2. Despite Genzardi's claim about a 'practical method', GT aimed to develop intellectual discipline rather than a means for communication. This leads to what is perhaps its most obvious characteristic for the modern reader, the *lack of authenticity*. The sentences GT uses were specially concocted to contain particular grammar points that were being taught. It is not surprising that sentences like this should be very unreal. Here are two sample sentences from recent writers which make the point: *The philosopher pulled the lower jaw of the hen* (from Howatt 1984: 145), and *The merchant is swimming with the gardener's son, but the Dutchman has a fine gun* (from Roberts 1998: 153). Hardly sentences for everyday use.

3. GT concentrates on *sentence-level practice*. But the sentences are often put into question and answer sequences, sometimes strung together on the page as if they form a passage. The result is what Howatt (1984: 143) calls 'manic interrogation' sequences. You may feel that the example in box 10.2 shows this. Box 10. 3 overleaf illustrates it even more clearly. To savour the full effect, try reading the sentences aloud as if they made up a dialogue:

165

> ### 10.3 'Manic interrogation'
>
> This example is also taken from Genzardi (1910: 174):
>
> *I am ready, and you? Not yet, wait a moment, please. What do you study at school? I study history and geography, and my sisters study music and drawing. At what o'clock do you dine? Ordinarily we dine at five, but today we dine a little later, because we are waiting for our uncle, who will arrive from Naples. What do you admire in this landscape? I admire all in it. Do you play any instrument? I don't play at all. Do your sisters sing? They sing a little. Why do you blame your school-fellows? Because they are not diligent at school. What does it matter to you, if they are diligent or not at school or elsewhere? Mind your own business.*

4. GT lessons characteristically begin with a lengthy grammar explanation, followed by examples. The method is highly *deductive*, and the sequence is RULEG. As we have already suggested, deductive methods nearly always imply *use of the learners' L1*. GT relies particularly heavily on the L1, and the example in box 10.2 shows this. Indeed, with the explanations given in the L1 and the liberal use of translations, there would almost certainly be more L1 than FL in the grammar–translation classroom.

5. Genzardi's book is intended for tourists wanting to speak the language, but the focus in much GT teaching is on the *written, not the spoken, language*. This comes about partly because of the use of classical-language teaching as the model, because classical Latin and Greek only really exist as written languages. Another reason goes back to the important influence of the universities, where written and not spoken language was felt to be appropriate for academic study. Howatt (1984: 134) makes the point that even today there is a tendency for academics to look down on teaching the spoken language, as if it were just giving foreign travellers a kind of phrase book.

6. What you have read in Chapter 3 will enable you to place GT at the mentalist rather than the behaviourist end of the learning-theory spectrum. But the practitioners of GT did not base their ideas on any coherent learning theory. GT is really rather *atheoretical*.

Quousque Tandem?

Towards the end of the nineteenth century, a group of linguists with a keen interest in language teaching formed a society with the express aim of reforming FL teaching practice. The society was called *Quousque Tandem*, a Latin phrase meaning literally 'how long is all this going to go on for?' The 'all this' refers to GT.[1] The reforms that took place around this time resulted in various groups of methods which, although they differ from each other, also have much in common. We shall consider them together.

10.4   Asking 'the seven questions'

Read this section bearing in mind our 'seven questions to ask'. Answer as many of them as you can in relation to the various methods covered.

One group of methods call themselves 'natural'. We have already come across the use of this word in relation to Krashen and Terrell's 'Natural Approach', mentioned in Chapter 6. The word suggests that a method carries into FL teaching some aspect of 'natural', first language acquisition. Box 10.5 tells the story of one language-teaching personality of the time, the Frenchman François Gouin (1831–96). In his book *L'Art d'Enseigner et d'Étudier les Langues'* (1880), he described the experiences which led him to develop one type of 'natural' approach, which came to be called the 'Series Method'.

10.5   Gouin and the flour mill[2]

François Gouin went to Hamburg to learn German. Being an earnest person he took with him a grammar book which he first memorized, together with 248 irregular verbs. But he was downhearted when he failed to understand a lecture given in German at Hamburg University. Gouin then went through a series of increasingly demanding and desperate activities culminating in his memorizing an entire dictionary. But he was still unable to understand much German.

Gouin returned to France in the summer to discover that during his short absence his three-year-old nephew had succeeded in mastering the rudiments of French (his first language), in a 'natural' way, apparently without any intellectual effort at all. Gouin spent the summer observing his nephew. He was particularly impressed by a trip they made to a flour mill. While there, the boy asked myriad questions, but then at home he kept silent, as if digesting the experience. After a suitable period of 'digestion', the child then started recounting the experience time and time again to everyone he met, rather in the style of the Ancient Mariner.

Gouin was here observing first-language acquisition at work, and looking for clues about how to teach foreign languages. For him, there were two salient features. The first was the child's 'direct organization of experience in linguistic terms'. The objects the child saw at the flour mill, and the activities he watched, were all directly encoded into words and phrases. This contrasted with the way Gouin had attempted to learn German; for him it was more the 'indirect organization of experience through the medium of another language'. The second important feature was that the child recounted the events at the flour mill as a sequence of happenings. This feature led Gouin to a language-teaching method called the Series Method, in which classroom events are talked about in the order in which they happened. Gouin was indeed responsible for the following sort of sequence that one often finds in classrooms to this day:

Teacher [to Maria]:	*Maria, go and close the window.*
T [to another student]:	*What is Maria going to do?*
Student 1:	*She is going to close the window.*
T [to another student]:	*What is Maria doing?*
Student 2:	*She is closing the window.*
T [to another student]	*What has Maria just done?*
Student 3:	*She has just closed the window.*

Gouin's parable also captures the Big Idea associated with another group of methods developed at this time – the Direct Methods. There is more than one Direct Method, but the best known is associated with a German who went to live in America in the 1870s. His name was Maximilian Delphinius Berlitz, and his method is still used in many places today, with many cities of the world still boasting their own 'Berlitz school'.

The Big Idea behind the Direct Methods lies in Gouin's notion of the 'direct organization of experience in linguistic terms'. A central characteristic of GT was that it approached the FL entirely through the L1. To illustrate the important difference between GT and Direct Methods in this respect, consider how a native speaker of English might learn a word like the French *maison*, meaning 'house'. In a GT course, the word in French would be approached 'through' the English word *house*. The association built up in the learner's mind (through translation exercises and by other means) would be between the words *house* and *maison*. This association is illustrated on the left-hand side of the diagram below. What the Direct Method teachers wanted was for a direct association to be made between the *object* (a house) and the French word *maison*, so that the learner 'experienced' the object as a *maison*. A *maison* would, in other words, come to be not the French word for *house*, but an object that people live in, with walls, windows and a roof. This direct association is shown on the right-hand side of the diagram:

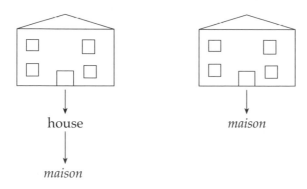

So while GT liberally uses the L1, Direct Methods avoid it altogether. This inevitably leads to two further features of the Direct Methods. The first is adherence to the 'here and now principle' we discussed in Chapter 5 (p. 81). With the L1 being avoided, teachers find it natural, even necessary, to concentrate on immediate surroundings in order to create comprehensible input. The problem for the Direct Method teacher comes when she has to talk about notions that take her beyond the here and now, and this leads some to say that Direct Methods are easy to use at the beginning stages but become more difficult as time goes on. The second feature of Direct Methods is that because they avoid use of the learner's L1, they are almost forced into being inductive rather than deductive. While GT was firmly RULEG, the natural and direct methods were equally firmly EGRUL. One of the guiding principles of the International Phonetic Association, an organization set up at around this time that was highly interested in language-teaching matters, was that 'in the early stages grammar should be taught inductively . . . A more systematic study of grammar should be postponed to the advanced stages of the course' (Stern 1983: 89).

Howatt (1984) calls Gouin and those like him 'individual reformers'. They were inspired individuals working alone. But as the setting up of the *Quousque Tandem* society indicates, there was a 'reform movement' which offered more organized resistance to GT. The movers and shakers were scholars who shared an interest in both language teaching and linguistics. Some of the important names are: Henry Sweet (British, 1845–1912), Otto Jespersen (Danish, 1860–1943), Harold Palmer (British, 1877–1949) and Wilhelm Viëtor (German, 1850–1918).

A major aspect of the reformers' work was to place emphasis on the teaching of the spoken language. This shift away from GT's emphasis on writing largely reflects the interests of reformers like Henry Sweet. As you will see in box 10.6 overleaf, he was a phonetician. Indeed, according to one writer at least, he 'taught phonetics to Europe'. One of his central axioms was that 'all study of language, whether theoretical or practical, ought to be based on the spoken language' (Sweet 1899/1964: 49). 'Most grammarians tacitly assume', he grumbles, 'that the spoken is a mere corruption of the literary language. But the exact contrary is the case: it is the spoken which is the real source of the literary language.' With views like this, it is natural that Sweet should advocate an emphasis on teaching the spoken language.

A further aspect of GT which linguists like Sweet reacted against was the important role given to the classical languages, particularly as the basis for analysis of modern languages. Sweet could get quite heated (and amusing) on this topic. He makes mention of a certain Professor Zupita in Berlin who, his supportive colleagues claimed, was not at all old-fashioned, and did not share the reverence for dead languages that GT exhibits. To demonstrate the professor's enlightened, modern attitudes, his chums point to the fact that he actually lectures on contemporary poems like Shelley's *Prometheus*

10.6 Henry Sweet – The Professor Higgins of *My Fair Lady*?

Henry Sweet was born in London in 1845. As a child he suffered from various physical defects, including extreme short-sightedness which made learning to read very difficult. He overcame these difficulties and went to study at Oxford. He spent most of his time there following his own academic interests, not those he should have been following, and as a result he left the university with a fourth-class degree (the lowest possible pass). Over the next few years he developed an interest in phonetics. According to C. T. Onions (1927: 519), 'he taught phonetics to Europe; he must, indeed, be considered to be the founder of modern phonetics'.

The great sadness of his life was that he never managed to become a professor, despite his obvious qualifications. The worst blow of all was when he failed to get the chair of comparative philology at Oxford. He did work as an academic in Oxford, but his disappointment over the chair made him very bitter. Bernard Shaw tells the story of how he persuaded the editor of a leading monthly review to commission a paper from Sweet on the importance of phonetics. 'When it arrived', Shaw (1916) says, 'it contained nothing but a savagely derisive attack on a professor of language and literature whose chair Sweet regarded as proper to a phonetic expert only. The article, being libellous, had to be returned as impossible.' Shaw also reports that in his appearance and behaviour, Sweet became 'a sort of walking repudiation of Oxford in all its traditions'. But along with the difficult aspects of his personality there was also a sense of humour. For example, he contemptuously described the Pitman system of shorthand as the 'Pitfall system'.

Bernard Shaw's play *Pygmalion* (popularized as the film *My Fair Lady*) includes a phonetician, Professor Higgins, who tries to teach the Cockney flower girl, Liza Doolittle, to speak 'proper' English. Shaw's Preface to the play is entitled 'A Professor of Phonetics' and is largely about Henry Sweet. 'Pygmalion Higgins', Shaw says (1916: 102) 'is not a portrait of Sweet . . . still, as will be seen, there are touches of Sweet in the play.'

Sweet's interest in phonetics was not at all confined to the theoretical. His 1899 book, *The Practical Study of Languages* was highly influential in the development of twentieth-century language-teaching methods, and was reprinted in 1964.

Unbound. But, Sweet says, investigations into Professor Zupita's lectures revealed that what he actually did was to get his students to translate *Prometheus Unbound* into Anglo-Saxon. So much for his modernism! In relation to language teaching, Sweet is devastatingly clear (1899/1964: 229):

The reader may be reminded once more that the question whether the study of dead or of modern languages affords the best training for the mind is one which has nothing to do with the question: Which is the best way of learning languages? The only question we have to deal with is whether the extension of the old methods of studying dead languages to the study of living languages would make the acquisition of the latter easier. Our answer to this question must be an unhesitating negative.

Another essential characteristic of the reformer linguists, including Sweet, was that they wanted to place FL teaching on a more theoretical footing, to sweep away the 'atheoretical' basis of GT. They were indeed language theoreticians with an interest in language teaching, and the theoretical footing on which they tried to place language teaching was related to the emerging science of speech sounds (phonetics). We shall see more clearly in the next section where this desire led.

A tool which became very important to the applied linguist's armoury is associated with the reformers, particularly the linguists Jespersen and Palmer (though it is not historically true to say that they 'invented' it). This tool is the <u>sentence pattern</u>. These patterns are characteristic sentence types associated with grammatical structures. As examples, here are some sentence patterns for the structure 'present tense of the verb BE'. These examples use the idea of the Noun Phrase. This is a group of words centred round a noun. A Noun Phrase may be one word (e.g. *dogs*) or more (*the dogs, the big dogs, the big ugly dogs*):

This is a + Noun Phrase
Is this a + Noun Phrase?
This isn't a + Noun Phrase

When an FL programme designer is preparing for teaching, she might first write a list of the structures to be taught, and one item might well be 'the present tense of the verb BE'. When it comes to the actual preparation of lessons, she will find that she needs to divide each structure up into a number of patterns, like the ones above. Sentence patterns are the building blocks of much teaching, not just in the Direct Methods. They became of central importance as a way of dividing grammar up into small segments for teaching purposes. This is the area of syllabus design, which we shall look at in detail in Chapter 12.

Audio-lingualism

Across the Atlantic now, to look at a method which, though it shares many characteristics with the reform methods, nevertheless has a clear identity of its own. It is called audio-lingualism (AL). We saw AL in action in Chapter 1's Classroom 4.

Practical need was the starting point for AL. Towards the end of the Second World War the Americans were deploying soldiers in different parts of the globe, especially in South-East Asia. The soldiers needed to learn languages, and this simple fact involved the Army Specialized Training Program (ASTP, started in 1943) in an exciting and unique language-teaching experiment. There were two new and important ingredients in the situation. The first was the sheer number of learners involved. According to Howatt (1984: 267) as many as 15,000 soldiers were enrolled, and this posed applied linguistics with a new set of logistical problems. The second element concerns the languages being taught; they were not the usual few 'run-of-the-mill' languages like French and German. There were 27 in all, and these included South-East Asian languages like Japanese and Korean – languages which North Americans and Europeans might describe as 'exotic' (a term which native speakers of Japanese and Korean might equally legitimately use to describe European tongues). From the teaching point of view these languages posed problems which more well-trodden languages – with their many published grammars and well-studied syntactic systems – did not pose. For students also the task was daunting, because exotic languages confront English-speaking learners with difficulties not encountered in languages more closely related to their own. Out of the ASTP emerged what is sometimes called the 'GI Method'; and out of that developed audio-lingualism.

In its early, heady days, two claims were made for AL – that it was 'scientific' and 'new'. We have already seen, in Chapter 3, that there is some justification for the first claim, because AL based itself on a combination of the new 'science of language' (structuralism) and the 'science of behaviour' (behaviourism). These two areas of scientific enquiry did indeed provide AL with theoretical underpinnings. The claim to newness is less justified, and the method owes much to what the reformers like Sweet and Jespersen were doing long before.

What does AL teaching look like? In box 10.7 is an example of part of a lesson.[3] It deals with two sentence patterns: HAVE + just + -ed, and HAVE + not + -ed + yet. Notice this way of describing sentence patterns. HAVE is written in small capitals to show that we are talking about the verb as a whole, including all its constituent forms (has, have and others). -ed is here a shorthand way of referring to the past participle of verbs, which usually end in -ed (e.g. worked, wanted).

What are AL's central characteristics? Rivers (1964), an important book on AL, lists six:

1. **Primacy of Speech**. We have already seen that linguists like Sweet gave importance to speech over writing. AL regards speech as 'primary' partly because it is the first medium the L1 child masters. Speech comes first and writing follows on. Over time AL developed firm views about the order in which the four skills should be introduced. It was believed that the

10.7 Picking up pens, opening doors, reading books...

Objectives: to teach the present perfect tense, with *just* and *yet*. Some examples:

I have just picked up the pen.   *I haven't picked up the pen yet.*
She has just opened the door.   *She hasn't opened the door yet.*
They have just read the book.   *They haven't read the book yet.*

Step 1   Demonstrating the sentence pattern HAVE + just + -ed
Actions are done in front of the class, sometimes by the teacher and sometimes by a pupil. For example, the teacher picks up a pen and says *I have just picked up the pen.* Then a pupil opens the door and the teacher says *She has just opened the door.*

Step 2   Practising HAVE + just + -ed
(a) **Drill**   Pupils form sentences from a table:

I We They He/she You	(to have)	just	(to close) the window (to switch on) the light (to play) football (to walk) home

(b) **Drill**   The teacher says sentences like the ones on the left below. Chosen pupils make HAVE + just + -ed sentences (as in the example on the right):

She's closing the window.   *She's just closed the window.*
She's going to switch on the light.
They will play football.

Step 3   Demonstrating and practising HAVE + not + -ed + yet
(a) **Demonstration**   Show a diary for the day:

7.30	get up	10.00	phone Bill
8.00	wash	12.00	visit Jane (for lunch)
9.00	eat breakfast	2.00	take dog for walk

Teacher says:

It's 8.30. I'm late. I haven't washed yet.
It's 9.30. Mary's late. She hasn't eaten breakfast yet.

(b) Drill Pupils form sentences from the table:

I			John	
		(to eat)		
We			the dog for a walk	
		(to phone)		
They	(to have) not		dinner	yet
		(to visit)		
He/she			Mary	
		(to take)		
You				

This is only part of a lesson. Think of what is needed to finish it (you can set 'homework' if you wish).

Think about this lesson in relation to our 'seven questions to ask' (on p. 162).

so-called receptive skills (listening and reading) should be approached before the corresponding productive ones (speaking and writing). Add this to the primacy of speech idea and you have the order: listening – speaking – reading – writing. This view is found most explicitly in textbooks like Alexander (1968), where the claim is that 'nothing will be spoken before it has been heard', and 'nothing will be written before it has been read' (p. xi).

2. **Stimulus–Response–Reinforcement (S–R–R) Model**. In Chapter 3 we saw that in behaviourism learning was regarded as the development of stimulus–response associations. Giving rewards (reinforcement) is important to the development of these associations – recall how Skinner's pigeons were rewarded ('reinforced') by food when they pushed the table-tennis ball in the right direction. Food pellets do not generally motivate language learners, but the S–R–R model did make its way into language teaching. In your own language-learning experience, you may have come across the kind of 'four-phase drill' shown in box 10.8.

3. **Habit formation through repetition**. Straight behaviourism, again. Here is a quotation from an evangelical advocate of AL, Nelson Brooks (1960: 142): 'the single paramount fact about language learning is that it concerns not problem-solving but the formation and performance of habits'.

4. **Incrementalism**. We also saw in Chapter 3 (p. 42) that to teach a complex behaviour (like table-tennis for pigeons), you divide the behaviour into pieces and *shape* it. The word incrementalism is used in this respect, 'incremental' meaning 'building up'. In language-teaching terms shaping involves dividing the language into structures and then into sentence patterns. You then teach the patterns one by one, only moving to the

10.8 Food pellets for language learning

In the four-phase language laboratory drill, a disembodied voice on tape says a cue word. The listening student puts the word in a sentence, following a given model. The correct answer is then given, and the sequence concludes with the student repeating this:

Disembodied voice:	*Table*	(1)
Student:	*This is a table.*	(2)
Disembodied voice:	*This is a table.*	(3)
Student:	*This is a table.*	(4)

(1) is the stimulus and (2) the response. In the example above the student response is correct, hence (3) has an element of reinforcement or reward to it; the pleasure of getting something right acts as a mental food pellet. In (4) the student has the further pleasure of repeating the right answer.

next when the previous one has been mastered. An important reason for teaching in small bits is to avoid errors. In behaviourism 'practice makes permanent' and errors performed might become engrained.

5. **Contrastive linguistics**. As we saw in Chapter 4, the behaviourist view of habits was that negative transfer, or interference, could occur from one language to another, and that this would prove troublesome for the learner. Heavy reliance was placed on contrastive linguistics to identify trouble spots.

6. **Inductive learning**. Because learning is a question of habit formation rather than problem-solving, explanation (when it does occur) is always a final stage. As Politzer (1961: 5, a strong advocate of audio-lingualism) has it: 'rules ought to be summaries of behaviours'. AL is clearly EGRUL, not RULEG.

AL was extremely widespread throughout the world up to the 1960s. It was often supported with great enthusiasm. As Cioffari (1962: 65, cited in Rivers 1964: 10) complains: 'small groups enthused with missionary zeal . . . have come to feel that they alone have the secret formula for bringing about improvement in the profession'.

What happened to AL after the beginning of the 1960s? It certainly did not die anything like a complete death, and teaching of the sort we saw in Chapter 1's Classroom 4 still continues in many places today. But two developments dampened the 'missionary zeal' mentioned above.

The first of these developments was research looking at the effectiveness of AL teaching. One of the hallmarks of the 1960s in applied linguistics was the number of large-scale research projects which involved comparing methods. These projects usually entailed teaching two competing methods in a number of classes over a long time, and then comparing the results through tests on student achievement. The hope was that research like this would answer the question it is perhaps natural for us all to ask: 'what is the "best" method for teaching languages?' Probably the best-known of these experiments involved comparing AL with a method known as *cognitive code*, already briefly mentioned on page 121. This was really a version of GT, and in fact Carroll 1966: 102 calls it 'up-to-date grammar translation theory'. The experiment is described in box 10.9.

10.9 Dampening the missionary's zeal

The experiment Scherer and Wertheimer (1964) describe compared the results of a lengthy period of AL teaching with a similar period of cognitive code teaching. The students were learning German at the University of Colorado. It was an experiment beset with many difficulties, and is indeed often quoted as an example of how *not* to do applied linguistic research. A main difficulty was the sheer size of the experiment and the impossibility of controlling all the variables. In terms of results, these were rather inconclusive, and certainly undramatic. The cognitive code group fared better at reading and writing, while the AL group were better in speaking and listening. It is often said that the major effect of the experiment was to quash the missionary zeal of AL supporters. If AL were indeed so vastly superior to any other method, one would expect this to shine through, whatever shortcomings there were in the experiment.

The second reason for dampened missionary zeal was that, as we saw in Chapter 3, Chomsky's views on language and language learning dealt a devastating blow to AL's theoretical underpinnings – behaviourism and structural linguistics. Without these supports, AL found it difficult to stand.

But what did Chomsky suggest replacing the discredited method with? On one level the answer is an anti-climactic 'nothing'. This is because Chomsky is the first to recognize that care is needed when applying the findings of linguistics to language-teaching matters. Here is what he says in Chomsky (1966: 52): 'I am, frankly, rather sceptical about the significance, for the teaching of languages, of such insights and understanding as have been attained in linguistics . . .' But, on another level, Chomsky's ideas had a very profound, though indirect, influence on language teaching. Arguably the time of greatest influence of these ideas is in the present. But an influence was first felt in the 1960s when his ideas were new. We shall consider this influence now.

Oiling a rusty LAD

Chomsky, as we saw in Chapter 3, credits the 'organism' (as opposed to the 'environment') with the major part of the work of L1 acquisition, achieved by means of LAD. The concept of an innate LAD was a powerful one in first language acquisition studies. But there was an apparent restriction on the use of the idea for foreign-language learning; namely that the life of LAD seems rather short. Like various biologically endowed mechanisms, LAD seems to have a 'critical period' – a time when it is called on to do its job, does it, then disappears from the scene. An enlightening metaphor might be to compare it to the stage of a rocket going into space. When a certain stage has done its job, it falls away and burns up. In the heady days of Chomsky and TG, there was much research and argument to show that the stage at which LAD falls away is around puberty (though research since then has suggested a much earlier age). Evidence comes from the study of (among other things) the way that certain brain malfunctions affect language before and after puberty. For example, if a child before puberty has a stroke and loses power of speech, there is a good prognosis for recovery, because LAD is still operating. A stroke after puberty is a far more serious affair, because LAD seems no longer able to do the job of restoring language.

Why cannot LAD be used for foreign-language acquisition? One might be able to argue that it can, as long as the acquisition takes place before puberty, before the LAD rocket stage has fallen off and burned up. But the clear and devastating argument against the use of LAD for foreign-language learning is that it cannot help in the very situation which is predominant in the FL field – language learning after puberty. Or is the argument so devastating? What happens if we change our metaphor and view LAD not as a rocket stage falling away but as a piece of machinery that, having done its job, has fallen into disuse and simply 'gone rusty'? If this is the case, then perhaps there is some way in which we can 'oil' LAD back into operation for the purpose of foreign-language learning.

How do you oil a rusty LAD? Three suggestions were put forward in the 1960s, two of them relatively minor in terms of their immediate impact on language-teaching practice (though much more major if you look forward to more recent times). One of the minor approaches was called the 'cognitive anti-method'. This is associated with the applied linguists Newmark and Reibel, whose 1968 paper is described in box 10.10 overleaf.

The second proposal for oiling LAD is related. In another two influential articles (1966 and 1971), Newmark develops what can be called a minimal strategy. He argues that language-teaching professionals conventionally do too much work. In their preparation for teaching they analyse the language into sentence patterns, chopping the language up into little pieces to make it more digestible for the learner. Then they produce complex programmes laying down what language items will be introduced in what order. But

10.10   How to oil a rusty LAD: Method 1

Newmark and Reibel begin their 1968 paper with the idea that L1 and FL learning are not substantially different. They do this by taking arguments that first and foreign-language learning *are* different, and arguing against them. For example: some claim that the child has much more time to learn the L1, than the FL student who perhaps learns for only a few hours a week. Newmark and Reibel counterargue by looking at how many other important and time-consuming things the child is doing at the same time – not only learning language, but concurrently developing on many different cognitive and physical levels.

Having dismissed a number of arguments in this way, they conclude that L1 and FL learning are comparable. They then observe that we already have a highly successful way of 'teaching' children their L1, evidenced by the fact that all normal children succeed in learning it. Why then do we not use this 'way of teaching' for an FL, rather that replacing it with 'unnatural' methods that have a very poor success rate? It is a mistake, in short, to give up a way of teaching which we *know* works for children, for one which *might* work for adults. We should instead try somehow to recreate in the FL classroom what happens for L1 learning. LAD will then do its work.

For Newmark and Reibel an important feature of the L1 situation is that the language the child receives is 'structurally random'. In conventional FL teaching there is usually finely tuned structural control. This means that in the lesson the teacher restricts her language to those grammar items she knows the learners are familiar with. As we saw in Chapter 5, caretaker talk is not finely tuned in the same way, and in this sense it is 'structurally random'.

Newmark and Reibel's arguments lead them away from the rigidly controlled grammatical teaching of AL, towards a loosening of the grammatical reins in the FL classroom. As Newmark says elsewhere (1963: 217): 'the whole question of the utility of grammatical analysis for language teaching needs to be reopened'. The very idea must have come as a shock in a language-teaching world still dominated by AL. Their suggestion is that structurally organized teaching should be replaced by 'situationally organized teaching'. This leads them to propose a version of the situational syllabus, something we shall consider in the next section.

why? All this, Newmark argues, simply serves to come between the learner and the language. If LAD can be oiled back into service, it is quite capable of working out ('analysing') the language for itself. Teachers should adopt a minimal strategy, restricting themselves to what caretakers do: providing roughly tuned input for LAD to work on. The title of Newmark (1966) says it all. It is *How not to interfere with language learning*.

These two 1960s proposals for oiling LAD were relatively minor in terms of immediate impact. The third was more substantial. It is the immersion teaching (or bilingual education as it is often called) which we have come across on various occasions. One aspect (possibly the most important) of this approach is that the main focus of attention in the teaching is not on language but on the other subjects in the curricula that are being taught *through* the FL. Language is acquired in an almost 'incidental' way; or, to put it in terms also used earlier in this book, there is high message-focus and low form-focus. Yet another way of expressing the same idea is to say that bilingual education involves a programme or syllabus expressed in 'other-than-linguistic' terms. If, as one of the concerned parents described in box 8.4 (p. 120), you asked to see the programme being followed by your child in the immersion programme, the piece of paper you received would not list sentence patterns nor any other language-related items. What it would list would be the topics to be covered under the subject headings – history, geography and so on. The phrase 'syllabus in other-than-linguistic terms' well captures the incidental nature of language learning in bilingual education.

These ideas, and the terminology associated with them, will resurface later in the chapter. Meanwhile we cross the Atlantic again, to consider some developments in Europe. The first involves an idea that was briefly mentioned in box 10.10 above – that of the 'situational syllabus'.

Situational and audio-visual language teaching

John Rupert Firth, who died in 1960 at the age of seventy, was Professor of General Linguistics at the University of London. One of his important ideas was the notion of 'context of situation' and the belief that the meaning of utterances is determined by the social setting in which they occur. This led Firth, and other European linguists, to advocate studying language in relation to the context in which it is being used. This social perspective differs from Chomsky's more psychological one, which tended to look at sentences divorced from their context. The emphasis on context in British and European linguistics led to two developments in language teaching.

The first development concerns syllabus design, the central topic of Chapter 12. A syllabus is a kind of organizational programme, a plan for teaching. By far the most common way of organizing teaching programmes is in terms of grammatical structures. As we shall see in Chapter 12, a structural syllabus is a programme plan stating which grammatical structures will be taught when. It leads to the sort of teaching in which a group of sentence patterns are covered in each lesson. The structural syllabus is found in AL, direct methods, and many other kinds of teaching.

One alternative to the structural syllabus is the <u>situational syllabus</u>. In this, the programme is stated in terms of situations, so that each lesson deals with the language associated with a different situation. Box 10.11 illustrates. Of course, books with situational syllabuses are also organized with grammar in mind. But the structural tuning tends to be rougher, and certainly not nearly so fine as in AL teaching.

10.11   Tourist haunts

Here are the names of some lessons ('units') from a situationally organized book intended for learners of English visiting Britain (Ockenden 1972):

On a bus	At a hotel
At a railway station	At a bank
At a garage	At a chemist's shop

A main justification for the situational syllabus comes from linguists like Firth. Language, the reasoning goes, is best learned and remembered when presented in contextual settings. Hence, in the 1950s particularly, some teaching materials use this format. It constitutes a minor revolution in syllabus design.

The second effect of the 'context of situation' notion was a method known as audio-visualism (AV). In many ways AV bears the hallmarks of other methods we have considered, particularly AL and the direct methods. It carries, for example, the primacy of speech element associated with AL. The new element relates to the notion of 'context of situation'. This method attempts to make language memorable not just by presenting it in context, but by making the context as 'vivid' as possible through the use of visual aids. Typically in AV tape and film strip are used. A dialogue is practised first without text but with accompanying visual aids so that a vivid connection is made between language and picture. Dialogues are often learned by heart, and then the language in them is expanded into new situations. Box 10.12 illustrates.

There are various versions of audio-visualism. The best known was first developed at CREDIF, the Centre de Recherche et d'Etude pour la Diffusion de Français, at Saint-Cloud near Paris. One of the method's leading proponents, Guberina, calls the movement 'structuroglobal'. The 'structuro' part indicates a connection with structural linguistics (and a similarity with AL). The word 'global' is added to indicate (in the words of van Els *et al.* 1984: 154) that 'every structure should be viewed as embedded in a situation of language use'. AV and situational teaching tend to be rather inductive because the context is intended to play an important role in determining the meaning.

10.12   The trouble with bikes

Here are two pages from *English for Children: Book 1* by Wild-Bicanic *et al.*, which describes the method it uses as 'audio-visual global and structural' (this name is explained above). The book is intended for young children learning English.

GOING TO SCHOOL

Hurry up, Betty!
Hurry up, Dick!

Are you ready?

Yes, Daddy, we're coming.

What's the time?

It's quarter to 9.

You're late for school this morning.

Come on, Dick. Here's your coat.

Have you got a hanky in your pocket, Dick?

No, I haven't.

Here's one.

Hurry up! You haven't got much time.

Wait a minute, Dad! We're coming.

Aren't you going by bike, Steve?

No, my bike's got a puncture.

I'm going by bus with you.

There's the bus. Run, children, run!

QUESTIONS AND ANSWERS

1. **Where're the children going?** — They're going to school.
2. **Are they late for school this morning?** — Yes, they are.
3. **What's the time?** — It's quarter to nine.
4. **Has Dick got a hanky in his pocket?** — No, he hasn't.
5. **Why isn't Steve going by bike?** — His bike's got a puncture.
6. **Who's he going with?** — He's going with his Dad.
7. **Are Betty and Dick going with them?** — Yes, they are.
8. **How're they going?** — By bus.
9. **Why must they run?** — Because it's late.

Notional/functional/communicative

In Chapter 3 we saw how, in the early 1970s, a 'sociolinguistic revolution' took place, where the emphasis given in linguistics to grammar was replaced by an interest in 'language in use'. Hymes's (1970) paper 'On communicative competence' was mentioned, with its exploration of the notion of 'the appropriate' as a dimension important in language studies.

The sociolinguistic revolution had a great effect on language teaching. To understand this effect, we shall return to a paper mentioned before – Newmark (1966). In it, Newmark expresses the discontent which language teachers were feeling towards the structurally oriented AL teaching of that time. The result of this teaching, Newmark says, is the student who may be entirely 'structurally competent', yet who is unable to perform even the simplest communicative task. This type of student will know her grammar well, and be able to produce structurally correct sentences without problems. But deposit her at an airport in the target-language country, and she may not know how to ask for a taxi, or request simple services. Newmark's amusing example of the 'structurally competent' but 'communicatively incompetent' student is the one who wants to ask for a light from a stranger in the street. There are various sentences that she might use, and Newmark suggest three. Notice that, although these sentences are entirely inappropriate, and would never be used by a native speaker, they are nevertheless perfectly grammatically correct. They are: *Have you fire?*, *Do you have illumination?* and *Are you a match's owner?*

What is the solution to the problem of the structurally competent but communicatively incompetent student? One answer (though not in fact the one explored by Newmark) is related to the field of syllabus design, and is associated with the work of an organization known as the Council of Europe. This organization has as part of its brief the unenviable task of fostering cooperation among member states in Western Europe (a little like trying to herd cats perhaps). In the early 1970s their Council for Cultural Cooperation brought together a team of language-teaching experts to look at the possibility of developing language-teaching systems for the teaching of all member-state languages. The team confronted the sociolinguistic complaints of those such as Hymes, and was responsible for the development of a type of syllabus which aimed to cater for the teaching of language in use – of communicative competence. In his 1973 paper, one member of the team, Wilkins, developed categories which might be used for a new type of syllabus oriented towards communicative competence. The two most important of these categories are illustrated in box 10.13.

10.13 New categories for new syllabuses

Here are some examples of Wilkins's two main category types. Can you see how these category types differ? Attempt to describe each and say what sort of 'item' each contains.

Category Type 1	Category Type 2
past time	greeting
frequency	inviting
dimension	making plans
location	expressing gratitude
quantity	complaining

Decide whether each of the following is a Type 1 or Type 2 category:

introducing yourself   possibility   futurity   asking for information

---

Wilkins called Category Type 1 above 'semantico-grammatical' and Type 2 'categories of communicative function'. Semantico-grammatical categories, or <u>notions</u> as they came to be almost universally called, are what one might in everyday English describe as 'concepts'. The functional categories, or functions, are what in everyday English we might call 'uses' of the language, and have something in common with the concept of 'speech acts' introduced at the end of Chapter 3 (p. 55). 'Possibility' and 'futurity' in box 10.13 are notions; 'introducing yourself' and 'asking for information' are functions.

The thinking behind the Council of Europe's work was that notions and functions would form the basis for syllabuses that listed these, rather than (initially at least) grammatical structures. This in turn would lead to a type of teaching in which each lesson would deal not with a structure, but with a concept or use. Box 10.14 gives an example of a 'functional' textbook.

10.14 What a functionally organized textbook looks like

Here is part of the contents page from a functionally organized textbook, Johnson and Morrow (1979). This shows what functional areas will be covered in the first nine teaching units:

1. Talking about yourself
2. Meeting people
3. Asking about things
4. Asking for things
5. Inviting
6. Making arrangements
7. Asking the way
8. Asking for help
9. Asking for permission

In which unit might Newmark's 'asking for a light' be covered?

It may well be that Unit 4 in the above, 'Asking for things' (or 'requesting services' as it might be called more formally) would cover the function of 'asking for a light'. The syllabus as a whole shows how Newmark's problem might be solved. It provides, in effect, a vehicle for teaching students how to 'be appropriate'; how to be communicatively competent. The development of the notional/functional syllabus had quite a dramatic effect on language-teaching syllabuses in the 1970s, and a large number of textbooks in the seventies and eighties are based on notional/functional syllabuses. We shall look in more detail at this syllabus type in Chapter 12.

The sociolinguistic revolution also left its mark on classroom techniques or 'methodology', and contributed significantly to what is commonly called *communicative methodology*. Part of that methodology came about as a consequence of the new syllabus types. It may sound odd to suggest that syllabuses should affect techniques – after all, you might say, syllabuses deal with the *what* of language teaching, and techniques with the *how*. But actually *how* and *what* can be intimately connected in language teaching. Consider the portion of a functional syllabus in box 10.14 for example. Unit 5 covers 'Inviting'. How can you practise 'inviting' in the classroom? Drills of the sort associated with AL can play a part. But quite soon you are going to have to say to your students: *Pretend that you are not in a classroom at all, but are walking down a street. You meet a friend you haven't seen for a long time. You want to invite him out for a meal. What do you say?* The exercise type you are involved in here is known as <u>role play</u>. In role-play exercises, students act out parts in a small-scale 'drama' specifically set up to practise chosen functions. Role play became an important technique in communicative methodology, almost as a direct result of notional/functional syllabuses and the aspects of language they focus on.

But it is possible to relate aspects of communicative methodology back to the sociolinguistic revolution in more general terms than this. Hymes attacked Chomsky for having an over-restricted view of linguistics. Look back to box 3.10 (p. 52) to remind yourself of how Hymes attempted to elaborate and enrich linguistics by adding extra dimensions to the notion of language competence. A similar point about over-restriction may be made in relation to language-teaching methodology. In the 1960s language teaching was concerned with a restricted range of skills. The most pervasive of these was the 'skill of being grammatical', which (as we saw in box 10.7, p. 173) methods like AL prized above all others.

One way of viewing what has occurred since then is in terms of development and enrichment. We shall pursue this theme fully in Chapters 13 and 14, but one example will be given now. It relates to the area of reading comprehension.

Not so long ago, reading exercises involved going line by line though a text, dwelling on the meaning of every word and structure until 100 per cent comprehension was achieved. The exercise in box 10.15 is not like this at all. The student has to read the guidebook description and follow the route on the map provided. To do this successfully, she will *not* have to understand every word of the text. Indeed, there will be very many difficult words that the learner can simply ignore. This is acceptable to modern eyes because we realize that in real life 100 per cent comprehension is rarely required. In fact, what the learner *does* need to be able to do in real life is to concentrate on extracting important pieces of information, ignoring other less important parts of the message, and not worrying too much about difficult words that are not relevant to the task in hand. The '100 per cent comprehension' school is actually a hindrance here, and in fact it prevents the learner from developing these skills. Exercises like the one in box 10.15 represent a significant development and enrichment of our idea of what skills are involved in language use.

Language-teaching theorists can use various questions as their starting point for the development of teaching procedures. A common one is 'what is language?', and we have seen in this section that the changing perception

---

10.15 A short tour round Oxford *from Functional English 1: Consolidation* by R. V. White (1979)

The exercise below (from White 1979) practises reading comprehension. The instructions to the student have been left out. What do you think the exercise involves doing? What is the student expected to do?[4]

Short Tour: 1 hour

Begin at Queen's College (39) *on the* **HIGH STREET**. The entrance to Queen's College opens onto the High Street. In style, the buildings of the college are neo-classical and contrast with those of nearby St Edmund Hall, founded in the 13th century. From Queen's, walk up Queen's Lane and turn right into the quadrangle of St Edmund Hall (48), the only remaining medieval hall at Oxford. The domestic scale of the buildings is of interest, giving us some idea of what the original colleges were like.

From St Edmund Hall, *continue along* **QUEEN'S LANE**, noting the ancient church, recently restored and now used as a library, to the right. Follow Queen's Lane where it turns left, passing between Queen's and New Colleges. A the junction of Queen's and New College Lanes, continue straight ahead and turn right into the entrance of New College (31). This college was new in the 14th century when it was founded by William of Wykeham, Bishop of Winchester. The college quadrangle is particularly handsome, while the chapel is one of the finest in Oxford.

From New College, *walk straight along* **NEW COLLEGE LANE** *to the junction with* **CATTE STREET**. At the junction, turn left and cross the street to the Bodleian Library (4), which is open to visitors from 9 to 5 on weekdays. This library, which houses more than 2,500,000 books, is one of the finest in the world. Originally founded by Humphrey, Duke of Gloucester, in 1444, it was restored and assisted by Thomas Bodley, an Elizabethan diplomat, in the late 16th century. Since that time, the Bodleian has received a copy of every book published in England.

From the Bodleian, *continue down* **CATTE STREET**, passing the Radcliffe Camera (40) on the right. This neo-classical building was built in 1737, and provides reading rooms for the Bodleian library. It is not open to visitors. The Radcliffe Camera stands in the middle of Radcliffe Square, with the Bodleian library at one end and the church of St Mary the Virgin (52) at the other, while Brasenose (6) and All Souls' Colleges stand on either side.

Continue down **CATTE STREET**, with the church to the right. A fine view of Oxford can be obtained from the tower, which is open to visitors. At the end of Catte Street, turn left into the High Street. Pass the entrance to All Souls' College to the left. There is a 15th century chapel at All Souls with beautiful stained glass. The twin towers of All Souls' College are a prominent Oxford landmark. They were designed by Nicholas Hawksmoor, a pupil of Christopher Wren. *Walk down the* **HIGH STREET** *as far as Queen's College where the tour started.*

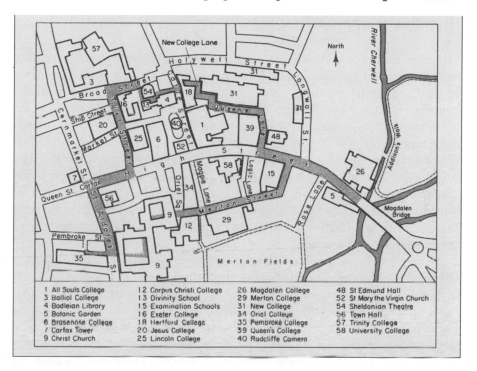

1 All Souls College	12 Corpus Christi College	26 Magdalen College	48 St Edmund Hall
3 Balliol College	13 Divinity School	29 Merton College	52 St Mary the Virgin Church
4 Bodleian Library	15 Examination Schools	31 New College	54 Sheldonian Theatre
5 Botanic Garden	16 Exeter College	34 Oriel College	56 Town Hall
6 Brasenose College	18 Hertford College	35 Pembroke College	57 Trinity College
7 Carfax Tower	20 Jesus College	39 Queen's College	58 University College
9 Christ Church	25 Lincoln College	40 Radcliffe Camera	

of language associated with the sociolinguistic revolution led to a particular view of language teaching. This view, encompassing the notional/functional syllabus and communicative methodology, might arguably be described as the European view of 'communicative language teaching' (CLT).[5]

But there is another question that theorists can use as their starting point. It is a question about learning, not about language. It is: 'how do people learn language?' While Europeans have largely been looking at the 'what is language?' question, theorists elsewhere (particularly in North America) have been more concerned with the nature of learning in their search for inspiration for language teaching. In the following section we return to the 'learning question'.

10.16 'How' methods and 'what' methods

Think back over the teaching methods that have so far been mentioned in this book. Make a list. Identify some that have been mainly motivated by the 'how do people learn?' question, and others motivated by the 'what is language?' question.

A warning: do not expect 100 per cent clear-cut results to your survey. It is natural that some methods should be motivated by both questions, or by some mixture of the two.

Humanistic approaches

The next group of methods we consider ask the 'learning question'. But, unlike others we have looked at, they answer it by appealing (in most cases at least) not to L1 learning, but to a set of principles associated with the concept of 'humanism'. Roberts (1998: 158) describes humanism in applied linguistics as 'language teaching respecting the integrity of learners, allowing for personal growth and responsibility, taking psychological and affective factors into account, and representing "whole person learning"'. The roots of humanism in language teaching are various. One central one is the 'discovery-learning' movement, particularly associated with the work of the educational psychologist Jerome Bruner. Discovery learning emphasizes the student's own activity and enquiry, rather than the transmission of information by the teacher.

An applied linguist who well expresses the principles of humanism is Gertrude Moskovitz. The title of her important book – *Caring and Sharing in the Foreign Language Class* (1978) – summarizes well the preoccupations of humanistic teaching. At the beginning of this book she expresses the discovery-learning view that the focus of conventional teaching is on 'information transmission', and that humanistic teaching helps students discover the personal meaning of the information that we so extravagantly provide them with.

Moskovitz's list of humanistic principles includes the following: student achievement of their full potential; striving for personal as well as cognitive growth; recognition of the important role of feelings; understanding the significance of self-discovery for learning; a belief that humans want to actualize their potential; recognizing the importance of healthy relationships with classmates; acknowledging that important factors in motivation are learning about yourself and increasing self-esteem.

Another influential book in the area is Earl Stevick's *Memory, Meaning and Method* (1976). It is worth pondering the book's last sentence, which says a lot about humanism in language teaching:

> Of the three subjects of this book, Memory is a by-product of Meaning, and Method should be the servant of Meaning, and Meaning depends on what happens inside and between people. (p. 160)

To put this in other words: meaningfulness is what makes things memorable, and hence learned. So the aim of methods should be to 'make meaningful'. Meaningfulness comes by thinking about people and how they relate to each other.

What are humanistic approaches like? Below is a rough guide to four of them.

THE SILENT WAY

The mover and shaker
Caleb Gattegno was an innovator in the field of mathematics teaching. He developed his views into language teaching and general education. He worked towards what he called his 'Science of Education'. His writings also have religious overtones. He wrote many books; one relating to language teaching is Gattegno (1972).

The 'Big Idea'
The teacher keeps silent for much of the time, withdrawing the verbal aid traditionally given to students.

What it looks like
The teacher says model sentences once only, and gets learners to repeat these. Mistakes are not corrected verbally. Various aids are used to make meanings clear.

Main characteristics
• It is hard work for the students, who have to be fully alert to make the most of what the teacher says and to play the major part in the learning. Learning through this method can be exhausting.
• The aids used include small coloured rods known as Cuisenaire Rods, introduced into language teaching by Gattegno from mathematics teaching. They can be used as simple pointers, or to make shapes, helping the learners deduce meanings for themselves.
• The method has many traditional aspects. These include use of traditional structural syllabuses

(to be discussed in Chapter 12). The teacher/learner relationship is also traditional. Roberts (1998: 288) says that 'though silent, the teacher directs and controls strictly'.

COMMUNITY LANGUAGE LEARNING (CLL)

The mover and shaker
Charles Curran was a specialist in counselling at Loyola University, Chicago. He developed a general model for learning, called Counselling-Learning. CLL is this theory applied to languages.

The 'Big Idea'
A parallel is made between teaching and psychotherapeutic counselling. The teacher is the counsellor or 'knower'; the learner is a 'client'.

What it looks like
See Chapter 1's Classroom 5 (p. 10).

Main characteristics
• An important role is given to translation from L1 (which is what the 'knower' does).
• Stages in the counsellor/client relationship are identified. These parallel stages of the growth of an individual – from childhood dependence, through adolescent rebellion, to adult independence.
• The method is interesting from syllabus design point of view, because the syllabus develops as the teaching goes along. There is no pre-determined syllabus at the beginning.

TOTAL PHYSICAL RESPONSE (TPR)

The mover and shaker

James Asher, psychology professor at San José University, California, developed this method.

The 'Big Idea'

- A link is made between physical actions and learning. This is associated with what happens in L1 acquisition, and in general learning. As Roberts (1998: 353) puts it: 'motor activity strengthens recall'.
- Comprehension skills are developed first. Learners do not produce language until well into the course.

What it looks like

See Chapter 1's Classroom 3 (p. 9).

Main characteristics

- It goes back to an approach developed by Harold and Dorothy Palmer in their 1925 book *English through Actions* (see p. 169 for previous mention of Harold Palmer).
- Centrality is given to the imperative as a structure. It is useful because the teacher can employ the imperative to initiate student actions. Roberts (1998: 353): 'learners execute teacher commands for about 120 hours before conversation is encouraged'.
- The method has traditional elements. The syllabus is grammar-based, and there is teacher control, especially over the input which learners receive.

SUGGESTOPEDIA

The mover and shaker

This method is associated with the Bulgarian psychiatrist and educator, Georgi Lozanov.

The 'Big Idea'

- Learning needs a stress-free environment, so attention is paid to furniture and surroundings.
- Use is made of background music, particularly Baroque slow movements.

What it looks like

Central to the teaching is the 'concert'. Students sit in comfort while a long dialogue is read by the teacher. Students have a copy of the text and an L1 translation. Soothing music is played. After the interval (no smoking or drinking allowed), the teacher reads the dialogue again, while students listen without being able to read the text. More conventional techniques are used before the concert.

Main characteristics

- Music therapy plays a central role. Richards and Rodgers (1986: 146) cite Ostrander *et al.* (1979: 115): 'East German researchers of Suggestopedia at Karl Marx University in Leipzig observed that slow movements from Baroque instrumental music featuring string instruments gave the best results'.
- Learners remember best from an authority, so the teacher must exude confidence. She should also be solemn, well-behaved and fastidiously dressed. Learners must avoid smoking and drinking.
- This method is not for everyone. Scovel (1979: 258) calls it a 'package of pseudo-scientific gobbledygook'.

Tasks and processes

We have seen on several occasions that Chomsky's ideas have had a powerful though indirect influence on language-teaching practice. Although this influence existed in earlier decades (notably the 1960s), it has been particularly strong in more recent times, when 'naturalistic' approaches to language teaching have been developed. Such approaches involve some parallel being drawn between natural L1 acquisition and FL learning. The word 'naturalistic' will bring Krashen and Terrell's 'Natural Approach' to mind, and indeed their approach is a good example of the manifestation of these ideas in recent times. It is one of a number, and we shall now turn to a further influential one, associated with work done in India.

The procedural syllabus

Prabhu is an applied linguist who worked in Southern India. In the late 1970s his concern to improve English language teaching in the region led him to find out about CLT and the notional/functional syllabus. He came to the conclusion that, while this movement was adding a valuable new (sociolinguistic) dimension to language teaching, it was not doing much to tackle the problem India faced, that structurally based language teaching was failing to teach structures! His thinking led him to undertake an experiment in language teaching often referred to as the Bangalore Experiment.

Prabhu's starting point is an answer to the 'learning question' that we have already come across. It is the idea – at first sight paradoxical – that the best way to teach grammatical structures is to focus, not on the structures themselves, but on 'meaning' or 'message'. If, the argument goes, classroom activities succeed in concentrating learners' minds on *what* is being said (message) rather than on *how* it is being said (form), then ultimately the structures will become absorbed. The relationship of this idea to what happens in L1 acquisition has already been discussed (p. 179).

It is where Prabhu takes this idea that is so novel. He argues that you cannot really focus on meaning if you are at the same time following a language syllabus. You cannot really expect your learners to concentrate on *what* is being said if your syllabus dictates that you should on that day be practising a certain tense. To give an example: you might decide to practise the simple past tense with your students by asking them on a Monday morning to tell you what they *did* at the weekend. The chances are that the students will recognize that you are not really interested in their message (what they actually did at the weekend) but on their grammar (using the simple past tense). 'Pretending to ask about message when you're really interested in form' is, Prabhu argues, a fruitless as well as a deceiving practice. This leads him to devise a language-teaching programme which does not list the language items that his course will use. He has instead a programme, or syllabus, of tasks. This task-based syllabus tells the teacher what kinds of activities she will be doing in class each day, but not what language items will come up. The idea is that whatever language is necessary to do the task will be used, and over time this language will be unconsciously absorbed.

You will by now have made connections between Prabhu's approach and the ideas on acquisition discussed both in Chapter 5 and earlier in this chapter. Others of those ideas find their way into his approach. His teachers in general model themselves on L1 caretakers, largely avoiding the kinds of activities (like drilling and error correction) that caretakers avoid.

10.17   What would *you* expect?

The following paragraphs describe what happened in the Bangalore experiment. Before reading these, think about what *you* would expect to happen if you taught in such a way. What would be the consequences of avoiding drilling and error correction? What about the idea of not having a language syllabus, but allowing whatever language is necessary for an activity to be used? What kind of benefits would you expect? What kind of problems would you predict? What kind of students would you produce?

Prabhu experimented with what is sometimes called the procedural, or 'task-based' syllabus over a number of years in India, first with intermediate students then with beginners. At first the children had severe problems with the lessons; they had never come across classes like that before. Box 10.18 reports, with commendable honesty, on the situation after a few months of using the procedural syllabus. It vividly demonstrates some of the problems met by anyone involved in classroom innovations.

10.18   How to oil a rusty LAD: Method 2?

The following extract is taken from the Bangalore Regional Institute of English Newsletter (1/2, 1979). It reports on what was happening in the experiment after a short time:

> Only a small number of children (about 8 in the class of 57) readily respond to the teacher's questions and regularly participate in the activities. The rest of the class is not only unresponsive and unsuccessful, but gives little evidence of having understood the tasks set or of wanting to tackle them. Whenever a task is set, they automatically look to the active eight to respond, joining in only when there is opportunity for a mechanical response (such as the

---

chorused *yes, sir*) or when they can merely repeat what one of the eight girls (or the teacher) has said. When attempts are made by the teachers to force the majority of the class to find and state their own answers, the answers received indicate wild, arbitrary guessing resulting from a lack of understanding of the task itself (as well as some resentment at being forced to be self-reliant). When homework is set (chiefly reading tasks) a majority of children either neglect to perform it or perform it perfunctorily). When groupwork is organised, those groups which include the bright girls leave the work entirely to them, while the others leave the task unperformed or unattempted. When tasks are set for each student to perform individually, girls resort to copying from the bright few and when the seating arrangement was changed to make this difficult they made no secret of their resentment . . .

Oh dear!

But shortly after the situation as recorded in box 10.18, the pupils began to come to terms with the new approach, and when it was formally evaluated, in Beretta and Davies (1985), the results show some advantages to this way of teaching. One of the main issues, of course, is whether naturalistic approaches like this lead to fossilization into a kind of pidgin. Prabhu (1987) describes the experiment and its background in detail.

When we spoke about bilingual education, the phrase 'syllabus in other-than-linguistic terms' was used (on p. 179) to describe the incidental nature of language learning in the approach. Prabhu's syllabus gives another clear example, because it lists tasks and not language items. A further piece of terminology, used by Breen (e.g. in 1983), can also be introduced here to describe the procedural syllabus. Breen's phrase is 'syllabus of means'. Most conventional syllabuses, Breen says, are syllabuses of 'ends'. That is, they are lists of the items that are to be taught. Although structural and notional/functional syllabuses differ from each other in important respects, they are both syllabuses of 'ends' – the structures, notions, functions listed are what is being taught. Prabhu's syllabus does not list ends. It is important to understand that it is not the aim of the teaching to increase the learners' proficiency in doing tasks. These tasks are not an end in themselves. They are means – vehicles for teaching something that is given no mention at all on the syllabus: language.

Process versus product

The term 'syllabus of means' well captures the present-day shift away from a preoccupation with the 'content' of language teaching towards an interest in 'activities done in class'. An anecdote will illustrate this shift. In the early 1980s, I visited South America. There I met many conscientious, committed English teachers who spent much out-of-class time discussing their work. In their case, one of the burning issues was in which school year the present perfect tense should be introduced. Issues like this – about language *content* – were being discussed throughout the world at that time, as they had been for many decades before then. Today the focus has changed and conscientious, committed English teachers world-wide are more likely to be discussing the kinds of activities that are used in class, asking questions like 'does this activity work?' or 'what happens when you use that activity with beginners?'

This focus of interest has led in two directions. The first is expressed by means of yet another piece of terminology, associated with a distinction made in educational studies between *product* and *process*. This distinction has been taken up by applied linguists, particularly Michael Breen. In his best-known paper on the subject (Breen 1984), he argues that language teaching has been over-concerned with the content or *product* of its teaching. Our teaching should, he continues, concentrate more on *process*. We need to consider *how* language is learned and used, and our syllabuses should be stated in terms of these processes. He draws a comparison between syllabuses and maps. In a product syllabus, he says (1984: 52), the designer 'draws a map beginning at the destination'. The process syllabus on the other hand would 'prioritise the route'. In Chapter 12, we shall look more closely at what is involved in 'process teaching'.

Task-based teaching

The second direction can be seen as the development beyond Prabhu of the task-based syllabus idea. Task-based teaching has become a subject of keen contemporary interest, and different task-based approaches exist today. Some differ substantially from Prabhu's, often not being based so centrally on the parallel with L1 acquisition. But one underlying principle holds for all the approaches – to place the emphasis firmly on activities or tasks that learners do in class. This emphasis is reflected in much current research which studies the characteristics of different sorts of activities. Crookes and Gass (1993a and 1993b), Skehan and Foster (1997), Long (1985) and Johnson (1996) are examples. It is possible that the late 1990s will be known in applied linguistics as 'The Age of the Task'.

We conclude our brisk walk by focusing on one particular task-based approach. It is related to the ideas about language learning, skill acquisition and automization discussed in Chapter 7. The $ra - 1$ (required attention minus one) formula was introduced in box 7.4 (p. 108). According to this formula, focus on form is progressively reduced until $ra = 0$, the point where full automization is achieved.

But how can this idea be put into practice? Specifically, how can we manipulate the amount of attention a learner gives to form? The answer is by developing tasks that in various ways take up more or less of the learner's attention. Two extreme instances will illustrate. Look back to box 10.7 (p. 173) and drill (b) in Step 2, which practises the pattern HAVE + *just* + *-ed*. It involves the learners in changing sentences like *She's closing the window* into *She's just closed the window*. The drill has complete form-focus, and the learner can give her full attention on getting the pattern right. Imagine now a second task which involves using the same pattern. In this, the class is shown a series of pictures on a chart. Each picture depicts a person 'just finishing' an action – one character may have 'just closed' a window, another 'just finished' her dinner, and so on. Each character's name is written under the picture. The activity is a memory game. The class are shown the chart for one minute only. Then it is taken out of view. Students work in pairs and must remember as many of the actions as they can, saying (or writing) sentences like *John has just closed the window, Mary has just finished her dinner*. The pair with the highest number of right answers wins the game. Because this task is presented as a game, and has a memory component, a good deal of the learners' attention will be taken up trying to remember who has just done what action. This means that less attention will be available for concentrating on the sentence pattern, and indeed it is quite likely that some learners who get the pattern right in the first task may get it wrong in the second.

There are a number of features that will make tasks more or less difficult, and much recent research into task-based teaching is looking at these. One outcome of this research will be to enable us to construct tasks for our learners which will put the $ra - 1$ idea into practice, so that we can progressively give our learners tasks where there are more and more things to think about, and consequently less and less attention available for form.

These ideas, as yet not fully explored, are associated with what might be called a 'cognitive approach to language teaching' (Skehan 1998 speaks of a 'cognitive approach to language *learning*'). The term 'information-processing approach' is also used (I use it in Johnson 1996 for example) because the $ra - 1$ idea recognizes that there is a processing dimension to language use. Think about those learners who get the HAVE + *just* + *-ed* pattern right in the first task above, but get it wrong in the second. Because they get it right once, there is a true sense in which they 'know' the pattern. So why do they get it wrong in the second task? It is because that task is more demanding, and this prevents them from being able to process what they know. Their problem is not one of *knowledge*, but of *processing ability*.

Perhaps this cognitive, or information-processing, approach is where the future lies. I certainly believe it offers exciting new dimensions. New? Remember Kelly at the beginning of this chapter? Historical investigation may well reveal that these ideas were being discussed in Aristotle's time.

Notes

1. This is the opening challenge in Cicero's address to the Senate on the Catiline conspiracy.
2. This description of Gouin's experiences is based on Diller (1971: 51 ff).
3. In order to provide a short, 'self-contained' example, this one has been invented.
4. The text is from a guidebook, and it describes a short tour round Oxford. The numbers in the text refer to numbered places on the map. Students read the text and follow the route of the tour on the map. They can be asked to mark the route in pencil.
5. The word 'arguably' is used because the term communicative language teaching has been used in very many different ways by applied linguists, and there is no agreement over its proper use. Some applied linguists will certainly feel that notional/functional syllabuses are a separate development, which should be kept apart from CLT.

Chapter 11

Contexts

Introduction

11.1 Language teaching and politics

One of the points that will be made in this chapter is that language teaching has a political side to it. Before reading the chapter, think what this might mean. What aspects of the language teaching operation might be regarded as political?

Those who are new to the language-teaching profession may (for a short while!) believe that becoming a good language teacher is only a question of equipping yourself with a good knowledge of the target language, learning how to conduct the sorts of activity which go on in classrooms, as well as acquiring more general teaching skills to do with managing classrooms and the people in them.

These aspects of language teaching are of course very important. But something that may not be immediately apparent to novice teachers is that language teaching has a social and even a political side to it. These aspects will be particularly important to the teacher who is a native speaker of the target language and who plans to go abroad to teach that language, perhaps to a culture that is entirely different from his own. He will find that there is an immense amount to learn about becoming a 'good' teacher which has nothing to do with nouns and verbs, or drills, or keeping discipline in class. But even teachers who are working within their own country, generally teaching a language that is not their own L1, will benefit from a realization that teaching a language is a social, and even a political, act. As Stern (1983: 284) puts it: 'language teaching can be looked upon as a deliberate intervention into ethnolinguistic relations which can be planned more or less efficiently and which, in this way, can contribute to the bilingualism of a society'.

In this chapter we shall look at language teaching as it operates within a society. We shall begin by looking at aspects of what is called 'foreign-language planning' – the decisions made by a society about language teaching. These decisions are usually made at a governmental, local or institutional level. They are unlikely to be made (yet at least!) by those reading this introductory book. Nevertheless teachers operating within the society will be better at their job for understanding why and how these decisions are made.

We shall then look at some issues of more direct relevance to individual teachers. These are largely issues to do with 'appropriate methodologies' – ensuring that the way we teach is in line with what is accepted within the society in which we work. A major aim of this chapter is to raise your awareness of how teaching practices have a social dimension.

Some questions language planners ask

Language planning is a large area which deals, on an 'official' level, with the language problems of a society. Box 11.2 lists some of the issues that concern language planners.

11.2 Some language planning questions

1. In a country where many languages are spoken, which language is to be the *lingua franca*? [As you will recall from Chapter 1, this term is used to describe a language used as means of communication between speakers of other languages. Examples we came across there were Hindi being used as a *lingua franca* in India, and French in some ex-French colonies.] Should one of the local languages be 'elevated' into the national language, or should a foreign language (e.g. English) be brought in for the purpose?
2. Changing the script. Because the Roman alphabet is so widespread, some countries (e.g. China) have taken steps to introduce it, causing an immense educational upheaval.
3. Changing spelling. As far back as the sixteenth century there have been attempts to standardize English spelling. There was a Simplified Spelling Society at the beginning of the twentieth century in Britain. Despite many efforts, we still continue in our eccentric ways. Look back to the poem in box 2.4 (p. 20) if you want convincing about eccentricity.
4. Controlling vocabulary. In some countries extensive efforts are made to control the influx of foreign words, as part of the effort to maintain the 'integrity' of the native language. France is often mentioned in this respect. Using an Anglo-Saxon word in French (speaking of *le weekend* for example) might be regarded by some as a quasi-treasonable offence.
5. What foreign languages should be taught in the country?

The last item in box 11.2 introduces the issue of foreign-language planning. It is not difficult to find examples in the history of language teaching where there has been bad foreign-language planning, or even none at all. It might be said (though not everyone would agree of course) that continuing to give such importance to Latin and Greek in Europe during the earlier part of the twentieth century, long after they served any obvious communicative purpose, is an example of bad planning. But, as time passes and the world gets smaller, nations are becoming more and more aware that deliberate language-teaching policies are required.

What sorts of questions do foreign-language planners ask? We shall here look at a few. They will show you that nouns, verbs, drills and discipline are indeed a small part of the overall language learning and teaching picture.

Which languages should be taught? A major consideration will of course be the learners' communication needs. These will in turn depend on whether the main use of the FL is likely to be for international communication, or for communication within the borders of the country. Sometimes there is a political dimension to the issue. In the days of the Soviet Union, for example, many Eastern European countries taught Russian; not so much perhaps for reasons to do with communicative needs, as a recognition of the existence of a sphere of influence. With the demise of the Soviet Union came widespread replacement of Russian by English as the first FL in that area. But the story is not over yet, because (as Jaworski 1998 notes) Russian is beginning to gain importance again in the area, as a *lingua franca* for trading purposes.

Another dimension to the question can be how closely related the L1 and target language are. For example, there are good reasons why languages like Japanese and Chinese should be taught in Western countries at the present time. Both provide a doorway into cultures whose economic influence is high now, and is likely to increase in the future. Although there are some signs that these languages are being taught more, they are not found as widespreadly in schools as perhaps their importance warrants. Why? One reason may well be their difficulty for speakers of Western languages, coupled with the important practical consideration of how much time would be available in schools to put aside for languages which are so difficult for these learners.

Which 'version' of which language? This is also a question that can generate heated debate. English is a good example. Countries where English is taught as the main FL may have agonized long and hard with one small corner of this problem – whether British or American English should be the norm. The Arabic-speaking Middle East for example, divides itself into British and American 'camps'. The standard, well-rehearsed arguments are: *for British English* – it is the 'real thing', the proper language, spoken by a respected, if elderly civilization; and *for American English* – English is an international language not because the British use it, but because it is the language of superpower America. Other English-speaking countries now are also in contention, for good reasons. If you live close to Australia, for example, then it may make sense to use Australian English as your norm.

Does the norm have to be associated with a native speaking country? Gone are the days when learners felt obliged to look towards a native speaking country for their norm. Why should not some local variety of English be accepted as the norm, particularly in situations where the foreign language is being used within borders as a *lingua franca*? There is no need for Indians to sound like the British Queen when they communicate with other Indians in English. Their own version of English (sometimes called Hinglish) is perfectly adequate. Once local varieties (of English, for example) become accepted as appropriate, so the role of the native speaker teacher becomes less crucial. It was not too long ago that The Native Speaker (very much with the capitals T, N and S) was accorded immense prestige world-wide. In some countries, Being A Native Speaker (worthy of capitals again) was more important than any teaching qualification or experience. It was a passport to travel the world as a teacher. Nowadays a more measured view of the matter is taken.

In which order of importance should foreign languages be placed? Many countries find it useful to specify this. So an 'important' Language A might be taught from an earlier age and for more hours weekly, and a 'less important' Language B started later and taught for fewer hours. Again, as well as actual communicative needs, other considerations may be relevant. Stern (1983: 278) gives the example of France, which has Spain, Germany, Italy and Britain as neighbours. The importance given to Spanish, German, Italian and English in different parts of France reflects this geographical reality. The influence of geography is also illustrated (as Stern again notes) in the Burstall Report, which we mentioned in Chapter 8 (p. 130). The report shows that children in the south of England have more positive attitudes towards learning French than those in the north. There are many parts of Scotland that are closer to Norway than they are to France. Indeed, they are closer to Norway than to London, but that's another story!

Who learns? is another important question. One provocative argument suggesting the folly of attempting to teach entire populations a language is illustrated in box 11.3 overleaf. It is difficult to escape the conclusion that sometimes reasons for language teaching stated in terms of utility actually mask political motivations to do with cultural imperialism. Colonial powers want their language to be taught in colonies, whether there is a need for it or not.

11.3 Too much English for too many people?

Rogers is a teacher and teacher trainer with experience in many parts of the world. In a provocative paper (Rogers 1982) he argues that too many students are taught English world-wide, for reasons that do not stand up to scrutiny. He looks at some of these reasons.

A main one is related to job prospects. Youngsters (and their parents) are told that English is the key to a decent job. But, Rogers says, if you actually look at the number of jobs available in a given country where English is necessary, it is often very small indeed. Hopes for employment are thus being cruelly raised.

The need for international communication is a second reason given. In an informal survey, Rogers asked his own trainee TEFL teachers how many of their own pupils will ever actually need English for communicative purposes. 'The replies', he says, 'suggest that only a very, very small percentage will need English for that purpose' (p. 146). A third reason is that students need English for academic purposes, to study at college or university, particularly overseas. Once again Rogers argues that the numbers involved are small. His example is Tonga, where according to one survey of the time, 'only two per cent of secondary school leavers actually need English for higher education overseas' (p. 146).

Rogers also points out how appallingly unsuccessful much English teaching is. A huge effort is made, for pathetic results. His illustration this time is Ethiopia, where he himself worked. The English level of first-year undergraduates (the 'cream' of school learners – those who make it to university) was very low indeed: 'very few of them could read English passages written within a 2,000 word vocabulary . . . Very few could write a correct sentence in English' (p. 148). Yet this was after 10 years of English, including 6 years with English as the medium of instruction.

One answer to this depressing situation might be, he argues, to restrict English to tertiary level students, who might be expected to have a real need for it. But he is realistic enough to concede that there are many pressures, not least from parents, for large-scale English language teaching to continue unchecked throughout the world.

How well? and *how much?* also need to be asked. Until recently, many societies had a simple view of level. Learners strove to attain near native speaker standards. But in many situations this is impracticable; there is not enough time for it to be anything like achieved. It is often also unnecessary, particularly in ESP situations. It is vitally important that airline pilots for example should have enough English for the crucial job of communicating properly with air-traffic controllers and others. But what the airline pilot does *not* have to do with English also needs to be recognized. For example, he does not need to read literature (for professional reasons anyway), or be able to articulate a political argument. Different levels, in different language areas, need to be accepted as aims for different types of learner.

Things foreign-language planners need to bear in mind

In order to answer the questions we have been considering, foreign-language planners – and the teachers who put their plans into action – need to know a lot about the *context* in which the teaching takes place. Context is all important, and applied linguists who try to make lists of the factors that are relevant to language teaching always include a set called 'contextual'. We need a framework for describing these factors. Stern's framework is shown in box 11.4. It is in fact an amalgam of two other models, from Spolsky *et al.* (1974) and Mackey (1970).

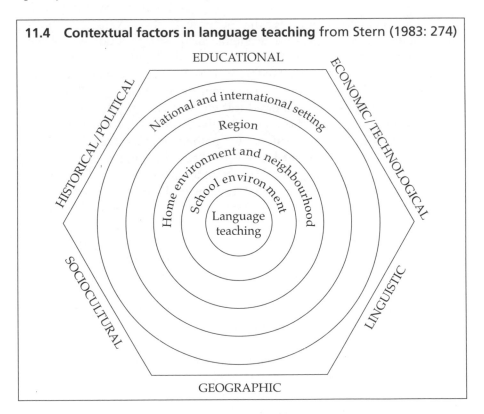

11.4 Contextual factors in language teaching from Stern (1983: 274)

Stern mentions a number of language-teaching situations that can illustrate the relevance of the factors in his model. They are: an English class for adult immigrants, French in a comprehensive school in Great Britain, English in a German primary school, Spanish in a US high school. Each of these situations occurs within a school environment, and teachers as well as administrators therefore need to know something about the school's policy on language teaching – how much importance is given to it, how it fits into the curriculum and so on. The school is located within a 'home environment and neighbourhood' and once again the teacher needs to know something about this. An oft-quoted example of how home and neighbourhood background can affect language teaching comes from Burstall's Report. Here is one finding from her study of French teaching in Britain: 'for pupils of both sexes in each group of primary schools, high mean scores on the Listening, Reading and Writing tests coincide with high-status parental occupation and low mean scores with low-status parental occupation' (Burstall *et al.* 1974: 24). And again (p. 31): 'children with parents in higher-status occupations receive greater parental support when they approach new learning experiences than do those with parents in lower-status occupations' (both these quotes are cited in Stern 1983).

We have already seen how region affects language teaching in our earlier example of language-teaching patterns in the regions of France, according to the neighbouring countries. Burstall again provides some interesting information. In her study it was consistently found that a high level of achievement in French was found in small rural schools, not large city ones. We have also seen earlier in this chapter how national and international factors are relevant to language learning.

The outer perimeter of Stern's model shows the six general factors that will influence the teaching. Box 11.5 puts some flesh onto these six categories:

11.5 Matching variables and examples

The six variables in Stern's model are:

1. sociocultural   2. historical/political   3. educational
4. economic/technological   5. linguistic   6. geographic

Below are six descriptions of these variables (one for each). The descriptions are nearly always based on examples we have already discussed. Try to match variables and descriptions.[1]

A Stern (p. 280) cites a study by Lewis and Massad (1975) entitled *The Teaching of English as a Foreign Language in Ten Countries*. The study points up important administrative differences between countries regarding the provision of language teaching. For example, the switch from primary to secondary school at that time took place at age ten in Italy, but age fourteen in Chile, Hungary and Thailand. In Sweden there was no switch (with pupils staying at the same school until at least the age of sixteen).

B Examples are: the different attitudes towards French in Southern England and in Scotland; and the languages taught in the different regions of France.

C Language planners, as well as teachers, have to bear in mind how much money is available for the language-teaching operation. Exciting and elaborate ideas about the use of video or computers will be quite useless in situations where the machines cannot be afforded.

D This variable includes factors like the relationship between success and parental occupation, as well as the esteem (or otherwise) in which the target language is viewed within the society.

E Japanese and Chinese are rarely taught in European schools, even though they are increasingly important languages.

F An example of this variable is the changing policies towards the teaching of Russian in Eastern European countries.

How do you plan foreign-language teaching? An initial look

We have looked at various considerations which need to be taken into account when answering the question: how do you plan foreign-language teaching? Important as these variables are, when we come to look at the details of foreign-language planning, one consideration becomes paramount – the communication needs of learners. To arrive at specific answers to the sort of questions raised in this chapter, we need to find a way of analysing learners' needs. It is the process of <u>needs analysis</u> that will tell us just how much, and for what purposes, our learners will need which foreign languages. We shall look in detail at needs analysis in the next chapter, which focuses on syllabus design. But to illustrate how the process can help with general language-planning issues, box 11.6 contains an example of how one study provided a profile of learner needs that led in the direction of very concrete suggestions for language-teaching practice in Holland.

11.6 Needs in Nijmegen (based on van Els *et al.*'s (1984) description of the work of Claessen and his colleagues in Nijmegen, Holland)

The late 1970s was a time of some upheaval in the Dutch language-teaching scene, as a result of some changes of educational policy. Some educationalists felt that these changes did not reflect the language needs of the country, and Claessen and his colleagues therefore undertook research to establish what these needs were. Needs were looked at in three ways, in relation to: (a) secondary schools; (b) trade, industry, public administration and tertiary education; and (c) other relevant areas. The researchers produced a list of 24 language-use situations, dealing with the areas of leisure, work and education. Here are three items from the list (taken from van Els *et al.* 1984: 168):

- light reading (illustrated periodicals, detective stories)
- writing a short business letter, asking for a report, registering at a congress
- having a conversation with a colleague or fellow-student on one's own special subject

The list of situations was given to relevant people – school pupils, staff of companies, government services and many others. They were asked how often these situations would be met for each of the major languages taught.

Van Els *et al.* list a number of findings of the research. Here are three:

1. There are different patterns of need for French, German and English. This includes different levels of required proficiency (something that the examination system did not take account of)
2. Learners found French more difficult than English or German, and hence many gave it up early at school. This problem might be answered by allocating more time to French than to the other languages
3. Minor needs for other languages – particularly Russian, Spanish and Italian – were revealed. Perhaps these minor needs could be catered for by making provision outside the school system available

What a teacher needs to know: appropriate methodology

Context is important not just for the language planner. Teachers need to know about context as well. Knowledge of context is most likely to be an issue in the case of the expatriate teacher going abroad – for example an Australian going to work in Africa. If he is to operate successfully in his new context he will have to understand it, and realize that it is different from his own. But sensitivity to context is also an issue for the FL teacher working in his own country. This is particularly true if he has been trained to use ideas and techniques that originate abroad. The fact is that many FL teaching situations involve the coming together of people and ideas from different cultures. When cultures meet, the result may be happy union. Unfortunately there is often also an element of clash. Language teachers must be ready to handle clash.

Someone who explores clash in detail is Holliday. His 1994 book is entitled *Appropriate Methodology and Social Context*. The book results partly from his experience working in Cairo as part of a joint British–American–Egyptian language–teaching project. During his stay, he took copious 'observation notes' on various classes he attended, as well as on other events relevant to his topic. Here is an extract from his observation notes on a class in a faculty of education in Egypt, conducted by a local lecturer. The extract well conveys his bewilderment on meeting a way of teaching alien to his own:

anyone walking in would have thought there was chaos because a lot of students were talking at once and the lecturer did not always seem to be in control . . . The lecturer asked some students to be quiet, but not some others who appeared to be talking out of turn . . . One particular student in a group which always seemed to be talking out of turn was clearly in contact with the lesson because they often initiated very cogent comments . . . The end of the lesson was left apparently without a concrete conclusion . . . (p. 38)

After the lesson Holliday discussed it with the local lecturer. She said that 'she knew exactly what was going on and that, yes, it was culturally normal to be talking and listening at the same time . . . and that although some students were talking a lot, perhaps only 60 per cent about the lesson, they were very much in touch. The ones she told to be quiet were [the ones who were] really off the point.'

This example shows the 'foreign-ness' an expatriate teacher experiences when going to work in a different cultural context. It is important to realize that this foreign-ness works in two directions. Individuals in the host culture are likely to find aspects of the expatriate's views as bizarre as he finds theirs. Many expatriate teachers are surprised by this. Here is a common scenario: our novice teacher, trained, let us say, in Canada, sets off for his first job abroad. In his suitcase, among his other private effects, he carries a set of views about language teaching and a collection of techniques provided by his training course. The shock he receives during his first few weeks of teaching abroad is not a trivial one. The 'locals', he discovers, are not as enthusiastic about the contents of his suitcase as he was expecting. In fact they are downright hostile to some of his favourite ideas and techniques. His reaction is as human as it is illogical. He blames the 'locals'. Muttering under his breath, he calls them 'backward', not yet ready for his advanced notions. He protests: *Certainly it is they, not I, who must change.*

Just to give an example, let us explore this issue in relation to one particular item in his baggage – the idea of groupwork. This technique has become very popular in recent years. In the past, classes were traditionally 'fully frontal'. That means that the teacher would stand at the front of the class, with the pupils in serried ranks facing him (sometimes the benches would actually be bolted down, as if deliberately to crush any attempt at communication in any direction except to the front). Interaction was traditionally teacher to pupil, one pupil at a time, perhaps occasionally (as in a Handel oratorio) alleviated by some choral work, with all the pupils repeating in a chant something that the teacher had said. In groupwork on the other hand, pupils work together in small groups (from 2 to 5 or more members). Most of the interaction in this configuration is pupil to pupil.

One of the obvious advantages of groupwork for the language teacher is that it increases the amount of learner talk possible in the classroom

– lots of people in the class can be speaking for lots of the time. This is particularly important if one holds the view that interaction is crucial for language learning (the 'Interaction Hypothesis' we mentioned in Chapter 6). Another major advantage is that students who are perhaps too nervous to speak directly to the teacher may be less inhibited when talking to their peers in a group. Long and Porter (1985) provide a list of the assumed advantages of groupwork for language teaching. The list is a long one, which is precisely why groupwork finds its way into our novice teacher's suitcase.

11.7   Grumbling about groupwork

As you have probably guessed, we are going to find that groupwork is not well accepted in the context where our novice teacher works. Given all the advantages to groupwork, how can it possibly be unpopular or unacceptable? Consider what the possible reasons might be.

Other techniques that are sometimes unacceptable or unpopular in particular contexts are role play and (in other contexts perhaps) drilling. Think what objections there might be to each of these.

Can you think of any other techniques (whether or not mentioned in this book) that might be controversial in any particular context?[2]

Our novice teacher's attempts to introduce groupwork may meet with some resistance. Why? He needs to know that the idea of groupwork has its origin, not in language teaching, but in the field of educational studies, where it is associated with a particular educational philosophy. The philosophy is one which attempts to shift the centre of 'power' away from the teacher, and to involve learners more in their own learning. It is part of a movement away from teacher-led classes towards more interactive, learner-oriented ones. Reynolds (1994) provides a good background to the concept of groupwork as used in education.

A number of writers have noted that some cultures are hostile to groupwork because it involves learner–teacher relations that are at odds with those held in the culture. Shamim (1996: 124), for example, notes that in Pakistan most classes are teacher-fronted. She gives three reasons for this. They are: (a) 'the teachers' lack of awareness and/or feelings of insecurity in using other types of classroom organization'; (b) 'the effect of culture, whereby the teacher is traditionally seen as an authority figure and is given respect for his or her age and superior knowledge'; (c) 'the view of teaching/learning that is prevalent in the community where teaching is viewed as transmission of knowledge'.

So our novice teacher may to his astonishment find that he is being accused of a kind of cultural imperialism. In his innocence he thought that groupwork was just a way of getting learners to talk more. He discovers that in fact it is a whole philosophy of education, even perhaps of life!

In an interview reported in Phillipson (1992), Widdowson discusses the general problem of which our groupwork example is a particular instance. He says that, although in recent years our expertise and awareness of various aspects of language teaching has increased impressively,

> where I think things have not been really effective has been in the mediation, the way in which these ideas have been integrated into local social, political and educational conditions of the countries where they are applied . . . We've tended always to make the same basic error, which is to assume that somehow it is the local conditions that have to be adjusted to the packaged set of concepts we bring with us rather than attempt to look into the real issues, practical as well as ideological, of implementation and innovation within these local contexts . . . I don't think we have brought into the operation [of language teaching] an awareness of local conditions nor an effective involvement of local people, so that one can see these as in some sense, even though enlightened and benevolent, well-meaning, but nevertheless to some degree impositional. (p. 260)

Recent writers, particularly Phillipson (1992) and Pennycook (1994) remind us that all too often language teaching can indeed be highly 'impositional', perhaps even constituting a form of cultural imperialism.

What is the answer? Should our novice teacher abandon his efforts to use groupwork, on the grounds that it does not fit in with the local cultural context? The issue is not a simple one, and in recent years there has been a growing literature on the subject of 'innovation', looking at how to introduce new ideas into a context in such a way that they will become accepted and 'sustainable'. Some books on this subject, like Fullan and Stiegelbauer (1991) deal with educational change in general; others (like Markee 1997) focus on language teaching.

Part of the answer lies in compromise and gradual movement. If the novice teacher is genuinely convinced about the value of groupwork, but does nothing to fit into local educational practice, he will get nowhere. He may have a degree of success if he manages to integrate small portions of groupwork into the local diet in a clever and subtle way. But even then, he needs to have the backing of others locally involved in the profession. You can argue that this backing is needed not just to ensure success, but also for ethical reasons. You should not try to change a context, you might say, unless that context wants to be changed.

What we have been discussing here may be called the relativism of methodologies. This is the idea that there is no one, 'best' way of doing anything. Instead, there are ways that may be more or less appropriate according to situation. Holliday uses the phrase 'appropriate methodology' to describe this idea. Box 11.8 looks at the issue from a slightly different viewpoint.

11.8 Methods as plausible fictions

In Johnson (1995) I discuss the idea that language-teaching methods can be viewed as 'works of fiction'. The paper begins by discussing what Widdowson (1980) says about linguistic theories. He makes the point that, when we compare such theories, we often talk in terms of truth, perhaps claiming that one theory is 'truer' than another. But, he argues, a criterion of truth cannot really apply here, and theories are better described using words like 'convincing', 'powerful' and 'plausible'. In this respect, theories are like fictions. Certainly we would not discuss a play like Shakespeare's *Hamlet* in terms of whether or not it is 'factually true'. We would use other words ('convincing' and so on) to describe it.

The same points, I say, can be made about language-learning theories and teaching methods. We may be tempted to describing one as 'better' than another, as if it were possible to apply some absolute criteria to them. But in fact these theories and methods 'are constructs which have more or less plausibility, more or less power, but not more or less objective truth. They are nearer to political beliefs than they are to empirical science.' (p. 5)

If a method is to succeed, it has to be regarded as 'convincing', 'powerful' and 'plausible'. To do this, it must fit in with the beliefs of the main participants in the teaching process, particularly the learners and the teacher. However objectively 'good' we may feel a method is, it will not succeed if the learners are not convinced by it. In this context I tell a cautionary tale about a group of students who came to study in England. The institution they attended 'was eager to use various modern "communicative" techniques. This did not at all fit the students' perceptions of how a language should be learned. There must be, they insisted, grammar, dictation and above all lots of pain, because learning a language (their experience told them) must be a painful process; without pain, learning could not be taking place. The situation reached deadlock, and in fact the learners simply left the institution involved.' (p. 6)

Appealing to a teacher's 'sense of plausibility' (the phrase is from Prabhu (1987)) is also very important. If a teacher does not believe in what he is doing, his performance is likely to be weak. The teacher will be 'like a cardboard fictional character in a second-rate novel' (p. 8).

We may all be tempted to believe that this message – that there are no 'best' ways of doing things – applies to other people, not ourselves. But what our own conviction persuades us is the 'best' may be just as culturally determined and as relative as the views we find so strange in other cultures. Really wise teachers are blessed with the sense to recognize what their own fictions are. And to recognize them as fictions, not facts.

Earlier in this chapter we took an initial look at the question: how do you plan foreign-language teaching? Our answer pointed up the importance of needs analysis. In the chapter about to begin we look more closely at this question, as it relates to the business of drawing up detailed language programmes specifying the content of courses, perhaps on a day to day basis. Detailed programme specification is the area of syllabus design. It is an area in which needs analysis continues to play an important role.

Notes

1. The intended matchings are: A3; B6; C4; D1; E5; F2. Because some of Stern's terms are rather general, other matchings may be possible.
2. In some countries, 'public performance', such as that required in role-play exercises, is not well-considered. Sometimes this view is combined with an attitude towards classroom learning where teachers, and not learners, are expected to do most of the talking. Drama, and discussion, techniques are often unpopular for similar reasons. As you will see in Chapter 13, many countries nowadays regard drilling as a discredited behaviourist technique, which is also thought of as very boring, and is hence frowned upon.

Chapter 12

Plans

Introduction

A good number of people who are professionally involved in language teaching will at one time or another in their lives have the responsibility of producing a syllabus, or part of one. But what exactly is a syllabus? In Chapter 10 we described it as an 'organizational programme, a plan for teaching'. We will now be more specific.

Being more specific involves some problems of terminology. An often-asked question is: what is the difference between a syllabus and a curriculum? For many, the term 'curriculum' is the wider of the two, referring, in White's (1988: 4) words to 'the totality of content to be taught and aims to be realized within one school or educational system'. 'Syllabus', on the other hand, tends to refer to the content of just one subject area. Although the terms may be differentiated in this way, the truth is that many applied linguists use them as synonyms. I was recently preparing a course with the official title of 'Curriculum Design'. As I was about to deliver the first talk, I checked through the handouts I had prepared. Half of them carried the official title. But the other half referred to the course as 'Syllabus Design'. I simply do not, in practice, distinguish the two terms. Another two difficult terms are 'syllabus design' and 'course (or programme) design'. Richards *et al.* (1985) describe the difference well. For them, syllabus design involves (as we shall see below) planning course *content*. Course or programme design involves other factors associated with implementation, including such issues as the timing (and indeed timetabling) of various course elements, and how the course will be evaluated.

Life is not made any simpler by the fact that, if you ask teachers or administrators what they use as a syllabus, you will get very different answers indeed. Taylor (1970) asked just this question and he notes that 'some were no more than one or two pages in length, others cover one hundred pages. Some were well laid out and carefully bound. Others were cramped and barely legible.' My own experience has been similar. On one occasion when I asked to see the syllabus used in a language school, a copy of George Orwell's *Animal Farm* was produced. This was the book that was being covered for an examination. On other occasions when I asked the same question I was given lengthy and glossy documents.

In all this diversity and terminological confusion, the main point to hold onto is that a syllabus is centrally a statement of *content*, stating what a programme will cover. In Chapter 10 we saw that the *what* and *how* of language teaching can be closely connected, so that a statement of content is likely to carry with it methodological implications. Syllabuses therefore rarely confine themselves to content. Often they talk about methodology as well, and are likely also to contain statements about aims and objectives, and even about the form of evaluation to be used for the teaching programme. But content remains the main element of most syllabuses.

We have also seen in earlier chapters that the terms in which content will be stated will change according to the view of language and/or language learning held by the syllabus designer. The clearest example of this, covered in some detail in Chapter 10, is the movement from structural to notional/functional syllabuses in the 1970s. This was related to a change in views as to what language is and what is involved in language use.

Chapter 10 provides a recent history of language teaching, and in it many different syllabus types were mentioned. The present chapter will take a more concentrated look at the major syllabus types, particularly the structural and the notional/functional. It will deal with the nuts and bolts of syllabus design. It will also try to give you a feeling of how syllabuses are actually constructed.

12.1 Nuts and bolts: an initial look

In some language-teaching textbooks, the contents page of the Teacher's Book reveals details of the syllabus. This page from Teacher's Book 1 of a course called *Now for English* is given below. I wrote these materials for primary level children, starting to learn English as a foreign language at the age of 8. Here are some questions to draw your attention to aspects of the contents page. Questions 1 and 2 are particularly important to our discussion; miss out the other ones if you wish.[1]

1. There are three columns. The titles of each column appear in the shaded boxes at the top. They have been omitted. What do you think they are for the first two columns? What about the third column? This is more difficult because we have not yet fully discussed the items that occur in this column. But go on: make a guess at what the title may be.
2. Though you cannot tell for sure without seeing more of the book, which of the three columns do you think tells you most about how the book is organized?
3. At regular intervals the book contains revision units. Identify these units, and the intervals at which they occur.

4. In Column 2, some items are given in italics. What do these items have in common? Other items are in capitals. What do they have in common? Say what the difference is between these two types of item.

5. Concentrate now on *verb forms*. Units 1 to 12 focus on one verb in particular. Which one? What are the two major tenses introduced in Units 13 to 25? Two uses of the verb *can* are introduced in the book. What are they? Think of a few sentences to illustrate each of these uses.

Contents page from Teacher's Book 1 of *Now for English* (Johnson 1983a)

Introductory lesson	*What's your name?* *My name's John.*	names (asking for names and saying who you are) colours countries of the world
1 Good morning everyone	*I'm Anne.* *I'm not Peter.* *Who's this?* *It's Sam.*	the characters of the book introducing yourself
2 Who's this?	*This is Mr Porter* *This is my father.* *he's/she's* numbers 1–10	family relations (talking about the family) children's ages
3 Oh Sally!	*What's this?* *It's a . . .* (positive, negative, interrogative, short answer)	objects commonly found in the street or house
4 What a mess!	*Whose is this book?* *Whose book is this?* *It's Sam's.* *It's his/her book.* *Is that/it your book?*	common classroom objects talking about who owns things
5 Kate's farm	*What colour is it?* *It's red.* *It's a red horse.* *this/that*	farm animals
6 Games to play	revision, and Progress Test 1	
7 Gee up, Sam	*I'm a . . .* *You're a . . .* (positive, negative, interrogative, short answer)	exciting jobs (talking about jobs)

8 Circus time	He's a . . . She's a . . . (positive, negative, interrogative, short answer)	the circus
9 Stop, Bella, stop	IMPERATIVE (positive negative)	simple actions giving orders
10 Shirts and skirts	What are these? They're . . . These are . . . PLURAL NOUNS NO ARTICLE + PLURAL NOUN / a + SINGULAR NOUN	articles of clothing
11 Cowboys and Indians	We're . . . You're . . . They're . . . (positive, negative, interrogative, short answer) numbers 11–20	cowboys and Indians
12 Games to play	revision, and Progress Test 2	
13 In the jungle	SIMPLE PRESENT (positive, affirmative, all persons) the	jungle animals talking about where people and animals live
14 What a noise!	SIMPLE PRESENT (negative, interrogative, all persons except 3rd person singular)	leisure activities asking about likes and dislikes
15 Kate's street	SIMPLE PRESENT (negative, interrogative 3rd person singular) numbers 20–60 here / there	shops and shopping asking for and giving information door numbers
16 Ghosts and monsters	There's/there are some PREPOSITIONS OF PLACE (in, on, under, behind)	rooms in the house furniture saying where things are
17 Let's have a picnic	some/any Is there/Are there? (interrogative, short answers)	picnics and food
18 Games to play	revision, and Progress Test 3	

19 Hurry up, Chris	days of the week *It's four o'clock.* *It's half past four.* *I go swimming* *on Mondays.* *at* + time *on* + day	days and times more leisure activities saying when things are done
20 Mr White's shop	uncountable *some/* countable *a how* *many/how much*	shopping and food talking about quantity
21 Catch, Bella	PRESENT CONTINUOUS (positive, affirmative)	describing everyday activities in the home
22 Funny Kate	PRESENT CONTINUOUS (negative, interrogative, short answer) sentences with DIRECT and INDIRECT OBJECTS	more everyday household activities

23 Hurray, I'm
   happy today
	It's sunny/wet/cold.
	ADVERBS OF FREQUENCY
	(*soon, always, sometimes,*
	often, never)
	PRESENT CONTINUOUS
	vs. SIMPLE PRESENT
		holidays
		weather
		saying how often things
		   happen

24 Games to play	revision, and Progress Test 4	
25 Sally's postcard	SIMPLE PRESENT vs. PRESENT CONTINUOUS telling the time – all times	telling the time
26 Fred's apron	*have got* (all persons except 3rd person singular) POSSESSIVE PRONOUNS (*mine, yours, his, hers*)	toys talking about who owns things

27 Well done,
   Chris
	can (= ability)
	more PREPOSITIONS
	of place (*over, inside, next to,*
	through, between)
	which + noun
		playground objects
		   and activities
		talking about ability
		describing where things
		   are

28 Good old Sally	OBJECT PRONOUNS (*him/her/them*) months of the year	months of the year birthday presents
29 Happy birthday	*have got* (3rd person singular) *can* (= permission)	talking about who owns things parties and party food asking for permission
30 Games to play	revision, and Progress Test 5	

215

The structural syllabus

Question 3 in box 12.1 above asks about how *Now for English* is organized. If you had the opportunity look more carefully at the book itself, it would become apparent to you that it's main organization is in terms of the structures. Each unit focuses on a number of grammatical structures. You can see (even from the contents pages, but more clearly by looking at the book itself) that these have been ordered and graded through the course. This is a way of saying that the book follows *a structural syllabus*. In this type of syllabus, the main organizing principle is according to language structures.

How are structural syllabuses actually constructed? One way to find out would be to interview someone who has designed syllabuses. At several points in my career I have done just that. So in the section below I interview myself. MAAL (Me as Applied Linguist) talks to MAMD (Me as Materials Designer). The discussion revolves around the *Now for English* syllabus that you have just seen.

MAAL interviews MAMD

MAAL: I'd like to know first of all, MAMD, why you decided to use a structural syllabus for your book. Why not a notional/functional or some other type?

MAMD: I thought about this for a very long time, and in the end decided that for a beginners' book it was important for the learners to be introduced to the grammar of the language in a systematic way. That means dealing with a different sentence pattern in each lesson or 'unit'. And that means a structural syllabus.

MAAL: Does that mean you ignored notions and functions?

MAMD: Not at all. But I didn't use them as my main 'organizing principle', my 'unit of organization'.

MAAL: Explain.

MAMD: Well, in each unit of the book the main focus is on a group of sentence patterns. For example in Unit 15 sentence patterns associated with the simple present tense are covered . . .

MAAL: (yawning) Yes, yes. I understand that.

MAMD: . . . but in the course of the unit the functions of 'asking for and giving information' are touched on, often using the simple present tense.

MAAL: So the main focus is on a grammar point, but notions and functions are borne in mind in your choice of language to put in the unit.

MAMD: Precisely.

MAAL: OK. Now tell us what the first stage in designing the syllabus for your course was.

MAMD: My course was to be a complete one, covering three years of teaching in three books. So most of the grammar of English was to be covered over the period. First of all, then, I wanted a list of all the important structures of English. Several books exist to help you with this. One very useful one is *English Grammatical Structure* (Alexander *et al.* 1975). This is a comprehensive list of English sentence patterns. The book was specially written with the purpose of helping syllabus designers.

MAAL: Once you had your list of structures, what did you do then?

MAMD: The next decision was to divide them into 'years', deciding which structures to teach in Year 1, Year 2 and Year 3.

MAAL: And how did you decide this?

MAMD: Well, I suppose that my main criterion, at the beginning at least, was to think about simplicity – teaching the simple structures before the more complicated ones.

MAAL: What some people call a 'simplicity criterion'.

MAMD: Exactly. Of course, it's difficult to apply this criterion in a strict way, and sometimes it's impossible to say whether one structure is more difficult that another. But it's a good starting point. Another criterion I used was frequency. I thought it would be a good idea to teach more common structures before less common ones. For example, there's some research that suggests that the 'simple' tenses (in sentences like *She eats chocolate* and *She ate chocolate*) are far more frequent than the 'continuous' ones (*She is eating chocolate* and *She was eating chocolate*). Many textbooks teach the present continuous before the simple present. I do it the other way round, partly because of these findings. There are other criteria we can use as well . . .

MAAL: I see. Don't these criteria conflict with each other?

MAMD: Yes they do. I'm afraid that syllabus design can be a messy business! Certainly it's rather more of an art than a science.

MAAL: I see. Well let's move on. So at the end of this stage, you have a list of structures assigned to Year 1, 2 or 3. What comes next?

MAMD: Of course a structure divides into many sentence patterns, so you have to make a list of the patterns associated with your structures, and decide in which order to teach them.

MAAL: Is that difficult?

MAMD: I'm afraid it is. Think about some of the main patterns associated with a tense – the simple present for example. First of all there's the basic form . . .

MAAL: Yes, yes. We can put these into a box; you don't have to go through them all, thank you very much . . .

MAMD: Now you may think it's sensible to teach the 'basic' form first of all, and the contents page of *Now for English* shows that I do this. But what that page doesn't show is that I introduce the receptive use of the question form in the same unit, so that the teacher can ask questions.

MAAL: Perhaps you should explain what you mean by the word 'receptive'.

MAMD: It means the learners should be able to understand, but not necessarily produce the form. As you know, reading and listening are the *receptive* skills, speaking and writing the *productive* ones. In my first unit on the simple present I have the class look at a jungle scene. The teacher asks questions like *Where do monkeys live?* and the pupils reply *Monkeys live in the trees.* So at this point the learners have to *understand* the question form and *produce* the 'basic' form.

MAAL: Sounds like gripping stuff!

MAMD: Well children are interested in monkeys and jungles, you know. Another issue at this stage is what is called 'pacing'. This is ensuring that there is some kind of balance through the book, in terms of what is introduced. Each of my books has 30 units, and these are divided into five 'sections' each with six units. The sixth unit of each section is a revision one, so each section has five units of new material and one of revision. I've tried to 'pace' the course so that no more than one major structure is introduced into each section. Usually the major structure will be a new tense. Then around this structure I spread the minor ones out – a sort of padding to fill the materials out.

MAAL: Can you give an example?

MAMD: Yes. In units 13 to 18 of Book 1, I introduce the simple present tense. But if you look at the contents page, you'll see that some other, more 'minor' structures are spread through these units: *some* and *any* for example.

MAAL: Yes. I see. Well thank you, MAMD. That was very interesting.

MAMD: But I haven't finished yet! There's much more to say.

MAAL: I'm sure there is. But we have to move on, I'm afraid.

12.2 Liking chocolates

Here are some of the main sentence patterns associated with the simple present tense in English:

'Basic' form (*positive affirmative*)	*She likes chocolates*
Negative	*She doesn't like chocolates*
Question (*interrogative*)	*Does she like chocolates?*

Note that all these examples use the third person singular (*she*). Think of the equivalent sentences using a different person (e.g. *they*). Identify the units in *Now for English 1* where these three patterns of the simple present are introduced. Finally, create similar sentences for the simple past tense; the 'basic' form would be *She liked chocolates*.

If you feel in the mood for a linguistic challenge, use the examples in this box to work out the rules for forming negatives and questions in English, for the simple present and simple past tenses of verbs similar to *like*.[2]

Criteria for structural syllabus ordering

MAMD gives us an indication of the stages involved in structural syllabus design. In their discussion, MAAL and MAMD also make mention of some of the criteria structural syllabus designers use for ordering the items on their syllabus. Here is a rough guide to the most common criteria:

SIMPLICITY CRITERION

What it is
It means moving from simple to complex structures

Comments
- We need to distinguish *formal* simplicity from *conceptual* simplicity. Formal simplicity relates to structure. For example, the present perfect is complex, involving part of the verb HAVE, plus part of the verb ending in *-ed*. A structure may be formally simple but conceptually difficult – the indefinite article, for example. It is formally simple (just put *a* or *an* at beginning of noun phrase). But it is *very* difficult to explain as a concept, if the learner does not have it in her L1.
- Linguists have sometimes tried to develop 'scientific' definitions of simplicity. But their attempts have never really worked. One reason is that what makes a sentence easy or difficult for you to process is not just a question of its structure. Many 'psychological' factors are also involved.
- Simplicity and complexity are complicated by contrastive linguistics. See Chapter 4 on the idea that a structure may be more difficult for the speakers of one language than another, according to the relationship between the target language and the learner's L1.
- See later in this chapter (p. 222) for a consideration of simplicity in relation to natural acquisition orders (discussed in Chapter 4).

SEQUENCING OR GROUPING

What it is
This involves putting things together that 'go' together.

Example 1
Some and *any*. Though the rule is a simplification, students are taught that *any* is used for negative and interrogative sentences: *Did she eat any chocolates?* and *She didn't eat any chocolates*, as opposed to *She ate some chocolates*. It makes sense to teach these words in the same or adjacent units.

Example 2
The movement from BE to the present continuous. Many coursebooks start with the verb BE. Three common sentence patterns are: *Helen is a painter; Is Helen a painter? Helen isn't a painter*.

Once these patterns have been learned, it is easy for the learner to go on to: *Helen is phoning her mum; Is Helen phoning her mum? Helen isn't phoning her mum*. So, in many textbooks, the present continuous immediately follows the verb BE.

FREQUENCY

What it is
This involves teaching the most frequently used forms first.

Comments
A 'frequency count' is a study which counts the frequency of items in a language. Many deal with vocabulary. West (1953), for example, is a dictionary which gives information about the frequency of a word's

different meanings. Some frequency counts deal with structures. An early example is George (1963). He finds that the 'simple' tenses (e.g. in *She eats chocolate* and *She ate chocolate*) far outstrip the 'continuous' ones (*She is eating chocolate* and *She was eating chocolate*). Perhaps this suggests the simple tense should be taught before the continuous ones? Many syllabuses teach them the other way round.

Recently, information about frequency has been taken from corpora [singular *corpus*]. A corpus is a huge collection of texts [spoken or written or both), held on computer. Two of the best known are the *British National Corpus* – about 100 million words – and the *Longman/Lancaster Corpus* – 30 million words. They can be used to calculate the frequency of words and structures.

UTILITY

What it is
This means teaching the most useful things first. 'Most useful' often means 'most frequent'. But sometimes a sentence pattern may not be frequent itself, but useful as a 'stepping stone' to learning other, more frequent patterns. Another sense of 'useful' relates to the classroom teaching process.

A 'stepping stone' example
See Example 2 under 'Sequencing or Grouping' above. Many structural books spend much time on the verb BE, practising sentences like *Helen is a painter; Is Helen a painter? Helen isn't a painter*. Teachers complain that sentences like this are rarely used in real life. But syllabus designers argue that once the verb BE has been mastered, various other areas of the language are opened up. So BE is a useful stepping stone to the use of the continuous tenses.

A 'classroom teaching process' example
Sentence patterns like *Open the door* (the imperative) and *What's this?* often occur early in courses, because they are so useful in the classroom. Once the imperative is learned, many classroom actions can be practised. Look back to the contents page of *Now for English 1* (p. 213) and note how early it is taught. The *what* question makes vocabulary practice easy (the teacher can point at objects and ask what they are).

TEACHABILITY

What it is
This is teaching structures that are easy to convey before ones that are difficult to teach. So it is simplicity from the *teaching* point of view.

Comments
All teachers know that some structures are easier to teach than others. The *some/any* distinction (see earlier) is a favourite for some teachers because it is easy to explain and practise. Other grammatical items, like the definite article, can be fiendishly difficult to teach.

A controversial statement to think about: perhaps with very difficult structures all you can do is expose learners to them, and offer explanations if asked, rather than trying to teach them in a formal way.

STRUCTURAL SYLLABUSES: POINTS TO PONDER

Conflicting criteria

The above criteria can conflict (which is why MAMD said that syllabus design can be a messy business). For example: should the simple present be introduced before or after the present continuous? Simplicity suggests perhaps that the continuous tense should come first (particularly if the verb BE has been thoroughly taught). But a frequency criterion might suggest teaching the simple present first (see mention of George's research above).

Does order matter?

Teachers used to agonize about the order in which to teach items. But does it matter? One point of view is that it *is* important that structures should be taught in separation, to give the teaching a focus. But whether Structure X is taught before Structure Y is perhaps less important.

Syllabuses and Swiss cheese

It is important to realize that you cannot teach everything. Syllabuses, like Swiss cheese, are full of holes. One reason for the holes is that teachers often decide that something does not need explicit teaching. For example, if we've taught *This is Helen's* and *This book is Helen's*, and *That is Helen's*, do we need to teach *That book is Helen's?* Another reason for holes is the immense difficulty of some linguistic items. The use of the definite article system in English is so complex, for example, that you cannot possibly teach all of it.

A recent perspective on the structural syllabus

In Chapter 4 we looked at morpheme acquisition studies which suggest that learners have their own order for learning structures – what amounts to an *internal syllabus*. The morpheme acquisition studies, and the Chomskyan tradition which inspired them, ask a challenging question that structural syllabus designers cannot avoid confronting. In box 4.12 (p. 72) we posed the question like this: 'what is the point in having an *external* syllabus if learners have their own *internal* one?'

There are a number of possible answers to this question. One is to say that since learners have their own internal syllabuses, we should abolish external ones, rather along the lines that Prabhu follows (as we saw in Chapter 10). A second possible answer would be simply to ignore the existence of the internal syllabus, and to continue following an external one regardless. We might for example point out that the morpheme studies were done in a naturalistic context, and argue that in the classroom situation, an external order for learning needs to be imposed.

A third possible answer is followed by a group of applied linguists of whom Manfred Pienemann is the best known. This answer involves making the external syllabus, as far as is possible, follow the order found in internal syllabuses. In other words, we would use the information given by the morpheme acquisition studies to decide on the order of structures introduced in textbooks.

Pienemann's research work investigates this possibility. In Pienemann (1985) for example he looks at three word-order rules in German. We shall call them Rules A, B and C. Acquisition-order studies show that these rules are acquired in the order A, then B, then C. In his own study, Pienemann takes two groups of learners of German as a foreign language. One group has learned Rule A but not Rule B, while the second group has learned both Rules A and B. He teaches both groups Rule C. He finds that, although both groups can pass a formal test on Rule C (after it has been taught), only the group that has learned Rule B actually uses Rule C in their own language outside class. In other words, if you want to learn Rule C properly, you need to have learned Rules A and B first.

Pienemann generalizes this finding into the belief that a learner will only really master a structure if her learning stage is nearing that item in her internal syllabus. Pienemann calls this the 'teachability hypothesis'. It 'predicts that instruction can only promote language acquisition if the interlanguage is close to the point when the structure to be taught is acquired in the natural setting' (1985: 36).

But how feasible is the idea of making external syllabuses follow internal ones? Certainly at the moment we do not have that much information about internal syllabuses (or how they might vary from learner to learner) for their influence to be that far-reaching. The morpheme studies deal with just a small part of language, and can give restricted guidance. Then there is another question: would a syllabus based on internal acquisition orders actually be that different from the ones we already have? Opinions differ on this. Pienemann himself suggests there will be a difference, and this is backed up by the research of Rogers (1994), who looks at seven textbooks teaching German as a foreign language, and finds that they do not follow what is known about natural acquisition orders of German. Hatch (1978) on the other hand is sceptical. She suggests that the differences would be small, and the effort of finding out about natural orders would, from the point of view of language-teaching syllabus design at least, not be worth making. Box 12.3 invites you to see how much one particular syllabus follows natural order:

12.3 Natural order and *Now for English*

Look back to box 4.11 on page 69. It gives the acquisition order of five morphemes of English. Now look at the contents page of *Now for English*, given on page 213. As far as you can tell, to what extent does this syllabus follow the acquisition order for the five morphemes?[3]

Despite reservations about the applicability of the teachability hypothesis, it does carry a very important message that syllabus designers ignore at their peril. It is that syllabus construction is not just the application of simplicity criteria, frequency counts and the rest. The notion of 'learner stage' is an important consideration. Whether this is measured in a formal way by acquisition-order studies, or is just based on teacher experience of the way learners progress, it should be in your thoughts as you design your syllabus.

Between the structural and the notional/functional syllabus came the situational syllabus. Here is a box about it, and about . . .

12.4 . . . learning to swim

As we saw in Chapter 10, between the structural syllabus (the subject of the last section) and the notional/functional (the subject of the next), comes the situational syllabus. You may wish to remind yourself of this syllabus type by looking back to page 180.

One of the major objections to the situational syllabus, raised by Wilkins (1972b) among others, is that it does not easily convey important generalizations about the language. A syllabus must be able to do this.

A rather absurd example will illustrate this point. It you are teaching someone to swim, it would make sense to deal with the different strokes in turn – beginning perhaps with the breast stroke, moving on to the crawl, and so on. Your 'swimming syllabus' would in this way be organized according to stroke. Imagine what a shock you would receive if you turned up as a learner to your first swimming lesson and were told by the instructor: *First of all on this course we're going to teach you to swim in a circular pool, then in a rectangular one, then in an oblong one.* A swimming syllabus organized according to shape of swimming pool would be ridiculous; no important generalizations about swimming would be captured through this organization.

As we shall see later in this chapter, this criticism can be raised not only in relation to the situational syllabus, but also for the notional/functional one.

Notional/functional (N/F) syllabuses

Needs analysis

In Chapter 10 we described the development of the notional/functional (n/f) syllabus by the Council of Europe team. We related it to the 'sociolinguistic revolution', to discontent with structural teaching in general, and with the structural syllabus in particular. In this section we shall look more carefully into the machinery of the n/f syllabus.

Selection is a big issue for this syllabus type. In structural-syllabus design selecting what to teach is very much a question of deciding on ordering. Remember what MAMD says about *Now for English*: over the three years of the course he feels he can teach all the major structures of English. This concept of total coverage – starting with beginners and proceeding over a period of time until all the structures of the language have been taught – is a common one in much language teaching. But it is not a concept that can be applied easily to n/f syllabuses. Take functions for example. It is clear that the uses to which a language can be put are very many. We simply cannot teach *all* the functions of English. We therefore have to find some means of identifying which functions to teach, and which to exclude, from our course.

The member of the Council of Europe team who considered this problem was the Swiss applied linguist René Richterich. His answer was to look at learners' *language needs*. He defines language needs as 'the requirements which arise from the use of a language in the multitude of situations which may arise in the social lives of individuals and groups' (1972: 32). But the key word in Richterich's definition – 'situation' – poses problems. One dictionary (the *Concise Oxford*) defines it as a 'set of circumstances', and van Ek (1973), thinking specifically about language use, talks of 'the complex of extra linguistic conditions which determines the nature of the language act'. The words 'set' and 'complex' convey the idea that the factors which go to make up a situation are complex and numerous. This suggests that if the concept of situation is to be really useful for syllabus design, it will have to be broken down into component parts. This is just what the Council of Europe does. The 'components of situations' as described by another member of the team, Jan van Ek (1975), are illustrated in box 12.5:

12.5   Part of the Council of Europe's needs analysis model

Here are the components of 'situation' (with some sub-categories) in the Council of Europe's framework:

Settings   There are two sub-categories of setting:

Geographical   which country the user wants to use the target language in. Some learners will want to use the target language in the country where it is an L1; others in a country where it is an FL. Country of use

---

may have important implications in our decision about what language items to teach.

Place   e.g. at the airport, in the hotel, in the office. These are the 'situations' of the situational syllabus.

Topics   What the user wants to talk about. We may find that a learner's needs are closely related to particular topic areas, like 'leisure activities' or 'business matters'. Topics can be important in the selection of notions and functions; they are clearly crucial in deciding what vocabulary to teach. As you saw in box 12.1 (p. 212), both topics and lexical areas appear in Column 3 of *Now for English*'s contents page.

Roles   The model identifies different sorts.[4] The most important of these are the *social roles*. Examples of social roles are 'stranger to stranger', 'customer to shopkeeper', 'doctor to patient'. As with the other categories in this, the social-role relationships a learner is likely to find himself in will affect the language it is most useful to teach.

So Step 1 of needs analysis à la Council of Europe involves listing the situations – broken down into settings, topics and roles – relevant to the learner in her use of the target language. Step 2 is to identify the language activities likely to occur in the situations. 'These', van Ek says (1975: 104) 'may be as comparatively "simple" as understanding the weather-forecast on the radio or as complex as summarising orally in a foreign language a report written in one's native language'. This second example illustrates for van Ek how the traditional division of activities into the four skills of listening, reading, speaking and writing is inadequate. Activities very often involve more than one skill. Step 3 is to list the notions and functions associated with the situations and activities. But there is an important Step 4. This is to identify the actual language forms most useful to express the notions and functions. The word <u>exponent</u> is used in this context; we say that such and such a form <u>expounds</u> such and such a function. To illustrate: in English (as in every language) there are very many ways to expound the function of 'greeting'. *Hi* and *Good morning* are two of them. These two differ very much in formality, and it may be that for particular students one is more appropriate than the other. You would let your needs analysis identify what exponent it would be appropriate to teach.

These four steps take us from situations to exponents, and provide a way of selecting the most relevant content for our language syllabus. To put a little more flesh onto these bones, imagine that you are developing a syllabus for a group of secretaries learning English. Box 12.6 invites you to undertake a mini-needs analysis for these learners:

12.6 Doing a mini-needs analysis

(a) Here is a short example of part of a needs analysis for a secretary.

    Step 1   **Components of situations**

    Setting   learner's L1 country; in the office

    Topics   hotel bookings, transportation arrangements, appointments

    Roles   stranger to stranger; secretary to boss

    Step 2   **Language activity**

        making phone calls to the FL country in relation to a business trip her boss is to undertake

    Step 3   **Identifying notions and functions**

    Notions   dates, times, futurity

    Functions   giving information, requesting information, making arrangements

    Step 4   **Identifying *exponents***

    She'll be staying for . . . days

    I'd like to . . .

    Could you please tell me . . .

    on + date; *at* + time; *will be* + *-ing*; *by* + form of transport

(b) Think of three more language activities in which this secretary may want to use her target language. For one of these activities, work through Steps 3 and 4 as above.

The Council of Europe's needs-analysis model was one of a number that were developed in the 1970s. You met another in box 11.6 (p. 204) where we took a brief look at the Nijmegen needs-analysis work. A further highly influential model was developed by John Munby. Munby's model (1978) was far more complex than the Council of Europe's one. It provided a sophisticated instrument that was used to analyse learners' needs in situations throughout the world.

The common core and the T-Level

Teaching a group of secretaries is an example of ESP (English for Specific Purposes). This type of teaching is very common nowadays, and many language-teaching institutions offer course with specialisms like 'English for airline pilots', 'French for diplomats', and 'German for scientists'. The modern world seems to expect, even demand, tailor-made courses of this sort.

One of the attractive features of ESP is that it is relatively easy to identify learner language needs. But this is not true of another very common teaching situation, called TENOR. This, as we saw in Chapter 1, stands for Teaching English for No Obvious Reason, and it includes all general courses, where the learners have divergent reasons for learning, or (as in many school situations) where we simply do not know what their eventual uses (if any) of the FL will be.

Needs analysis does not work easily for TENOR students because their needs are unknown. How then can you do the job of selection which the notional/functional syllabus seems to require? The Council of Europe's answer lies in the concept of the 'common core'. All learners, whatever their eventual uses of the FL, will (the argument runs) need a certain common core of notions and functions. In the functional area, these are particularly uses associated with general socializing, like 'greeting', 'requesting information', 'inviting'.

The Council of Europe needed to develop a language-teaching system that would work in the many highly diverse situations met throughout the member countries. Flexibility was all important, and the Council's needs were met by a unit/credit system. In this, teaching units deal with distinct areas of language use. Learners select which units to cover according to their particular language needs. Credits are given for units completed and, when a number of credits have been gained, a qualification is awarded.

The system identifies five levels of proficiency. The lowest was called the 'Threshold Level' (or 'T-Level'), though later a lower level called 'Waystage' was introduced. Next up is 'basic', then 'general competence', 'advanced' and 'full professional'. The idea is that each level should have a common core unit, plus additional specialized units. Van Ek was given the task of developing a syllabus for the common core of the Threshold Level. His document, called *The Threshold Level*, is a landmark document in n/f syllabus design. It appeared in two forms: van Ek (1975) for the adult learner, and van Ek (1978) for the secondary school student.

One of the advantages of n/f is that until you start to consider actual exponents, you are dealing with ideas (like 'situation', 'notion' and 'function') which are non-language-specific, and can therefore be applied to the teaching of many languages.[5] Consequently the notions and functions you identify as useful for a German learning English are likely to be equally useful to the Briton learning German, the American learning Spanish, the Italian learning French. This means that a document like the Threshold Level can exist in a number of versions, for different languages. So it is that, alongside the T-Level, there are comparable documents in other languages – the French *Niveau-Seuil*, German *Kontaktschwelle*, Spanish *Nivel Umbral* and Italian *Livello Soglia* for example.

12.7 Getting to know the T-Level

The T-Level specification (van Ek 1975) consists of a series of lists. We have dealt with the most important of these, which are:

A Topics   B Settings
C Roles   D Activities
E Functions   F Notions
G Form (exponents)

Below are some items of the sort found in the T-Level. Put these under the categories above; there are two for each category. You can do this by matching letters and numbers – e.g. if you think 'hobbies' is a notional category, you would write F5.

1. booking a hotel room over the phone
2. airport
3. questions using Wh- words (*when, where, why,* etc.)
4. quantity
5. hobbies
6. friend/friend
7. duration (length of time)
8. language institute
9. apologizing
10. types of accommodation
11. private person/official
12. should/ought to
13. expressing gratitude
14. understanding announcements via public address systems (e.g. in an airport)

For each category A to G, think of two more examples that you might expect to appear in the common core of the Threshold Level.[6]

Uses of n/f syllabuses

Are there any teaching situations in which the n/f syllabus is particularly useful? One clear, and very large, audience was immediately apparent when n/f syllabuses came into existence. In fact, it was the audience *for which* n/f came into existence. These were the learners suffering from the epidemic of 'syntax syndrome' that (as we saw in Chapter 10) Newmark diagnosed so well. These students knew their grammar, but lacked communicative ability. They existed in droves around the world, a legacy of structural teaching. N/f teaching was able to add a communicative dimension to their knowledge, to 'activate' this knowledge so that it could be used for doing things with language. Because of the size of this audience, very many n/f courses are pitched at the intermediate level and above, the assumption being that the learners already know their grammar. Implicit in this approach is a view of language teaching that became very common. It is a two-stage model. At Stage 1 you teach the grammar of the language using a structural syllabus. At Stage 2 you use a functional syllabus to teach language use, activating the structures taught at Stage 1.

What about other, more specialized, uses of n/f? We have already discussed ESP. As we have seen, because of n/f and needs analysis, we are able to say to our students: 'We have analysed your needs, and are teaching you just those parts of English that are relevant to those needs.' Though ESP existed before n/f, the two concepts worked very well together. They were essentially twins who grew up together.

There is another type of course which is becoming increasingly widespread throughout the world. We met it in Chapter 1 with the Chinese student Zhang. He has just six months in which to bring his English up to a particular standard. What he requires might be called an 'urgency course'. Its essence is to teach a large amount of language in a short space of time. The urgency course is popular, because the world is full of people in Zhang's circumstances.

The traditional approach to the urgency course is not very satisfactory. Often a textbook intended for a long course would be used, and abandoned when time ran out. So learners following a book like *Now for English* might cover the verb BE and not much else. N/f provides a much better way of selection, again by looking at needs – this time urgent ones. One common version of the urgency course is the pre-sessional course. This gives language training to students about to follow some study programme in which the FL is the language of instruction. Many pre-sessional courses are held in the target-language country. It is possible to predict the learners' urgent needs as from the moment they arrive. They will, for example, soon want to open a bank account, to search for accommodation, to register at the Health Centre (in Britain they will probably have caught a cold in the first few days). These needs can form the basis of highly relevant teaching in which the notions and functions urgent for them are introduced.

In the 1970s and early 1980s, it is no exaggeration to say that n/f syllabuses dominated syllabus design in language teaching. Ministries of Education world-wide jostled to change their syllabuses from structural to n/f, and private language schools would boast of their up-to-date notional/functional-based teaching.

The bubble had to burst. When it did, this was not just the result of theoretical objections to the notional/functional syllabus, but also of concrete problems encountered by practitioners – the teachers who actually went into classrooms to teach with n/f textbooks. Box 12.8 gives two anecdotes to illustrate these problems.

12.8 Down with notions and functions: two anecdotes

Some time in the early 1980s, I was invited to sit in on a planning meeting at a major language-teaching institution in Italy. The purpose of the meeting was to select the teaching books for the coming year. Because it was the early 1980s, I was confident that fashion would dictate that all the chosen books would be notional/functional. But I was wrong, and in the event almost all the books were structurally based. One teacher, who had been using n/f books for a number of years, explained: 'in n/f books the students learn lots of phrases, but they don't come out of the lesson with one major thing learned. In structural teaching they do.' This objection is grounded in the fact that it is difficult to make clear and strong generalizations about language use. So if you are not careful, your n/f lesson ends up providing not very much more than an elaborate phrase book (ten ways of 'inviting', five ways of 'making plans', and so on). The problem with phrase books is that you are not taught any general knowledge that enables you to go beyond the phrases given. The phrase book may tell you how to ask for a cup of tea, but what happens if you want a cup of hot chocolate?

The second anecdote makes the same point. In the late 1970s a colleague and I were writing n/f materials to be taught on a pre-sessional course.[7] One lesson dealt with one of those urgent activities – opening a bank account. The campus bank set aside a lunch hour for arriving overseas students to open accounts, and in the morning of that day we taught our group of recently arrived students some language appropriate to that activity. One sentence we introduced and drilled was *Good morning. I'd like to open a bank account please*. At lunch time I thought I would go to the bank and eavesdrop on the results of the morning's lesson. One short dialogue was most depressing. The bank clerk knew of course that the students all wanted to open accounts, so she said to one student: *Hello. You want to open an account I expect*. The reply that came back was the drilled one: *Good morning, I'd like to open a bank account please*. Hardly a successful piece of dialogue! The learner had produced, parrot-like, the taught opening to the interaction. She did not have the knowledge to handle the unexpected.

Use of the phrase 'strong generalizations' in the first anecdote may rightly remind you of what was said in box 12.4 (p. 223) about generalizations, syllabuses and learning to swim.

The bubble may have burst. But, as we shall see in the next section, n/f never disappeared, and indeed it is almost inconceivable today to produce a syllabus without a notional/functional dimension. The heady days of notions and functions and nothing else may have gone. But the movement has left its mark.

Units of organization, and the multidimensional syllabus

We saw in box 12.7 that the T-Level document is in effect a series of lists. of settings, topics, roles and the rest. It is sometimes described as a syllabus inventory rather than as a syllabus. It can be used to construct syllabuses, but it is not a syllabus in itself.

It is certainly true that notional/functional was the syllabus type that most commonly came out of the T-Level in the late 1970s. But it is important to realize that very many sorts of syllabus could be based on a syllabus inventory like this. You could in fact use any of van Ek's lists as the basis for a syllabus, producing a setting-based syllabus, or topic-based, role-based or structure-(exponent-)based ones. To form a topic-based syllabus, for example, you would simply take the list of topics, and organize your course so that each unit covered one topic area. To use a phrase of MAMD's, you would be making the topic your 'unit of organization'. It is important also to realize that in choosing one unit or organization, you are not ignoring the other types of item on the inventory. MAMD chooses the structure as his unit of organization, but (as he points out on p 216) functions are not ignored. Similarly, a topic-based syllabus would be constructed around topics; but settings, roles and the rest might play their part in the construction of the course. In Johnson (1982) I deal at length with the idea of 'unit of organization'.

Syllabus designers and textbook writers today commonly follow similar procedures to van Ek's, producing their own syllabus inventories. But, because of the burst bubble, the resulting syllabuses are rarely exclusively notional/functional. They are more often hybrids, or mixtures. They are sometimes called multidimensional syllabuses. The basis of the multidimensional syllabus is that it has more than one unit of organization. There are two main ways these syllabuses can be produced from an inventory like the T-Level. In the first, you can shift the focus at different points in the course. You might for example have some structural units followed by the occasional unit dealing with a situation; later you might change the focus yet again with some functional units. Morrow and Johnson (1979) uses this method.

The second way is very common nowadays. It is to have more than one focus operating in each part of the course. A widely used textbook which follows this solution is Swan and Walter (1985). The table below is taken from what they call the 'map' of their Book 2. It shows what is covered in the first five units of the course. You will recognize most of the item types listed in the first row:

	FUNCTIONS AND SKILLS	NOTIONS, TOPICS AND SITUATIONS	GRAMMAR	PHONOLOGY
In unit	Students will learn to	Students will learn to talk about	Students will learn or revise these grammar points	Students will study these aspects of pronunciation
1	Make introductions; ask for and give information; describe people; listen for specific information	Themselves and their interests; people's appearance and behaviour	Simple present; *be* and *have*; *have got*; adverbs of degree; *like . . . ing*; no article for general meaning	Hearing unstressed syllables in rapid speech
2	Make commentaries; express doubt and certainty; take part in simple discussions	Appearance of things; beliefs	Present progressive; contrast between simple present and present progressive	/i/ and /iː/; pronunciations of *th*
3	Narrate; express past time relations	Accidents; basic office situations	Regular and irregular past tenses; past progressive; *when-* and *while-* clauses; ellipsis	Hearing final consonants; pronunciations of the letter *a*
4	Describe; compare	Similarities and differences; people's appearance	Comparative and superlative of adjectives; *than* and *as*; relative clauses with *who*; *do* as a pro-verb; compound adjectives	Decoding rapid speech; stress, rhythm and linking
5	Ask for things without knowing the exact word; make and reply to suggestions, requests and offers	Shopping; household goods; clothes	*At a +* shop; *a thing with a . . .*; *a thing for . . . ing*; modal verbs; infinitive with and without *to*	Rhythm and stress; /ei/ versus /e/; spellings of /ei/

Many other examples could be given. Littlejohn and Hicks (1996) for example also have a 'map' of their course. This shows that the book is divided into a number of 'themes'; in our terminology these are 'topic areas'. Each of these is divided into five units, called: topic; language focus; activity; cultural matters; revision and evaluation. These terms are slightly different from those of the T-Level, but there is much common ground. Syllabuses like this are also commonly found in books dealing with specific skills (like reading or writing). An example is Haarman *et al.* (1988). Their book teaches reading skills for social science students. Its contents page indicates that three main types of organizational category run alongside. One of these deals with structures and other linguistic items, and is called *language work*. The second comes under the name of *approaching the text*. It covers different types of reading skill, like skimming (quickly reading for gist) and scanning (reading for specific information). The third category, *intensive reading*, also deals with skills, but covers specific strategies like 'inferring the meaning of words from context' and 'note taking'.

12.9 Spotting how a textbook is organized

You might think it easy, but it is in fact very difficult to tell just by a quick glance how a textbook is really organized. As we have seen, the contents page can help, but often it will tell you very little, because unit names do not always reveal much about organization. Column 1 of *Now for English*'s contents page (on p. 213) is a good example. The units have names like 'Oh Sally!' and 'What a mess!', that are not very revealing. Beware also of what a book says about itself. Many books *say* they are functional, and contain units bearing functional titles like 'Describing people' or 'Introducing yourself'. But the unit on 'Describing people' may in fact be a unit about the verb BE followed by an adjective, as in *He's tall*, and *She's thin*. Similarly, 'Introducing yourself' may just consist of BE plus a name – *I'm Keith*.

How to tell the true from the false? The secret lies in the concept of 'unit of organization'. You need to look closely at the lessons themselves, to see what they are really covering. If there is a clear structural thread running through a unit, while the functions within it seem to be disorganized, then that unit at least is a structurally based one. Looking at all the units in a book should enable you to say something certain about its underlying syllabus.

You are invited to look closely at a textbook that you know. Try to work out the syllabus it is based on. This may take you some time!

Conclusion

For many people, syllabus design is a dry, yawn-inducing subject. Whether or not this chapter has succeeded in stifling the yawns, it has hopefully indicated how much has happened in syllabus design in recent decades. Much of what has happened has been an enrichment and a 'complexification'. Syllabuses once could be short, simple documents, listing structures to be taught, in order. Nowadays, they are likely to be based on large-scale syllabus inventories with many different sorts of lists.

But it is also true to say that along with developments in syllabus design has come an interest in the *how* of language teaching – in methodology. At this point in the book, we imagine you have your syllabus ready and waiting. You now have to go into the classroom and teach it. But how?

12.10   Find the missing syllabuses

At the end of Chapter 10 three sorts of syllabus are mentioned that have not been covered in the present chapter. Go back to Chapter 10 and identify what these are.[8]

You might also like to make a list of all the different syllabus types that have been mentioned in the book as a whole. This may help to convince you what a rich and complex area syllabus design is.

Notes

1. Column 1 is entitled 'Unit', and the column just gives the unit names (like the chapter titles of a book). Column 2 is 'Main teaching points (structures)'. This column lists the structures to be covered in each unit. Column 3 is 'Topics (lexical areas) and functions'. The concept of 'topic' will be discussed later in the chapter.

   The answer to Question 2 will be given in the following section.

   The revision units are 6, 12, 18, 24 and 30. In Column 2 the items in italics are sentence patterns. Those in capitals are structures. Sentence patterns and structures were discussed on page 171. The first twelve units focus particularly on the verb BE. The simple present and the present continuous are introduced in Units 13–25. *Can* to indicate ability is introduced in Unit 27. Example sentences might be: *She can swim well; Anne is only four, but she can already write her own name.* In Unit 29 *can* is used to indicate permission. Examples: *Can I open the window please? Pauline can go to the party as long as she's home by midnight.*

2. The simple present tense is covered in Units 13–17. Unit 13 deals with the basic form. The third-person negatives and interrogatives are introduced in Unit 15. The negative and interrogative simple past would be *She didn't like chocolates*, and *Did she like chocolates?* To form negatives and interrogatives (from the basic form), you need to use part of the verb *do*. It is this verb that shows the tense (*did* in the simple past) and carries the negation (*didn't*). The main verb *like* appears in the

'infinite' form, without an ending. In the interrogative, the subject (*she*) comes between part of the verb *do* and the main verb *like*.

3. The indefinite article is first met in Unit 3, and the definite article in Unit 13. The difference between the two is not mentioned as a point to be covered in the syllabus. *-ing* is first met in Unit 21, *-s* plural in Unit 10, *-'s* possessive in 4 and *-s* 3rd person simple present in Unit 13. This order is very different from the natural order shown in box 4.11.

4. This treatment of the Threshold Level has been adapted from the original in various ways. Van Ek (1975) in fact identifies two sorts of roles. As well as the social roles, there are also 'psychological' ones. If you count these two types of role as separate (as van Ek on occasion does), there are four 'components of situations': settings, topics, social roles, psychological roles. In addition, notions are divided into general and specific (topic-related) ones. A further component, not touched on in this treatment, is 'degree of skill'.

5. This sentence illustrates that the term 'n/f' can be used alone, without the word 'syllabus' following. This usage is continued in the following pages.

6. The matchings are: A–5, 10; B–2, 8; C–6, 11; D–1, 14; E–9, 13; F–4, 7; G–3, 12.

7. The colleague was Keith Morrow and the materials were a pilot version of what eventually became Morrow and Johnson (1979).

8. These are the procedural syllabus (mentioned on p. 191), the task-based syllabus (p. 192) and the process syllabus (p. 194).

Chapter 13

Ways and means

In Chapter 7 we identified two processes important in the mastering of a foreign language – declarativization and proceduralization. This chapter is about how we, as teachers, might help learners with these processes. With declarativization we are concerned with showing learners how some aspect of language 'works'. There are various ways this can be done. One is by actually 'presenting' the aspect to learners, by showing them examples, or giving them some kind of explanation. It would also include a procedure common today known as 'language awareness', where we try to find ways of drawing learners' attention to language items. We shall use the term 'conveying language' to refer to all these different ways of showing how a language works. This may seem a curious term, and is not one generally used in the literature. But it does capture the diversity of the activities that can achieve this aim in a classroom. The term we shall use in relation to procedural knowledge is less curious – it is 'practising language'. This also captures a range of procedures, from very controlled drilling to activities like discussions, where learners are free to express themselves however they wish. In this chapter we shall look at techniques which are often, though not always, suited to teaching *spoken* English. In Chapter 14 we shall look at the teaching of other skills.

CONVEYING LANGUAGE

Some ways of conveying language

Two characteristics can be associated with the good presentation of new language. One of them is *clarity*. The language point you are conveying to your learners needs to be clear. The second one is *memorability*. For the point to remain in the learners' heads, it needs to be presented in a memorable way. When I was at school, my history teacher wanted our class to understand the hardship suffered by workers during the British Industrial Revolution. He did so by dropping to the floor and crawling on all fours between the rows of desks, to show what it was like inside a coal mine. That was memorable. I still remember it.

13.1 Teaching prepositions . . . with an army of helpers

In Chapter 12 (p. 214) you saw that in unit 16 of *Now for English* four prepositions of place were introduced: *in, on, under* and *behind*. Imagine that you have to introduce these prepositions, and their basic meanings, to a group of learners who have never met them before. Think of as many different ways as you can of how you might do this.

If you wish, choose one of these ways and develop it to the stage where you would be ready to go into the class and teach the prepositions.

For the purposes of this box, imagine that you have an army of helpers at hand, together with access to whatever equipment you need for your presentation. An excellent artist is at your disposal if you need any pictures, and recording facilities are available if you decide you want to use a dialogue recorded on tape. We can even find video equipment for you, should you need it.

Unfortunately, these two characteristics often lead in opposite directions. Clarity often suggests keeping the language content down to a minimum, so that the new item can be focused on without a cluttering context. Baldness and focus are key words. Memorability, on the other hand, often leads in the direction of a full context, trying to make the presentation as alive and meaningful as possible. Richness and discursiveness suggest themselves as key words. As we now consider some of the main modes of presentation available in language teaching, make a point of thinking of each in terms of the possibilities for clarity and memorability.[1]

One way of conveying information about language is by **explanation**. Here, a language rule is explained to the learners in explicit terms. It is associated with highly deductive teaching approaches like GT. Box 10.2 (p. 163) suggested what GT explanations can be like.

A potential problem with explanations is that they can be highly intellectually challenging, thus making them inaccessible to many learners. This inaccessibility can be heightened by the use of linguistic words – like *noun, adverb, noun phrase* – which some learners will simply not have come across before. We use the word metalanguage to describe such 'language about language'. Explanation can be useful to introduce something for the first time, as the starting point for the proceduralization process. They can give the learner a kind of 'mental map' of what is to be learned. Fitts and Posner (1967) give a non-linguistic example. They report how the time taken to lead novice pilots up to their first solo flights can be reduced by more than half by giving an initial explanation in which the manoeuvres involved are discussed and explained.

But over-complex explanations can be particularly troublesome as a starting point, and it is very easy for them to become so long and contorted that they actually hinder performance. You can probably think of examples from your own experience, again related to non-language skills – learning how to serve in tennis for example, or how to drive a car perhaps. A tennis instructor may give such elaborate instructions on what to do (*Hold your arm at an angle of x degrees, with the wrist moving flexibly in an up and down position. The racquet should be pointing directly ahead . . .*) that the learner not only fails to serve, but also risks a nervous breakdown at the same time. As the skill psychologist Holding (1965) succinctly puts it: 'it is possible to disrupt the operator's performance in a quite lasting way by the over-elaboration of instructions'.

Simplicity is clearly an important characteristic for good grammar rules. What others are there? Swan (1994) is one of the few people who have tried to draw up a list of the characteristics a good language-teaching rule should have. He lists six in all. One of them is indeed *simplicity*; another is that the rule should be *true*. Easier said than done, of course, and these two may conflict with each other. Often the language teacher has to simplify a rule to make it clear, but in so doing may arrive at a statement that is 'economical with the truth'. The *some/any* rules we saw in the 'rough guide on syllabus design criteria' in Chapter 12 are a case in point. The rule that *any* is always used in questions (like *Did he eat any chocolates?*) is not strictly true, and you can doubtless think of your own examples where *some* is used in a question. The following explanation (from Murphy 1990: 140) clarifies the difference between *any* and *some* in questions. It also gives a good example of the kind of explanation favoured by many teachers nowadays. It *is* an explanation, but the 'explaining' element is quite short, and is supported by examples.

In most questions (but not all) we use **any**:

- Is there **any** ice in the fridge?
- Did they make **any** mistakes?
- Are you doing **anything** this evening?
- I can't find Ann. Has **anybody** seen her?

We normally use **some** (*not* **any**) when we *offer* things (**Would you like some . . . ?**):

- A: Would you like **some** coffee?
  B: Yes, please.
- A: Would you like **something** to eat?
  B: No, thank you. I'm not hungry.

or ask for things (**Can I have some . . . ? / Can you lend me some . . . ?** etc.):
- 'Can I have **some** soup, please?'   'Yes, of course. Help yourself.'
- 'Can you lend me **some** money?'   'I'm sorry, I can't.'

The explanation above has elements of a second common way in which language is conveyed. This is by means of key sentences. Box 13.2 gives a further illustration:

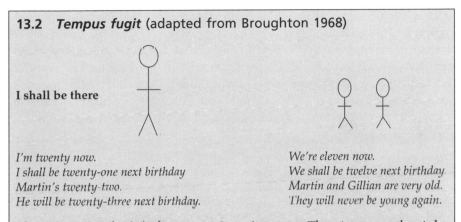

13.2 *Tempus fugit* (adapted from Broughton 1968)

I shall be there

I'm twenty now.
I shall be twenty-one next birthday
Martin's twenty-two.
He will be twenty-three next birthday.

We're eleven now.
We shall be twelve next birthday.
Martin and Gillian are very old.
They will never be young again.

The picture on the left shows a girl aged twenty. The picture on the right shows two eleven-year-old boys. What structure is being introduced in these sentences? What forms of the structure are presented? The first person singular (*I*) is illustrated. What other persons? Notice the different forms the verb has for the different persons.

What *meaning* does the presented form have? How is that meaning conveyed in the key sentences? Be precise about this; various measures are used to make learners understand how the new verb is used.[2]

Think about clarity and memorability. Give the key sentences points out of ten for each.

Good marks for clarity, perhaps. But memorable? The words 'baldness' and 'focus' spring to mind, certainly more than 'richness' and 'discursiveness'. There is an attempt at a joke (*They will never be young again*); but no one (including the textbook writer) would expect the learners to be excitedly telling their family about these key sentences when they return home after the lesson.

Dialogues/written texts are another extremely popular way of presenting new language in textbooks. Sometimes these are as bald and focused as the key sentences above, little more than a collection of sentences intended to convey a grammatical point. We shall see an example of such a dialogue in box 13.4.

In the following example of a written text, a great deal of effort has been put into making the text interesting and hence memorable. Like a number of books mentioned in Chapter 12, these materials (Powell and McHugh 1991) specify the contents of each unit in terms of various items – in this

239

case topics, structures/lexis and functions. The topic for this unit is 'non-verbal communication', and before the text is read there are various warm-up activities geared to focus the learners' attention on the topic, and to arouse interest in it. For example, they are asked to explain various gestures used in their own countries. Warm-up activities like this provide useful contextualization for dialogues and texts. The passage, which is then read, is likely to contain much material that is new to the learner. Apart from the new structure that is being introduced, there will be unknown words and phrases. At this stage the emphasis is on memorability rather than clarity. The focusing comes later, in Exercise 3. This contains an explanation, and the learner is referred back to the text to find instances of the structure being taught.

It's not what you say . . .

Non-verbal communication, or body language, refers to ways of communicating without words, gesture, facial expression and posture are all norms of non-verbal communication. The meanings of some forms of body language are the same all over the world: when people are happy, they smile; when they are sad or angry, they frown or scowl. Nodding the head, or moving it up and down, is almost universally used to indicate *yes*. Shaking the head from side to side to indicate *no* is also a universal gesture and may be learned in infancy – when a baby has had enough milk, he turns his head from side to side to show he doesn't want any more. Shrugging the shoulders is another universal gesture used to show that a person does not know or understand what you are talking about. Verbal language is different from culture to culture, however, and so the non-verbal language may also differ. A gesture may have a clear meaning in one culture, but be meaningless or have a completely different meaning in another culture.

[Exercises 1 and 2 are omitted]
3 *Language focus* **infinitive of purpose**

a Look at these examples:
   1 Nodding the head is used *to indicate* 'yes'.
   2 A baby turns his head from side to side *to show* he . . .
     To + **infinitive is used to talk about the reason or purpose for doing something.**
b Finish these sentences.

Example People nod their head to indicate 'yes'.

1 People wear smart clothes to __.
2 Women wear make-up to __.
3 People go to the cinema to __.
4 In my country, people __ to show they're pleased to meet you.
5 In my country, people __ to mean 'goodbye'.

Write two more examples of your own.

Teacher actions/descriptions can also be used to convey language to learners. Box 13.3 illustrates:

13.3 Teaching righteous indignation

Coulavin (1983, cited in Ur 1996) gives an example of how a teacher can use an incident from his own life to help teach language. She says:

It can happen to anyone who commutes – a traffic jam, a last-minute phone call, a car that won't start – and you realize you are going to be late for a lesson . . . However, attack being the best form of defence, I recently found a way to turn my lateness to good account. A full ten minutes after the start of the lesson, I strode into the classroom and wrote on the board in huge letters

YOU'RE LATE!

Then I invited the students to yell at me with all the venom they could muster and we all laughed. So I wrote:

You're late **again!**

and

You're **always** late!

So we practised these forms. They seemed to get a real kick out of putting the stress in the right place . . . when we had savoured the pleasure of righteous indignation, I proposed that everyone should write down the accusations most commonly levelled at him (or her). A rich and varied selection poured out such as:

You **always** eat my sweets!

You've lost the keys!

You haven't lost the keys **again!**

Teacher actions/descriptions are techniques suited to some structures more than others. One of the structures it *is* commonly used for is teaching the present continuous tense. One major use of this tense is to describe actions taking place at the present moment (*contiguous* actions). Since contiguous actions can be done in class, a common technique for conveying the tense's meaning is for the teacher to perform a series of actions, and to commentate on them as they are being done: *I am walking to the door, I am writing on the blackboard* and so on. Other members of the class then do the same actions, and the teacher produces sentences like *He is walking to the door, They are writing on the blackboard*. This procedure makes the contiguous action meaning of the tense very clear.

But the procedure has a danger, which Widdowson (1972) discusses. He makes the point that although this way of presenting the tense clarifies its *meaning*, it says nothing about how the tense is actually *used*. In fact the use made of the tense in the examples just given is to 'commentate on your own actions and the actions of others'. Since everyone in the class can see what is happening, this use is unnatural and – if you look at it in terms of natural communication – even a little silly. It certainly leaves the learners without any feeling for when the tense is really used. Widdowson uses the terms signification and value for what we have called meaning and use above. He makes the point that learners need to be taught not just the signification but also the value of the grammar they are learning. This insight contributed significantly to the development of a communicative approach to language teaching.

How can we avoid the danger Widdowson discusses? Textbook writers nowadays take more care to ensure that the language of their texts is used in communicatively appropriate ways. In *Now for English*, for example, I introduce the present continuous tense through a dialogue that describes contiguous actions. I attempt to make this natural through choice of the situation. The children have played a trick on their friend Sally, hiding something in her school desk. They are concealed behind desks in the classroom, waiting for Sally to come in. One of their number is peeping out from behind a desk and reporting to the others what is happening (*She's opening the door. She's coming in . . .*). Commentating on actions is natural when the person being 'commentated to' cannot see what is going on.

Widdowson's discussion raises the point that even in structural teaching we need to think about naturalness of language to situation. How much more so when we are teaching a function, like 'asking for permission', for example. In functional teaching, an essential part of the teaching point is to indicate the situations in which the exponent being taught would be used. 'Naturalness to situation' is not just important. It is what is being taught.

13.4   Beckett, Pinter or EFL?

It is easy, and unfair, to make fun of dialogues from less recent books because they do not have the same aims as books today. The dialogue below was clearly produced to contain examples of grammatical structures, and not to teach anything about communicative value. But, though unfair, it may be useful for you to look, for a moment, at the dialogue as a piece of communication. Do this by thinking about what people would *really* say in the situation presented. Then compare it with what the dialogue has.

To start you off: as the dialogue unfolds it becomes clear that Y is a rail passenger (not a rail employee). One would not usually approach another passenger and say the first sentence without (at the very least) an introductory *Excuse me*. And is *It goes to Millville* a likely answer to that particular request? Go through the dialogue considering it in this way, to the point where the interactants say goodbye and apparently get on the same train together.

AT THE STATION

X: *Does this train go to Newtown?*
Y: *No, it goes to Millville.*
X: *Where is the train to Newtown?*

> Y: *It comes at a quarter to three.*
> X: *When does it go to Newtown?*
> Y: *Every half hour, and on Sundays it goes every two hours.*
> X: *When does the bus go to Newtown?*
> Y: *The bus goes from the bus station every fifteen minutes.*
> X: *Are you going to Newtown?*
> Y: *Yes, I go there every day. Where do you come from?*
> X: *I come from Puerto Rico.*
> Y: *When did you come to this country?*
> X: *I came here in April last year.*
> Y: *This is our train. Goodbye.*
> X: *Goodbye.*

In most of the examples we have so far considered, the teacher or textbook is directly 'presenting' a language item to learners. Allowing learners, with guidance from the teacher, to find out for themselves is a popular precept today, and has given rise to the procedure mentioned at the beginning of this chapter – 'language awareness' or 'consciousness raising'. Rutherford and Sharwood Smith (1985: 274) define the second of these as the 'deliberate attempt to draw the learner's attention specifically to the formal properties of the target language'. The exercise on p. 244 (from Wright and Bolitho 1993) gives an example of this highly inductive technique.

Here the (quite advanced) learners are given a text and asked various questions (ten in fact) designed to draw attention to a structure – the passive. The learners are asked, at the top of the page, to count the number of passives in the text. This introduces an interesting point about the passive in English. One way of viewing 'normal' passives is that they come from active constructions: so the active *John opens the door* becomes the passive *The door is opened (by John)*. There are constructions in English that look like passives, because they use the verb BE followed by a form ending in *-ed*. The *is based* in the first paragraph of the text above would be an example. But perhaps these are better viewed as 'BE + adjective' constructions rather than as 'normal' passives. By asking the learners to count the passives, these constructions and their nature would clearly come to light.

A number of applied linguists today believe that language awareness or consciousness raising is important for language learning. Schmidt and Frota (1986) report on some fascinating evidence concerned with the process they call 'noticing'. They observe Schmidt's own learning of Portuguese. He keeps a diary of his own learning, together with tapes of input and output. Diary and taped data were compared at intervals, and the conclusion is that he and his fellow researcher 'found a remarkable correspondence between my reports of what I had noticed when Brazilians talked to me and the linguistic forms I used myself' (p. 140). This leads to the conclusion that 'conscious processing is a necessary condition for one step in the language-learning process, and is facilitative for other aspects of learning'.

Teaching

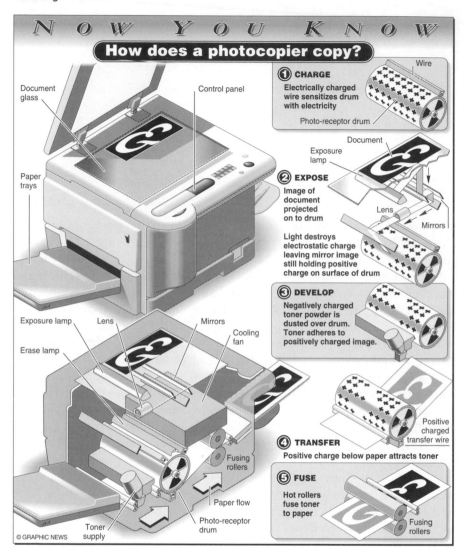

NOW YOU KNOW

How does a photocopier copy?

Document glass
Control panel
Paper trays

Exposure lamp
Lens
Mirrors
Cooling fan
Erase lamp

Toner supply
Paper flow
Photo-receptor drum
Fusing rollers

© GRAPHIC NEWS

① CHARGE
Electrically charged wire sensitizes drum with electricity
Wire
Photo-receptor drum

② EXPOSE
Image of document projected on to drum
Document
Exposure lamp
Lens
Mirrors

Light destroys electrostatic charge leaving mirror image still holding positive charge on surface of drum

③ DEVELOP
Negatively charged toner powder is dusted over drum. Toner adheres to positively charged image.

④ TRANSFER
Positive charge below paper attracts toner
Positive charged transfer wire

⑤ FUSE
Hot rollers fuse toner to paper
Fusing rollers

CATEGORY: Science and Technology
IPTC CODE: SCI,OVR :Science
SUBJECT: Now you know/copier
ARTISTS: Duncan Mil, Russell Lewis, Phil Bainbridge, Julie Hacking (research)
ORIGIN: GRAPHIC NEWS
TYPE: Monochrome / Adobe Illustrator version 3.2
SIZE: 3 columns by 195mm deep
DATE: August 13, 1993
SOURCES: Minolta
GRAPHIC #: 1705

STANDARD MEASURES (SAU)

Width	Picas	millimetres
1 col	12p5	52.3
2 col	25p7	107.7
3 col	38p9	163.2
4 col	52p	219.0
5 col	65p1	274.4
6 col	78.p3	329.7

GRAPHIC NEWS

Utopia Village, 7 Chalcot Road, London NW1 8LH, United Kingdom.
Tel: +44 71 722 4673. Fax: +44 71 586 3567

13.5 Induction versus deduction

An issue associated with conveying language is induction versus deduction. We briefly touched on this in Chapter 10, where we saw that induction involves moving from particular to general (EGRUL), while deduction is RULEG. The issue also relates to the empiricist/rationalist controversy we looked at in Chapter 3, and has to do with the role given to conscious learning.

Rivers (1964) uses the terms analogy (learning by generalization from examples) and analysis (learning by understanding rules). She looks at the pros and cons of each. In favour of analogy she cites the dictum associated with Aristotle: 'there is nothing in the mind that was not first in the senses', together with Politzer's 1961 statement (we saw it in Chapter 10) that 'rules ought to be summaries of behaviours'.[3]

Rivers notes that the danger with analogy is overgeneralization, when the learner mistakenly broadens the scope of the rule. A learner might, for example, be taught that the word *there* can replace a noun phrase starting with *to*. So *I go to the university* becomes *I go there*. Overgeneralization would occur if the learner were to change *I speak to my friend* into *I speak there*.

In favour of deduction Rivers cites Wertheimer's (1945: 199) statement that 'to live in a fog . . . is for many people an unbearable state of affairs. There is a tendency [to desire] structural clearness, surveyability.' The danger of deduction is that (declarative) *knowledge about* will be mistaken for (procedural) *knowledge how to*. A problem that plagued language teaching for a very long time was the false assumption that, if a learner understands a rule, he will be able to use it without problems. The eminent professor from overseas whom we met in box 7.1 (p. 105) shows that this is not true.

There seems little point in heated debate about whether inductive is overall better than deductive or vice versa. It is rather like arguing how many angels can sit on the average pinhead. Perhaps it is a question of learning style; maybe some learners are naturally inductive, others naturally deductive. One might even be able to make statements about different learner groups. It seems likely that children, for example, are able to learn better inductively than deductively. One might also be tempted to think that intelligent learners learn better with rules, less intelligent learners without rules. Recall in this respect the findings of Chastain (1969) linking success in cognitive-code learning with intelligence. But Rivers has a counterargument: 'students of low intelligence are, of course, much happier just repeating what is given to them, and do not feel a strong compulsion to understand what they are doing, but the same low intelligence also makes it hard for them to see analogies'.

Go back over the various ways of conveying language we have illustrated in this section. Consider whether each is better described as inductive or deductive.

Practising language

If you are fortunate (or perhaps unfortunate) enough to live next door to a pianist, you may be aware of how much practice most musicians do. You will also have noticed what a variety of types of practice there is. Worst, from a neighbour's point of view, are probably the scales. For what seems like hours the single-minded pianist goes up and down his instrument playing tedious, mind-numbing sequences of notes. But on other occasions he plays 'the real thing' – actual pieces of music written for performance. Sometimes he stops and repeats bits, but occasionally he plays the pieces from beginning to end. These may even be enjoyable to listen to.

Language learning can involve a similar variety of practice types, which have much in common with the musician's equivalents. Similar to the scales are what are called drills – highly repetitive, controlled, tedious and mind-numbing (but for the learner this time, not his neighbour). In fact one applied linguist, Debyser (1974) has made the parallel explicit by using the word *scales* to refer to a type of repetitive practice that includes the language learner's drills. At the other end of the spectrum is doing 'the real thing', and in the case of language this means using language for those activities language is usually used for – holding conversations, having discussions, writing letters, and so on.

In this chapter we shall look at two practice types, and we shall stay with the names 'scales' and 'the real thing' to suggest that they have parallels in other areas of skill learning. But our concentration on just two types should not disguise the fact that between the extremes there are many intermediary stages – forms of practice that are not as controlled as drills, nor as open-ended as free communication.

Scales (drills)

Five characteristics of scales

What are scales like? As we shall see later, the following five characteristics will help to distinguish them from 'the real thing':

(a) **Repetitive** Scales depend for their effect on being done lots of times. *How many times can I get my learners to repeat an item in ten minutes?* is the question teachers ask in this respect. This characteristic shows the centrality of drilling in a behaviourist-based approach (like AL) where the importance of repetition was paramount. The search for an answer to the 'How Many Question' may lead you in the direction of pairwork, because in a pair each student can produce more language than when you have to deal with the class as a whole. It might also lead you in the direction of techniques like the substitution table, illustrated below. Those of you who are mathematically inclined might like to work out how many different sentences can be formed from this table:[4]

	atlas dictionary	you asked for	has	been	mislaid lost
The		he wanted			
	photographs maps		have		borrowed stolen

from Byrne (1986: 34)

(b) **Relative meaninglessness** As we shall see later, efforts can be made to inject some meaningfulness into scales. But they are in themselves relatively meaningless. This is partly because of their repetitive nature. To make practice meaningful often requires time, to create a context and provide the opportunity for the learners to become immersed in the situation. Individual drills tend to be 'nasty, brutish, short . . . and meaningless' (to develop Thomas Hobbes's description of the life of man).

(c) **Part practice** Scales tend to focus on one small area of language (a single sentence pattern, for example), and practise it in isolation. Again, there is the influence of behaviourism here. The word 'isolative' is sometimes used to describe this characteristic; another key word (met in Chapter 10, p. 174) was 'incrementalism' – the procedure of gradually building language up bit by bit.

(d) **Indirect** Very often drills bear little resemblance to the overall behaviour we are trying to develop ('the real thing', sometimes called – rather ghoulishly – the *terminal behaviour*). Scales are not real piano playing, and you would indeed feel cheated if you went to a piano recital where a series of scales was performed. Similarly, drills are not what people do when they speak or write to each other. The value of these practice types is that they are felt to contribute indirectly and cumulatively to the terminal behaviour. They are stepping stones.

(e) **Controlled** Scales usually provide the learner with very little freedom indeed to say what he wants to say. There is no room for improvisation.

Meaninglessness and meaningfulness

13.6 Buying books you don't read, cooking food you don't eat

In the two exercises below, from Dakin (1973), the teacher (or language laboratory tape) says the sentences on the left, and the learners produce the sentences on the right. To ensure that you understand how each drill works, invent one more item for each, giving the actual sentences both teacher and learner would say. Be sure also that you are clear on what is being practised here.

(i) You bought the book.   *I have already bought the book*
    You didn't read it.   *but I haven't yet read it.*

    You cooked the food.   *I have already cooked the food*
    You didn't eat it.   *but I haven't yet eaten it.*

    You saw him.   *I have already seen him*
    You didn't meet him.   *but I haven't yet met him.*

(ii) You bought the record.   *I haven't yet listened to the*
    You didn't listen to it.   *record that I bought.*

    You received a letter.   *I haven't yet answered the*
    You didn't answer it.   *letter that I received.*

    You made some mistakes.   *I haven't yet corrected the*
    You didn't correct them.   *mistakes that I made.*

Would you describe these drills as 'meaningful' or 'meaningless'? Why?

These are Dakin's examples of meaningless drills. For him the revealing characteristic is that you could do them without actually knowing what key words mean (like *buy* and *read* and *see*), though you would of course have to know how to form the appropriate parts of these verbs (*bought* and *seen*, etc.).

Dakin is critical of the meaninglessness of many drills developed in the audiolingual tradition, pointing out that they can be done in totally mechanical fashion, without any regard for meaning. He talks about the *tumtetum effect*, and illustrates this by means of a foolish parody of a drill using nonsense words. In this, the teacher says the 'sentence' *Tum tumtete tonk te*, which the learner repeats. The teacher then gives some words to replace *tonk*, and the learner produces new 'sentences', like this:

TEACHER   LEARNER
Tum tumtete tonk te   *Tum tumtete tonk te*
    konk   *Tum tumtete konk te*
    bonk   *Tum tumtete bonk te*
    honk   *Tum tumtete honk te*

We have already made the point that a degree of meaninglessness is in the very nature of drilling, and that you are unlikely to be able to make any drill highly meaningful. But there are degrees of meaningfulness, and most teachers today would argue for 'as meaningful as possible'.

But how can this be done? For Dakin, some meaning can be injected by making the learner relate his responses to a context. In one of his examples (1973: 61), he shows a series of pictures of a girl named Felicity. The pictures are in pairs. In the first of each pair, Felicity is doing something – eating a fish, climbing a mountain, combing her hair. In the second, she has just completed the action. Learners look at the pictures and say sentences like *Felicity is eating a fish* or *Felicity has just eaten the fish*. Having to relate the sentences to a picture makes them more than simple tumtetum.

Nowadays we strive for more meaningfulness than this. Some attempt would be made to introduce an element of problem solving, interpretation of some information given, or just plain fun. Box 13.7 illustrates some more recent drills of this sort.

13.7 Three ways to practise saying 'no'

Here are three drills. They have in common that they are all practising simple negative sentences.

The first is from Ur (1988: 181). The teacher, with students' help, draws a picture on the blackboard. Perhaps it will show a scene containing many objects and people. In turn, students then ask the teacher to erase objects. One student, for example, may say *Alice doesn't have a hat*, whereupon Alice's hat is erased from the picture. This continues until the picture is entirely erased.

The second is also from Ur (1988). In this game, one student volunteer comes to the front of the class and is asked questions. He must answer these without using the word *no*. All questions must be answered with full sentences (answers like *Not really* or *Never* are unacceptable). So the volunteer may be asked *Does the President of the United States live in Canada?* His answer may be *The President of the United States does not live in Canada* (p. 189).

The third is adapted from *Now for English* (Johnson 1983a), a book intended for young children. A picture shows six objects (e.g. a train, a bus, a car, a plane, a ship, a bicycle). A pupil volunteer must identify one of these objects by saying what it is *not*. He might, for example, say *It isn't a train. It isn't a bicycle. It isn't a car. It isn't a ship. It isn't a plane. What is it?* The first pupil to put up his hand and answer becomes the next 'volunteer'.

In Chapter 10's section on 'the humanistic approaches' (p. 188) we came across a quotation from Stevick (1976), part of which dealt with the concept of meaningfulness. He said that 'Meaning depends on what happens inside and between people'. Finding out about your classmates – their habits, way of life, likes, dislikes – has become a major activity type in foreign-language teaching. Questionnaire, quizzes and mini-surveys are techniques for doing this. In Hover (1986) for example, learners are asked to find out about how healthy their classmates are. This is done by means of a questionnaire asking about eating habits and amount of exercise taken. As with magazine quizzes of this sort, you are given a score at the end, and it is possible to find out who is the healthiest person in the class. Such activities are particularly useful for practising functions like 'finding out about/expressing likes and dislikes', 'expressing preferences'. This reminds us that, although all the drills we have seen in this section focus on structural areas, there is certainly such a thing as the functional drill. You might like to ponder how you would devise a drill practising 'inviting people' and 'accepting/declining invitations'. What would your functional drill look like?

Communicative drills

In Johnson (1980a) I argue that 'conveying information' is often an essential part of communication (though by no means always – perhaps you can think of some exceptions). In a situation where people give each other information they already know, this essential element is missing. There often needs to be an 'information gap'. For communication truly to take place, in many situations people need to be telling each other things they do not already know. One way of viewing communication is as 'bridging an information gap'.

Many language-teaching exercises, like the one in box 13.8, lack an information gap:

13.8 Telling your partner what he can see

This drill is taken from Broughton (1968). The students work in pairs, one asking and the other replying. Do the exercise alone in your head, working out what would be said for each picture.

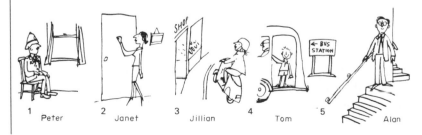

1 Peter   2 Janet   3 Jillian   4 Tom   5 Alan

Ask:

Is	Janet Tom Peter Alan Jillian	standing sitting	by the window? on the stairs? by the door? on the bus? on the scooter?

Answer:

Yes, No,	he she	is isn't

In this exercise both students are looking at the same page. So Student A is asking questions to which he already knows the answers, and Student B is supplying answers which he knows A already has. However useful the drill may be as structural practice, it is, from a communicative point of view, a charade. No information is changing hands.

Here is my modified version of this exercise:

13.9   Telling your partner what he can't see

This is an 'information-gapped' version of the drill above. Can you figure out how it works? Clue: creating an information gap involves use of a sheet of paper. The procedure is described under the box.

A.

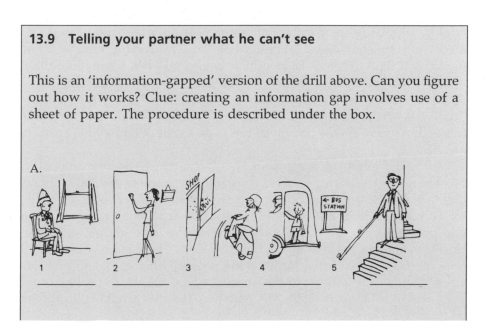

Ask your partner a question, and write names under the pictures.

Who's that	standing sitting	by the window? on the stairs? by the door? on the bus? on the scooter?

B. Give your partner information

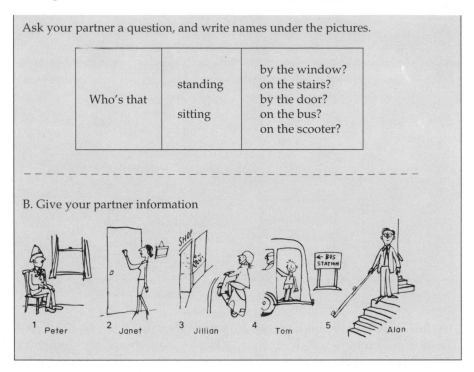

1 Peter   2 Janet   3 Jillian   4 Tom   5 Alan

To do this exercise, Student A covers the portion of the page below the dotted line with a piece of paper. Student B covers the top of the page in the same way. By asking the students to look at different parts of the page (and by supplying one picture without names), an information gap is created. Now Student B does not know what A will ask, and A does not know how B will reply. There is an information gap, and hence communication – viewed as a 'bridging of the information gap' – becomes possible. Student A asks questions like *Who's that sitting by the window?* and B replies *Peter*. Student A writes the information under Picture 1. When the exercise is finished, A uncovers the bottom of the page to check that all his answers are right.

Why is the information gap important? One reason is motivational. It must be rather tedious for students constantly to be telling each other things that they already know, and can in fact see before their very eyes – a recipe for boredom indeed. But more important is that without an information gap present, important communicative processes may not get practised. Consider Student A's role in the box 13.8 drill. There is no reason at all why he should even listen to, let alone process what is said to him. He already knows the answers to the questions he is asking. In fact, he could very well block his ears while B is replying. The drill would still proceed without problems. Ear-blocking is not an action associated with communicative behaviour!

Like the exercise in box 13.8, the one in box 13.9 is a simple drill: it practises one structure which is repeated a number of times. But I call it a 'communicative drill' because, having an information gap, it does involve communicative processes. The participants have to listen and process what they are told. Exercises like this are nowadays very common. Here is another example:

13.10   Spending money

The information-gap exercise below is taken from Read and Matthews (1991). How exactly does this drill work? If you wish you can write teacher's notes for this exercise, specifying exactly what happens at each stage (clue: the pair of scissors (overleaf), in the middle of the exercise page is very important).[5]

As the pair of scissors shows, there are different ways of creating an information gap, other than by asking students to conceal part of the page. A further common technique is to have information on different pages of a book. One student looks at one page, his partner at another. Some publishers have even gone as far as publishing two books, one used by Student A in each pair, and the other by Student B. A good example of this is Watcyn-Jones (1981).

12   LAST DAY OF THE SALES

The notion of a 'communicative drill' does not please everyone. Harmer (1982) for example argues that the concepts of drilling and communication are incompatible. The essence of communicative teaching is message-focus, he claims, and drills cannot of their nature be message-focused. It is in essence the same sort of argument that (as we saw in Chapter 10) led Prabhu in the direction of his procedural syllabus.

Mention of the procedural syllabus introduces another issue that has rumbled on just below the surface of many recent approaches to language teaching. What these approaches have managed to do is to find ways of placing emphasis on message- (as opposed to form-) focus. The information-gap exercise is one small example of this. At various points in this book we have touched on reasons why emphasis on message-focus is beneficial. But it is not without its disadvantages. The main, and obvious one is that learners may become satisfied with their performance in an FL as long as they manage to get their message across, and irrespective of the 'quality' of the language used to do this. Earlier (p. 99) I called this the 'Fish-and-Chips Syndrome'. To recap a learner might go into a café and say *Give me fish and chips*. If the result is a plate of fish and chips, then the utterance is successful as a piece of communication. This would not be true if the waitress were to bring a glass of lemonade, or if he were to say *Sorry. What do you want?* But, even if *Give me fish and chips* succeeds as communication, it is poor English, and most teachers would not be satisfied if their learners produced it. The danger of too much message-focus is that communicatively successful, but poorly expressed language may result. This issue also came up on page

193, where we noted in relation to the Bangalore experiment the danger that a procedural syllabus may result in an elaborate pidgin. What is the answer? Some (H. Johnson 1992 for example) have discussed the possibility of using message-focused activities which nevertheless involve the learner in having to 'stretch' his language and use it accurately. The whole question of how to handle form (accuracy, correctness) within message-focused practice is a fascinating one of great current interest. It is discussed in Foster and Skehan (1999) for example.

Yes, but do scales work?

> ### 13.11   The Big Question
>
> Do scales work? This is, surely, the Big Question.
>
> Think first about your experience as a foreign-language learner. Have you found drills to be of any value? Then think in more abstract terms. Can you learn a musical instrument without doing scales? What about a language without doing drills? If your answer is different for music and language, then what is the difference between learning a language and a musical instrument?
>
> Are there likely to be any bad consequences in learning a language without *ever* doing drills? What about learning a language using *nothing but* drills as practice?

Almost all of the recent discussion in language teaching about the pros and cons of drilling has been within the behaviourism versus cognitivism debate. We have already explored these positions, and discussed the connection between drilling and behaviourist theory. We have met the basic assumption of audiolingualism that 'foreign language learning is basically a mechanical process of habit formation' (Rivers 1964: 31), and in Chapter 10 we encountered Nelson Brooks's view (1960: 142) that 'the single paramount fact about language learning is that it concerns not problem solving, but the formation and performance of habits'. In Chapter 3 (box 3.6, p. 48) we also considered the cognitivist case against learning as habit formation. You will recall the L1 example of the child who repeated a wrong sentence (*Nobody don't like me*) eight times, yet despite such repetition presumably eventually moved on, when ready, to the correct form.[6]

In more recent times, there has been some actual research into the role of practice in learning. Box 13.12 summarizes a piece of small-scale research done by Ellis. He concludes that, at least in the situation he considers, there is little observable value to practice.

13.12 Practice makes less perfect?

Ellis (1984) reports on a study done in London on thirteen children, aged between 11 and 15. He was interested in the development of Wh-questions, and wanted to know what effect some formal teaching would have on that development. Three one-hour lessons were given to the children, teaching the different meanings of *who, what, where* and *when*, and practising the formation of questions with these words. The learners were then given a 'test', which involved them in making up some Wh- questions about a picture of a classroom scene. The improvement in Wh- question formation was not dramatic for the group as a whole (perhaps to be expected after such a small amount of teaching). But some pupils did show much more improvement than others.

Ellis was interested to find out whether those who had improved had been the ones who had 'practised' most in the lessons. Amount of practice was measured by looking at the number of times the teacher had nominated a pupil to produce a question. Those who participated most were called 'high interactors'; those who participated least, 'low interactors'.

Was there a relationship between amount of interaction and improvement in the Wh-form? The answer was yes. 'It was', Ellis says (p. 146), 'the low interactors, rather than high interactors, who progressed.'

To the extent that interaction means practice, the suggestion is that those who practised least did best!

Ellis is the first to admit that the amount of research done into the value of practice is small, and cannot lead to firm conclusions. There are many questions still unanswered. One relates to Pienemann's notion of learnability. Perhaps practice will have value only if the item being practised is close to the point at which it would be acquired in the 'natural order'. Then there is what Ellis (1994: 621) calls the 'delayed effect hypothesis' – the idea that the value of practice (or indeed instruction in general) cannot be expected to appear for a while. This is an attractive idea. I certainly find with learning a musical instrument that practising some tricky sequence does not pay off for quite a while. In fact the practice sometimes has an immediate bad effect, making me play the sequence worse. Perhaps this is because practice makes the conscious mind pay attention to the sequence, which may have an initial inhibiting effect.

Is there any real alternative to scales, apart from adopting a Prabhu-like approach? Many applied linguists today (including Ellis; see 1994: 643) regard language-awareness or consciousness-raising activities as being potentially more effective than scale-like practice. Such activities might be useful as an initial step in learning (recall what Schmidt and Frota say about the value of noticing). But they might also be beneficial at some later stage. I can certainly recall instances in my own foreign-language learning experience where focusing in a conscious way on structures I had already come across and used was an extremely valuable procedure. Perhaps you have had similar experiences?

The real thing

Scales may have their place, but the chances are that your answers to box 13.11's questions will reveal a feeling that some other type of practice will also be necessary for successful foreign-language learning. In this section we consider another practice type. We shall ask three questions about 'real-thing practice': *what* it is, *why* it is important, and *how* we can introduce it into the classroom.

What it is: five characteristics of real-thing practice

13.13 Lost in the desert

Read this description of an exercise called *Desert Dilemma*, taken from Harmer (1991: 130):

THE SITUATION
It is about ten o'clock in the morning in July, and you have just crashed in a small aeroplane in the Sonora desert in Northern Mexico. The pilot and co-pilot are dead and the aeroplane is a burnt-out shell. One of the passengers is injured.

The aeroplane had no radio, and the survivors think that they were about 100 kilometres off course when they crashed. Just before the crash the pilot told the passengers that they were 120 kilometres south of a small mining camp.

From experience you know that daytime temperatures can reach 43° centigrade (110° Fahrenheit) and night-time temperatures reach freezing. All the passengers are dressed in light clothes. The area is flat and arid as far as the eye can see.

Instructions
The following is a list of items that came out of the crash in good order:

Flashlight with four batteries	*Jack knife*
Detailed pilot's chart of the area	*Large plastic poncho*
Compass	*Instrument to measure blood pressure*

> *Loaded .45 pistol*   *One red and white parachute*
> *Bottle of 100 salt tablets*   *One quart of water per person*
> Book Edible Desert Animals   *One pair of sunglasses per person*
> *Two bottles of vodka*   *One overcoat per person*
>   *One pocket mirror*
>
> *Now do the following:*
>
> (a) *Individually write down a list of the seven most important items on this list to ensure survival and/or rescue.*
>
> (b) *Agree with the other members of the group what these items are.*
>
> Be sure you are clear on how the exercise would work in class. Think about what sorts of things the students will say when they do the exercise. Also think about 'management' details, like how big the student groups would be.
>
> Look back to the five characteristics of scales found on page 246. Consider this exercise in relation to each characteristic. What is your conclusion? Is *Desert Dilemma* a scale?

No, *Desert Dilemma* is not a scale. Your conclusion is likely to have been that it has none of a scale's five main characteristics. This leads us to a characterization of real-thing practice in which the contrast with scales could not be more marked:

(a) **Non-repetitive** Real-thing exercises do not rely on repetition for their value. In fact any particular activity of this type is often just done once, or possibly twice. This is not just because their value does not lie in repetition, but also because by their very nature they are time-consuming activities. Think how long it would take to set up and execute *Desert Dilemma* in class.

(b) **Meaningful** Although the situation of a desert air crash is an unlikely one, *Desert Dilemma* has been developed in the expectation that the situation will engage the learners; the result should be discussion that is lively and even earnest. As we noted earlier in this chapter, creating meaningfulness is a time-consuming business, which is one reason for (a) above.

(c) Real-thing practice is **whole practice**. Scales concentrate on small segments of behaviour. In the real thing, the learner 'puts it all together'.

(d) **Direct** At this stage, we make efforts to practise the terminal behaviour itself – actually using language in simulations of real situations. It is the real thing, in fact. The word 'simulation' is important in this respect. A lot of real-thing practice involves the learners in pretence: *pretending* that you have had an air crash, *pretending* you are the director of a company chairing a board meeting, and so on. There are similarities between this kind of exercise and the practice given to novice pilots in aircraft simulators. Both attempt to reproduce the conditions of real activities, but in a safe environment – the classroom or the simulating machine.

(e) **Free** In real-thing practice, the learners are allowed to express their ideas, thoughts, feelings, in line with their wishes and capabilities. The teacher's role is not to insist that any particular language item is used.

Why the real thing is important

In much audiolingual teaching, there was no real-thing practice. New structures were introduced and drilled. Then you went on to the next structure. The belief seems to have been that once a structure has been thoroughly drilled, no further exercising will be necessary; the structure will make its way from controlled classroom practice into everyday use without any further effort. Arguably one of the major insights of recent years in applied linguistics is the realization that the transfer from controlled classroom practice to free outside use is extremely difficult to achieve. Much work has to be put into it. This has led in recent times to importance being given to real thing practice. Indeed, if any practice type nowadays has to sing for its supper, it is the scale (pun intended).

There are three reasons why real-thing practice is important. The first is the *need for freedom*. It is partly a revised view of errors that has led to our realization of the importance of this. We have seen (in Chapter 4) that, in the behaviourist model, errors were to be avoided at all costs. Nowadays we have the cognitive reaction to this to take into account. We know that, in L1 acquisition, errors disappear on their own with time. Their occurrence is therefore nothing to worry about; indeed, it may be seen as useful for the learning process (a general view of learning captured in the expression that 'we learn through our mistakes'). In addition to all this is the realization, mentioned in Chapter 10 in association with communicative methodology, that learning a language involves mastering many types of skill, not just grammatical ones. We now realize the importance of risk-taking skills and the development of strategic competence.

Being prepared to take risks is indeed a vital part of language learning. The learner who is not prepared to do this may never open his mouth. One of the risk-taking skills is circumlocution: being able to express an idea when you do not have the real words to do so. You also have to have the confidence to start sentences when you do not know how to finish them. I remember vividly a problem I had learning German, a language in which verbs sometimes come at the end of sentences. I would often start a sentence, but then realize with increasing dread as the sentence went on, that I did not know what verb should go at the end. There would be a silence where the verb should be. 'Communicating with inadequate means' is a skill that every language learner needs to develop.

Errors will occur, and risk-taking skills only be developed, if we loosen the reins that control learners, allowing them the freedom to express themselves as they wish. This means real-thing practice.

The second reason for the importance of this practice type is the *need for meaningfulness*. We saw in our historical survey how recent humanistic methods value meaningfulness, and the last sentence of Stevick (1976) was cited in this context (on p. 188): 'Memory is a by-product of Meaning, and Method should be the servant of Meaning, and Meaning depends on what happens inside and between people'.

It is not only humanistic approaches that attach importance to meaningfulness. Meaning- (or message-) focus plays an important part in many recent approaches, including CLT. One extremely common strategy for communicatively oriented teachers (discussed in Harmer 1991, and in many other places) is to make the starting point for language practice the learner's desire to say something, the desire to 'mean'. From this point of view, a crucial part of the teacher's role is to create situations in which the learner will want to communicate. Language teaching is seen as the process whereby the learner is taught how to say what he has decided he wants to say. It is a process of 'learning how to mean'.

We have already seen that, although some drills may be more meaningful than others, there are limits to the extent this can be achieved. Meaningfulness means real-thing practice.

A third reason for the importance of the real thing is the *need for fluency practice*. The concepts of fluency and accuracy have been much discussed recently in language teaching (for example in Christopher Brumfit's influential 1984 book, which is subtitled *the roles of fluency and accuracy*). What do these terms mean? You may wish to attempt your own definitions before reading on.

13.14 What you really, really want to say

'Language teaching', we have just said, 'is seen as the process whereby the learner is taught how to say what he has decided he wants to say.' The *Desert Dilemma* simulation in box 13.13 above is an attempt to put learners in a situation where they will have a desire to communicate.

Or will they? You could argue that *Desert Dilemma* is unlikely to engage the learner very much, because the situation is 'externally imposed' on him by the teacher or textbook. H. Johnson (1992) takes this very 'aircraft crash' situation and explores ways in which the learner may be encouraged to participate more in the construction of the simulation. One of her suggestions is that the list of items surviving the crash can be agreed on by the class, rather than being given in the exercise. Look back at *Desert Dilemma* and try to think of other ways in which the exercise may be modified to increase learner participation in its construction.

One dictionary (Richards *et al.* 1985) defines accuracy as the 'ability to produce grammatically correct sentences'. Correctness is certainly a central idea, although it is possible to broaden use of the term to apply to different aspects of language use, not just the grammatical:

13.15 Different ways of being wrong

Imagine that you stop a stranger in the street and ask them the time by saying *Excuse me, can you tell me the time?* The following seven replies are all 'inaccurate'. Each may be seen as involving different aspects of language use. Identify what these aspects are.

(1) *It are five o'clock*
(2) *It's five o'clock* ('five' is pronounced with an 'f' sound at the end, rather that a 'v' sound)
(3) *It's five hours*
(4) *Yes, I can, thanks.* [Person walks away]
(5) *Yes, I would. It's five o'clock.*
(6) *Yes, darling. It's five o'clock.*
(7) *There are fairies living in the woods.*

In the case of the first answer, the inaccuracy is syntactic; in the second it is phonetic. We may say that the third relates to the lexical or semantic use. The fourth is an interesting case. The person here (probably deliberately) is mistaking what is intended as a request for a service as a request for information. It is a functional or pragmatic inaccuracy. There are different ways of regarding (5). One is to see it as a cohesion error – the person is simply not 'following on' grammatically from the question asked. In (6) the error is an interpersonal one – you do not normally address strangers as 'darling'. As in (5), there is a lack of 'following on' properly in (7), but here it relates to sense not grammar, and we would therefore speak (as we hastily departed) about incoherence.

The word 'fluency' is far more problematical, and is used in a large number of different ways. The aspect of it we shall focus on here is what we shall call 'combinatorial skill'. This in turn may be defined as the skill of 'getting many things right at the same time'. This skill is not easy. Because drills are 'part practice', they can be used to develop individual aspects of the language one by one. The learner may be able to handle each aspect perfectly adequately in isolation, but may come completely unstuck when aspects are combined. It is extremely common to find learners getting something right in a drill, and wrong in a conversation. A parallel can be made with learning a musical instrument. The learner may be able to play a note completely in tune when it occurs in a scale, and he is concentrating on just that. But when he is playing an actual piece, many things have to be done at the same time. The timing must be right, as well as the dynamics (loudness and softness), and the sound quality. With all these things to attend to, the note in question may slip out of tune.

The literature on general skills learning has something to say about combinatorial skill. Peterson (1975) for example notes that for some skills, doing many things at the same time is an important component. Piloting an aircraft is an example. Landing a plane involves many actions undertaken within a short time span. These include lowering the flaps and the undercarriage, adjusting for height and position. Language, as we have seen, is also in this category. A linguist who particularly focuses on this characteristic is Halliday. He talks about the language user being involved in 'simultaneous selection', and notes that speaking involves 'planning that is . . . simultaneous in respect to all the functions of language' (1970: 145). Box 13.15 above gives some idea of the different levels on which you have to get things right when you take part in a conversation. With such skills, Peterson says, 'the sooner the skill can be performed as a whole, the better will be the results' (p. 94). It is in real-thing practice that the learner has the chance to 'put it all together' – to say things that are accurate and appropriate on all linguistic levels at the same time.

An implication in what Peterson says is that real-thing practice should be begun early. This has not always been the case in language teaching. Sometimes this type of practice has been left to the very end. When I learned French at school, it was not until after several years, when all the grammar had been learned, that I was allowed actually to use the language in anything resembling real communication. A parallel could again be made with learning a musical instrument. An approach which did not allow the learner to tackle an actual piece of music until a high degree of skill had been achieved in all the 'parts', would fail to develop combinatorial skill.

How to practise the real thing: a rough guide to three exercise types

ROLE PLAY AND SIMULATION

What they are
In role play, learners play characters, often following instructions given on 'role cards'. For example, Learners 1, 2 and 3 might be friends wanting to go on holiday together. They discuss possible destinations, then phone up Learner 4, a travel agent, to make bookings.

In a simulation, learners are themselves in an invented situation. The *Desert Dilemma* exercise in box 13.13 is an example. However, many writers use the terms 'role play' and 'simulation' interchangeably.

Comment
Wilkins (1973) makes a distinction between the 'language of reporting' and the 'language of doing'. An example of the first is the sentence *The manager threw the drunk out of the restaurant.* This reports what happened. An example of the second is

Get out, or I'll call the police, the words actually used to throw the drunk out. Wilkins makes the point that reporting is easy to set up in class, and most traditional exercises involve it. But (he argues) we need to practise the second as well, and for this we need exercises like role play. See the comments on page 185 above about *pretending*.

Reading
For discussion of these techniques in language teaching, see Sturtridge (1981).

COMMUNICATION GAMES

What they are
According to Richards *et al.* (1985: 118) a game in language teaching has the following characteristics. It involves: (a) a particular task or objective; (b) a set of rules; (c) competition between the players; (d) communication between the players by spoken or written language.

Examples
Many popular games can be used for language teaching. For example, *Twenty Questions* and *Charades*. Board games (and card games) can also be used, usually with some adaptation to make sure that language is introduced. See box 13.16 overleaf for an example.

Comment
Games of all sorts use the concept of the information gap. An example is the child's game of *Put the tail on the donkey*. In this, a child is blindfolded and has to pin a cardboard tail onto a picture of a donkey. The child who

puts the tail nearest to where it should be is the winner. Blindfolding is a way of creating a physical information gap. With this example, think whether a language element could be introduced, to make it into a language teaching game. The game in box 13.16 is also centred around an information gap.

Reading
For general discussion, including a short classification of games, see Maley (1981). Two collections of games to practise specific grammar points are Rinvolucri (1985) and Ur (1988).

DISCUSSIONS AND DEBATES

Examples
These can be informal affairs involving activities like finding differences between pictures. Social and moral issues (e.g. for and against fox hunting) can also be involved. A hoary old favourite is the *Balloon Debate*, where learners represent well-known figures flying together in a hot-air balloon. The balloon is losing height, and people have to be thrown out to keep the balloon safe. Learners argue for the character they represent remaining on balloon.

Comment
Debates and discussions need careful preparation for success. Learners do not automatically have opinions on all topics and, even if they do, these are not usually expressed without some coaxing. It is sometimes necessary to use stimuli (e.g. visuals), or to start with a survey of opinions

round the class – or to use some other means for allowing thoughts to be mustered.

Reading

Ur (1981) is a classic; an excellent collection of ideas for discussions.

13.16 Battleships and zoos

The game below is taken from *Now for English*, the book for eight-year-old children mentioned in Chapter 12. The game is closely based on a traditional one called *Battleships*. The traditional game is for two players. Each has a collection of different warships – e.g. three cruisers, two aircraft carriers, four destroyers, etc. Each player has a grid, like the ones below but larger. Players place their warships on the grid, one in each square. Ships of the same type (e.g. all the cruisers) must be in adjacent squares. The aim of the game is for a player to find out where all his opponent's ships are (and hence 'destroy' them). This he does by saying the number of a square. The opponent has to say whether the square has a ship in it. Players take it in turns to ask about squares. They keep a note of where their opponent's ships are by using a second grid.

The language-teaching version below does not use ships of war. First decide how this version works. Then think what language the game could be used to practise. It needs to be more than just saying numbers (as above), but should be quite simple because the learners are near-beginners. If you wish you can try to write Teacher's Notes explaining (with an eye for detail) how the game can be played in class.[7]

UNIT 12

Put the animals in cages.

monkeys   elephants   tigers   seals

My Zoo

1	2	3	4	5
6	7	8	9	10
11	12	13	14	15
16	17	18	19	20

My friend's Zoo

1	2	3	4	5
6	7	8	9	10
11	12	13	14	15
16	17	18	19	20

44

Activity sequences

The three Ps

In this chapter we have considered two types of classroom activity which we have called *conveying language* and *practising language*. The second of these has been subdivided into *scales* (or *drills*) and *real-thing practice*. How can these activities be sequenced? In what order should they go?

One activity sequence has been accepted by applied linguists and practised by teachers for many decades. The sequence is often referred to as 'the three Ps', standing for presentation → practice → production. You will probably be able to make immediate associations between these Ps, and the activities we have been discussing. At the *presentation* stage, the item to be taught is introduced. This is a version of our 'conveying language'. It is then *practised* in drills, or scales (the name 'manipulation' is also used for this stage). The *production* stage – our 'real-thing practice' – is likewise known by different names; van Els *et al.* (1984: 264) note 'transfer', 'comprehension and development', while 'free practice' is also commonly used.

265

One of the language-teaching methodologists who did much to popularize discussion of the three stages in recent times is Don Byrne, particularly in Byrne (1986).

13.17   From P to P to P

PPP has various sequences embedded within it. Here are some of these:

from understanding to doing
from reception to production
from controlled to free
from informant to conductor
from conductor to guide

Identify exactly where these sequences are found. You might, for example, want to say that presentation is 'controlled' but practice and production are 'free'. These sequences are discussed in the paragraph below (where you will find that the example answer above is not really right!).

One sequence embedded in PPP is 'from understanding to doing'. At the presentation stage, the learner's effort is in grasping what is being taught; it is then practised at the second and third stages. The movement from Stages 1 to 2 and 3 also therefore implies a transition from reception to production – from listening or reading in the first P to speaking or writing in the second and third. Another embedded sequence is from controlled to free, particularly in the movement from second to third P. Byrne (1986) and others associate different teacher roles with each of the Ps. At the presentation stage, the teacher acts as an *informant*, providing learners with information they did not previously have. At the second stage the teacher is often a *conductor* (as in the musical sense), pointing at students as he wants them to speak, in the same way that a conductor points at the instrumentalists in an orchestra. At the production stage the teacher is a *guide*, facilitating but not rigidly controlling what goes on; making sure the practice runs smoothly, but not interfering too much.

The PPP sequence has not been without its critics. Some describe it pejoratively as a 'transmission model', because it is based on a view of learning in which knowledge is 'transmitted' from learner to teacher. (You may wish to remind yourself of what Moskovitz says on page 188 about 'information transmission'.) Transmission models have fallen out of favour in recent years, and the PPP sequence has therefore also lost its place in the sun.

But what are the alternatives to PPP? Brumfit (1979 and elsewhere) offers a possible candidate. He suggests that the most lasting impact of communicative language teaching is replacement of the traditional PPP sequence with the one shown in box 13.18:

13.18   Three Ps: but in which order?

Below is what Brumfit (1979: 183) calls a 'reversal of traditional methodological emphases'. Think of the sequence below in terms of the traditional
three Ps. In which order do these come below?

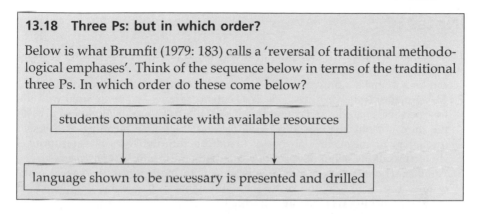

Brumfit's sequence is production → presentation → practice. Its starting point
is some kind of free production exercise. So, at the beginning of the lesson,
the learners might be asked to do a role-play exercise, or play a game, or
hold a discussion. This would happen without any linguistic preparation.
The teacher would listen to their performance, and on the basis of it would
decide what needed to be presented and practised.

There are advantages (and disadvantages as well) to this exciting proposal.
One advantage is that the learners really do have the chance to develop
strategic competence, and practise the risk-taking skills we discussed earlier
in this chapter. At the first stage they really are in a risk-taking situation,
being asked to say things that they have not been taught how to say. In
Johnson (1980b) I call the procedure the 'deep-end strategy'. There are two
ways to teach someone how to swim. One of them is the behaviourist way
of teaching strokes bit by bit, and slowly shaping the behaviour. The other
way is to throw learners in at the deep end. Those who survive learn how
to swim. Those who don't . . . !

Here, to finish the chapter, are some connections. In Chapter 7 we presented a view of language teaching which gave centre stage to the processes of declarativization and proceduralization, and introduced two
'pathways', called DECPRO and PRODEC. How does traditional PPP fit
into this? Presentation is clearly associated with declarativization, and
the other two Ps with proceduralization. Traditional PPP is a DECPRO
sequence – you start off giving your learners some 'information' about
language (presentation), which you then set about proceduralizing. But
DECPRO (and PPP with it) is not what happens in the L1 situation, and we
found it necessary to identify a second 'pathway', associated with acquisition, which we call PRODEC. It is possible to see the deep-end strategy as
a version of PRODEC.

You may also wish to think about the notion of a 'transmission model'.
What would a *non*-transmission model be like? Is there any way in which
the deep-end sequence is 'non-transmission'?

Notes

1. One major weapon in the fight for memorability is by chance not well represented in the examples given. This is the visual aid. Pictures of all sorts (including videos) can help to make a presentation vivid, thereby contributing to memorability.

2. The structure is the verb *shall/will*. The sentences show *shall* being used with the first persons, singular and plural (*I* and *we*). It also shows *will* being used with the third persons singular and plural (*he* and *they*). One meaning of *shall/will* (though by no means the only one) is to indicate futurity. The sense of futurity is shown by talking about ages, and by contrasting *now* and *next birthday*.

3. Another scholar whose name is associated with induction is the seventeenth-century Czech who is known by the Latin name of Comenius. His views on language teaching were highly influential.

4. The horizontal lines in columns 2 and 4 separate the singular from the plural forms. They indicate to the learner that, if he chooses an item above the line in Column 2 (e.g. *dictionary*), he must select the item above the line in Column 4 (*has*). Many substitution tables do not have such lines.

5. Students remove the page from their books, and cut it in half (where the scissors indicate). Student A keeps the top half, Student B the bottom half. Student A knows about the prices in 'His 'n' Hers', but not in 'Wow'. For Student B it is the other way round. Both students ask questions like *How much do socks cost in His 'n' Hers/Wow?*, and write down the prices in the spaces provided. At the end of this stage, both students have all prices, in both shops, marked. They can then see which shop is cheaper for which items, and so plan their shopping. They can also work out how much they will spend.

6. Young children do in fact indulge in a kind of 'drilling', known as 'crib talk'. Alone in their cribs or cots, they often practise sequences of sounds and words in a drill-like way. This phenomenon has been described in Weir (1962).

7. Students work in pairs. Each has a certain number of animals to 'put in his zoo', as indicated at the top of the page – five monkeys, two elephants and so on. He must put them in cages (the numbered boxes in the top diagram), by writing the first letter of the animal's name. So an 'M' in box 1 and an 'E' in box 2 would mean that there is a monkey in cage 1 and an elephant in cage 2. The same animals must be in adjacent cages. So all the monkeys must be together – e.g. in cages 1, 7, 3, 8, 13. A student must not let his partner see where he is putting the animals. The object of the game is to be first to find out where the partner has put his animals. Students take turns to ask questions like: *Is there an animal in cage 1?* The partner replies *No*, or *Yes, it's a monkey*. The lower diagram is used to keep track of where the partner's animals have been found. The language used in this exercise can be varied according to what the teacher wants to practise. For example, instead of *Is there an animal in cage 1?*, students could ask *Do any animals live in cage 1?*

Chapter 14

Skills

The four skills

Speaking, writing, listening and reading are the four skills. Most of the example activities we looked at in the last chapter were in the context of the first of these. Now we shall focus on the other three.

There are two conventional ways of dividing the four skills up. The first is into medium, with listening and speaking occurring in the spoken medium, reading and writing in the written medium. The second division is into the receptive skills of listening and reading, and the productive skills of speaking and writing. This use of the terms 'receptive' and 'productive' is probably self-evident. But beware of the once-used terminology which called the productive skills 'active' and the receptive skills 'passive'. As we shall see in this chapter, listening and reading are in fact highly 'active' processes. You are invited to write the words *Speaking Listening, Reading* and *Writing* inside the box below, to indicate how they stand in relation to these divisions:[1]

	Spoken	Written
Receptive		
Productive		

In some approaches to language teaching, the four skills are treated separately. There is a listening comprehension lesson, a speaking lesson, a reading and a writing lesson. There are obvious advantages to doing this. For one thing, learner needs are likely to be different for each. Also, each skill poses its own problems, which will sometimes benefit from separate treatment.

But it is important to realize that there are similarities and interconnections between the skills as well. In this chapter we shall treat listening and reading together, because both involve common processes of *comprehension*. Also, when we look at teaching techniques, we shall often find that listening exercises can be used, with small changes, for the teaching of reading as well, and vice versa. In addition there are processes common to the productive skills, so that techniques for the teaching of speaking can, with modifications, sometimes be used for writing. But there is another set of interconnections to think about. In a later section we shall touch briefly on the idea that to be a good writer, it helps to be a good reader. Understanding your reader, knowing what she is expecting next, and how she will interpret what you write are skills essential for good writing. One might even go so far as to say that teaching good writing involves teaching someone to be a good reader. All this adds up to the fact that, although it is sometimes useful to look at the four skills separately, we must not forget ways in which they are similar, and how they interconnect.

The comprehension skills

The comprehension process

Things have developed a lot in the teaching of comprehension in the past few decades. One of the main agents of change has been psycholinguistics. A major concern of this branch of linguistics is with the way we process language. What procedures do humans follow when they try to understand a piece of speech or writing? The answer to this question has changed rather dramatically in recent decades, and this change has had its effect on language teaching. To understand it, we need to do a little psycholinguistics.

To simplify discussion, we shall here talk sometimes of reading, sometimes listening, though most of what is said applies equally well to both these skills. We shall use the word *text* to apply to pieces of language that are spoken as well as written. As a prelude to discussion, you are invited to read the passage given in box 14.1:

14.1   Reading about a peace march taken from Bransford and Johnson (1973, cited in Clark and Clark 1977: 163)

Read this passage quickly through. What you have read will be discussed later.

A peace march
The view was breathtaking. From the window one could see the crowd below. Everything looked extremely small from such a distance, but the colourful costumes could still be seen. Everyone seemed to be moving in one direction in an orderly fashion and there seemed to be little children as well as adults. The landing was gentle and luckily the atmosphere was such that no special suits had to be worn. At first there was a great deal of activity. Later, when the speeches started, the crowd quietened down. The man with the television camera took many shots of the setting and the crowd. Everyone was very friendly and seemed to be glad when the music started.

Here is the common-sense, layman's view of reading: a text is a collection of words – the little black marks on the page – grouped into phrases, sentences, paragraphs. In order to understand the text, what the reader needs is the linguistic knowledge necessary to decipher the little black marks. According to this view, meaning is something that resides in the text itself. The reader prises the meaning out of the text, like an oyster out of its shell.

Associated with this view of reading is a model of comprehension processing which was a focus of psycholinguistic thought before the 1970s. The procedure described in this model has come to be known as <u>bottom-up</u>. In bottom-up processing, the starting-point is the text itself. The reader attends to individual words and structures in the text, from these gradually building up an interpretation of the whole. Imagine, for example that you read the following sentence (from Clark and Clark 1977): *The farmer put the straw on a pile beside his threshing machine.* Processing this in a bottom-up way, you would identify that a farmer is (roughly speaking) a person engaged in agricultural pursuits, and that the word *the* is signifying that some particular farmer is being spoken about. You would then move on to the word *put*, identifying it as describing a past action, of 'placing', or 'setting down'. When you came to the word *straw*, you would consult your internal dictionary, which would tell you that the word has at least two meanings – 'grain stalk' and 'drinking tube'. You would hold these two meanings in your mind until a later stage when you were considering the meaning of the whole sentence. You would then doubtless decide that the first meaning was the one intended here. You would continue through this sentence in the same manner, word by word, in a process involving what was traditionally called <u>parsing</u>. The term 'bottom-up' is used because in this process you begin at the 'bottom', with the text itself. Another term used by psychologists for the same process makes this notion even clearer. It is 'data-driven processing'.

But 'Strange Occurrences' take place when readers set to work on texts. We shall explore some of these. They will lead us to conclude that the bottom-up processing model is an incomplete and inaccurate representation of comprehension.

Strange Occurrence 1 is that it is possible to understand every word of a text and still not know what it is about. We have already come across this idea, in Chapter 2 where we discussed the notion of 'rules of use'. When the old Croatian lady said *Where are you going?* to me, I understood her grammar and the signification of her words, but failed to identify their pragmatic 'value' as a greeting. In this example, cultural knowledge is important. Here is another example where the knowledge required is not cultural but specialist. It is taken from an article describing how a player of a wind instrument – the oboe – made improvements to his instrument. In these sentences he is describing a problem with conventional oboes, and what he did about it:

> Another feature to fall by the wayside is the 'butterfly' for left little finger. The left-hand E flat with its ungrateful pivoting is no one's favourite key. So, with those passages in mind with E flat and A flat in close succession, the touches for these notes are mounted cheek by jowl and pivoted sympathetically (though on different joints, as is normal) . . . Finally, the lower tier of touches duplicates others for the right little finger . . .[2]

Understood?

Strange Occurrence 2 is that it is possible not to understand some parts of a text, yet still know what it is about. The other day our dog Bertie chased a sheep on the hill behind our house. I said to him: *Now you know you shouldn't do that. That's naughty. I've told you not to chase sheep. If I catch you doing that again there'll be trouble.* He did not understand many of these words. But he knew I was angry, and he knew why. He understood the underlying message perfectly. In case you are unconvinced by an example of listening involving another species, have a look at the exercise in box 14.2:

14.2 Biners injured

This exercise, taken from Grellet (1981: 36), is based on an article that appeared in the *Daily Telegraph*. It shows how it is possible to understand the gist of a text when not all the words are understood:

The following text contains a number of imaginary words. Can you guess their meaning?

TRAIN DERAILED

Plicks are believed to have caused the dolling of a two-car diesel passenger train yesterday. The train, with 24 biners on board, hit a metal object and ratteol 100 yards of track before stopping four pars from Middlesbrough. Three people were taken to hospital, one slightly ropped, the others finding from shock.

(*Daily Telegraph*)

Strange Occurrence 3 is that it is possible to understand a message even when there is no evidence for your interpretation in the actual words on the page. The example we met in Chapter 2 (p. 33) involved the exchange:

A: *There's the doorbell*
B: *I'm in the bath.*

This small snatch of dialogue has a 'subtext' that reads:

A: *There's someone at the door. Can you go and open it?*
B: *No I can't, because I'm in the bath.*

You might say that this exchange is 'about' who will answer the door. Yet answering the door is not in fact mentioned. The word <u>inferencing</u> is commonly used to describe what the reader or listener does here.

What the Strange Occurrences so far suggest is that the black marks on the page play only a part of what we do when we read (or listen). It is beginning to be clear that the reader or listener brings a lot of herself with her to the job of interpreting. Strange Occurrence 4 illustrates just how far this can go. It is an example of how it is possible to think you have been told something that was not in fact said at all. In 1932 the psychologist Bartlett told some American Indian folk tales to British subjects, asking his listeners immediately to retell the stories in their own words. Coming from a very different culture, these stories would have been very odd indeed to the British listeners, containing many details which would bewilder them. The fascinating result of his experiment was that the listeners changed the stories to fit in with their own expectations. This even involved adding details to make the stories conform to listener expectations. One story, for example, describes how an Indian was wounded in battle. How he was wounded is not stated in the original, but some British listeners add the detail that it was by an arrow. This is because the listeners know that bows and arrows are the means Indians use for fighting. Their embellishments make it clear that the subjects came to the stories with some already existing set of expectations which played a major part in how they 'understood' the story.

Strange Occurrence 5 is exemplified in the text you read in box 14.1 on page 270 (deliberately put earlier so that you would not be alerted to the possibility of any 'Strange Occurrence' in it). Did you notice a sentence in it that does not relate to the title, or indeed the rest of the passage? It is the sentence about the space landing. In Bransford and Johnson's experiment people failed to recall that sentence well. It is as if they blotted it out because it did not fit into their expectations, aroused by the title. When Bransford and Johnson changed the title of the passage to 'a Space Trip To An Inhabited Planet', subjects' recall of that same sentence was much better. This example shows that readers are able to ignore something said in a text if it does not fit in well to expectations. It is almost as if they had not read it.

Our final Strange Occurrence, number 6, is that different people will take different 'information' out of a text. There can be many reasons for this, and in some circumstances you will perhaps not find this strange at all. You will probably accept, for example, that no two individuals will comprehend a play like Shakespeare's *Hamlet* in quite the same way. But on a more banal level, one major reason for this phenomenon relates to the *reason* why the person is reading or listening. The example in box 14.3 overleaf shows how individuals with different reasons for listening will extract different pieces of information from the same message. They are listening *for* different things. Therefore, perhaps, they are listening *to* different things.

14.3 Catching a train

The scene is a crowded railway station in London at 10.00 one morning. The following message comes over the tannoy: *The train at Platform 5 is the 10.30 to Edinburgh.* For many listening to this announcement, it will be of no importance and they will give it little attention; their travel plans do not involve Edinburgh, or Platform 5. Among those who attend more carefully are three individuals. Here is what they say to themselves when they hear the announcement:

Passenger A: *Ah, so it's Platform 5 I need.*
Passenger B: *So this is the Edinburgh train. Where does mine go from then?*
Passenger C: *Right. So I've got half an hour then. Time to go off and buy some coffee.*

We might say that each passenger takes different information out of the same message. For each, specify what you know about each passenger, including what you think they *do* and *do not* know just before the announcement is made. One thing you might surmise about Passenger A, for example, is that she is travelling on the Edinburgh train (or seeing off someone else who is travelling on it). Then say what piece of information contained in the message is important for each passenger.[3]

The Edinburgh train example shows how our purpose for listening/reading involves us in being *selective* with our attention. We do not pay equal attention to everything we hear or read. As Faerch and Kasper (1986: 265) put it: 'the principle that "all input must be accounted for" applies to computational but not to human information processing'.

Our purpose is also likely to set limits on how much we actually need to understand. Most purposes are not likely to be highly rigorous, demanding anything like 'total comprehension' (whatever that might be). *Partial* understanding is usually enough. Take the word *Ayatollah* as an example. *The Cambridge Encyclopedia* (Crystal 1990) defines this as 'a Shiite Muslim religious title . . . referring to a clergyman who has reached the third level of Shiite higher education, is recognized as a mujtahid, and is over 40'. Most readers from non-Muslim societies will doubtless not know this, and few would be able to come up with such a precise definition. So there is a sense in which they do not 'understand' the word. But few of us actually need such a precise definition. We may know that an Ayatollah is a religious leader in Islam, and this restricted knowledge is probably enough to ensure comprehension of the text in which we come across the word. There is, in other words, a level on which we *do* understand the word. Full comprehension is rarely required by a reader, or for that matter possessed by the writer.

Taken as a whole, our Strange Occurrences clearly indicate that, although the text itself is of course important for reading comprehension, what the reader brings to the text is also very important. This is why the bottom-up model cannot alone account for comprehension. As early as the 1930s and the work of Bartlett that we referred to above, psychologists were concerned to develop a processing model which would take account of the listener/reader's role in comprehension. The model that emerged involves a type of processing called <u>top-down</u>. This term captures the idea that the starting point is within the mind of the listener/reader and, as with 'bottom-up', there is another term psychologists use which clarifies the meaning – 'concept-driven processing'.

An important notion in top-down processing is what Bartlett (1932) calls <u>schemata</u> (singular *schema*). These may be described as the 'mental frameworks' we hold as individuals, and which we bring with us when we read or listen to a text. In the case of the British listeners to Bartlett's American Indian stories, the schemata are about American Indians, their lives, and the weapons they use when they fight. It is from the American Indian schema of some listeners that the arrow makes its way into the story. Schemata play an important part in comprehension, even from an early stage in the process. Comprehension does *not* follow a totally bottom-up pathway, and we do *not* logically work through all possible interpretations of a text (as a machine might) before deciding what it means. Instead, we take short cuts. We use background knowledge to select the most likely interpretation, often without even being aware of other possible interpretations. Our agricultural sentence: *The farmer put the straw on a pile beside his threshing machine* is a good example of this. We saw that the word *straw* has at least two possible meanings, and that in purely bottom-up processing we would note these meanings when we came to the word, only deciding at a later stage which was intended. This is the way an intelligent computer might process the sentence. But the likelihood is that, faced with a sentence like this, we would not even consider the second meaning. Words like *farmer* and *threshing machine* would immediately invoke our 'farmyard schema', and in this the word *straw* has only one meaning. Comprehension is a process of *making sense of a text*, in the most cost-effective (but not necessarily the most thorough) way.

How do bottom-up and top-down processing relate to each other? There have been various models of comprehension which have encompassed both bottom-up and top-down processing (one of which was developed by the cognitive psychologist Anderson (1983), whose work we met in Chapter 7). It is important to realize that all recent models involve *both* types of processing. It may be that in different situations one will be more prominent that the other. Faerch and Kasper (1986: 264), for example, suggest that in highly predictable contexts top-down may be used more, while in situations where little context is provided we tend to be more bottom-up. But overall, both are needed. Even the highly skilled reader/listener will engage in bottom-up processing and, although some of the examples we have given of top-down processing have ended in inaccuracies (British listeners adding possibly wrong information to the Indian stories, for example), this type of processing is also vital. It enables us to interpret texts in realistic time (not going through the various interpretations of each word, for example).

The paragraph above is about L1 processing. What about comprehension in a foreign language? How does the learner need to be equipped if she is to be a good reader/listener? Let us think first about the different types of knowledge she will need to bring to a text. High on the list, and not to be forgotten, is knowledge of the target language. A non-native listener/reader's problems with a text may be due largely to deficiencies in banal but vital areas like vocabulary and grammar. As Eskey (1988: 94, cited in Paran 1996) puts it: 'Good readers know the language. They can decode . . . both the lexical units and syntactic structures they encounter in texts . . .' But knowledge of the target language needs to go beyond the understanding of words and structures in isolation. There are the 'rules of use' which enable you to interpret what is actually being 'said' in a message. To understand these, an important component will be background knowledge. The aspect of this that we have focused on is schemata, though psychologists and applied linguists have introduced various other concepts to refine and develop this notion of background knowledge.[4] Hedge (1985) divides background knowledge into general knowledge, subject-specific knowledge and cultural knowledge. The learner will need varying quantities of these according to the texts being read or listened to. She will also need *reasons* for listening or reading. You may wish to look back over the examples given in association with each of our Strange Occurrences and try and specify, for each, which of the things we have discussed in this paragraph the reader is bringing to the text.

Think now about the skills the learner will have to develop. Applied linguists have developed numerous lists of skills, many of which are, in Williams's words (1998: 334) 'vague' and 'overlapping'. Some are also very long: Grellet (1981) uses Munby (1978) – a book mentioned in Chapter 12 – and has a reading skill list with no less that nineteen items on it. Some commonly listed skills are clearly related to bottom-up processes, like *word recognition*, and *understanding word meaning*. Others equally clearly involve top-down processing, like *applying schemata to texts*, *predicting* and *inferencing*. Then there are skills associated with understanding of general message. Williams (1998: 333) mentions *identifying main ideas* and *following the development of an argument* in this category. Important characteristics for some of these skills are 'being selective' and 'being partial' – the capacity to focus on some pieces of information and ignore others, particularly in relation to a given purpose for reading/listening.

Does the FL learner need more bottom-up or more top-down practice? As we have seen both are important, and what the learner requires can often best be assessed by looking at what she has already been given. Many learners suffer from a surfeit of bottom-up. This develops in them the habit of processing word by word, and refusing to progress if one word is not understood. So if they do not know what a *pile* is in our *The farmer put the straw on a pile beside his threshing machine*, they would give up before *threshing machine* was ever reached. These learners desperately need training in top-down. But in recent years, top-down listening and reading have been fashionable, and there is the danger of developing a breed of learners who are expert in applying schemata to texts, without too much regard for what the texts actually say. This danger is well expressed in Paran (1996) who argues the need for attention to bottom-up skills. There must be a diet of both.

Facilitating comprehension

Bottom-up skills

Traditional comprehension exercises focus on bottom-up processing. At their worst these can be of the *Cat sat on the mat* variety. The text tells the students that the cat sat on the mat. Then a series of questions ask such things as *Who sat on the mat? What did the cat do? Where did the cat sit?* More imaginative approaches ask questions about a variety of different linguistic levels. There is also room for exercises practising skills in isolation. Box 14.4 (overleaf) gives an example. Grellet (1981), a useful source of ideas on reading comprehension, has a large collection of exercises dealing with specific skills like *deducing the meaning and use of unfamiliar lexical items through understanding word formation*, and *developing word comprehension* speed.

Understanding communicative value, and main points

The result of nothing but the *Cat sat on the mat* type of comprehension questions will be learners who are not trained to recognize the communicative functions in a text. One way of achieving this is by giving a list of sentences and asking which captures most clearly what is being said in a given part of the text. This exercise can be made more meaningful by making sure that all the sentences listed say things that are mentioned in the text. The learners have to distinguish important from secondary information. This silly example stays with the cat and mat theme: imagine a listening passage containing the utterances *Just look at my beautiful mat. It's filthy all over. There's no doubt about it. The cat sat on the mat.* You might give learners the following three sentences, asking which most clearly captures what the speaker is saying:

14.4   A word recognition exercise from Paran (1990, cited in Paran 1996)

This exercise deals with the skill of word recognition. Notice how different typeweights (roman, italic, bold) and typefaces are used. Because word recognition is a skill that has to be done at speed, this exercise is timed.

Word recognition (timed exercise)
In each exercise, circle the word (or words) which exactly matches those printed in bold.
1 **ensure**
   a. *insure*   b. sure   c. **insurance**   d. **ensure**
2 **on board**
   a. aboard   b. **abroad**   c. **on board**   d. *a board*
3 **superstitious**
   a. *superstition*   b. **superstitious**   c. *cuperstitions*   d. surreptitious
4 **applies**
   a. **applied**   b. *apples*   c. **applies**   d. apple
5 **omen**
   a. *men*   b. **omen**   c. **omens**   d. *amen*
6 **extremely**
   a. **extremely**   b. **extremity**   c. extreme   d. *extremes*

(a) The speaker is expressing her fondness for her mat

(b) The speaker is blaming the cat for making a mess

(c) The speaker is stating that no part of the mat is now clean

The correct answer is (b). But notice that the other two sentences express ideas that are also present in the text.

There are two traditional exercise types which are sometimes branded as old-fashioned, but which can be very useful in this context. The first is translation. This has, according to Cook (1998b: 359), 'been dismissed by almost all twentieth-century theories and methodologies'. But translation is now enjoying a revival, because we have come to realize that being able to translate a passage well involves a clear understanding of the writer's intention. A good translator has to understand functions and speech acts, not just the signification of individual words and sentences. The second traditional exercise is particularly useful for facilitating understanding of the intention of a text as a whole. It is *précis* or summary writing. As with translation, this has a dusty, old-fashioned air about it. But in order to be able to write a good summary, you have to have understood what the main points of a text are, distinguishing them from other, less important points that are also made in it.

Forming or activating schemata

In cases where students do not have background knowledge appropriate for the understanding of a passage, ways of giving it to them need to be found. Here is how one book (Foll 1990) does it. His Unit 4 has two reading passages dealing with Italian history and culture. Before the passage is a section called *Starting off*. The instructions read: 'Both extracts are set in very specific cultural backgrounds. Before you read the extracts, see how much of this specific cultural knowledge you have by answering the following questions. If there are any you cannot answer, consult an encyclopaedia, or ask someone who knows' (p. 26). There are eight questions. They include: *In the Catholic religion, who is Our Blessed Lady?*, and *Where is the Colosseum? What was it originally used for?* Pre-reading or pre-listening exercises are also a common way of activating background knowledge that learners already possess. The 'non-verbal communication' activity mentioned on page 239 is an example, and Exercise 4 in box 14.7 (p. 282) is another. The next time you are in a library containing FL textbooks which specialize in reading or listening, take some off the shelves. The chances are that they will contain pre-reading/listening activities. There is one book, Hess (1991), that consists of nothing but 'pre-text' activities. It provides a set of games, discussions, activities involving looking up information, that will 'motivate, challenge, and arouse curiosity' (p. ix) before texts are read or heard.

Developing predictive skills

Part of the top-down process is to be able to make sensible guesses as to what is coming next in a context. Good readers and listeners can do this. One exercise type which helps develop predictive skills is called cloze. A cloze test or exercise is one in which learners are given a text with some words missing. Trying to guess what the words are is a form of prediction. In many instances of cloze, single words are deleted at regular intervals (e.g. every seventh word). The exercise in box 14.5 (overleaf) is of a type sometimes called selective cloze. Here words are not omitted at regular intervals, and the omissions have been chosen to make the learner think about the content and organization of the text. The gaps are all of the same length, though what fills them may be one word, or a whole chunk of text. In exercises like this, it does not matter if the learner cannot guess the actual words; more important is whether the gist of what is missing can be predicted. Try the exercise yourself. The passage is taken from Chapter 1 (p. 4), so you can check your version against the original.

An extreme version of cloze is found in the exciting computer-based game called *Storyboard*. The game is based on a text. The title is given, and perhaps an opening sentence to start things off. The rest of the text appears as a series of blanks, one for each word. The learner has a certain amount of

> ### 14.5   What's missing?
>
> Learner number one is Zhang. He lives in the Sichuan province of main-land China. He has a bachelor's degree from _____ in business stud-ies, and he wants to do a master's degree overseas. He has _____ universities in Britain, the United States and Australia, and there is the chance that he may receive some scholarship money. _____ all the universities require him to take an internationally recognized English test before _____, and his score on the test must be very high. It is now January, and _____ is in June. He does not enjoy language learning at all, but his situation explains very well why _____ spent in the (for him) tedious business of _____ his English.

money with which to 'buy' words. The learner asks whether a particular word appears in the text (by typing it onto the screen). If it does, all occur-rences of it replace the appropriate blanks. The learner tries to replace all the blanks to form an entire text, before her money runs out. Though the game is a little tedious to prepare without a computer, it can be done. You may like to try it with a friend. You need to identify a text and turn it into blanks. As your friend makes guesses, you check the words in the original, and write them in to the blanked version.[5]

Purposeful comprehension

Some, but not all, of reading and listening is for a specific purpose – to find out some specific piece of information for example. One major dif-ference between the way comprehension used to be practised and how it is practised nowadays is that we now commonly state a clear reason why a passage should be read or listened to; it is purposeful comprehension. Sometimes a textbook will proclaim this in its title: Scarbrough (1984) for example is entitled *Reasons for Listening*, while Davies and Witney's (1979) book is *Reasons for Reading*. We saw an example of a purposeful reading exercise in Chapter 10 (box 10.15, p. 186). We made the point there that purposeful comprehension is important because it teaches the invaluable skill of 'not trying to understand everything'. Learners who do not have this skill really will suffer terribly. One group of students I tried the exer-cise in box 14.6 with did not get further than the first line of the 'Girl in a raincoat' passage. Two words held them up: *limping* and *pale*. They would not continue reading till they knew what the words meant. In situations like this, perhaps the teacher should do what goes against the mentality of the pedagogue – withhold information, by saying *Sorry, I'm not going to tell you what it means*. The point is that knowing what *pale* means is not relevant to the task in hand (the word *limping* is admittedly more relevant); and the

14.6 Ghosts

This exercise is an abridged version of one found in a textbook specially for reading: Castrillo *et al.* (1988). The unit is about 'Ghosts'. It starts with a pre-reading exercise of the sort we have discussed, aimed at activating the learners' 'ghost schemata'. Then there is a chart:

Title	Ghost of	Seen by	At/in (place)	In (time)	Why did it/ they haunt that place?	What did it/they do?
	A girl					
					There had been a battle there	
				Around 1728		
		Its owner, Norma Kresgal		Not mentioned		
					They had possibly been buried there	Looked fixedly

On the next page are five passages. Here are three of them:

GHOSTS

Lesson of death

Twelve schoolboys were shocked to see their classmate John Daniel sitting at his desk. For seven weeks earlier John had been found dead 200 yards from his home in Beaminster, Dorset. His death had been recorded as 'from natural causes' after his mother said he suffered from fits.

After questioning the 12 boys, local magistrate Colonel Broadrep ordered the body to be exhumed, and an inquest in 1728 revealed that John had been strangled. The murderer was never caught.

Girl in a raincoat

A limping blonde girl in a pale raincoat has startled several motorists on the A23 road north of Brighton, Sussex. In 1964 one driver saw her dash to the central reservation and vanish. In 1972, several people said they saw her north of the village of Pyecombe. She may be the ghost of a young girl killed in a motor cycle accident in the area.

Ghostly barking

Norma Kresgal, of New York, was awakened by the barking of Corky, her collie dog. But Corky was dead. Mrs Kresgal got up to investigate – and found that the house was on fire.

The learners are asked to read the passages and fill in the chart. Where a specific piece of information is not given, learners write *Not mentioned*.

learner who goes from the beginning to the end of the text insisting on 100 per cent understanding is not just misunderstanding the nature of comprehension; she is also going to fare badly in the target language country.

The exercise exemplified in box 14.6 is of the type called 'information transfer' (IT).[6] IT exercises work by asking the learner to transfer information from one representation to another – from a passage to a table in the case above. Box 14.7 gives some other examples of IT exercises. Some of these are reading, some listening. But in all cases the exercises could be modified to practise in the other medium.

14.7   Five information transfer exercises

For each exercise, state what the transfer is *from* and *to*. For example, in exercise 1 it is from letter to application form.

1. The learners are given two letters from individuals applying to join a sports club. Blank application forms are supplied, and the learners use the information in the letters to fill out the forms. This is reading comprehension, but a listening comprehension component can be added, by using taped telephone conversations instead of the letters (from Morrow and Johnson 1979).
2. An exercise for young children. A picture shows a space ship with an astronaut doing various activities, like eating breakfast, exercising, going to bed. There is a clock beside each picture, but with the hands missing. Learners listen to a tape describing the *Astronaut's Day*. It tells them what the astronaut does and at what time. They use this information to put hands on the clocks (from Scott 1980).
3. Unit 5 in Greenall and Pye (1991) is entitled *Childhood Dreams*. The thematic link running through the unit is childhood dreams and whether they have been realized. There is a pre-reading exercise where learners are asked about their own childhood dreams. Then there are pictures of five famous individuals. There are five short reading passages, in which each individual talks about themselves, mentioning their present work as well as their childhood dreams. Learners read the passages in order to fill in a table giving information about 'dreams, and what actually happened'.
4. Lindop and Fisher (1988) have a passage describing how a British couple adopt a boy called James. The sequence of events in the actual week of the adoption is described in great detail. Accompanying the passage is a table showing the days of the week on the left and the events of the week on the right, in jumbled order. Learners match days and events by drawing lines from one to the other, left to right.
5. You have already met the fifth example, in a box in Chapter 10. Spend a few moments trying to find it.[7]

A particularly imaginative form of information-transfer exercise, pioneered by Geddes and Sturtridge (1979 and 1982), has come to be known as jigsaw listening and reading. In this, the class divides up into groups, with each group listening to or reading a different text. The groups then come together and pool their information, to complete the 'jigsaw'. Unit 9 of Geddes and Sturtridge (1982) for example, is about a giant, mysterious creature known as the Sasquatch. Three groups of learners read three different passages (printed on different pages of the book, to preserve an information gap). There is a table to complete with information about the Sasquatch – where it lives, what it eats and so on. Each group can only fill in part of the table from the information they read. The groups then combine, and together complete the table.

14.8 On a point of order

Perhaps you find yourself saying: *Yes, purposeful comprehension, which is very selective and partial, is very important. But I want something more. I think learners need to spend time studying texts, even in a bottom-up, form-focused way.*

A sensible standpoint. But, if you want to practise *both* comprehension for a specific purpose *and* detailed textual study, then the order in which you do it is important. If you do the detailed analysis first, then your learners will never practise selecting, being partial, ignoring the unwanted. You need to do it the other way round. First set a specific reason for comprehending, then do the more detailed study of the text.

Writing

In the previous section, the point was made that listening comprehension exercises can be turned into reading comprehension, and vice versa, usually without much difficulty. To some extent the same is true for speaking and writing exercises, and for this reason a number of the techniques introduced in Chapter 13 can be adapted for writing practice. For example, nearly all the practice-stage exercises, including the information-gap ones, can be modified just by asking the students to write down sentences rather than saying them though, since writing is a longer process than speaking, you have to bear in mind how time-consuming some drills will be. You are invited to pick out at random a few of the example exercises introduced in Chapter 13, and think how they could be converted into writing exercises. Choose real-thing exercises as well as scales.

The teacher can, then, use speaking exercises for writing practice, and indeed, as Byrne (1988) notes, a major and respectable use of writing is as a reinforcement to what is done in speech practice. It also, incidentally, has the great advantage of being visible evidence of effort. A written exercise can be taken home to a parent as proof of work done. Speaking practice suffers from a lack of documentary evidence.

But most writing is more than speech written down. There are many aspects of writing that are different from speech. Box 14.9 asks you to consider some of these, and box 14.10 gives a summary of some of the more important ones. This latter box needs treating with care. What the differences between speaking and writing are depends on what kind of speaking and what kind of writing we are considering. A formal spoken lecture will have certain characteristics in common with a written essay, while an informal note to a spouse about what shopping she should buy on the way home will have certain characteristics in common with spoken conversation. Box 14.10 looks at rather formal writing and rather informal speech and, if you vary this, the differences will disappear. For example, it may be true that contracted forms do not appear often in writing an academic essay, but this would not be true about a note to a spouse.

14.9 Complaining in speech and writing

In box 9.12 (p. 156) you read the comments of a subject complaining bitterly about the think-aloud technique for collecting data. That transcribed version was modified and slightly abridged. The transcription below is a more accurate representation of what she actually said. It does not contain punctuation, because there is no punctuation in speech.

> the main problem erm was that I was so aware of the need to keep talking that I didn't get a chance to think about erm anything through and I was I was desperate to be able to switch off sit back think about it in peace and quiet think something through and I knew I wasn't going to be able to come up with anything not wonderful not even satisfactory really through this necessity to keep talking and it is drivel I found that if I mentioned an idea if I hadn't had to talk about it I would have been rejecting it within within seconds probably as rubbish.

Imagine that this subject is asked to write a report on her problems with think-aloud techniques. How would she express what is said in the above extract? Either write a paragraph, or compose one in your head. Think about how the written and spoken versions differ.

Use what you have done as a spur to think in more general terms about the differences between speech and writing.

The existence of these differences carries a clear message. When we are teaching speaking, we are *not* at the same time teaching writing. Writing is indeed more than speech written down.

14.10   Some differences between speaking and writing

(a) General

   (i) learned vs. taught. Everyone learns to speak. Not everyone learns to write; it has to be taught

   (ii) writing is more 'organized'. Why?

      (a) there is less 'redundancy'. The reader cannot rely on repetitions to clarify. The writer is often not given immediate feedback. In speech, if something is unclear, your interactant immediately tells you, and you can rephrase your message

      (b) permanence of the written medium and knowledge of scrutiny. When you write something, you know it is there for ever. It is also available for others to scrutinize and 'pick over'. But (presidents of the United States note) tape recordings are changing this situation, by making speech potentially permanent

      (c) writing is often 'fuller'. You are less certain of what knowledge you share with your reader, because her identity is often more vague

(b) Linguistic

   (i) some structural differences: e.g. contracted forms are less common in writing (so we may say *didn't* but write *did not*)

   (ii) no intonation, stress, or gestures to help clarify meaning in writing. We have to find other ways of achieving what these things manage. Note also that there is no punctuation in speech

(c) Functional

Perhaps more 'language of reporting' in writing than speech. Certainly a needs analysis of speaking and writing uses would identify different purposes and notions/functions.[8]

Teaching the 'joining-together' skills

Of the differences described in box 14.10, the one that perhaps has the most implications for teaching is that writing is more organized. Part of what this implies is that attention has to be given to the 'joining-together' skills of cohesion and coherence. We discussed these concepts in Chapter 2. There we noted that a passage is more than a sequence of individual sentences. We spoke of two types of rules of discourse, concerned with grammatical unity (cohesion) and sense unity (coherence). If you need to remind yourself of the difference between these concepts, look back to box 2.16 on page 32.

How can we teach cohesion and coherence? Some of the exercises we considered under the receptive skills can be useful here. Cloze activities (the one in box 14.5, p. 280 for example) can be extremely useful in drawing the learner's attention to passage organization, particularly if the teacher carefully selects what words to omit from the text, so as to focus on organization. Another technique involves giving the learner sentences in isolation, and asking her to join them together. This technique is known as sentence combining (SC). Box 14.11 illustrates two SC exercises:

14.11 Two versions of sentence combining

(a) One version of SC involves taking a text and dividing it into separate sentences, repeating information where necessary. The learners have to join the sentences together. Try it:

take a passage
subtract sentences from the passage
the passage with sentences subtracted will not be coherent
the passage with sentences subtracted will not be cohesive
give the passage with subtracted sentences to the learners

Now find another passage (in this book or from elsewhere). From it create a series of sentences as above, suitable for an SC exercise.

(b) In another version of SC you give the learners an opening sentence, then a series of choices as to what will follow. Hamp-Lyons and Heasley (1987: 52), for example, have an exercise with the following instruction:

Read the beginning of the text and choose one sentence from the two which follow it. Keep choosing one sentence from each two, continuing the text as you think the writer might have written it.

According to the kind of sentences you offer as a choice, this exercise can be used to practise coherence or cohesion.

SC involves a process of what might be called 'passage assembly', and this process is highly productive as a technique for practising the 'joining-together' skills. Here is another example. The discussion the students will have while doing the activity below will be about cohesion and coherence:

14.12 Smuggling jewels

This description of an exercise is taken from Johnson (1981: 103). It uses a passage from Newland (1974):

Take a short passage (pieces of narrative are ideal) and write each sentence of it on a separate card. Mix the cards up and give one card to each

---

student. The students must order the cards to make the original passage. If there are more students than cards, have more than one set of cards available with the students working in groups.

As a second best, present the sentences to the students in jumbled order on one piece of paper. The students must number the sentences in the correct order. Here is an example using a passage taken directly from a reader. The sentences are presented below in jumbled order:

> *After a few minutes the man got out of the car and went into the phone box.*
> *They watched as the merchant and Mrs Perkin left the flat.*
> *This is it, Jan, said the man in the car to his friend.*
> *She was talking to a diamond merchant.*
> Yes, I'll keep them here in the company's flat, *replied Mrs Perkin.*
> *He went to the window and looked out.*
> *In the street he saw a red car by a public telephone.*
> *The merchant smiled.*
> You won't want to lose these, *he said. Is there a safe place for them?*
> *Mrs Perkin was visiting Amsterdam on business to buy some diamonds.*

Listen to the kind of discussion the students have while doing this type of exercise. It is highly detailed discussion about specific aspects of cohesion and coherence.

A further set of techniques popularly used for teaching joining-together involve passage *re*-assembly. Hedge (1988: 136) gives an example. She asks learners to analyse a given text . She does this by providing a number of statements describing what is done in the text, like *supporting an argument with an example*, and *making a general statement*. Learners write a number beside each statement to show how the text is organized. She then suggests a new opening sentence for the text, and asks how the order would change if the passage started in that way. This is actually quite a natural task. As you may have discovered from your own experience at academic writing, you often find yourself rewriting paragraphs, perhaps to begin in a different way. Different beginnings often require total reorganization of paragraphs – an exercise in cohesion and coherence.

This last exercise is an example of another set of productive writing techniques which involve performing various operations on already existing texts. In this example the 'operation' involves a change in opening sentence, but many other sorts of changes can be suggested. You can suggest a change in writer intention, a change of standpoint, a change of style or tone. In Johnson (1983b) I describe an approach to the teaching of writing which involves constantly asking learners questions like: *Why did the writer say X (and not Y)? What difference would it have made if she had written Y and not X? What would the writer have said if she had wanted to emphasize A instead of B? If the reader misunderstands Sentence X in a certain way, how may it be changed to eliminate misunderstanding?* I relate this approach to Aristotelian rhetoric. This is defined by Grierson (1945) as 'the study of how to express oneself correctly and effectively, bearing in mind the nature of the language we use, the subject we are speaking or writing about, the kind of audience we have in view . . . and the purpose, which last is the main determinant'. In the approach we are exploring how these various 'determinants' exert influence on texts. Candlin has a vivid way of describing approaches like this. They involve, he says, 'gutting reality'.[9]

Notice that various of the exercises we have considered in this section do not always involve very much actual writing. In fact, many of them inhabit a twilight world somewhere between reading comprehension and writing practice. They involve understanding why a text has been written in such a way, and then thinking about changes to it. This twilight world brings us back to a point made at the beginning of the chapter, that reading and writing are intimately connected. Understanding the structure of a text, for example, makes you a good reader, and helps to make you a good writer too.

Process writing

In Chapter 10, mention was made of the *process syllabus*. This type of syllabus is based on the distinction between product and process, and the idea that language teaching should be more interested in the latter than the former. The area in which a focus on process has been particularly pursued is writing. Process writing is today an accepted, indeed common approach. In it, attention is focused on the processes writers go through when producing texts, and these are practised in class. One book particularly influential in the area is White and Arndt (1991). Here are the major writing processes they identify (p. 4):

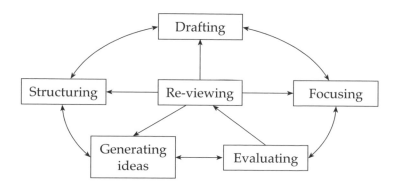

White and Arndt suggest a wealth of techniques for practising these in class, and box 14.13 exemplifies some associated with three areas:

14.13 How to generate, focus and structure (some techniques based on White and Arndt 1991)

A technique to facilitate *generating* – 'getting the ideas flowing':

Brainstorming is thinking quickly and without inhibition to develop a few buzz words and ideas. It should be 'free-wheeling, unstructured and non-judgmental' (p. 18; a little like Virginia Woolf for language teaching). It can be a 'snow-ball' activity – learners work alone (writing ideas on cards), then pool ideas in pairs, then in groups (developing and refining a list). The class comes together. Each group selects their 3 favourite ideas, which are written on the blackboard.

Techniques to facilitate *focusing* – deciding on the central idea(s) (answering the reader's question: *What are you trying to tell me?*):

Loopwriting. This is usually done using *fastwriting*, which is a written version of brainstorming. The learner does some fastwriting, to produce a few lines of text. She then writes a sentence summarizing what she has said. The summary acts as a stimulus to produce more text (a second 'loop'), which is then summarized in turn. The technique helps learners to focus on what they want their main points to be.

Conferencing often follows loopwriting. It involves going through what you've written with the teacher or fellow students. It helps to bring ideas into the open.

A technique to facilitate *structuring* (organizing ideas into groups and deciding in what order to present them):

Once a set of ideas has been decided on, learners work together to think of several different ways of organizing them. They then decide on the best way, given an agreed purpose.

In our treatment of writing we have focused on just some of the skills involved. These have been chosen partly because they are the ones that have most interested applied linguists and teachers in recent years. Another reason is that they are skills particularly associated with writing and may not receive attention in a course with a bias to teaching the spoken language. But do not forget that there really is much more to teaching writing than developing the joining-together skills and the processes of composition that we have covered. Among many other things, a good writer must have a grasp of basic sentence construction, and somehow or other this needs to be taught.

Sometimes (though not always!) in language teaching what you teach gets learned, and what you do not teach does not get learned. In the late 1970s, when much attention was given to teaching cohesion, one sometimes found the strangest examples of student writing resulting. An essay might contain very many (unnaturally many in fact) sophisticated 'link expressions', like *however, moreover, nevertheless, on the other hand*. But between these elegant link expressions might be the most awful English, full of errors. This was the result of teaching the joining-together skills and not much else. Beautiful joints, holding nothing together.

Notes

1. This is how the four skills are categorized:

	Spoken	Written
Receptive	Listening	Reading
Productive	Speaking	Writing

2. From Garnett, W. 1992 'A Back-to-the-Drawing-Board Oboe'. *Double Reed News*, 19: 22–5.
3. For Passenger A, the important information is *Platform 5*. Passenger B wants to travel to somewhere other than Edinburgh. She is perhaps standing on Platform 5, having thought that her train went from there. She now knows she was wrong. *Edinburgh* is an important piece of information for this passenger. Passenger C knows that the Edinburgh train is leaving from Platform 5. She is catching the train (or seeing off someone who is travelling on it). She's not sure what time it leaves. The important piece of information for her is *10.30*.
4. As well as schemata, two other concepts, known as scripts and scenarios are used to describe aspects of background knowledge. If you want to know more about schemata, scripts, scenarios and comprehension processes in general, Brown and Yule (1983) is a good read.
5. *Storyboard*, and other computer games, are described in a number of places, including Higgins and Johns (1984).
6. I discuss information transfer exercises in Paper 15 of Johnson (1982).
7. In example 2 the transfer is from tape to picture. In 3 and 4 it is from passage to table. The fifth exercise is in box 10.15, on page 186. The transfer there is from passage (guidebook) to map.
8. For a lengthier discussion of speech/writing differences, looked at from a slightly different perspective, see Chapter 6 of Short (1996).
9. Candlin's phrase was used in a personal communication.

Chapter 15

Tests

Introduction

It is an unfortunate truth that those who populate the world of foreign-language education divide themselves into two camps, which rarely meet except on the verbal battlefield. They are the Teachers and the Testers. When they do meet in battle, the Teachers are inclined to say things like *Let's learn to teach before we learn to test* and (unkindest cut of all) *We deal with people, you deal with statistics*. The Testers on the other hand sometimes regard the Teachers as rather a vague lot, well-meaning perhaps, but who tend to be unspecific about their aims and objectives, and on finding out whether they have been met. As a result, Testers and Teachers sit in differ-ent parts of the staff common room. The Testers think the Teachers are talking over coffee about whether Maria and Giovanni in Class 1 are dating, while the Teachers think the Testers are discussing what mark out of ten to give their coffee – for flavour, cost and overall quality.

It is natural that individuals with different outlooks and interests should be drawn towards either the teaching or the testing field. But the kinds of stereotypes just mentioned can be dangerous if they lead us to believe that the one field can do without the other. So it is vital for teachers to recognize the necessity for testing, and the potential value of tests for teach-ing. Testing is important for almost all the people involved in the education process. The learner wants to know how well he is doing, and wants the 'piece of paper' at the end of the course that will help open professional doors. The teacher wants to know not only how the learner is progress-ing, but also how he, the teacher, is succeeding in his job. Then there are parents, educational authorities and countless others who have some interest in the learner's progress. This includes the all-important outsider – the potential employer, or the university administrator (to mention just two), who rely heavily on what tests tell them about learner proficiency levels.

Another reason why testing is important for teaching is to do with the phenomenon known as <u>washback</u>, or backwash. This is the effect that testing has on teaching. For better or worse, tests and exams exert control over what goes on in classrooms. This is because very many language-teaching classes are geared more or less directly to the tests or examinations the learners will end up taking. Teachers must often 'teach to' a test. If the test is a bad one (or the teacher is too narrow in his interpretation of it), the result may be negative washback, where we can say that teaching suffers because of the test coming at the end of the course. But if the test is a good one, and its nature well understood by the teacher, the effect on the teaching may be very positive. There will be positive washback.

So teachers need testers. Perhaps the two groups should even learn to love one another, or at least to sit together in the staff common room.

15.1   Tests you have known

Think about your own experiences with language tests. Have some that you have taken been better than others? Use your personal experiences as the starting point to think about what makes a good test . . . and what makes a bad one.

Types of test

We have already come across one type of test, the aptitude test, in Chapter 8. This, we saw, did not measure any actual performance or level of achievement, but attempted to measure potential – how well a learner might progress if he were to learn a language. Though some of the test types we shall be concerned with in this chapter do have a similarly forward-looking component to them, they all focus more on what has been done, on what level of achievement or proficiency a learner has reached.

Writers on testing sometimes divide test types into two broad categories, within which sub-categories are recognized. These broad categories are *achievement* and *proficiency* tests. *Achievement* tests are concerned with how well a learner has done in relation to a particular course or programme. They usually come at the end of programmes, and are deliberately based on the content covered in it. *Diagnostic* tests are also concerned with achievement, or lack thereof. They are often geared to assess the success of some small stretch of teaching, and perhaps to suggest where remedial work will be required. Achievement tests are useful to the teacher as well as the learners; they indicate how well teaching has succeeded, and where improvements need to be made.

Proficiency tests do not relate to any specific content or programme. They are tests of what level has been reached in the language, and stand independent of any course. Their results are statements to the world about what a learner can do. Sometimes proficiency tests may have a particular end user in mind. For example, there may be a proficiency test at the end of a pre-sessional course which states the extent to which a learner is ready for a specific area of use – studying an academic subject in the foreign language. Alternatively, they may be more general statements of level. The well-known Cambridge tests (First Certificate and Proficiency – see the final section of this chapter) are of this type, and have no specific end user in mind. Indeed, part of their value is that they have come to be generally recognized as statements of overall proficiency that have validity in very many situations. *Placement* tests are a particular sort of proficiency test. They are given at the beginning of language-teaching programmes, to help with decisions as to which classes learners should be put into. Though these tests are generally concerned with proficiency, they can be drawn up with the coming teaching programme in mind. So, to stay with the pre-sessional example, a placement test for such a course would perhaps want to tap the language skill areas that are to be covered on the course. For example, if the learners are to be studying *taking lecture notes* as one component of their course, then the placement test might measure present proficiency in that area.

Approaches to language testing

The psychometric approach

We have seen at various times in this book the way that structural linguistics and behaviourism has had its effect on language education. Testing is no exception, and the approach to testing predominant in the 1960s (particularly associated with Lado 1961) was one which owed much to these traditions. There was an emphasis on the testing of language structure, usually (as in audiolingual language teaching) in decontextualized, sentence-level form. There was also emphasis placed on being scientific (recall Bloomfield's preoccupation with this in Chapter 3). Importance was hence given to objective and accurate measuring, and the word <u>psychometric</u> (meaning 'psychological measuring') is often used to describe this approach. Another expression associated with this form of testing is <u>discrete</u> <u>point</u>. As with behaviourist teaching, individual items are focused on discretely – that is, one at a time.

In psychometric testing the *multiple-choice question* is given pride of place, so much so that it attracts its own technical terminology, given in box 15.2 below. You might imagine that it is extremely easy to write good multiple-choice questions. Box 15.2 also illustrates that this is wrong.

15.2 How to write bad multiple-choice questions

Example 1 Here is a passage taken from Chapter 1 (p. 8). The multiple-choice question below it is a bad one. Why?

Naiman *et al.* (1978) make mention of one girl in Canada who had many qualities that suggest she should be a good foreign language learner. Her teachers described her as 'attentive, very jovial and relaxed, obviously enjoying some of the activities'; French was, she said, her favourite subject, and outside the classroom she would listen to French radio and would talk to her friends in French, just for fun. She was not afraid of making mistakes, was very motivated, and a hard worker. Everything is there to make her a good learner, except that she lacked something – talent (aptitude) perhaps. As a result she was second lowest in her class.

This passage is about:

A   a girl studying French in Canada

B   a highly motivated language learner

C   a person possibly lacking in language aptitude.

D   a poor language learner

Example 2 This is taken from Heaton (1988: 32). It is also used by Alderson *et al.* (1995: 49):

Select the option closest in meaning to the word underlined:

He began to <u>choke</u> while he was eating the fish.

A   die

B   cough and vomit

C   be unable to breathe because of something in his windpipe

D   grow very angry

What is wrong with this question? Alderson *et al.* give three reasons – see Note 1 at the end of this chapter.

Example 2 can be used to illustrate three pieces of technical terminology. The sentence itself (*He began to choke . . .*) is known as the *stem*. Then there is the *correct option* (in this case probably intended to be C), and the *distractors* (options A, B and D).

Multiple-choice questions have many advantages. If well constructed, they provide clear-cut right and wrong answers, thus avoiding endless agonizing debates about whether a particular answer is correct or not. They are also very easy to mark, which is particularly important when a large number of test results are required in a short space of time. But they have many disadvantages. Here are some mentioned by Baxter (1997) and Weir (1990):

- the format makes it possible to have a reasonable chance of guessing the correct answer. Sometimes, if the questions have been poorly constructed, it may even be possible to arrive at the correct answer without referring to the text
- we saw in box 15.2 above that it is very difficult to write good multiple-choice questions. It is sometimes also difficult to invent an adequate number of good questions from a text
- multiple-choice items will only test a restricted number of skills. Some grammar points are difficult to test in this way. Think for example about the difference between *some* and *any* (we discussed this on p. 219). If you write a test item, you will have a correct answer (perhaps it will be *some*), but it may be difficult to think of more than the one obvious distractor (*any*). Other activities, like writing, involve whole areas of skill that it is difficult to imagine being tested by multiple-choice
- multiple choice can lead to harmful washback. A teacher working to the test may decide to base too much classroom work on multiple-choice exercises

Integrative testing

The reaction against discrete-point testing can be related to the 'sociolinguistic revolution' that had its effect on language teaching. It was largely the work of John Oller, whose 1979 book launched a strong attack on the psychometric, discrete-point approach.

The starting point for the change was the realization that there were interesting correlations between the results of discrete-point tests and tests which have come to be known as *integrative* (or holistic). These are tests that deliberately do not attempt to isolate discrete items or skills and test them separately. They are concerned with a learner's performance when using language skills together. The correlations are interesting because integrative tests are relatively easy to construct. What is the point, the argument ran, in struggling to set up discrete-point tests based on small differentiated areas of language competence, when a simply constructed cloze test will do the same job?

The technique that has pride of place in the integrative world is the cloze test. In Chapter 14 we looked at cloze used as an exercise, and the version illustrated in box 14.5 (p. 280) was a selective cloze exercise. In *numerical cloze* words are deleted at regular intervals (perhaps every seventh word will be removed). Try the one in box 15.3 overleaf. Notice here how the first few sentences are given, to provide a context. Notice also how the passage is set out. The blanks are numbered, and the answers are to be written on the right. This makes marking easy; the marker holds a piece of paper with the correct answers beside what the learner has written, and writes a tick or cross beside each.

15.3 A numerical cloze

You will find the original passage on page 9, and the answers are given for convenience in Note 2.

Classroom 1 is in Canada, and the pupils are nine-year-old children. Their native language is English, but this is hard to believe as you listen to what goes on during the school day. From the time they arrive till the time they leave, the pupils are spoken to almost entirely in French. They are greeted by their teacher (1) _____ French, their lessons are conducted in (2) _____ , teachers speak to them in the (3) _____ and the dinner hall in French, (4) _____ say goodbye to them at the (5) _____ of the day in French. When (6) _____ pupils started at this school, they (7) _____ replied to the teachers in English (8) (_____ is, the teachers spoke French and (9) _____ pupils responded naturally in English), but (10) _____ time this has changed, and now the pupils themselves are increasingly using French.

(1) _____
(2) _____
(3) _____
(4) _____
(5) _____
(6) _____
(7) _____
(8) _____
(9) _____
(10) _____

Cloze tests can be marked in one of two ways. In the 'exact' method, the marker insists on the very words that appeared in the original. This makes marking very quick, with no need to agonize whether a particular answer is correct or not. But the method may not appear very fair, and certainly an educated native speaker would score less than 100 per cent marked like this. The alternative is the 'acceptable' method, where words which did not in fact appear, but are perfectly acceptable, are considered as right. For example, the actual word used for (7) in the passage in box 15.3 is *themselves*. You may well have chosen a word like *always*, which fits the context equally well. By the exact method you would be marked wrong, by the acceptable method you would be marked right. The acceptable method does of course involve agonizing, and sometimes lengthy, debate among markers about whether something a learner has written is acceptable or not. But the interesting thing is that whichever method is used does not seem to make much difference as far as *ranking* the learners by result (putting them in order) is concerned.

Though cloze tests are usually associated with reading comprehension, they can be used with spoken texts as well. All you need is a transcription of spoken English (a conversation perhaps) to put your blanks into. A book which provides a collection of spoken cloze texts is Garman and Hughes (1983).

Because the words in a numerical cloze are deleted in a mathematical way (every seventh word, for example, may be taken out), these missing words will represent different grammatical categories and types of vocabulary. The passage in box 15.3 illustrates this well, and you are invited to look through it quickly to identify some of the word categories (nouns, verbs, etc.) that have been deleted. This is one sense in which cloze is 'holistic' and not 'discrete-point' – no one area of language is focused on, and different linguistic levels are involved. As we have noted, the findings of Oller and others seemed to suggest that these tests yielded results that were comparable to those of discrete-point tests. How can this be? Maybe there exists some underlying language competence that makes its appearance in both cloze-type tests and in discrete-point ones. This view was put forward by Oller as the Unitary Competence Hypothesis (UCH). According to it, all tests, integrative and discrete-point are tapping the same competence, so whatever kind of test you give will yield similar results. As Baker (1989) puts it: 'all tests, whatever their label, measure this general factor'. The inevitable result of this view was that integrative tests, being so easy to construct, began to take the place of discrete-point ones.

Cloze may have pride of place among the integrative testing techniques, but there are others. Included in Oller's (1976: 156) list are translation, essay and oral interview. Two further ones are worthy of mention. One might be seen as a version of cloze, and is known as the C-Test. In this version, the second half of every second word is deleted. This type of test suffers from a face validity problem, meaning that those who take it may feel bewildered as to what it is testing. Try the example in box 15.4 and see whether you agree:

15.4   A C-Test (you will find the original passage on p. 9)

In this example, *exactly half* of each second word is deleted when the full word has an even number of letters. *Exactly half plus one* are omitted when the word has an odd number of letters. This follows the example given in Alderson *et al.* (1995: 56).

*In **Classroom 2**, the teenage English pupils are learning Italian. The book they are using is full of extremely complicated grammar rules, explained in English. The tea____ spends so____ twenty min____ of t____ lesson expla____ the gra____ point o____ the d____, in Eng____, using diag____ on t____ blackboard, a____ plenty o____ grammatical te____ (talking o____ 'tenses', 'no____', 'adv____' and t____ like). (Original on p. 9)*

If you follow the exact scoring method with a C-Test, native speakers are likely to achieve higher marks than with cloze, though your experience with box 15.4 may lead you to realize that the answers are not always obvious or easy. There is research to suggest that C-tests yield valid and reliable results (Klein-Braley and Raatz 1984).

Another integrative technique is dictation. Though this was decried in the 1960s because it was unclear exactly what it was testing, later research showed it to be of value, and in the 1980s it enjoyed a revival. Davis and Rinvolucri (1988), a book full of interesting dictation techniques, is evidence of this revival. A potential advantage that it has over cloze is that it includes a listening component. It is also easy to administer. But it is difficult to score. It takes a very long time to mark a dictation, and all kinds of difficult decisions may loom. Is a small misspelling, for example, as serious as completely missing out a word? The potential for heated debate is endless.

Towards the mid-1980s, doubts began to be expressed regarding the UCH. Particularly, the statistics that led to the initial correlations between discrete-point and integrative tests were questioned, and it began to be felt that tests like cloze were not living up to their expectations. Baker (1989: 71) gives an interesting account by drawing an unusual parallel – with the assessment of elderly people's health. If we wanted to find out how healthy a group of elderly people are, we might use generally accepted ('discrete-point') tests like taking blood pressure or measuring weight/height ratio. An alternative ('integrative') test would be to send them all on a one-mile run. This would certainly yield information about health, and doubtless correlations could be found with blood-pressure tests. But these correlations would *not* lead us to assume that 'health is unitary'. Not only would correlations be expected; we would also expect there to be advantages to the generally accepted methods, because they would help us to isolate the causes of any ill health.

A number of writers today continue to see advantages to integrative tests like cloze, particularly in situations when some idea of general proficiency is what is required (as in placement testing, for example). But integrative tests, and the UCH underpinning them, are no longer assumed to have the power once attributed to them.

Communicative testing

Communicative Language Teaching, which we discussed in Chapter 10, finds its parallel in Communicative Language Testing. A common basis to both is an interest in the uses to which language is put, and in many so-called communicative tests, learners are asked questions about the function of utterances rather than their grammatical structure. Box 15.5 illustrates.

15.5 Testing appropriateness

Harrison (1983: 100) provides an example of how some tests try to find out whether a learner can make responses which are appropriate to context. The example comes from the Certificate Examination set by ARELS, the (British) Association of Recognised English Language Schools.

In the test the learner hears a number of questions or comments, either on tape or said by the examiner. The learner is asked to 'reply in a natural way' after each one. Responses are recorded on tape. Here are three of the items:

1. *Hasn't it been a marvellous summer!*
2. *Do you know if the banks are open on Saturdays?*
3. *I'd love one of those cream cakes, but I really shouldn't. I'm on a strict diet.*

What do you think is the expected answer for each of these three items? One of the issues for language testing would come to light if the learner were to answer item 3 by saying *Well don't have it then. Perhaps you should show some self-control.* Later in this chapter, in box 15.10 (p. 309) you will see some more examples of this issue.[3]

A second aspect of communicative testing is the importance it gives to text and task authenticity. As we saw in Chapter 13, CLT revolted against the kind of dialogue found in box 13.4 (p. 242) – the one where two people were asking rudely about trains to Millville. Thought was given to ensuring that language was used in a manner appropriate to its context. It was also felt to be important that the language introduced should be useful. A process of needs analysis would ensure that what was taught would be not just authentic, but relevant also. Similar preoccupations made themselves felt in the testing world, and affected not just language, but task selection also. It was part of the spirit of the time to argue that tasks given in tests should be similar to those undertaken in the real world. Morrow, whose 1977 document was important in the development of communicative testing, well represents this spirit.

This point introduces a distinction made in testing circles between *indirect* and *direct* tests. It is the same difference that was discussed in Chapter 13 when we spoke about indirect and direct relationships to the 'terminal behaviour' in scales and real-thing practice. Indirect tests measure abilities thought to be important to the terminal behaviour, but they do not attempt to simulate the behaviour itself. One of Hughes's (1989) examples of indirect testing is Lado's (1961) method of testing pronunciation by a paper and pencil test where pairs of words which rhyme have to be identified. Aspiring poets apart, people do not usually spend much time identifying rhyming words as part of their everyday routine. Direct tests try as far as possible to replicate the actual terminal behaviour in the test itself. Here is an example:

15.6 *Get* and *give*

Baker (1989: 13) gives an example of what might be called 'direct testing' from the Oxford Syndicate's Preliminary Test in English. It involves using an English-English dictionary to help solve reading problems. In the relevant part of the test, learners are given two dictionary entries, for the words *get* and *give*. These are quite lengthy, and cover many uses of these words. As is usual in dictionaries, each use is numbered, with a definition and an example given. So use (1) of *get* is 'have something' (as in *Peter's got a huge house*), while use (2) is 'buy or procure' (as in *I'll get some wine from the supermarket on the way home*). Learners are given ten sentences containing one of the two verbs. They are asked to write beside each sentence the number corresponding to the use as it appears in the dictionary. So, to continue the example above, a sentence like *Don't forget to get some sugar at the shop* would have the number (2) written beside it.

This part of the test is direct because using a dictionary in this way is an activity that many learners will undertake regularly.

A further characteristic of communicative tests is that they tend to treat the four skills separately, providing information about a learner's performance in each. This characteristic relates to the process of needs analysis. At the beginning of Chapter 14 we saw (in passing) that a needs analysis may well provide different specifications for each of the four skills. This is because a learner's writing needs, for example, will be different from his speaking needs. Notional/function teaching claimed that it would produce syllabuses and teaching that was sensitive to these differences in needs. In communicative testing this idea led to language tests which were also sensitive to skill differences. So the questions behind communicative tests are often not general ones like *What is this learner's English like?*, but more specific ones: *What is this learner's spoken English like? What about his reading, listening, writing?* The result is what is known as profile reporting, where learners are given separate scores for each of the four skills, together perhaps with descriptions of skill levels achieved. Good examples are two tests widely used to assess English for the purposes of academic study. These are the British IELTS test (International English Language Testing System) and the American TOEFL (Test of English as a Foreign Language). As well as an overall mark, scores for each skill are given, and these individual scores may play a part in whether a student is accepted to study at an institution. For example, because writing is an important activity in academic study, a university might insist that Zhang (the Chinese student we met in Chapter 1) should get a particularly high test score for writing. Notice that behind this procedure of treating the four skills in separation is a view quite contrary to the UCH we considered earlier. The underlying view seems to be a <u>divisible competence hypothesis</u>, suggesting that language competence has separate components that need to be tested separately.

Mention of needs analyses and the different specifications they will yield introduces a further distinction often made by testers, between *norm-referenced* and *criterion-referenced* tests. The former is a test in which the learner's score is measured against others who have taken the same test. The learner may be given a 'position' or 'ordering' in relation to the others; he might have come third, or tenth in the class for example, or be in the top (or bottom) 10 per cent. Many of the big, internationally recognized tests operate in a norm-referenced way. Even though an actual ordering of candidates in relation to each other may not be stated, the outside world develops an understanding of how to interpret test scores. So, for example, a score of 40 per cent on a given test will over time come to be meaningful to the world outside.

Norm-referenced tests do not make any direct statement about what a learner will be able to 'do' in terms of language or its uses. Tests which do this are criterion-referenced. They are the ones that are usually based on some form of needs analysis and a resulting syllabus specification. The results of the test are expressed in terms of whether the learner has mastered the content specification. So a pass will mean that the learner can do X, Y and Z and a fail will mean that he cannot.

Concepts of test construction

How do you construct a test? There are four characteristics which a good test should possess. These are validity, reliability, discrimination and feasibility. We shall look at each in turn.

Validity: five types

Heaton (1988: 159) defines validity as 'the extent to which [a test] measures what it is supposed to measure *and nothing else*'. If a test is valid, the outsider who looks at an individual's score knows that it is a true reflection of the individual's skill in the area the test claims to have covered. There are different sorts of validity. *Content validity* is about what actually goes into the test. To have content validity, a test's content must be seen as representative of the subject area being covered. In an achievement test, for example, the course content must clearly be represented in the test itself. This raises an important issue which all tests must face – the question of *sampling*. A test cannot of course deal directly with every single item covered on a programme. Such a test would be impossibly long. The test must operate by selecting sample items from the total content (of a programme for example), and making a statement which in effect says that, if a learner knows the sample material, it is a reasonable assumption that he has grasped the entire material. Good sampling is very important. It fails if the test items are regularly perceived of as covering just one small area of the total behaviour If this happens, bad washback will occur, because only that small area will get taught in future. For example, if a test is supposed to cover both speaking and writing, but in fact regularly only deals with written skills, then it will not be long before speaking quietly disappears from the school curriculum training for the test. To achieve content validity it is important for the tester to draw up a detailed *content specification* – in effect a list of everything the test will cover. He then needs to ensure that this specification is sampled in an even way over time. We shall consider how to draw up content specifications in a later part of this chapter.

Heaton's definition of validity specifies that the test should measure what it is supposed to measure, and nothing else. The 'nothing else' can indeed be very hard to eradicate. Imagine, for example, a test of written English which involved learners in writing an essay with the title: 'Discuss the idea that a healthy body means a healthy mind (Juvenal's *mens sana in corpore sano*)'. The point is that there is much more to writing a good essay on this topic than having good English. In particular it involves the ability to structure an argument. There might well be a case for testing this in an academic context. But, if we are dealing with general learners, and are interested mainly in the quality of their English, this test would be inappropriate. A similar point might be made about the *Balloon Debate* we met in Chapter 13. The game may well stimulate classroom discussion. But it would be a poor way of testing, since it involves the ability to persuade, as well perhaps as requiring some knowledge of celebrities. It is possible to investigate content validity through research. One method for this is followed in Alderson and Lukmani (1989). They give testers a list of the skills supposed to be being tested in some test items, and ask them to identify which skills are in fact being tested by which item. This is a way of making sure that what the tester thinks is being tested is in fact what the test focuses on.

Content validity involves the judgements of professionals regarding whether a test covers what it should cover. *Face validity*, on the other hand, is to do with what the world thinks of the test. It relates again to that all-important figure in the testing world, the outsider. He must be able to look at a test and, as a layperson, be convinced that it is a test giving valid information about language use. Indirect tests are naturally the ones that are most likely to be condemned as having poor face validity. If you followed a course in phonetics, you might (or might not!) emerge convinced that a good test of pronunciation in a foreign language would be to ask learners to write FL words in phonetic script. But it is doubtful that a layperson would share this view, and he might well condemn the test as the production of 'experts who think they know everything . . .'

Face validity is a phenomenon that is sometimes highly related to a specific environment. We met an example of this in Chapter 10, though it was concerned with teaching, not testing. We saw how the pupils in the early days of Prabhu's experiment clearly did not regard his approach as having face validity. Box 10.18 (p. 192) gives a vivid expression of this. Recall also the comments about appropriate methodology in Chapter 11. What is important is not what you do, but how people *perceive* what you are doing.

We have seen that one way in which CLT has had an effect on testing is to give importance to needs analysis, and careful selection of content in relationship to terminal needs. Consequently, one important characteristic of communicative tests is that their content relates clearly to what the learner will have to do in the outside world. From this communicative point of view, face validity is (as Heaton 1988 points out) something more than a question of public relations. It is a declaration of the *authenticity* of the test.

Construct validity deals with the relationship between a test and a particular view of language and language learning. As an example of low construct validity, imagine a test which today claimed to measure ability to communicate orally. You know from your reading of earlier chapters that the notion of communicative competence has had a very special and detailed interpretation since the 1970s. If the test ignored that interpretation and consisted of nothing but a series of multiple-choice questions dealing with structural aspects of the language, we would say that it lacked construct validity.

Empirical validity (or criterion-related validity as some call it) deals with how the test relates to other testing measures. A test should not yield results that are dramatically at odds with the results of other forms of assessment. These 'other forms' include teacher perceptions of learner achievement and, though teachers will be prepared for the odd surprise when their learners' test results are known, they will rightly be suspicious if these results dramatically conflict with their own judgements at every turn. It will be important for a new test to establish its empirical validity early on. One way of doing this will be to use it together with another, well-established test, to see whether the results compare. A test may also be said to have *predictive validity* where its results yield some information about the future. It may be particularly useful to find out whether placement tests, for example, have any predictive validity. Once a course has been run, you can go back and find out whether the placement test did in fact (in the light of subsequent learner performance) lead to the 'right' placement decisions being made.

Reliability

'The reliability of a test', Harrison (1983: 10) says, 'is its consistency. There would be little point in trying to measure people's waists with a piece of elastic. What is needed is a tape measure which stays the same length all the time . . .' Reliability has two main sides to it. One is to do with marking, and ensuring that different markers give comparable marks to the same script, as well as that the same markers give the same marks on two different occasions. Testing mythology is full of anecdotes about what effect a good lunch will have on the score a candidate receives, as well as about the effects of time of day (some people – including markers – are more alert in the morning, while others feel most awake in the evening). Second is test/retest reliability. This ensures that same test will give the same results on two different occasions. This will not happen if, for example, the test is poorly constructed and the instructions can be interpreted in more than one way. It may also not happen if the conditions under which the test is administered are different on the two occasions.

It is a relatively simple matter for you to find out whether you have these two sorts of reliability. Comparing the marks of different markers, as well as giving a marker the same paper to mark on different occasions will give you information about marking reliability. One way of establishing whether test/retest reliability exists would be to repeat a test with the same group after a period of time (during which no language teaching had taken place). Alternatively, parallel forms of the same test can be given to the same group, in the expectation that they will get the same marks.

How do you create reliability if it does not exist? For marking, it is partly a question of training, to ensure that your markers use clear criteria in a consistent way. As an added safeguard, the system should allow for tests to be marked by more than one marker where this is felt necessary. Professional testing organizations expend a great deal of effort to make sure that both these things happen. Box 15.7 lists some of Hughes's (1989) suggestions in relation to both the forms of reliability we have been describing:

15.7 How to be reliable. Some suggestions adapted from Hughes 1989

- take enough samples of behaviour
- do not allow candidates too much freedom
- write unambiguous items
- provide clear and explicit instructions
- ensure that tests are well laid out and perfectly legible
- candidates should be familiar with format and testing techniques
- provide uniform and non-distracting conditions of administration
- use items that permit scoring which is as objective as possible\make comparisons between candidates as direct as possible\provide a detailed scoring key
- train scorers
- agree acceptable responses and appropriate scores at outset of scoring
- identify candidates by number, not name
- employ multiple, independent scoring

The tension between reliability and validity

Both reliability and validity are important for a test. As S. McDonough (1998: 188) puts it: 'reliability is essential in a test, because without it one cannot believe the results . . . but it is useless unless the test is valid as well, for without validity one does not know what has been tested'. It is relatively easy to achieve reliability at the expense of validity. To make a test reliable, you aim for clear, 'unadventurous' questions where there are no doubts about the correct answers. So, for example, a spelling test in which the learner has to underline the correct spelling of a word is likely (if properly constructed) to be reliable. But if this test is put forward as a measure of writing skills in general, including 'high-order' skills such as cohesion, coherence, and organizational ability, then it is not likely to be considered valid. This is an extreme example, but at various points in test construction, the tester is likely to find a conflict between reliability and validity. This conflict may be expressed in the form of a question you find yourself asking: *Do I make this test item clear and unambiguous (suggesting reliability) or more related to what language users actually have to do (suggesting validity)?* It is a little like the conflict between clarity and memorability that we saw in Chapter 13.

A number of writers suggest that it is better to create a test that is initially valid, and then seek ways of making it reliable, rather than creating a reliable test and trying to make it valid. The dog must wag the tail.

Discrimination and feasibility

Tests need to be able to discriminate between students – to tell the good from the bad, or those who have reached a certain level from those who have not. In some situations, discriminative ability may take a back seat – a class diagnostic test for example may (if the teaching has been successful) simply come up with the result that all students have learned successfully. But even in this situation, the test needs to have the potentiality for recognizing students who have not succeeded. In other testing situations, a good degree of sensitivity to different student levels is required, and a good spread of scores is expected. One way of achieving this is to ensure that a wide spectrum of questions of varying difficulty is covered, so that different levels of attainment can be discerned. Individual test items, as well as whole tests, should also be able to discriminate. Testers need to be aware of how each item behaves in relation to the test as a whole. If one item consistently brings up different results from the test as a whole, perhaps its future needs to be considered.

The notion of feasibility relates to administrative issues and, because tests can play such an important role in people's lives, it needs to be taken very seriously. A test which uses tape recordings to measure listening comprehension, may have a very high degree of validity and reliability. But, if half the centres where the test is taken have potentially faulty tape recorders, then the test is a non-starter. Testing is sometimes the art of the possible.

Test production

We have seen that tests operate by sampling from a specification. A first step in test production is therefore to produce a specification. This is a kind of syllabus for a test. Like other types of syllabus, it can take many forms. Heaton (1988: 13) gives two examples which show how test specifications, like teaching syllabuses, reflect different views of language. One example is based on a grammatically oriented course. It simply lists the structures that have been taught, and gives some statement about their relative importance. His second example is also a list, but of functions, not structures, again listed with weightings. Syllabus inventories like the Council of Europe's *Threshold Level* can be used as the basis for test specification.

Because of the purpose it has to serve, it is natural that a test specification should give information additional to that found in a teaching syllabus. Box 15.8 illustrates:

15.8   A battery for academic French

Alderson *et al.* (1995: 14) invent an example of a test specification for part of a test of French for postgraduate studies. Their specification appears under eight headings. Here are six of them:

General statement of purpose
This describes the test battery (collection of tests) in general terms, saying who it is for, and what its aims are.

The test battery
The tests making up the battery are described, with details like the length of each test given, how they will be administered and scored.

From this point onward the specification focuses on the reading test alone.

Test focus
The level of reading at which the test will operate is here stated. The skills to be focused on are also stated. These include *skimming* and *scanning* (see p. 233 for the difference between these), and such skills as

---

'distinguishing fact from opinion', and 'understanding the communicative function of sentences and paragraphs'.

Source of texts
Much detail is given concerning the nature of the texts to be used. This includes details of the content areas they should cover, statements about whether they should be completely authentic (or modified a little for testing purposes), and their length.

Item types
The number of items to be included in the test is stated, together with guidelines about what type of items they should be. A list of possible item types is given. This includes 'identifying appropriate headings, labelling or completing diagrams, tables, charts, etc., gap filling'.

Rubrics
This gives guidelines about what instructions should be given to the learner, including the language level of these instructions (it would of course be silly to have instructions for doing the test that were linguistically more complex than the level being tested!).

A complete (and more complex) framework for test specification is given in Bachman (1990: Chapter 5). Alderson *et al.* (1995: 24 onwards) contains a useful collection of test specifications for actual tests.

Another ingredient which test specifications usually contain is a *rating scale*. This states what levels of performance are expected for various grades or bands to be achieved. We have already mentioned that the practice of profile reporting results in statements in relation to each of the four skills. Statements of levels of performance often need to go even further than this, and divide up each skill into component parts. Box 15.9 (overleaf) contains part of a statement of levels of performance for oral skills.

One problem with rating scales like this is that by concentrating on details, they may lead the tester to ignore overall learner performance – a case of not seeing the wood for the trees. One answer is to use (together with, or instead of, the type of rating scale we have seen) an *impression scale*. This allows the tester to form a general impression of performance, and base marking on that. Guidelines can be given to help the tester structure his impressions.

An issue which rating scales like this raise is the amount of training that is needed to ensure reliability of marking. If you wanted to use the scale given in box 15.9, for example, you would need to make sure that all markers agreed on their interpretations of all the statements given in relation to all the categories.

15.9 A rating scale for spoken interaction

Weir (1995) gives an example of a rating scale developed for a test known as TEEP (Test of English for Educational Purposes). This test identifies four levels of performance – 0, 1, 2 and 3. The categories for rating are:

A Appropriateness
B Adequacy of vocabulary for purpose
C Grammatical accuracy
D Intelligibility
E Fluency
F Relevance and adequacy of content

Under each of these categories, four statements are given, characterizing what a learner must do to reach each of the four levels. Below are the statements just for levels 1 and 2, in each category. The statements have been abridged in some cases, and their order has been mixed. For each statement, decide which of the categories above it measures. When you have done this for all categories, you will have two statements per category. Decide which of the two statements is for level 1, which for level 2. For example, if you think the first statement below is about fluency, and characterizes Level 2, you would write E2 beside it.[4]

(i)   Misunderstandings may occasionally arise through inappropriateness, particularly of sociocultural convention
(ii)   Inadequacy of vocabulary restricts topics of interaction to the most basic
(iii) Responses of limited relevance to the task set
(iv)   Responses characterized by sociocultural inappropriateness
(v)   Some grammatical inaccuracies; developing a control of major patterns
(vi)   Rhythm, intonation and pronunciation require concentrated listening, but only occasional misunderstanding is caused or repetition required
(vii) Some misunderstandings may arise through lexical inadequacy or inaccuracy . . . though there are signs of a developing active vocabulary
(viii) Utterances hesitant and often incomplete . . . sentences are for the most part disjointed and restricted in length
(ix)   Understanding is difficult, and achieved often only after frequent repetition
(x)   Utterances may still be hesitant, but are gaining in coherence, speed and length
(xi)   Responses for the most part relevant to the task set, though there may be some gaps or redundancy
(xii) Syntax is fragmented and there are frequent grammatical inaccuracies . . . confusion of structural elements

Notice in passing how difficult it is to balance different aspects of learner performance. Consider the example in box 15.10:

> ### 15.10   A choice between evils
>
> Imagine an oral test being given to a group of students on a visit to Britain. Below are three (invented) answers to one of the tester's questions:
>
> Tester: *How long have you been in Britain?*
> Student A: *Another three months.*
> Student B: *I been here since two week.*
> Student C: *It very cold and rain.*
>
> Describe each answer, saying how it is right and wrong. How would you characterize the difference between the three answers? And the Big Questions: How you would mark these responses? Which answer is 'least bad', which worst? Once you have decided this, think how you might give general instructions to markers to ensure that in this particular case the least bad answer gets a better mark than the worst.[5]

Testing the four skills

We have spent time looking at various components a test must possess. But what do tests actually look like? In this section we shall briefly consider testing in relation to the four skills. Part of the purpose will be to give a flavour of what kind of techniques are used in language testing. Not surprisingly, there will be many overlaps with language-teaching techniques – another reason why testers and teachers really should talk to each other.

In Chapter 14 we noted that there are similarities and differences between the four skills, suggesting that there will be similarities and differences in the techniques used to teach them. So it is also with testing. Here is a rough guide to the testing of the four skills:

TESTING RECEPTIVE SKILLS

Issues

Receptive skills are easier to test in an objective way; problems of the sort found in box 15.10, for example, can be avoided. But they are more difficult to test in a direct way. This is because listening and reading are naturally covert activities (an idea discussed on page 150), and there is usually no visible or audible outcome from them. A difference between listening and reading is that speech is transient. Unless a transcript is provided, the learner cannot go backwards and forwards over

309

the text to search for a piece of information. If you provide a transcript, you will not be testing the ability to process listened-to language quickly.

TECHNIQUES

Information transfer Look back to box 14.7, which contains a collection of IT exercises. Think about how each of them could be used for the testing of first reading, then listening.

Note taking This has the advantage of being direct (and therefore having face validity as well as leading to possible beneficial washback). The learner can be given skeleton notes (with some blanks in it) of a 'lecture' which he listens to on tape. The task is to fill in the blanks. Note taking can be used for reading too.

Matching Learners can for example read or listen to a passage describing a picture. Four slightly different pictures might be shown. Learners have to decide which one is being described.

Passage assembly (or reassembly). This is a teaching technique we looked at in Chapter 14. It can be used for testing reading. For example, the exercise in box 14.12 ((p. 286) with sentences on one piece of paper in jumbled order) can be used as a test item.

TESTING SPEAKING

ISSUES

This poses many problems. It can be a very time-consuming business – a nightmare with a big test where thousands of learners have to be tested quickly. Also there are the many different levels on which performance has to be assessed. As we saw earlier, (in box 15.9, p. 308) marking schemes which recognize different levels are needed. In addition, there are difficulties involved in marking objectively with face-to-face contact. Hughes (1989: 113) puts it this way: 'it is obvious that scorers should not be influenced by such features as candidates' pleasantness, prettiness, or the cut of their dress. The truth is that these are hard to exclude from one's judgement – but an effort has to be made!'

TECHNIQUES

Oral interview This is where the examiner asks the learner questions about himself, and perhaps also about a passage or picture sequence given in advance. This is a traditional technique.

Role play and simulation are now also popular (see p. 262 for discussion of these techniques in relation to teaching). The learner can be given a role card just before the test, asking him to act a role. The tester can also play a character in the role play. Here is an example of an instruction (from Carroll and Hall 1985: 51): 'You are at Amsterdam (Schipol) Airport having just missed the 1320 flight to Brussels where a friend, Mr Raymond, has arranged to meet you.

You now want to do two things – make arrangements for a later flight and contact Mr Raymond in Brussels. Please explain your situation at the Information Desk.'

Imitation This was one of the French proficiency tests given in the large Good Language Learner study (Naiman *et al.* 1978) we saw in Chapter 9. The tester says a series of sentences to the learner, each longer than the one before. The learner repeats each sentence. The idea is that the longer the sentence the learner can repeat without error, the higher his level. A very indirect test, with little face validity. But it has the advantage of being quick to administer, and might be used in a situation where rough and fast decisions are needed (for example as a placement test for a course which has to begin almost immediately).

For a thorough treatment of oral testing techniques, see Underhill (1987).

TESTING WRITING

ISSUES
As with speaking there are many different levels that have to be taken into account, including spelling, vocabulary use, grammar, treatment of content, stylistic appropriateness, and organizational skill. Also, as with speaking, there are plenty of side-issues to distract the marker. A notorious one is handwriting. Though there may be circumstances in which handwriting should be assessed, it is peculiarly common for a marker to find that poor handwriting unjustly leads to a judgement about poor content.

The kind of banding system which we saw earlier (in box 15.9) should be drawn up for writing as well as speech (though the aspects of performance being judged will of course be different). In one writing test discussed by Hughes (1989: 95), the following aspects are specified: communicative quality, organization, argumentation, linguistic accuracy, linguistic appropriateness.

As with speech, there is no reason why this 'analytic' way of marking should not be supported by a more 'impressionistic' judgement, where the marker allows himself to express an overall 'feeling' for the learner's achievement.

TECHNIQUES
Many of the techniques already discussed are suitable for the testing of writing (including, yet again, the ubiquitous Information Transfer exercise). Note the point made on page 288 – that many teaching exercises inhabit the 'twilight world' somewhere between reading and writing, and are useful to both. So **passage assembly**, an item mentioned above under 'Testing Reading' is relevant for writing also.

Picture stimulus Heaton (1988: 142) illustrates how a picture can be the basis for a writing test. His example shows a map of an accident 'black spot'. Various features indicate why accidents happen there – for example, there is a bus stop just by a crossroads, so cars sometimes overtake stationary buses very close to the crossroads. Learners are asked to write a letter to a local newspaper describing the dangers of the 'black spot'.

Some important tests

One of the major British Examining Boards is UCLES, the University of Cambridge Local Examination Syndicate, and they administer a number of tests which have come to be accepted world-wide. Of their range, the two best known are the First Certificate in English (FCE), and the more advanced Certificate of Proficiency in English (CPE). This latter is in some countries of the world regarded as an important qualification for non-native teachers of English to possess. A test specifically geared for non-native teachers is the UCLES Cambridge Examination in English for Language Teachers (CEELT). The British ARELS organization (Association of Recognized English Language Schools) also has a much-used range of tests, particularly their three-level Examinations in Spoken English and Comprehension.

In the United States there is a set of levels for speaking proficiency known as the ACTFL Proficiency Guidelines. There are four levels, which deal with a number of languages.

For testing suitability for academic study, the two best-known tests have already been mentioned. They are the British Council's IELTS and the American TOEFL. Very many institutions of tertiary education in the English-speaking world have entry qualifications regarding English language proficiency that are stated in terms of scores on the IELTS and TOEFL tests.

S. McDonough (1998) gives a more comprehensive list of current tests.

ENVOI

The poet Geoffrey Chaucer sends his poem *Troilus and Criseyde* into the world with the words: *Go, litel bok, go, litel myn tragedye* ('Go little book, go my little tragedy'). The word *litel* here always caused bewilderment to me as a student, given that the poem is some 8239 lines long! Did Chaucer intend the poem to be shorter? Certainly this book was intended to be 'little'. But it grew. Ironically, now that it is time to stop, I am aware only of what it has not covered. Hopefully you will be sufficiently stimulated by what it contains to find out for yourself about what it does not contain.

Notes

1. The multiple-choice question in Example 1 is bad because all the alternatives given are right! You need to be sure that, although alternatives may contain *elements* of truth, there is one – and only one – right answer.

   Alderson *et al.* point out firstly that answer C in Example 2 is much longer than the other answers, and looks like a dictionary definition. A candidate who wanted to guess might well choose it. Secondly, answer B does give a passable definition of *choke*, and a learner could be forgiven for choosing it. Thirdly, we do not in fact know that the man did not choke through anger. Though it is likely that a fish bone caused the problem, something we do not know about might have made him angry over his dinner.

2. The deleted words are: (1) in; (2) French; (3) playground; (4) and; (5) end; (6) the; (7) themselves; (8) that; (9) the; (10) over time.

3. In British English the expected answers might be along the following lines:

   1. *Yes, it really has. Absolutely wonderful.*
   2. *No, most banks are closed on a Saturday.*
   3. *Oh go on! You can start your diet again tomorrow.*

4. The expected matchings are:

(i) = A2	(ii) = B1	(iii) = F1	(iv) = A1
(v) = C2	(vi) = D2	(vii) = B2	(viii) = E1
(ix) = D1	(x) = E2	(xi) = F2	(xii) = C1

5. Student A's answer is perfectly correct grammatically. He seems to have misunderstood the question, thinking he has been asked *How long will you be in Britain?*

   Student B has understood the question, but his answer has three mistakes in it. Perhaps he thinks that the tense he needs is the simple past (which is wrong), and he has formed it by saying *been* instead of *was*. Or he has simply misformed the present perfect tense (the right one to use), leaving out the auxiliary *have*. The tense in sentences like this causes many students problems, partly because in some languages the present tense would be used – I *am* here since . . . Secondly, this student has misused the word *since*. The words *for* and *since* are confusing for many students, because their own languages do not mark the distinction these words signal. *Since* is used with a 'point in time' (*since Monday, since 1970*), while *for* is used with a 'period of time' (*for a week, for three years*). So *for* should be used here. Finally, Student B commits the common error of missing the final -s off the plural *weeks*.

   As for Student C . . . He has first of all misunderstood the question completely, perhaps thinking that since the British have a reputation for talking about the weather, any question he is asked will be on that topic. He also omits the verb *be* – a common mistake. His final sin is to assume that *rain* is an adjective as well as a noun. *Rainy* would be the appropriate word to use here.

   Which answer is 'least bad', which worst? If an important criterion for you is whether messages have been properly conveyed, then Student B is the only one who understands what he has been asked. According to this criterion, he would be the 'least bad'. Student A at least knows that he is being asked about a period of time. Worst from the comprehension point of view is Student C, who does not even understand the general topic area of the question. From the point of view of grammar, Student A does not make any mistakes. Both Students B and C make more than one mistake, with B perhaps producing the grammatically least accurate sentence.

But is grammar more important that understanding messages, or vice versa? There is no simple answer. Many would argue that the latter should be given more attention, in which case you would need to instruct your markers accordingly. Notice that in this case 'misunderstanding the message' is to do with *listening* not *speaking*. If you want your test to deal specifically with speaking, then you have to decide to what extent you should consider the ability to understand.

References

Abercrombie, D. 1949 'Teaching pronunciation' *ELT* III/1: 1–11. Reprinted in Abercrombie, D. *Studies in Phonetics and Linguistics* Oxford: Oxford University Press, 1965: 28–40.

Alderson, J. C. and Lukmani, Y. 1989 'Cognition and levels of comprehension as embodied in test questions'. *Reading in a Foreign Language* 5(2): 253–70.

Alderson, J. C., Clapham, C. and Wall, D. 1995 *Language Test Construction and Evaluation* Cambridge: Cambridge University Press.

Alexander, L. G. 1968 *Look, Listen and Learn: Teacher's Book 1* London: Longman.

Alexander, L. G., Allen, W. S., Close, R. A. and O'Neill, R. J. 1975 *English Grammatical Structure* London: Longman.

Allwright, R. L. 1984 'Why don't learners learn what teachers teach? The interaction hypothesis'. In Singleton, D. M. and Little, D. G. (eds) *Language Learning in Formal and Informal Contexts* Dublin: IRAAL, 3–18.

Anderson, J. R. 1982 'Acquisition of cognitive skill' *Psychological Review* 89/4: 369–406.

Anderson, J. R. 1983 *The Architecture of Cognition* Cambridge, Mass.: Harvard University Press.

Austin, J. L. 1962 *How to Do Things with Words* Oxford: Oxford University Press.

Bachman, L. F. 1990 *Fundamental Considerations in Language Testing* Oxford: Oxford University Press.

Bailey, N., Madden C. and Krashen, S. D. 1974 'Is there a "natural sequence" in adult second language learning?' *Language Learning* 21: 235–43.

Baker, D. 1989 *Language Testing: A Critical Survey and Practical Guide* London: Edward Arnold.

Bartlett, F. C. 1932 *Remembering* Cambridge: Cambridge University Press.

Baxter, A. 1997 *Evaluating Your Students* London: Richmond Publishing.

Beretta, A. and Davies, A. 1985 'Evaluation of the Bangalore project'. *ELT Journal* 39/2, 121–7.

Berko, J. 1958 'The child's learning of English morphology' *Word* 14: 159–77.

Bialystok, E. 1990 *Communication Strategies* Oxford: Blackwell.

Bloomfield, L. 1933 *Language* New York: Holt.

Boas, F. (ed.) 1911 *Handbook of American Indian Languages: Part 1* Bulletin 40, Bureau of American Ethnology, Smithsonian Institution, Washington, DC.

Borger, L. and Seabourne, A. E. M. 1966 *The Psychology of Learning* Harmondsworth: Penguin.

Bransford, J. D. and Johnson, M. K. 1973 'Considerations of some problems of comprehension'. In Chase, W. G. (ed.) *Visual Information Processing* New York: Academic Press, 383–438.

Breen, M. P. 1983 'Prepared comments to Johnson, K. Syllabus design: possible future trends.' In Johnson, K. and Porter, D. (eds) *Perspectives in Communicative Language Teaching* London: Academic Press, 58–66.

References

Breen, M. P. 1984 'Process syllabuses for the language classroom'. In Brumfit, C. J. (ed.) *General English Syllabus Design* ELT Documents 118. Oxford: Modern English Publications with the British Council, 47–60.

Brooks, N. 1960 *Language and Language Learning: Theory and Practice* New York: Harcourt, Brace & World.

Broughton, G. 1968 *Success with English* Harmondsworth: Penguin.

Brown, H. D. 1973 'Some limitations of C-L/CLL models of language teaching' *TESOL Quarterly* 11: 365–72.

Brown, R. 1973 *A First Language: The Early Stages* Cambridge, Mass.: Harvard University Press.

Brown, R. and Hanlon, C. 1970 'Derivational complexity and order of acquisition in child speech'. In Hayes, J. (ed.) *Cognition and the Development of Language* New York: Wiley, 1–53.

Brown, G. and Yule, G. 1983 *Discourse Analysis* Cambridge: Cambridge University Press.

Brumfit, C. J. 1979 ' "Communicative" language teaching: an educational perspective'. In Brumfit, C. J. and Johnson, K. (eds) *The Communicative Approach to Language Teaching* Oxford: Oxford University Press 183–91.

Brumfit, C. J. 1984 *Communicative Methodology in Language Teaching* Cambridge: Cambridge University Press.

Budner, S. 1962 'Intolerance of ambiguity as a personality variable' *Journal of Personality* 39: 29–50.

Burstall, C., Jamieson, M., Cohen, S. and Hargreaves, M. (1974) *Primary French in the Balance* Slough: NFER.

Byrne, D. 1986 *Teaching Oral English* (2nd edition) London: Longman.

Byrne, D. 1988 *Teaching Writing Skills* (2nd edition) London: Longman.

Canale, M. and Swain, M. 1980 'Theoretical bases of communicative approaches to second language teaching and testing' *Applied Linguistics* 1: 1–47.

Cancino, H., Rosansky, E. and Schumann, J. 1978 'The acquisition of English negatives and interrogatives by native Spanish speakers'. In Hatch, E. (ed.) *Second Language Acquisition* Rowley, Mass.: Newbury House.

Carroll, J. B. 1965 'The prediction of success in foreign language training'. In Glaser, R. (ed.) *Training, Research and Education* New York: Wiley.

Carroll, J. B. 1966 'The contributions of psychological theory and educational research to the teaching of foreign languages'. In Valdman, A. (ed.) *Trends in Language Teaching* New York: McGraw-Hill 1966, 93–106.

Carroll, J. B. 1967 'Research problems concerning the teaching of foreign or second languages to younger children'. In Stern, H. H. (ed.) *Foreign Languages in Primary Education* Oxford: Oxford University Press 1967, 94–109.

Carroll, J. B. 1973 'Implications of aptitude test research and psycholinguistic theory for foreign-language teaching' *Linguistics* 112: 5–13.

Carroll, J. B. and Hall, P. J. 1985 *Make your own Language Tests: A Practical Guide to Writing Language Performance Tests* Oxford: Pergamon Press.

Carroll, J. B. and Sapon, S. 1959 *Modern Language Aptitude Test* New York: Psychological Corporation.

Castrillo, J. M., Cerezal, N. and Suarez, C. 1988 *Reading Tasks* London: Longman.

Chastain, 1969 'Prediction of success in audio-lingual and cognitive classes' *Language Learning* 19: 27–39.

Cheng, P. W. 1985 'Restructuring versus automaticity: alternative accounts of skill acquisition'. *Psychological Review* 92: 214–23.

Chomsky, N. 1957 *Syntactic Structures* The Hague: Mouton.

Chomsky, N. 1959 'Review of Skinner, B. F. *Verbal Behaviour' Language* 35: 26–58.

Chomsky, N. 1965 *Aspects of the Theory of Syntax* Cambridge, Mass.: MIT Press.

Chomsky, N. 1966 'Linguistic Theory'. In Lester, M. (ed.) *Readings in Applied Transformational Grammar* New York: Holt, Rinehart, Winston 1970, 51–60.

Chomsky, N. 1987 'The nature, use and acquisition of language'. Lecture delivered to the Open University, 1987.

Cioffari, V. 1962 'The influence of the language institute program – past, present, and future' *Modern Language Journal* XLV: 65.

Clark, H. H. and Clark, E. V. 1977 *Psychology and Language* New York: Harcourt Brace Jovanovich.

Clyne, M. 1991 *Community Languages: the Australian Experience* Cambridge: Cambridge University Press.

Cook, G. 1998a 'Pragmatics'. In Johnson, K. and Johnson, H. (eds) *Encyclopedic Dictionary of Applied Linguistics* Oxford: Blackwell, 249.

Cook, G. 1998b 'Translation in language teaching'. In Johnson, K. and Johnson, H. (eds) *Encyclopedic Dictionary of Applied Linguistics* Oxford. Blackwell, 359–60.

Cook, V. J. and Newson, M. 1995 *Chomsky's Universal Grammar* Oxford: Oxford University Press.

Corder, S. P. 1967 'The significance of learners' errors' *International Review of Applied Linguistics* 9: 149–59.

Coulavin, A. 1983 'Excuses, excuses' *Practical English Teaching* 4/2: 31.

Crookes, G. and Gass, S. M. 1993a *Tasks and Language Learning: Integrating Theory and Practice* Clevedon: Multilingual Matters.

Crookes, G. and Gass, S. M. 1993b *Tasks in a Pedagogical Context: Integrating Theory and Practice* Clevedon: Multilingual Matters.

Cross, T. G. 1977 'Mothers' speech adjustments: the contribution of selected child listener variables'. In Snow, C. E. and Ferguson, C. A. (eds) *Talking to Children* Cambridge: Cambridge University Press, 151–88.

Crossman, E. R. F. W. 1959 'A theory of the acquisition of speed-skill' *Ergonomics* 2.

Crystal, D. (ed.) 1987 *The Cambridge Encyclopedia of Language* Cambridge: Cambridge University Press.

Crystal, D. (ed.) 1990 *The Cambridge Encyclopedia* Cambridge: Cambridge University Press.

Cummins, J. (1980) 'The cross-lingual dimension of language proficiency: implications for bilingual education and the optimal age issue' *TESOL Quarterly* 14: 175–87.

Dakin, J. 1973 *The Language Laboratory and Language Learning* London: Longman.

Davies, E. and Whitney, N. 1979 *Reasons for Reading* London: Heinemann.

Davis, P. and Rinvolucri, M. 1988 *Dictation: New methods, new possibilities* Cambridge: Cambridge University Press.

Debyser, F. 1974 'Simulation et réalité dans l'enseignement des langues vivantes'. *Études*, 105.

Diller, K. W. 1971 *Generative Grammar, Structural Linguistics and Language Teaching* Rowley, Mass.: Newbury House.

Dobson, L., Pugh, A. K. and Howatt, A. P. R. 1981 'Language teaching'. In *Language Learning and Language Teaching* (Block 3 of 'Language in Use' course). Milton Keynes: Open University.

Dörnyei, Z. and Csizér, K. 1998 'Ten commandments for motivating language learners: results of an empirical study' *Language Teaching Research* 2: 203–30.

References

Dulay, H. and Burt, M. 1973 'Should we teach children syntax?' *Language Learning* 23/2: 245–58.

Dulay, H. and Burt, M. 1974 'Natural sequences in child second language acquisition' *Language Learning* 24/1: 37–53.

Dulay, H., Burt, H. and Krashen, S. D. 1982 *Language Two* New York: Oxford University Press.

Ellis, R. 1984 'Can syntax be taught? A study of the effects of formal instruction on the acquisition of Wh- questions by children' *Applied Linguistics* 5: 138–55.

Ellis, R. 1994 *The Study of Second Language Acquisition* Oxford: Oxford University Press.

Ellis, R. 1997 *Second Language Acquisition* Oxford: Oxford University Press.

Ellis, G. and Sinclair, B. 1989 *Learning to Learn English* Cambridge: Cambridge University Press.

Ervin-Tripp, S. 1974 'Is second language learning like the first?' *TESOL Quarterly* 8/2: 111–27.

Eskey, D. 1988 'Holding in the bottom: an interactive approach to the language problems of second language learners'. In Carrell, P., Devine, J. and Eskey, D. (eds) *Interactive Approaches to Second Language Reading* Cambridge: Cambridge University Press.

Eysenck, H. J. 1965 *Fact and Fiction in Psychology* Harmondsworth: Penguin.

Faerch, C. and Kasper, G. 1986 'The role of comprehension in second-language learning' *Applied Linguistics* 7: 257–74.

Fennell, J. L. I. 1961 *The Penguin Russian Course* Harmondsworth: Penguin.

Fitts, P. M. and Posner, M. I. 1967 *Human Performance* Belmont, Calif.: Brooks Cole.

Flick, W. 1980 'Error types in adult English as a second language'. In Ketterman, B. and St Clair, R. (eds) *New Approaches to Language Acquisition* Heidelberg: Julius Groos.

Foll, D. 1990 *Contrasts* London: Longman.

Foster, P. and Skehan, P. 1999 'The influence of source of planning and focus of planning on task-based performance' *Language Teaching Research* 3/3.

Fullan, M. G. and Stiegelbauer, S. 1991 *The New Meaning of Educational Change* London: Cassell.

Gardner, R. C. 1985 *Social Psychology and Second-Language Learning: The role of attitudes and motivation* London: Edward Arnold.

Gardner, R. C. and Lambert, W. E. 1972 *Attitudes and Motivation in Second-Language Learning* Rowley, Mass.: Newbury House.

Garfinkel, H. 1967 *Studies in Ethnomethodology* New York: Prentice Hall.

Garman, M. and Hughes, A. 1983 *English Cloze Exercises* Oxford: Blackwell.

Garnett, W. 1992 'A back-to-the-drawing-board oboe'. *Double Reed News*, 19: 22–5.

Gattegno, C. 1972 *Teaching Foreign Languages in Schools: The Silent Way* (revised edition) New York: Educational Solutions.

Geddes, M. and Sturtridge, G. 1979 *Listening Links* London: Heinemann.

Geddes, M. and Sturtridge, G. 1982 *Reading Links* London: Heinemann.

Genesee, F. 1976 'The role of intelligence in second language learning'. *Language Learning* 26/2: 267–80.

Genzardi, N. E. 1910 *The English Tourist in Italy: A practical and easy method of learning and speaking Italian* Turin: Paravia.

George, H. V. 1963 'A verb-form frequency count' *English Language Teaching*, 18: 1.

George, H. 1972 *Common Errors in Language Learning: Insights from English* Rowley, Mass.: Newbury House.

Gillette, B. 1987 'Two successful language learners: an introspective report'. In Faerch, C. and Kasper, G. (eds) *Introspection in Second Language Research* Clevedon, Avon: Multilingual Matters, 267–79.

Goh, C. 1998 'Strategic processing and metacognition in second language listening'. Unpublished PhD thesis, Lancaster University.

Grauberg, W. 1971 'An error analysis in the German of first-year university students'. In Perren, G. and Trim, J. (eds) *Applications of Linguistics* Cambridge. Cambridge University Press, 1971.

Green, P. S. 1975 (ed.) *The Language Laboratory in School* Edinburgh: Oliver and Boyd.

Greenall, S. and Pye, D. 1991 *Reading 2* Cambridge: Cambridge University Press.

Grellet, F. 1981 *Developing Reading Skills* Cambridge: Cambridge University Press.

Grierson, H. J. C. 1945 *Rhetoric and English Composition* London: Oliver and Boyd.

Guiora, A. Z., Brannon, R. C. L. and Dull, C. Y. 1972 'Empathy and second language learning' *Language Learning* 22: 111–30.

Haarman, L., Leech, P. and Murray, J. 1988 *Reading Skills for the Social Sciences* Oxford: Oxford University Press.

Halliday, M. A. K. 1970 'Language structure and language function'. In Lyons, J. (ed.) *New Horizons in Linguistics* Harmondsworth: Penguin.

Halliday, M. A. K. 1975 *Learning How to Mean* London: Edward Arnold.

Hamp-Lyons, L. and Heasley, B. 1987 *Study Writing* Cambridge: Cambridge University Press.

Harley, B. 1989 'Functional grammar in French immersion: a classroom experiment'. *Applied Linguistics* 10: 331–59.

Harmer, J. 1982 'What is communicative?' *ELT Journal* 36/3: 164–8.

Harmer, J. 1991 *The Practice of English Language Teaching* London: Longman.

Harrison, A. 1983 *A Language Testing Handbook* Basingstoke: Macmillan.

Hatch, E. 1978 'Apply with caution' *Studies in Second Language Acquisition* 2: 123–43.

Hawkins, R. 1998 'Learning strategies'. In Johnson, K. and Johnson, H. (eds) *Encyclopedic Dictionary of Applied Linguistics* Oxford: Blackwell, 195–7.

Heaton, J. B. 1988 *Writing English Language Tests* London: Longman.

Hedge, T. 1985 *Using Readers in Language Teaching* London: Macmillan.

Hedge, T. 1988 *Writing* Oxford: Oxford University Press.

Hess, N. 1991 *Headstarts* London: Longman.

Higgins, J. and Johns, T. 1984 *Computers in Language Learning* London: Collins.

Hogan, R. 1969 'Development of an empathy scale' *Journal of Consulting and Clinical Psychology* 33: 307–16.

Holder, P. (ed.) 1966 Franz Boas's *Introduction to Handbook of American Indian Languages* and J. W. Powell's 'Indian Linguistic Families of America North of Mexico'. Lincoln: University of Nebraska Press.

Holding, D. H. 1965 *Principles of Training* Oxford: Pergamon Press.

Holliday, A. 1994 *Appropriate Methodology and Social Context* Cambridge: Cambridge University Press.

Holmes, J. 1992 *An Introduction to Sociolinguistics* London: Longman.

Hover, D. 1986 *Think Twice* Oxford: Oxford University Press.

Howatt, A. P. R. 1984 *A History of English Language Teaching* Oxford: Oxford University Press.

Hughes, A. 1989 *Testing for Language Teachers* Cambridge: Cambridge University Press.

Hughes, A. and Trudgill, P. 1996 *English Accents and Dialects* London: Arnold.

References

Hymes, D. 1970 'On communicative competence'. In Gumperz, J. J. and Hymes, D. (eds) *Directions in Sociolinguistics* New York: Holt, Rinehart and Winston.

Jakobovits, L. A. 1970 *Foreign Language Learning: A psycholinguistic analysis of the issues* Rowley, Mass.: Newbury House.

James, C. 1980 *Contrastive Analysis* London: Longman.

Jaworski, A. 1998 'Language planning'. In Johnson, K. and Johnson, H. (eds) *Encyclopedic Dictionary of Applied Linguistics* Oxford: Blackwell, 185–7.

Johnson, H. 1992 'Defossilizing' *ELT Journal* 46/2, 180–9.

Johnson, K. 1977 'Teaching appropriateness and coherence in academic writing'. In Johnson, K. *Communicative Syllabus Design and Methodology* Oxford: Pergamon Institute of English, 1982, 176–82.

Johnson, K. 1980a 'Making drills communicative'. Reprinted in Johnson, K. *Communicative Syllabus Design and Methodology* Oxford: Pergamon Institute of English, 1982, 156–63.

Johnson, K. 1980b 'The "deep-end" strategy in communicative language teaching'. In Johnson, K. *Communicative Syllabus Design and Methodology* Oxford: Pergamon Institute of English, 1982, 192–200.

Johnson, K. 1981 'Writing'. In Johnson, K. and Morrow, K. (eds) *Communication in the Classroom* London: Longman, 93–107.

Johnson, K. 1982 *Communicative Syllabus Design and Methodology* Oxford: Pergamon Institute of English.

Johnson, K. 1983a *Now for English* Walton-on-Thames: Nelson.

Johnson, K. 1983b 'Communicative writing practice and Aristotelian rhetoric'. In Freedman, A., Pringle, I. and Yalden, J. (eds) *Learning to Write: First Language/ Second Language* London: Longman.

Johnson, K. 1995 'Methods as Plausible Fictions'. *CRILE Working Paper, No. 23*, Centre for Research in Language Education, Lancaster University, 1995.

Johnson, K. 1996 *Language Teaching and Skill Learning* Oxford: Blackwell.

Johnson, K. and Morrow, K. 1979 *Approaches* Cambridge: Cambridge University Press.

Johnson, K. and Morrow, K. 1981 *Communication in the Classroom* London: Longman.

Kaplan, R. B. 1966 'Cultural thought patterns in inter-cultural education' *Language Learning* 16: 1–20.

Keenan, E. L. and Ochs, E. 1979 'Becoming a competent speaker of Malagasy'. In Shopen, T. *Languages and Their Speakers* Philadelphia: University of Pennsylvania Press, 113–239.

Kelly, L. G. 1969 *25 Centuries of Language Teaching* Rowley, Mass.: Newbury House.

Klein-Braley, C. and Raatz, U. 1984 'A survey of research on the C-Test' *Language Testing* 1: 134–46.

Krashen, S. D. 1977 'The monitor model for adult second language performance'. In Burt, M. K., Dulay, H. C. and Finocchiaro, M. (eds) *Viewpoints on English as a Second Language* New York: Regents, 152–61.

Krashen, S. D. 1981 *Second Language Acquisition and Second Language Learning* Oxford: Pergamon.

Krashen, S. D. 1982 *Principles and Practice in Second Language Acquisition* Oxford: Pergamon Institute of English.

Krashen, S. D. 1983 BBC *Horizon* programme 'A Child's Guide to Language'.

Krashen, S. D. and Terrell, T. D. 1983 *The Natural Approach* New York: Pergamon and Alemany.

Krzeszowski, T. P. 1990 *Contrasting Languages: The Scope of Contrastive Linguistics* Berlin: Mouton de Gruyter.

Labov, W. 1966 *The Social Stratification of English in New York City* Washington, DC: Center for Applied Linguistics.

Lado, R. 1957 *Linguistics across Cultures: Applied linguistics for language teachers* Ann Arbor, Michigan: University of Michigan.

Lado, R. 1961 *Language Testing* London: Longman.

Lambert, W. E. and Klineberg, O. 1967 *Children's Views of Foreign Peoples: A Cross-national Study* New York: Appleton.

Lambert, W. E. and Tucker, G. R. 1972 *Bilingual Education of Children: The St Lambert experiment* Rowley, Mass.: Newbury House.

Lambert, W. E., Hodgson, R. C., Gardner, R. C. and Fillenbaum, S. 1960 'Evaluation reactions to spoken languages' *Journal of Abnormal and Social Psychology* 60/1: 44–51.

Lee, W. 1968 'Thoughts on contrastive linguistics in the context of language teaching'. In Alatis, J. (ed.) *Report on the Nineteenth Annual Round Table Meeting on Linguistics and Language Studies, Georgetown University* Washington DD: Georgetown University Press.

Lenneberg, E. 1967 *Biological Foundations of Language* New York: Wiley.

Lennon, P. 1989 'Introspection and intentionality in advanced second-language acquisition' *Language Learning* 39: 375–95.

Lewis, E. G. and Massad, C. E. 1975 *The Teaching of English as a Foreign Language in Ten Countries* New York: Wiley.

Lightbown, P. M. 1987 'Classroom language as input to second language acquisition'. In Pfaff, C. W. (ed.) *First and Second Language Acquisition Processes* Rowley, Mass.: Newbury House.

Lindop, C. and Fisher, D. 1988 *Something to Read 1* Cambridge: Cambridge University Press.

Littlejohn, A. and Hicks, D. 1996 *Cambridge English: Student's Book 2* Cambridge: Cambridge University Press.

Long, M. H. 1983 'Native speaker/non-native speaker conversation and the negotiation of comprehensible input' *Applied Linguistics* 4: 126–41.

Long, M. H. 1985 'A role for instruction in second language acquisition: task-based language training'. In Hyltenstam, K. and Pienemann, M. (eds) *Modelling and Assessing Second Language Acquisition* Clevedon: Multilingual Matters, 77–100.

Long, M. H. and Porter, P. 1985 'Group work, interlanguage talk and second language acquisition' *TESOL Quarterly* 19: 207–28.

Lott, D. 1983 'Analysing and counteracting interference errors' *English Language Teaching Journal* 37: 256–61.

Lukmani, Y. 1972 'Motivation to learn and language proficiency' *Language Learning* 22: 261–73.

Lyons, J. 1970 *Chomsky* London: Fontana/Collins.

McCarthy, M. 1990 *Vocabulary* Oxford: Oxford University Press.

McDonough, J. 1998 'Learner training'. In Johnson, K. and Johnson, H. (eds) *Encyclopedic Dictionary of Applied Linguistics* Oxford: Blackwell, 193–5.

McDonough, S. 1998 'Language testing'. In Johnson, K. and Johnson, H. (eds) *Encyclopedic Dictionary of Applied Linguistics* Oxford: Blackwell, 187–92.

McDonough, S. H. 1981 *Psychology in Foreign Language Teaching* London: Allen and Unwin.

Mackey, W. F. 1965 *Language Teaching Analysis* London: Longman.

Mackey, W. F. 1970 'A typology of bilingual education' *Foreign Language Annals* 3: 596–608.

References

McLaughlin, B. 1987 *Theories of Second-Language Learning* London: Edward Arnold.

McLaughlin, B. 1990 'Restructuring' *Applied Linguistics* 11/2, 113–28.

McLaughlin, B., Rossman, R. and McLeod, B. 1983 'Second-language learning: an information-processing perspective' *Language Learning* 33: 135–58.

McNeill, D. 1970 *The Acquisition of Language* New York: Harper and Row.

Markee, N. 1997 *Managing Curricular Innovation* London: Allen and Unwin.

Maley, A. 1981 'Games and problem solving'. In Johnson, K. Morrow, K. (eds) *Communication in the Classroom* London: Longman, 137–48.

Mehrabian, A. 1970 'The development and validation of measures of affiliative tendency and sensitivity to rejection' *Educational and Psychological Measurement* 30: 417–28.

Messick, S. 1970 'The criterion problem in the evaluation of instruction: assessing possible, not just intended, outcomes'. In Wittrock, M. C. and Wiley, D. E. (eds) *The Evaluation of Instruction: Issues and problems* New York: Holt, Rinehart and Winston.

Miller, G. A. 1974 'Psychology, language and levels of communication'. In Silverstein, A. (ed.) *Human Communication* New York: Wiley.

Montgomery, C. and Eisenstein, M. 1985 'Real reality revisited: an experimental communicative course in ESL' *TESOL Quarterly* 19: 317–33.

Morrow, K. 1977 *Techniques of Evaluation for a Notional Syllabus* London: Royal Society of Arts.

Morrow, K. and Johnson, K. 1979 *Communicate 1 and 2* Cambridge: Cambridge University Press.

Moskovitz, G. 1978 *Caring and Sharing in the Foreign Language Class* Rowley, Mass.: Newbury House.

Mukkatesh, L. 1977 'Persistence in fossilization' *International Review of Applied Linguistics* 24: 187–203.

Munby, J. 1978 *Communicative Syllabus Design* Cambridge: Cambridge University Press.

Murphy, R. 1990 *Essential Grammar in Use* Cambridge: Cambridge University Press.

Naiman, N., Fröhlich, H., Stern, H. and Todesco, A. 1978 *The Good Language Learner* Toronto: Ontario Institute for Studies in Education: Research in Education Series, 7.

Nemser, W. 1971 'Approximative systems of foreign language learners' *International Review of Applied Linguistics* 9: 115–23.

Neves, D. M. and Anderson, J. R. 1981 'Knowledge compilation: mechanisms for the automization of cognitive skills'. In Anderson, J. R. (ed.) *Cognitive Skills and their Acquisition* Hillside, NJ: Lawrence Erlbaum Associates, 57–84.

Newland, M. 1974 *The Diamond Smuggler* Ranger Fiction Series, Range 3. Basingstoke: Macmillan.

Newmark, L. 1963 'Grammatical theory and the teaching of English as a foreign language'. In Lester, M. (ed.) *Readings in Applied Transformational Grammar* New York: Holt, Rinehart and Winston, 1970, 210–18.

Newmark, L. 1966 'How not to interfere with language learning'. Reprinted in Brumfit, C. J. and Johnson, K. (eds) *The Communicative Approach to Language Teaching* Oxford: Oxford University Press, 160–6.

Newmark, L. 1971 'A minimal language-teaching program'. In Pimsleur, P. and Quinn, T. (eds) *The Psychology of Second Language Learning* Cambridge: Cambridge University Press, 11–18.

Newmark, L. and Reibel, D. A. 1968 'Necessity and sufficiency in language learning' *International Review of Applied Linguistics* 6/2: 145–64.

Newport, E. L., Gleitman, H. and Gleitman, L. R. 1977 'Mother, I'd rather do it myself: some effects and non-effects of maternal speech style'. In Snow, C. E. and Ferguson, C. A. (eds) *Talking to Children* Cambridge: Cambridge University Press, 109–50.

Ockenden, M. 1972 *Situational Dialogues* London: Longman.

Oller, J. W. 1976 'A program for language testing research'. In Brown, H. D. (ed.) 'Papers in second language acquisition' *Language Learning*, 4: 141–66.

Oller, J. W. 1979 *Language Tests at School* London: Longman.

O'Malley, J. M. and Chamot, A. U. 1990 *Learning Strategies in Second Language Acquisition* Cambridge: Cambridge University Press.

Onions, C. T. (1927) 'Henry Sweet'. In Davis, H. W. C. and Weaver, J. R. H. (eds) *Dictionary of National Biography, 1912–21* Oxford: Oxford University Press, 519–20.

Ostrander, S., Schroeder, L. and Ostrander, N. 1979 *Superlearning* New York: Dell.

Oxford, R. 1990 *Language Learning Strategies: What every teacher should know* Rowley, Mass.: Newbury House.

Palmer, H. and Palmer, D. 1925 *English through Actions* Reprinted edition: London: Longman Green, 1959.

Paran, A. 1990 *Reading Comprehension: Year 1, Burlington Proficiency Series* Limassol: Burlington Books.

Paran, A. 1996 'Reading in EFL: facts and fictions' *ELT Journal* 50/1: 25–34.

Pennycook, A. 1994 *The Cultural Politics of English as an International Language* London: Longman.

Peterson, L. R. 1975 *Learning* Glenview, Ill: Scott, Foresman.

Phillips, J. 1973 'Syntax and vocabulary of mothers' speech to young children: age and sex comparisons' *Child Development* 44: 182–5.

Phillips, D. and Sheerin, S. 1990 *Signature* London: Nelson.

Phillipson, R. 1992 *Linguistic Imperialism* Oxford: Oxford University Press.

Pickett, G. D. 1978 *The Foreign Language Learning Process* London: British Council.

Pienemann, M. 1985 'Learnability and syllabus construction'. In Hyltenstam, K. and Pienemann, M. (eds) *Modelling and Assessing Second Language Acquisition* Clevedon, Avon: Multilingual Matters, 1985.

Pimsleur, P. 1968 *Language Aptitude Battery* New York: Harcourt Brace and World.

Pimsleur, P., Sundland, D. M. and McIntyre, R. D. 1964 'Under-achievement in foreign language learning' *International Review of Applied Linguistics* 2/2: 113–50.

Politzer, R. L. 1961 *Teaching French: An introduction to applied linguistics* Boston: Ginn.

Powell, D. and McHugh, M. 1991 *Compact* London: HarperCollins.

Prabhu, N. S. 1987 *Second Language Pedagogy: A perspective* Oxford: Oxford University Press.

Pritchard, D. F. 1952 'An investigation into the relationship of personality traits and ability in modern language' *British Journal of Educational Psychology* 22: 157–8.

Read, C. and Matthews, A. 1991 *Tandem Plus* Walton-on-Thames: Nelson.

Regional Institute of English 1979 *Newsletter 1 (Special Series)* Regional Institute of English, South India, Bangalore (mimeo).

Reynolds, M. 1994 *Groupwork in Education and Training* London: Kogan Page.

Richards, J. C. 1971 'A non-contrastive approach to error analysis'. In Richards, J. C. (ed.) *Error Analysis* London: Longman 1974.

Richards, J. C. 1985 'The secret life of methods'. In Richards, J. C. *The Context of Language Teaching* Cambridge: Cambridge University Press, 32–45.

References

Richards, J. C. and Rodgers, T. S. 1986 *Approaches and Methods in Language Teaching* Cambridge: Cambridge University Press.

Richards, J., Platt, J. and Weber, H. 1985 *Longman Dictionary of Applied Linguistics* London: Longman.

Richterich, R. 1972 'Definition of language needs and types of adults'. In Trim, J. L. M., Richterich, R., Van Ek, J. A. and Wilkins, D. A. *Systems Development in Adult Language Learning* Strasbourg: Council of Europe, 29–88.

Ringbom, H. 1978 'The influence of the mother tongue on the translation of lexical items' *Interlanguage Studies Bulletin* 3: 80–101.

Rinvolucri, M. 1985 *Grammar Games* Cambridge: Cambridge University Press.

Rivers, W. M. 1964 *The Psychologist and the Foreign Language Teacher* Chicago: University of Chicago Press.

Roberts, J. T. 1998 'Humanistic approaches'. In Johnson, K. and Johnson, H. (eds) *Encyclopedic Dictionary of Applied Linguistics* Oxford: Blackwell, 158–61.

Robinson, D. N. 1995 *An Intellectual History of Psychology* Third edition London: Arnold.

Rogers, J. 1982 ' "The world for sick proper" ', *ELT Journal* 36/3: 144–51.

Rogers, M. 1994 'German word order: a role for developmental and linguistic factors in L2 pedagogy'. In Bygate, M., Tonkyn, A. and Williams, E. (eds) *Grammar and the Language Teacher* New York: Prentice Hall, 132–59.

Rubin, J. 1975 'What the good language learner can teach us'. *TESOL Quarterly* 9: 41–51.

Rutherford, W. and Sharwood Smith, M. 1985 'Consciousness-raising and universal grammar' *Applied Linguistics* 6: 274–82.

Savignon, S. 1972 *Communicative Competence: An experiment in foreign language teaching* Philadelphia: Center for Curriculum Development.

Scarbrough, D. 1984 *Reasons for Listening* Cambridge: Cambridge University Press.

Scherer, G. A. C. and Wertheimer, M. 1964 *A Psycholinguistic Experiment in Foreign Language Teaching* New York: McGraw-Hill.

Schmidt, R. 1983 'Interaction, acculturation and the acquisition of communicative competence'. In Wolfson, N. and Judd, E. (eds) *Sociolinguistics and Second Language Acquisition* Rowley, Mass.: Newbury House.

Schmidt, R. W. and Frota, S. 1986 'Developing basic conversational ability in a second language: a case study of an adult learner of Portugese'. In Day, R. (ed.) *Talking to Learn: Conversation in second language acquisition* Rowley, Mass.: Newbury House.

Schoenfeld, A. H. 1985 *Mathematical Problem Solving* Orlando: Academic Press.

Schumann, J. 1978 *The Pidginization Process: A model for second language acquisition* Rowley, Mass.: Newbury House.

Scott, W. 1980 *Are you Listening?* Oxford: Oxford University Press.

Scovel, T. 1979 'Review of *Suggestology and Outlines of Suggestopedy*' *TESOL Quarterly* 13: 255–66.

Selinker, L. 1972 'Interlanguage' *International Review of Applied Linguistics* 10: 209–31.

Selinker, L. and Lamendella, J. 1978 'Two perspectives on fossilization in interlanguage learning' *Interlanguage Studies Bulletin* 3: 143–91.

Shamim, F. 1996 'In or out of the action zone: location as a feature of interaction in large ESL classes in Pakistan'. In Bailey, K. M. and Nunan, D. (eds) *Voices from the Language Classroom* Cambridge: Cambridge University Press.

Shapira, R. G. 1978 'The non-learning of English: a case study of an adult'. In Hatch, E. (ed.) *Second Language Acquisition* Rowley, Mass.: Newbury House.

Shaw, G. B. 1916 *Preface to Pygmalion* Republished by Penguin, Harmondsworth, 1941.

Shiffrin, R. M. and Dumais, S. T. 1981 'The development of automatism'. In Anderson, J. R. (ed.) *Cognitive Skills and their Acquisition* Hillside, NJ: Lawrence Erlbaum Associates, 111–40.

Short, M. 1996 *Exploring the Language of Poems, Plays and Prose* London: Longman.

Sinclair, J. and Coulthard, M. 1975 *Towards an Analysis of Discourse* Oxford: Oxford University Press.

Skehan, P. 1989 *Individual Differences in Second-Language Learning* London: Edward Arnold.

Skehan, P. 1998 *A Cognitive Approach to Language Learning* Oxford: Oxford University Press.

Skehan, P. and Foster, P. 1997 'Task type and task processing conditions as influences on foreign language performance' *Language Teaching Research* 1: 185–211.

Skinner, B. F. 1957 *Verbal Behaviour* New York: Appleton Crofts.

Smith, D. M. 1972 'Some implications for the social status of pidgin languages'. In Smith, D. M. and Shuy, R. W. (eds) *Sociolinguistics in Cross-Cultural Analysis* Washington DC: Georgetown University Press.

Smith, N. and Tsimpli, I-M. 1991 'Linguistic modularity? A case study of a "savant" linguist' *Lingua* 84: 315–51.

Smith, N. and Tsimpli, I-M. 1995 *The Mind of a Savant* Oxford: Blackwell.

Smith, N., Tsimpli, I-M. and Ouhalla, J. 1993 'Learning the impossible: the acquisition of possible and impossible languages by a polyglot *savant*' *Lingua* 91: 279–347.

Snow, C. E. 1972 'Mothers' speech to children learning language' *Child Development* 43: 549–65.

Snow, C. E. and Ferguson, C. A. (eds) 1977 *Talking to Children: Language input and acquisition* Cambridge: Cambridge University Press.

Spada, N. 1986 'The interaction between types of content and type of instruction: some effects on the L2 proficiency of adult learners' *Studies in Second Language Acquisition* 8: 181–99.

Spada, N. 1987 'Relationships between instructional differences and learning outcomes: a process–product study of communicative language teaching' *Applied Linguistics* 8: 137–61.

Spolsky, B. 1969 'Attitudinal aspects of second language learning' *Language Learning* 19: 271–85.

Spolsky, B. 1989 *Conditions for Second Language Learning* Oxford: Oxford University Press.

Spolsky, B., Green, J. B. and Read, J. 1974 'A model for the description, analysis and perhaps evaluation of bilingual education' *Navajo Reading Study Progress Report No. 23* Albuquerque, NM: University of New Mexico.

Stern, H. H. 1975 'What can we learn from the good language learner?' *Canadian Modern Language Review* 31: 304–18.

Stern, H. H. 1983 *Fundamental Concepts of Language Teaching* Oxford: Oxford University Press.

Stevick, E. 1976 *Memory, Meaning and Method* Rowley, Mass.: Newbury House.

Stevick, E. 1989 *Success with Foreign Languages* New York: Prentice Hall.

Stratton, P. and Hayes, N. 1988 *A Student's Dictionary of Psychology* London: Edward Arnold.

Sturtridge, G. 1981 'Role-play and simulations'. In Johnson, K. and Morrow, K. (eds) *Communication in the Classroom* London: Longman 126–30.

References

Swain, M. 1985 'Communicative competence: some roles of comprehensible input and comprehensible output in its development'. In Gass, S. and Madden, C. (eds) *Input in Second Language Acquisition* Rowley, Mass.: Newbury House, 1985.

Swan, M. 1994 'Design criteria for pedagogic language rules'. In Bygate, M., Tonkyn, A. and Williams, E. (eds) *Grammar and the Language Teacher* London: Prentice Hall, 45–55.

Swan, M. 1995 *Practical English Usage* Second Edition Oxford: Oxford University Press.

Swan, M. and Walter, C. 1985 *The Cambridge English Course* Cambridge: Cambridge University Press.

Sweet, H. 1899/1964 *The Practical Study of Languages. A Guide for Teachers and Learners* London: Dent. Republished by Oxford University Press in 1964, edited by Mackin, R.

Tarone, E. 1977 'Conscious communication strategies in interlanguage'. In Brown, H. D., Yorio, C. A. and Crymes, R. C. (eds) *On TESOL '77* Washington, DC: TESOL.

Taylor, P. H. 1970 *How Teachers Plan Their Courses* Slough: NFER.

Taylor, B. P. 1975 'The use of overgeneralization and transfer learning strategies by elementary and intermediate students of ESL' *Language Learning* 25: 73–107.

Thomas, J. 1983 'Cross-cultural pragmatic failure' *Applied Linguistics* 4/2: 91–111.

Tran-Chi-Chau 1975 'Error analysis, contrastive analysis and students' perceptions: a study of difficulty in second language learning' *International Review of Applied Linguistics* 13: 119–43.

Underhill, N. 1987 *Testing Spoken Language: A handbook of oral testing techniques* Cambridge: Cambridge University Press.

Ur, P. 1981 *Discussions that Work* Cambridge: Cambridge University Press.

Ur, P. 1988 *Grammar Practice Activities* Cambridge: Cambridge University Press.

Ur, P. 1996 *A Course in Language Teaching* Cambridge: Cambridge University Press.

van Ek, J. A. 1973 'The "Threshold Level" in a unit/credit system'. In Trim, J. L. M., Richterich, R., van Ek, J. A. and Wilkins, D. A. *Systems Development in Adult Language Learning* Strasbourg: Council of Europe, 89–128.

van Ek, J. A. 1975 *The Threshold Level* Strasbourg: Council of Europe.

van Ek, J. A. 1978 *The Threshold Level for Schools* London: Longman.

van Els, T., Bongaerts, T., Extra, G., van Os, C. and Janssen-van Dieten, A-M. 1984 *Applied Linguistics and the Learning and Teaching of Foreign Languages* London: Edward Arnold.

Vigil, N. A. and Oller, J. W. 1976 'Rule fossilization: a tentative model' *Language Learning* 26/2: 281–95.

Wardhaugh, R. 1970 'The Contrastive Analysis Hypothesis' *TESOL Quarterly* 4: 123–30.

Watcyn-Jones, P. 1981 *Pair Work: Activities for Effective Communication* Harmondsworth: Penguin.

Weir, C. J. 1990 *Communicative Language Testing* London: Prentice Hall.

Weir, C. J. 1995 *Understanding and Developing Language Tests* New York: Phoenix ELT.

Weir, R. H. 1962 *Language in the Crib* The Hague: Mouton.

Wertheimer, M. 1945 *Productive Thinking* New York: Harper.

West, M. 1926 *Bilingualism (with Special Reference to Bengal)* Calcutta: Bureau of Education, India, Occasional Report 13.

West, M. 1953 *A General Service List of English Words* Revised and enlarged edition. London: Longman.

White, L. 1991 'Adverb placement in second language acquisition: some effects of positive and negative evidence in the classroom' *Second Language Research* 7: 133–61.

White, R. V. 1979 *Functional English* Walton-on-Thames: Nelson.

White, R. V. 1988 *The ELT Curriculum* Oxford: Blackwell.

White, R. V. and Arndt, V. 1991 *Process Writing* London: Longman.

Widdowson, H. G. 1972 'The teaching of English as communication' *ELT Journal* 27/1, 15–19.

Widdowson, H. G. 1980 'Models and fictions' *Applied Linguistics* 1/2, 165–70.

Widdowson, H. G. 1996 *Linguistics* Oxford: Oxford University Press.

Wild-Bicanic, S., Nonvciller, V., Pervan, M. and Stojsavljevic, A. 1968 *English for Children: Book 1* Zagreb: Skolska Knjiga.

Wilkins, D. A. 1972a *Linguistics in Language Teaching* London: Arnold.

Wilkins, D. A. 1972b 'Grammatical, situational and notional syllabuses'. Reprinted in Brumfit, C. J. and Johnson, K. (eds) *The Communicative Approach to Language Teaching* Oxford: Oxford University Press, 1979: 82–90.

Wilkins, D. A. 1973 'An investigation into the linguistic and situational common core in a unit/credit system'. In Trim, J. L. M., Richterich, R., van Ek, J. A. and Wilkins, D. A. *Systems Development in Adult Language Learning* Strasbourg: Council of Europe, 129–43.

Williams, E. 1998 'Teaching reading'. In Johnson, K. and Johnson, H. (eds) *Encyclopedic Dictionary of Applied Linguistics* Oxford: Blackwell, 330–5.

Witkin, H. A., Dyk, R., Faterson, H. F., Goodenough, D. R. and Karp, S. A. 1962 *Psychological Differentiation* New York: Wiley.

Wright, T. and Bolitho, R. 1993 'Language awareness: a riming link in language teaching education?' *ELT Journal* 47/4, 292–304.

Index